The Complete Book of Collection Letters, Telephone Scripts, and Faxes

The Complete Book of Collection Letters, Telephone Scripts, and Faxes

Cecil J. Bond

McGraw-Hill, Inc.

New York   San Francisco   Washington, D.C.   Auckland   Bogotá
Caracas   Lisbon   London   Madrid   Mexico City   Milan
Montreal   New Delhi   San Juan   Singapore
Sydney   Tokyo   Toronto

Library of Congress Cataloging-in-Publication Data

Bond, Cecil J.
　The complete book of collection letters, telephone scripts, and
faxes / Cecil J. Bond.
　　　p.　cm.
　Includes index.
　ISBN 0–07–006605-1
　　1. Collecting of accounts—United States—Handbooks, manuals, etc.
　2. Commercial correspondence—United States.　3. Collection laws—
United States.　I. Title.
　HG3752.7.U6B66　1994
　658.8'8—dc20　　　　　　　　　　　　　　　　93–48991
　　　　　　　　　　　　　　　　　　　　　　　　CIP

1 2 3 4 5 6 7 8 9 0　DOH/DOH　9 0 9 8 7 6 5 4

PN 0-07-006617-5
PART OF
ISBN 0–07–006605-1

The sponsoring editor for this book was David Conti, the editing supervisor was Fred Dahl, the designer was Inkwell Publishing Services, and the production supervisor was Suzanne Babeuf. It was set in Palatino by Inkwell Publishing Services.

Printed and bound by R. R. Donnelley & Sons Company.

 This book is printed on recycled, acid-free paper containing a minimum of 50 percent recycled de-inked fiber.

This publication is designed to provide accurate and authoritative information in regard to the subject matter covered. It is sold with the understanding that the publisher is not engaged in rendering legal, accounting, or other professional service. If legal advice or other expert assistance is required, the services of a competent professional person should be sought.

　　　　　—From the declaration of principles jointly adopted by a committee of the
　　　　　American Bar Association and a committee of publishers

Contents

Preface

A key element in the success of any business or company that offers credit terms to its customers is the timely collection of accounts receivable. There may be other good and reliable sources of cash (venture capitalists, banks, private investors, public shareholders, etc.) but unless a high percentage of the cashflow requirement is generated from accounts receivable, the long-term prognosis for success is not good.

The Complete Book of Collection Letters, Telephone Scripts, and Faxes gives credit grantors the tools and the hands-on guidelines necessary to substantially increase the flow of cash from the company's receivables accounts. The timely collection of accounts receivable balances is of major significance in reducing interest charges when money is borrowed to supplement cashflow.

The hands-on approach of *The Complete Book of Collection Letters, Telephone Scripts, and Faxes* enables the credit administrator to work more effectively to resolve the problem of accounts that do not turn over as rapidly as they should. The book provides guidelines for minimizing the chances that unsatisfactory accounts will find their way into the Bad Debt Account. It also includes:

More than 400 letters and other collection tools which range from gentle reminders to final demands for payment, including scripted examples of collection calls that allow the creditor company to focus more effectively on specific problems and problem accounts.

Scripted examples of collection visits to customers whose accounts are past due, with emphasis on guidelines that will keep the conversation focused on immediate payment of the past-due account balance.

Examples of how fax messages may be incorporated into a successful collection effort.

The Complete Book includes guideline material that will help the credit administrator to collect current and past-due balances while maintaining an appropriate level of control over the account relationship. The tools are in these pages, arranged and referenced so that they can be identified and accessed promptly. Will *The Complete Book of Collection Letters, Telephone Scripts, and Faxes* ensure that your company will never lose another accounts receivable dollar? Not unless you are the person who reported seeing the tooth fairy do a fly-by over a dentist's office in Peoria, Illinois, on August 10, 1969. If you are that person, anything is possible.

Apply the following questions to your company's collection effort and then decide whether it is handling the problem of slow-pay accounts as effectively as it might.

1. Does your company have an effective procedure for collecting past-due balances?

2. Do you know how to write collection letters that generate payments?

3. Do you know how to structure and control telephone collection calls?

4. Do the records of your collection letters and telephone calls enable you to know what was said on a specific date, what was promised on that date, and whether the customer responded as he or she agreed to do?

5. Does your collection program effectively integrate letters, telephone calls, fax messages, and personal visits?

6. Do you confirm payment arrangements negotiated during the course of a telephone conversation with a letter or a memo?

7. If your company does not have a clearly defined program for collecting past-due accounts receivable—a program that makes it obvious to customers that there is ongoing monitoring of account balances—how can you expect accounts with a chronic cashflow problem to handle their payment responsibility in an acceptable manner?

8. Are you able to recognize the fine line that exists between a collection procedure that is legal and one that is not?

9. Do you know what constitutes harassment and the potential for legal action to collect general or punitive damages when false or damaging statements are made?

10. Based upon what you now know, is it possible that you might write or say something that, quite inadvertently, would include one or more elements of a provable intent to damage the reputation of a debtor-customer?

The Complete Book of Collection Letters, Telephone Scripts, and Faxes covers a focused spectrum of hands-on tools that will enable your company to collect its accounts receivable balances with a minimum of delay, stress, and hassle. This book includes "how to" guidelines for creating your own collection materials, or you can quickly adapt any of the letters, scripted telephone calls, scripted personal visits, or fax messages to any of your company's collection situations. All of the instructional, guideline, and descriptive material presented is in a form that is easy to understand

and easy to use. It enables the reader to select promptly and effectively from a strong menu of collection tools and options.

This book offers criteria that will enable your company to avoid the costly trap of having credit department people devote a disproportionate amount of their time to a limited number of problem accounts; it is a misdirected focus of time and energy that can work to the detriment of the total collection effort. Minimizing the number of collection problems and reducing the DSO (Days Sales Outstanding) is a must if the financial fitness program of your business or company is to achieve its goal. *The Complete Book of Collection Letters, Telephone Scripts, and Faxes* contains the answers you need to achieve your credit and collection goals.

Acknowledgments—Special Thanks to ...

David Conti, sponsoring editor for this book and the three that preceded it, for making the editor-author relationship a professional and a personal pleasure.

My daughter, *Coralyn Bond,* for once again monitoring several hundred pages of manuscript to minimize the number and the magnitude of punctuation and other errors.

Gabby, who will never read this but whose companionship during the writing of my four books helped enormously.

Cecil J. Bond

How to Use the Disk

The disk that comes with this book is easy to use.

If you own an IBM personal computer (PC, AT, etc.) or an IBM compatible and use MS/DOS (Microsoft Disk Operating System), you can make use of this disk. This disk itself is 3.5-in., double-sided, high-density.

Getting started is simple. After turning on your computer (and you have "C:>" prompt in DOS), insert the disk into the 3.5-in. drive (usually called the a: drive, but it could also be b:). Type:

    md c:\letters

This will create a directory called "Letters" on your hard drive. Then type:

    c: [Enter]
    cd\letters [Enter]
    copy a:[or b:]\letters*.* c:\letters   [Enter]

You will see files being copied from the disk to the hard drive. You can now store the floppy disk as a backup.

When you run your word processing program, these files may be loaded from the "Letters" directory. Note that the filenames are "letter8-," "letter9-," and so on. Any form found in Chap. 8 of the book will be found in the file entitled "letter8-." Chapter 9 forms will be in "letter9-," and so on.

You may want to organize your files differently (perhaps create a separate file for each form), or select only some of the files for storage on your computer's hard drive. Having all the forms available on the hard drive makes it easier for you to tailor them to your needs—and keeps the original disk safe if you mistakenly delete something.

The forms have been saved in ASCII, so that they can be imported into most or all word processors. To call up a form on your screen from the floppy disk or the hard drive, access the directory name, and then type the filename.

For example, suppose you want to access something from the file letter8- in the book. For floppy disk users, the pathname is

a: [or b:]\letters\letter8-.

For hard disk users, it is

c:\letters\letter8-.

If your word processor contains default margins, the letter should appear on the screen with line wraps at those margins. If your word processor does not contain default margins, the lines of the letter may run off the right edge of the screen. If so, simply define the margins you want, and the line wraps should be adjusted accordingly.

Part 1

How to Minimize Your Company's Collection Problems

Collection problems can have their roots in one or more of the steps that must be taken to effectively assess, and subsequently to monitor, the financial and business health of your credit accounts. What are the guidelines for minimizing the problem of slow-pay accounts receivable? They include:

- A strong, clearly defined credit policy, and a credit management team whose goal it is to adhere to it.
- A comprehensive screening procedure that includes input from current suppliers, credit reporting agencies, the banker, financial statements, and such other data as may be available and/or pertinent.
- Avoiding the pressure—from your own marketing department or from the applicant—for a credit decision that offers too much too soon.

The goal for any company is to have a strong accounts receivable base that makes a major contribution to the monthly cashflow requirement of the creditor/supplier company. Accounts that have become a part of the receivables problem cannot be justified on the basis of an incomplete new account information form, inadequate supplier data, a bank that was reluctant to furnish helpful data, or any other unacceptable excuse. Use good screening techniques and guidelines to evaluate credit applicants, and monitor existing accounts within parameters that reflect a strong dedication to maximize the quality of the receivables.

It is not possible to avoid the occasional loss of an accounts receivable balance. If the company's credit policy is geared to reasonable degrees of exposure, an occasional loss is an inevitable part of the process of selling goods and/or services on credit. If a company's business plan projects annual growth at a fixed percentage or a specific dollar figure, the credit department is expected to find ways to approve whatever level of credit is necessary to attain those goals of growth.

Under no circumstances should the company's management urge or direct the Credit Department to approve accounts, or levels of credit exposure, that are not acceptable within the context of the company's credit policy. Suppose, for example, that the company is looking for dramatic sales figures, perhaps racing toward a first public offering of the company's stock? Nothing—absolutely *nothing*—should be said or done by the company's management to pressure the Credit Department to make decisions that are unwise—decisions that exceed the parameters for a *quality account* as defined by the company's credit policy.

Among the guidelines for minimizing the problem of slow-pay or no-pay accounts is a *comprehensive screening procedure*. The tools that follow can be very helpful in screening your credit applicants, setting up account controls, and monitoring their performance.

1

Is It Really a Creditworthy Account?

A *creditworthy account* is one that has a record of paying the bank on time and paying for its supplier purchases within terms or close to terms. It is an account that has done nothing to generate negative comments among suppliers, credit reporting agencies, or the bank. An evaluation by the supplier of the applicant's credit and financial references should enable the supplier to offer a mutually realistic credit line.

Assigning a credit line to an applicant incorporates no guarantee that the account will continue to prosper or continue to pay account balances in a satisfactory manner. Changes occur that impact the stability of a company. Few businesses or industries are immune from the possibility that the value to customers of a product or a service will at some point be diminished by the introduction of something better. Management changes may occur in a customer company, some of which may not work out for the best. The national economy, or the economy in the area served by the customer, may lose its momentum, causing a downturn in business and a dramatic reduction in the quantity of product(s) sold. There are no guarantees; but, if the applicant has been evaluated carefully and thoroughly, and a program of ongoing monitoring attaches to every one of your accounts, the chances are good that you will have an accounts receivable aging sheet that is loaded with *creditworthy accounts*.

The tomorrows that follow today may prove as successful for your accounts as they have in the past, but, then again, they may not. And if they are not, it is to be hoped that the constant monitoring of receivables will pick up signs of individual account weakness long before they become a threat to the safety of your company's receivables dollars.

A Good Company Credit Policy?
Don't Deviate from It!

Every company or business must take appropriate measures to ensure that receivables accounts can deliver a high percentage of the company's cashflow requirement. If the company's credit policy and collection procedures have been well structured, the best way to accomplish that goal is to adhere to the guideline parameters. The business plan will determine the credit policy for your company, which will be one of the following:

- *Restrictive*—reflects the policy of a company that is unwilling to take risks greater than minimal, a company whose plan is for growth that is tightly controlled.

- *Moderate*—a more conventional mix of good accounts (discount or prompt), average accounts (pay within terms to 10 or 20 days slow), and slower accounts (ones that pay consistently 20 to 30 days past due).

- *Liberal*—a potentially high-risk credit policy that puts sales growth first and the quality of receivables (and safety of the company's receivables investment) a distant second. It is a credit policy that, if allowed to generate any amount of momentum, can accelerate to a point where cashflow becomes a trickle and the ability of the company to survive becomes the victim of a format for self-destruction.

Every company must take measures to ensure that receivables accounts are of a quality consistent with the company's business plan, and are consistent with a credit policy that derives its shape and purpose from the business plan. *Internally generated cash* is the buzz phrase that means the best and the easiest way for a company to save interest dollars, and interest dollars saved are dollars that filter down quickly into the bottom line of the company's financial report. If your company's credit policy and collection procedures are good, then you must stay within the parameters of those guidelines to maximize the results.

Example 1: If the credit policy of Company A is moderate (accepts accounts that pay discount, prompt, to 20 or 30 days slow), the credit manager should not approve the credit request of an applicant whose payment record with other suppliers is seldom less than 30 to 45 days past due. If Company A's cashflow is linked to the expectation that accounts receivable will be paid within or near terms, any major deviation from that expectation will have a significant impact upon the amount of internally generated cash. How, then, when internally generated cash is so severely impacted, does Company A supplement this shortfall of cash from accounts receivable? It must borrow from the bank, an act that raises the annual cost (interest charges) of money borrowed to augment the shortfall of cash generated from receivables. It is an action that has as its product an unacceptable erosion of funds that were projected to make their way into the company's bottom line.

Example 2: The credit policy of Company B states that the company will assume no credit risk that does not fall within the parameters of its moderate credit policy, utilizing the same criteria for *moderate credit policy* that has been applied to Company A. The owner(s) or management of Company B has made it clear that the credit manager has no latitude to deviate from the guidelines for acceptable credit accounts set forth in the company's credit policy. When the course is set properly by the company's top management, credit administrators should have no difficulty in synchronizing their performance to the requirements of the company's credit policy. Internally generated cash should minimize the use of borrowed money and meet goals set by the company's management.

The effort to minimize your company's collection problems should not restrict unrealistically the types of accounts that can be sold on credit terms. Your own company's goals for growth and financial health demand a credit policy that does not excessively restrict sales: That it does, in fact, service the dual purposes of increasing growth—within the format of the company's business plan—and enhancing financial stability with a credit policy that addresses itself to goals stated in the business policy.

Examples 1 and 2 should not be construed to mean that factors other than the *payment record with other suppliers* should determine whether an applicant for credit is or is not accepted. There is much additional data that goes into the evaluation of a prospective account. They include:

- A bank's experience.
- The quality and depth of management.
- The potential for stability and growth of the company.
- Acceptance and stability of the product line(s).
- Information and data supplied by a credit report agency (D & B, NACM, Etc.).

The information from each of these areas is relevant to making the decision that is right for your company.

The Value of a Good Screening Process

When a prospective credit granter has gathered and evaluated information from credit reporting agencies, suppliers, banks, financial statements from the preceding three years, and any relevant antecedent information pertaining to the personal history of principals or key executives, the question: Is it *really* a creditworthy account? must be addressed. And, if within the context of the company's credit policy it is determined that the applicant is creditworthy, is the credit line that can be assigned going to be high enough to satisfy the applicant's requirements for product(s)?

CREDIT POLICY

The XYZ Company is committed to a growth pattern that is moderate in terms of our industry's standards. We do not seek to take unnecessary or unusual financial risks, nor do we wish to promote growth at levels beyond our financial capabilities, beyond the capabilities of our present plant facility, or beyond our ability to add good, productive people. Our company is dedicated to a pattern of solid, steady growth, and to a company policy that incorporates the highest standards of personal and business integrity and ethics in our relationships with fellow employees, with all segments of the general public, with our customers, and with our suppliers.

It is our commitment to manufacture products of the highest quality for the targeted market level and to act responsibly and positively in our relationships with other members of our industry. We do not intend to become a major player in our industry, but it is our goal to make the XYZ Company a positive factor in how the consumer perceives our industry. In a phrase, we are not a "fast buck" company. We are in business for the long haul and we expect this attitude to guide and motivate the interaction of employees to each other, in their contact with the public, and in every decision-making and production area of our company.

The following guidelines will help the Credit Department to channel its efforts toward making the expected contribution:

Credit terms should not be offered to accounts that do not meet the criteria for a low-risk receivables base.

Account evaluation procedures shall be geared to an annual bad debt loss (percentage of sales) that is not in excess of the average for our industry.

The Credit Manager's decisions regarding any sales or credit line may be reviewed by the Treasurer (or VP of Finance) if requested to do so by the Sales Manager (or VP of Sales).

The Credit Department shall work effectively with all departments and levels of company management to ensure a continuity of company objectives.

Any question that the Credit Manager might have regarding the application of this credit policy to a specific account is to be discussed with the Treasurer.

Credit policy will be reviewed periodically by senior management to ensure that the company's goals remain unchanged as they impact the Credit Department.

Credit department personnel should, whenever possible, be a positive force in our effort to build strong customer loyalties and relationships.

The Credit Department shall expedite the processing of credit decisions, within the context of an appropriate input of necessary data and an appropriate time frame in which to evaluate that data.

The Treasurer (or VP of Finance) will monitor the effectiveness of methods used by the Credit Department to achieve its goals.

_____   _____
Date   Title

When the applicant requests a specific credit line but the analysis of reference and other data falls short of qualifying the applicant for the requested line, the credit granter may do one of two things: (1) summarily reject the applicant's bid for the requested line of credit, or, if the applicant qualifies for a lower-than-requested opening line, the credit granter could (2) arrange to ship increments of the total order (lower dollar amounts and more frequent shipments and payments).

The second approach has the positive effect of enabling a supplier to save a good piece of business while adding a customer at a level of credit exposure that is realistic for the supplier and adequate for the customer's needs. An applicant or a customer may be *credit worthy* to a certain dollar level and an unacceptable risk at a higher level. The circumstances of individual accounts and account situations will determine what is and what is not acceptable.

The letters and forms shown in the following pages include a credit policy, gathering and evaluating new account information (see letter 1.1), accepting new accounts, assigning credit limits, and letters thanking key people in the customer firm for their business.

No precollection phase of the creditor-customer relationship is more important than the proper screening and evaluating of new account applications. Whether a high or a low percentage of this book ultimately has relevance in the context of collecting, your past-due accounts receivable balances generally have their roots in the initial evaluation of certain risk factors that are not a part of every account.

These are tools that are indirectly related to the collecting of accounts receivable balances. They can, however, be of more than incidental assistance as you pick your way through the minefield of acceptable, questionable, and unacceptable credit accounts.

Assigning a Credit Line

When a credit line is assigned to a customer—whether it is a temporary line assigned to cover needs until credit data has been received and evaluated, or until the first *permanent* line has been assigned—the letter advising the customer that a temporary credit line has been assigned is usually the first contact with the customer for a department other than sales/marketing. It is an opportunity for your department to welcome the customer and to enhance the company's image with a good first impression.

Letters 1.2–1.15 are examples of letters that assign a credit line and welcome the customer.

1.1   [date]

Mr. Leonard Carter, Controller
Company Name
Street Address (or P.O. Box No.)
City, State, Zip Code

Re: Credit Application and Financial Statements

Dear Mr. Carter:

We can expedite the processing of credit reference data if you will complete the attached Account Information Sheet and return it, with a copy of your most current financial statement, at your earliest convenience.

We appreciate the confidence your company has expressed in our products by giving us a first order. It is our hope that this is the beginning of a long and a mutually satisfactory business relationship.

Sincerely yours,

Credit Manager

1.2   Attention of Mr. Alan Carlson, Purchasing Manager

Dear Mr. Carlson:

Our thanks for your first order and for the credit information that accompanied it.

Your order should arrive at your warehouse sometime today. Because the credit information forwarded with the purchase order was so comprehensive, we were able to release the order and also to assign your company a temporary credit line of $_____.

The credit information that was attached to the purchase order has been inserted on the enclosed New Account Information Sheet. Please complete the form at your earliest convenience and return it in the enclosed envelope. At that time the temporary credit line will be reviewed and a permanent line assigned.

We appreciate your interest in our products. Our goal is to provide a level of service that matches the quality of our products. Please advise me if your company has any experience that does not meet or exceed that goal.

Sincerely,

1.3   Attention: Charles Wilburn, Purchasing Manager

Dear Mr. Wilburn:

It is my pleasure to welcome your company to our family of customers.

To help us expedite the process of checking reference data and assigning a permanent credit line, please complete the attached New Account Information sheet and return it in the enclosed envelope. Meanwhile, a temporary credit line of $_____ is available to cover interim purchases.

Our goal is to give our customers a quality of service that meets or exceeds the quality standards of our fine products (services). Should your company experience an incident or a situation that is not satisfactory or is at odds with our goal of excellent service, please contact me at your earliest convenience.

Sincerely,

1.4   [date]

Attention: The Purchasing Manager

Dear Mr./Mrs. _____:

Thank you for the first order. It will be shipped on our open account terms of Net 30 days.

Attached is a copy of our New Account Information Sheet. Please complete and return it as soon as possible so that we may verify references and assign a credit line to the account.

Until references have been verified and a credit line established, orders after the first one will be processed on COD terms. Your prompt and detailed assistance with the requested references will assist our effort to expedite the establishing of a credit line.

Sincerely yours,

Credit Manager

Enclosure

1.5   [date]

Company Name
Street Address (or P.O. Box No.)
City, State, Zip Code

Dear Mr./Ms. _____:

Thank you for your prompt response to our request for credit references and credit reference data.

We have assigned your account a temporary credit line of _____ on our standard sales terms of _____. Our account experience will be reviewed at the end of 90 days, and if our experience and your product requirements indicate the need for an increase, we will hope to do it at that time.

Your interest in our products is greatly appreciated. We anticipate a long and a mutually rewarding relationship.

Sincerely,

Credit Manager

1.6   Attention: Mr. Alan Carson, Purchasing Manager

Dear Mr. Carson:

We thank you for the first order and welcome you to our family of customers.

A temporary credit line of $_____ has been assigned until data received from your credit references has been received and reviewed. We should have no problem increasing the credit line to a figure more compatible with what we hope will be your long-term requirement.

The combination of our products and your company is a natural one—one that has the qualities necessary for it to become a long and a mutually profitable one.

Sincerely,

Credit Manager

1.7   [date]

Company Name
Street Address (or P.O. Box No.)
City, State, Zip Code

Dear Mr. Cameron:

A current check of the information in our customer credit files has revealed that many of these files are incomplete. In that category is our file of information on your company.

The attached Account Information Sheet, when completed and returned with a copy of your most recent financial statement, will give us the appropriate balance of background and current business information.

Your cooperation is appreciated.

Sincerely,

Credit Manager

1.8   [date]

Company Name
Street Address (or P.O. Box No.)
City, State, Zip Code

Dear Mr./Ms. _____:

It is my pleasure to advise you that we have set an opening credit line of $5000.00 for your account. This should not be construed as a maximum figure for use over the long-term but rather an opportunity for our two firms to become better business acquaintances before we consider increasing the line.

Please call if I can assist you in any way. We greatly appreciate your interest in our product(s) and anticipate a mutually successful long-term association.

Sincerely,

Credit Manager

1.9   [date]

Company Name
Street Address (or P.O. Box No.)
City, State, Zip Code

Dear Mr. Carter:

Let me first thank you for the order your company has placed with us. We appreciate the confidence in our products that this order represents.

It is our policy to process the first order or two from a new customer on a COD basis. This is not a reflection on the credit worthiness of customers who are new to us. It is simply a recognition of the fact that we are new to each other and must be as prudent in our approach to open account terms as we feel sure you are.

Please complete the attached Account Information Sheet (also the Resale Form), attach a copy of your most recent financial statement, and return documents to this office in the enclosed stamped self-addressed envelope.

When reference data has been processed, we hope to offer a mutually acceptable credit line on our standard terms of 2%/10 days/Net 30.

Sincerely,

Credit Manager

1.10   [date]

Company Name
Street Address (or P.O. Box No.)
City, State, Zip Code

Dear Mr./Ms. _____:

Our company's line of products has recently been added to the merchandise carried by your branches in _____, _____, and _____. We are also about to conclude agreements with the branches in _____, _____, and _____, which means that we shall be shipping product(s) to those locations before the end of this month.

Before we inadvertently create a mess for ourselves and for your department, a list of the "bill-to" addresses for the branches listed above will be appreciated. Our sales reps have obtained some information but we prefer to assure ourselves of accurate information by contacting your office before invoices are mailed.

If there is ever a time or a situation when this office might be of assistance to your department, please do not hesitate to contact the undersigned.

Your assistance is greatly appreciated.

Sincerely,

Credit Manager

1.11   [date]

Company Name
Street Address (or P.O. Box No.)
City, State, Zip Code

Dear Mr./Ms. _____:

A review of our files indicates that we do not have a completed Resale Card (Sales Tax Exemption Number) for your account.

To avoid having California State Sales Tax charged to your invoices, please complete, sign, and return the enclosed Resale Card.

We appreciate your prompt attention to this request.

Sincerely,

Credit Manager

1.12

Credit Limit Update

Customer Name _____   Acct. # _____

Present Limit $ _____   Aging as of _____

Date Approved   _____   Current $ _____

Approved By   _____   30-60 $ _____

60-90 $ _____

90 plus $ _____

D&B Rating   _____   Balance $ _____

Date of Last Financial   _____   Last 6 Months' Sales $ _____

Terms, Aging and Pay History _____

New Limit Requested $_____   By Date _____   By Whom _____

Reason for Requested Change _____

_____

_____

Recommendation _____

_____

_____

Amount   *Approval*

_____   By _____   Date _____

_____   _____   _____

Net Review Date _____

Input to System By: _____   Date _____

[company letterhead]

Corporate Guarantee

The XYZ Company [address], agrees to guarantee payment for purchases made by its subsidiary, [name and address], from the [creditor/supplier company's name and address], during the period from _____ through _____ inclusive.

Should the [subsidiary company] fail to make payment or payments within the Net 30 Days sales/credit terms of the [creditor/supplier company], the [parent/guarantor company] will upon notification received from the [creditor/supplier company], and upon receipt of invoices for which the payment claim is made, promptly pay the submitted past due invoices as covered by this agreement.

It is understood that payment for invoices is subject to verification of the quantities ordered and received, the prices quoted and billed, and such other obligations and requirements as may be a part of the agreement between the [subsidiary/purchaser company] and the [creditor-supplier company].

Dated _____   by _____
                                                                                        Treasurer, XYZ Company

1.14   **Credit Lines**

Account Number	Name and Location	Date Originally Assigned	Amount Originally Assigned	Date Reviewed	Current Credit Line

1.15   [date]

Company Name
Street Address (or P.O. Box No.)
City, State, Zip Code

Gentlemen:

A review of the information in our credit file indicates a need to upgrade our decision-making data.

The following list pinpoints information that was either not requested when your account was opened or has become outdated. In order that we may do the best possible credit job for your company and ours, it is important that we promptly receive the indicated information.

___ *Current Financials (Statement of Income/Profit and Loss)

___ Trade References (three major suppliers with whom you are currently doing business)

___ Bank Reference (name, location, telephone number, and bank officer most familiar with your account)

___ Business Plan

*This important information will be treated in strict confidence.

Please address the requested information to the attention of the undersigned.

Sincerely,

Credit Department

Some Reasons for Refusing Credit

1. Other suppliers report slow payment experience.
2. Company/business is expanding too rapidly.
3. Principals/management do not have enough experience.
4. Financial data is incomplete or inadequate (financial statements and bank information is not comprehensive).
5. The business is not established.
6. Businesses already established in the applicant's market area are causing strong competitive pressure.
7. The economy in the applicant's market area is in a cycle of recession. This diminishes the chances for a new business to succeed.

Intradepartment Memo

To: Department Personnel
From: Credit Manager
Subject: Processing New Account Information

1. Review your holding file every Friday afternoon.

2. Pull all file folders that are 10 days or more older than the date on the New Account Information sheet.

3. Pull all file folders for which you have received either (a) a bank response and one supplier reference response or (b) no bank response but two supplier responses.

4. Give me the file folders in the category covered by paragraph 2 (above) each Monday morning. Give me the file folders in the category covered by paragraph 3 (above) as rapidly as they meet minimum processing requirements (*a* and *b* in paragraph 3).

5. Credit references are to be contacted by telephone whenever possible, and as rapidly as possible. If telephone numbers are not listed on the New Account Information sheet, but street and city information are given, reference requests should be mailed promptly to the listed companies.

6. If you receive a New Account Information sheet that includes references names but no telephone number or city or street information, contact the sales representative and have him or her obtain the missing information.

These instructions are to be followed without change unless change is authorized by me.

_____   _____
Credit Manager   Date

1.17   [date]

The above-named firm has given your name as a credit reference to assist them in establishing an account with us. We greatly appreciate your help and pledge that any information given to us by your company will be treated in strictest confidence.

Sold from		Method of Payment:	
Highest Credit	_____	Discounts	_____
Owing	_____	Prompt	_____
Past Due	_____	Slow	_____
Terms	_____	Pays by Note	_____
		Pays on Account	_____

Remarks _____

_____

_____

_____

_____

Sincerely,

Credit Manager

Please complete and return to:

Credit File Control Sheet

Identification _____

Name (and/or Trade Style) _____

Billing/Payments Address _____

Documents in File

Credit App. (Date) _____   App. Rec'd _____   Contacted _____

Security Documents _____   UCC Filing: Date _____

Location _____

(*Continued*)

Credit Reports   (Report Date)   (Update Requested)   (Update Rec'd)

D & B _____

NACM _____

Other _____

Bank Reference _____

Trade Reference _____

_____

Financials, Bus. Plan, etc. _____

Comments _____

(Territory Rep) _____

Authorization _____

Credit Requested: _____

First Order _____

Anticipated High Credit _____

Credit Line

Amount _____   Special Instructions_____

By_____   Date _____

Experience Analysis @ _____ : _____

_____

_____

Experience Analysis @ _____ : _____

_____

_____

Request for Special Terms

Date _____

To Be Completed by Sales:

Customer Name _____

Customer Address _____

_____

Term Requested _____

On (P.O. or Invoice Number) _____

Reason _____

_____

_____

Requested by _____

- -

To Be Completed by Credit Department:

Date Account Opened _____

Financial Statement (Date) _____

D & B Rating _____

Our Payment History with This Company _____

_____

Comments and Recommendation _____

_____

Approved _____   Approved _____

1.19   **Memorandum**

[date]

To:

From: Credit Department

Subject:

My telephone conversation this date with _____ indicates that the listed unit/system is not operating within specifications, and payment will not be released until it is.

Job No. _____

Invoice No. _____

Invoice Date _____

Invoice Amount _____

Customer P.O. _____

Type of Unit/System _____

Customer's Description of Problem _____

_____

_____

_____

Please advise what corrective action has been/will be taken to help expedite payment of invoice.

_____

— —

To:

I have taken/I am initiating the following corrective action.

_____

_____

_____

Accounts Receivable Aged Trial Balances
as of 11/26/XX

Customer Name/Number	Document Date/Number	Total Amount	Aging			
			0-30	31-60	61-90	91 & Over
406	405-555-1098	1140.00			1140.00	
Gladings Co.	8/28/XX 12345	1,140.00			1140.00	
	9/24/XX 12418	936.00			936.00	
	10/31/XX 12522	1488.00	1488.00			
	11/04/XX 12345	1,140.00–			1140.00–	
		1488.00	1488.00	0.00	0.00	0.00
414	213-555-1053					
Gladstone Co.	10/30/XX 12508	748.10	748.10			
	11/14/XX 12508	748.10–	748.10–			
		0.00	0.00	0.00	0.00	0.00
415	916-555-3902					
Gold Star Ind.	9/30/XX 12438	108.00		108.00		
	10/10/XX 12463	112.00		112.00		
	11/10/XX 12541	135.00	135.00			
	11/21/XX 12438	108.00–		108.00–		
		247.00	135.00	112.00	0.00	0.00
421	415-555-2956					
Gopher's	9/24/XX 12420	180.00			180.00	
	11/18/XX 12420	180.00–			180.00–	
		0.00	0.00	0.00	0.00	0.00
425	800-555 3618					
Graystone, Inc.	10/27/XX 12493	46.50	46.50			
	11/07/XX 12493	46.50–	46.50–			
		0.00	0.00	0.00	0.00	0.00
427	213-555-5827					
Gregorio's	10/30/XX 12515	292.50		292.50		
		292.50	0.00	292.50	0.00	0.00

1.21

Past-Due Balances

Account Name	Acct. No.	Current 0-30	31-60	61-90	91 & Over	Total

Credit Hold

To

Ship To _____

Bill To _____

S.O.# _____

Amount of Order_____ Shipping Date _____

Reason for Hold _____

Requirement for Release _____

_____   _____
Date   Credit Manager

1.22   [date]

To Our Customers:

We have no desire to project the image of a whining, complaining or ungrateful supplier. Our customers are much too important for us to slide into any of those unpleasant behavioral attitudes. This is meant only to be a mutual self-help suggestion, and
if it works for you it will automatically work for us.

When you receive an invoice that lists a quantity of product that does not agree with
the quantity you received, please do not change the invoice and pay what you
calculate to be correct. It may be correct, but call us with the information so we can
promptly issue a credit, mail it to you, and protect your discount on the specific
invoice for 10 days beyond the normal discount period. Issuing the credit simplifies
our bookkeeping and should also simplify yours if for one reason or another we
calculate two different amounts for the goods billed but not received.

Are there errors or questions regarding the price quoted to you and the price billed?
Please contact this department as soon as you notice the discrepancy—and before
the invoice is input for payment. We'll either promptly correct the problem with a
credit for the difference or have our sales representative call you to discuss or clarify
any misunderstanding that may have occurred.We can do our best job for you when
your telephone call puts the matter of correcting our mistake or problem exactly
where it belongs—in our lap. Many thanks for your cooperation.

Sincerely,

Cecil Bond
Credit Manager

Unwise Credit Decisions

Few obstacles are more detrimental to a strong and a constant flow of internally generated cash than a credit manager who succumbs to pressure—whether from applicants or from the company's own marketing people—and makes decisions that prove to be unwise.

It matters not whether the credit policy is restrictive or moderate because it imposes upon the credit manager specific limitations regarding the quality of the accounts receivable. The limitations for a moderate credit policy will be somewhat more liberal than those for a restrictive policy, but there will be limitations that cannot be bent or broken if the integrity of accounts receivable is to be maintained within the context of the credit policy. With a liberal credit policy, there is far more latitude when determining what can and cannot be accepted, but there must be some realistic parameters for declaring accounts to be *acceptable* if receivables is to have the credibility that is necessary to give it legitimacy in the company's list of assets.

Unwise credit decisions can cost a company money in the areas of increased interest dollars, fees to third-party collection agencies, and the loss of a high percentage of account dollars when a customer files for bankruptcy protection. At such a time, there are few assets other than those to be shared among secured creditors. The loss of a receivables balance to the bad debt account is the most devastating result of an unwise credit decision. A credit manager whose company has a moderate or "main stream" credit policy cannot avoid an occasional loss to the bad debt account. Operating within a moderate credit policy and never losing an account is indicative of a credit policy that is too restrictive for the parameters of a moderate credit policy.

Costly mistakes are often related to, but not always the result of, incomplete information or limited data evaluation skills. There are applicants who will give you ambiguous statements, managed data, and slanted facts; you might encounter one or all of these toxic ingredients in the broad base of material that you must use. Although your company's money is always on the line when you release an order, it is never more at risk than when a first order is released before all pertinent facts have been checked and are found to be satisfactory.

No statistic is available to cover the number of people who will say or do whatever is necessary to get a company to give them a line of credit. There is also no statistic to cover the number of accounts whose performance with your company will fail to measure up to the quality of the experience reported by some other suppliers. Sometimes it's as simple as whether your product(s) is as important to the customer as the product(s) of another supplier. In any money crunch, major suppliers—key suppliers—will always get their money much closer to credit terms than suppliers whose product(s) is less important.

Do not give way to pressure from the applicant or from the Sales or Marketing Department of your own company. You must process applications for credit and make credit decisions as rapidly as good management practice will allow, but you must control the tempo of the decision-making process. Do not give in to the thought that just this once you can waive getting financial statements from the applicant, or waive getting meaningful information from the bank. Do not do it! Do not allow yourself to accept the absence of a key document or the absence of key pieces of information from a bank of supplier sources.

Collecting Receivables

Collecting receivables—the process of getting your company's money from a customer when it is due, when it is past due, or before it slips into the financial morass of bankruptcy or bad debt—becomes a reality from day one of the creditor/customer relationship. It does not matter that it may be 15, 30, or more days after the date of sale before payment for the new receivables obligation becomes due.

What is important is that the new receivables balance (*every* receivables balance) is accepted free of any mental reservations regarding the customer's ability to pay. From the outset of the relationship there should be no major concern that the account will turn into a collection problem. When a credit line is granted or a credit line is increased, the credit granter should have no reservations regarding the ability of customers to handle their credit obligation in a satisfactory manner.

A Strong Customer Base—Good Cashflow

The goal of any good credit management program is to minimize the number of days it takes to collect accounts receivable balances and maximize the amount of cash generated from those balances. Collecting account balances within terms, or as close to terms as possible, is a challenge that the credit manager/administrator must meet successfully if the company or business is to hold the cost of money at the lowest level consistent with its requirement.

Accounts receivable must be collected at a rate that reflects two things: the company's terms of sale and the company's credit policy. If the company's credit policy is other than restrictive, either moderate or liberal, the payment pattern of some accounts will require extra collection effort. It is essential that people who have the collection responsibility must do so with diligence, a knowledge of good collection practices, a knowledge of the payment patterns of the company's major accounts, and a solid program for dealing promptly, fairly and effectively with accounts whose payment pattern requires that extra collection effort.

A strong receivables base—one that consistently delivers a high percentage of the company's monthly cash requirement—is an enormous plus for any business or company. It has enormous importance to a company breaking out of its start-up mode and to the company entering, or immersed in, an ongoing cycle of growth, and to the company with many years of well-managed growth and financial success. It is essential that customers who have been granted the privilege of buying goods or services on credit terms are not allowed to abuse that privilege. Customers whose payment pattern is inconsistent with credit terms and credit policy should not be allowed to extend their abuse to the point where profits from sales to accounts in the *abuser* category—or money generated to sustain cashflow—is diminished to a degree that is not acceptable.

There is no guarantee that an account will continue to prosper and continue to pay account balances in a satisfactory manner. Changes occur that impact the stability of a company:

- Management changes
- The industry need or acceptance of a product
- The national economy or the economy in the area serviced by the customer
- Other relevant causes for unanticipated problems

The tomorrows that follow today may be as successful for your applicant and for your customers as they have been in the past—or they may not. And if they are not, it is to be hoped that the constant monitoring of receivables by the people who administer credit will pick up individual signs of account weakness long before they can become a threat to the safety of your company's receivables dollars.

Part 2

Collection Techniques: Commercial Accounts

2

Legitimate and Reasonable Collection Methods

The collection decisions that you made yesterday and the yesterdays before that will settle ultimately into one of three categories: the good, the fair, and the ugly. Unless you change the guidelines for a particular account, your experience with the account probably will not change measurably. From that earliest point when you relied solely upon the experience of others, your experience with the account gradually became of primary importance. What peer credit managers are doing and experiencing will always be relevant to your own decisions, but secondary to your own experience. Your evaluation will become the determining factor in any decision to continue selling on the terms and dollar level you first assigned, or, if your company's account experience indicates you should, to make an upward or a downward adjustment.

Watch for signs. Any account that requires two or three collection calls each month, particularly after a long period of an acceptable payments pattern, warrants careful monitoring. When such a customer begins to slip, dig for answers. You don't need a medical degree to know when the vital signs begin to falter. If changes are occurring in the way an account makes its payments, ask for reasons why.

Occasionally you will have an account whose response to your strongest in-house collection effort is verbal abuse. Hold your temper, but take that response as your cue not to drag out your in-house collection effort. Assign the account to a collection agency, one that specializes in commercial accounts. For a variety of reasons (especially to avoid having a formal collection assignment picked up by credit reporting services, or having a suit become a matter of public record), the first notice from a collection agency can sometimes jar the delinquent account into sending all or part of the money that you have been trying to collect. When that happens, and your collection service agreement specifies "10 days free demand," the usual collection fee of 20 to 35 percent (percentages vary from one agency to another and according to the dollar amount of the assignment) is not applicable. What happens if the demand letter sent to your customer by the collection agency draws a *payment in full* response within 10 days of the collection agency's letter? With the "10 days free demand" provision, there is no collection charge. Remember, however, that when one of your customers is sliding, whatever the collection service gets for you is that much more than your own effort generated. If the agency collects your money, it earns its fee.

Professional Effort and Conduct

It is imperative that personnel in the credit department who have the responsibility for collecting receivables balances should put forth their best and most professional effort. What are the ingredients for a *best and most professional effort*? The following is a list of the major ingredients:

1. *Tact:* The ability to address the problem and move the conversation toward a commitment for payment and not appear to force the issue or apply obvious amounts of pressure.

2. *Perseverance:* The ability to persist in or remain constant to the purpose or goal of collecting the past due balance(s), and to do it without causing the customer/debtor to become resentful or antagonistic.

3. *Tenacity:* The ability to hold firm to the goal of collecting past due balances from the customer and refusing to be put off by contrived and untruthful reasons for nonpayment of overdue balances.

4. *Creative Solutions:* The ability to work within the financial circumstances of a customer/debtor and to fashion a payment program acceptable to the customer and to the supplier/creditor.

5. *Mutually Beneficial Compromises:* To recognize and to accept a less than perfect solution or plan as the best obtainable for all parties of interest.

6. *Sense of Responsibility to Customers:* A sense of responsibility to customers who, through no fault of their own, suffer a sudden, but reversible, cashflow problem.

The levels of urgency for collecting past due accounts can be established by reversing the value of the scale of 1 to 10.

Example: The customer is relatively new to your company, has not been in business long enough to have established a trend, is consistently past due with your company and other suppliers, and receivables aging is lengthening. The level of urgency, after reversing the weight of the scale, may be somewhere between 6 and 9. If past due balances are really stretching, you could be looking at an 8 or a 9; when the aging is closer to terms, the risk level might be no more than 6 or 7. What is considered a 10? Unrelated to the popular interpretation of a 10, this level on the scale triggers the all-out, little short-of-panic effort to collect past-due balances from an account whose pyramiding inability to pay suppliers is indicative of an imminent filing for protection under Chapter 11. It might also instill a fear of a midnight evacuation of the office, store, and/or warehouse—and no forwarding address! A 10 is any situation where the loss of receivables dollars could be an imminent probability.

Number one through five are reserved for accounts whose pattern of occasional and modest past-due balances poses no threat of loss. These are accounts whose cashflow may vary among them from consistently good to those accounts whose cashflow is not always equal to the monthly cashflow requirement of the business. These accounts should be watched as individual accounts but as a group there should be no ongoing trend downward and no reason to consider that any "1 to 5" account is in the short term a candidate for business failure.

Procedures and Goals

(The following is a guideline [fine tune for your own business or company] for distributing the work load within a Credit Department. It should minimize the amount of time that staff members devote to collecting past-due receivables as it will maximize results when a collection procedure becomes necessary).

1. The Aged Trial Balance Report of customer accounts should be split into sections of approximately equal size, not equal in the number of accounts assigned to each account section supervisor, but approximately equal in the work load assigned to each supervisor. As growth warrants, accounts on the receivables reports can be realigned between sections.

2. Certain major accounts (to be designated by the Credit Manager) will be handled by the Credit Manager or the Assistant Credit Manager. The Assistant Credit Manager will monitor the accounts that are assigned to him or her and make the necessary telephone or letter contacts.

3. The Assistant Credit Manager (or if there is no assistant, the Credit Manager) will monitor the work of the section supervisors, answer questions that are within the range of his or her experience and authority and refer other questions to the Credit Manager. Section supervisors will have access to the Credit Manager, but to avoid any appearance of undercutting the authority of the Assistant Manager, such contact must be through the Assistant Manager.

4. Aged Trial Balance Reports (whether on a once a week, twice a week, or more frequent schedule) will be delivered to the Credit Manager's office. He or she will make appropriate notations on the assistant Manager's copy, then pass that copy and copies for the section supervisors on to the Assistant Manager.

5. The Assistant Manager will see that appropriate notations are included on the copy received by each section supervisor. These comments will address the

sequence of collection priority—the type, timing, and progressive strength of the collection actions to be taken—and the point in a given collection situation where the Credit Manager has indicated he or she will review the effort to that point and authorize a written *final demand*. Other notations regarding special actions or special effort will also be made on section supervisors' copies by the Assistant Manager.

6. Section supervisors will use call sheets in each account file folder to briefly recap collection and other conversations with the customer or the customer's employees. Customer folders, with recaps of these conversations, will be put on the Assistant Credit Manager's desk at the close of each business day. Payment commitment data will be transferred from individual file folders by the Assistant Manager to a list that will be put on the Credit Manager's desk by 10:00 the following morning. The Credit Manager will then enter payment commitment data on a form (Receivables Projection Form) which will be attached to the currently applicable master copy of the accounts receivable aging report.

7. Customer folders that require review will be put on the Credit Manager's desk at the end of each business day. If special action is indicated, it will be detailed in a note which will be attached to the folder or discussed with the Assistant Manager. Folders will be returned to section supervisors for the indicated action. (If standard action has been or seems about to be productive, the Assistant Manager will initial the account *calls recap sheet* and return it to the section supervisor without additional comment.)

8. If a collection call or letter triggers any form of unreasonable or abusive customer response, the conversation or letter will be brought to the attention of the Credit Manager as soon thereafter as is practicable.

9. Every Monday morning in a 30-minute session, the Credit Manager will discuss with the Assistant Manager and account sections supervisors both the positive and negative results of the previous week's work, where the emphasis is to be placed during the current week, and what is expected from these and other collection actions. (If a procedure or an approach does not seem to be working or is less effective than it was in the past, the Monday morning meeting is the time for fine-tuning, correcting, or changing a procedure with the goal of improving the effectiveness of each call.)

10. Credit clearances will continue to be the overview responsibility of the Credit Manager, but the Assistant Manager has the authority to authorize the open-account release of goods to a maximum of 10 percent above established credit limits. When a credit request is not in line with prior order clearances, or when there is any question regarding open balances or payment history, the credit decision will be deferred until the Credit Manager is available. (If, in one of the above-described situations, the Credit Manager is not available to make the decision, it will be referred to the Financial Officer.)

11. In every collection and/or past-due situation, the initial goal is to collect the balance(s) and to retain enough customer goodwill so the customer can continue to be serviced on terms somewhere between COD and Open Account. In some situations it will be obvious that the emphasis of the effort is to collect the past-due balance(s): the customer has reached a point in the downward slide where there is no thought of future business, and the objective is to collect what is owed to the creditor and walk rapidly away from the customer. (The Credit Manager will indicate at the outset of the collection effort, or at some point during that effort, where there is a customer to be saved or whether the only objective is to save the creditor's dollars.)

Sequential Collection Procedure for Accounts Receivable

No one collection procedure is the right fit for every company or every industry. The following is an effective procedure that can be easily adjusted to meet the requirements of your own company's financial requirements.

1. Statements will be mailed each month to all accounts.

2. When customer balances pass from the *Current* to the *Over 30* column on the Aged Trial Balance Report, a first collection call will be made.

3. When customer balances reach the *Over 45* point on the Aged Trial Balance Report, a second collection call will be made.

4. When customer balances reach the *Over 60* column on the Aged Trial Balance Report, a collection letter will be sent to the customer. Five to eight days after the collection letter has been mailed, the credit department person who has responsibility for the account will make a collection telephone call.

5. There can be some variation from the above (the spacing of letters and telephone calls,and the substituting of a collection letter for the first or second telephone call) based upon the following criteria of priority and/or urgency:
   a. When balances are in two or more columns, the urgency is based upon the combination of dollars and aging. (All balances are past due, or open balances are a combination of current and past due.)
   b. Past experience with the account plus the past and current experience of other suppliers. If report data isn't current (D & B, NACM, etc.), those reports should be updated.
   c. The quality of the customer's response to the first letter or telephone call; key person not available, no return telephone call, etc.
   d. Whether there appears to be a trend downward in the customer's business.
   e. Whether cashflow seems to have been impacted by any single factor or a combination of extremely rapid growth, the loss of a key person or key personnel, or the loss of what may have been a long-standing advantage in the marketplace.

f. Any product-related litigation that might involve the potential for a damaging financial settlement or that might incorporate the possibility of a negative impact on the customer's marketplace image. These are some of the factors that influence the timing and the amount of effort that we put into collecting past-due balances. They are some of the factors that dictate how much time and effort company credit department personnel will expend on an account before the account is assigned to an outside collection agency.

6. When a customer's balance or a part of that balance reaches the *Over 90 Days* column on the Aged Trial Balance Report, the credit manager will have taken one or more of the following steps:

   a. Orders would have been held when the account became 45- or 60-days past due. The quality of your experience with the account in the past and what you are able to ascertain regarding the account's present condition will determine the exact timing of a hold on orders.

   b. If a satisfactory payment arrangement is worked out with the customer (payments every week or every two weeks which reduce the total open balance while allowing for the release of some goods; a payment arrangement of two dollars for every one dollar of goods released, etc.), then the *hold* on the release of orders can be eased.

   c. If an account falls increasingly deeper into the category of slow-pay accounts and the problem is not just a temporary cashflow problem, but is the result of some new, adverse business problems, then the Credit Manager will monitor the account's trend with the person who has responsibility for the account.

7. When an account has a past-due balance that has reached the *Over 120 Days* column, it may already have been a third-party (outside collection service) collection assignment for 30 or more days. The Credit Manager will review each week all accounts on the past-due lists of department personnel with responsibility for accounts. As some accounts begin to slide deeper into the past-due columns, action appropriate to the specific account will be authorized by the Credit Manager.

8. When an account has been assigned to a collection agency, the company's products will not be available to the assigned account until the account has been paid in full. Unless there are unusual extenuating circumstances that would justify a change in the credit policy, the account may buy products on COD terms, but will not be allowed to buy products on credit terms.

Caution: There are no inflexible criteria for handling most credit and collection problems. The primary criterion is the company's credit policy which sets parameters of some latitude and flexibility, not the least of which is the department's need and mandate to deal fairly and honestly with the company's credit customers, and the phrase *company's credit customers* includes virtually every customer who buys on a regular basis.

Department staff with account responsibility will monitor all accounts on an ongoing basis, prorating time and energy to focus on major customers with an account or a payment problem, accounts with a lower dollar volume and some new or recurring payment problems, and an increasingly diminishing amount of time on the lower-to-lowest dollar volume accounts.

You should not expect to lose a single dollar in bad-debt write-offs that could have been avoided with solid, diligent monitoring and collection procedures. The customer is king, but his or her crown diminishes in size and importance as it relates to the quality (payment performance) of the account.

3

Legal Collection Methods

The law is specific as it relates to what a creditor can and cannot do to collect past-due balances; there is occasional difficulty, however, when it comes to defining whether a specific letter, telephone call, or other collection action stayed within the law or slipped over into an area that is unacceptable.

There is a limit beyond which a company cannot escalate the collection effort without incurring the probability of a legal response (restraining order, law suit, etc.). The people who own or manage a company or business may have treated your company quite badly, but you must be sure that your collection effort remains within the boundaries of legal and ethical conduct. In that same context, never use the services of a commercial collection agency whose reputation for operating ethically, and within the law, is not well known. Your company could incur liability because of the questionable or blatantly illegal practices of an agency whom you have designated as an authorized representative. Problems of this nature can get very complicated and quite expensive if a suit goes to trial and the judge or jury is persuaded that the actions of your company, or of the company's designated representative, were illegal. Such a verdict can only result in a substantial monetary award in favor of the plaintiff company.

How can credit managers ensure that their collection effort is legal within the most rigid interpretation of the laws governing illegal collection practices? The primary canon of conduct is that you do not threaten an individual or a company: do not make threatening or intimidating telephone calls to the residence of the owner, manager, or any other employee; say nothing that is not factual when asked by another company for your experience with an account. Never offer derogatory opinions or remarks regarding the management, personnel, or conduct of the business, and never put yourself or your company in the position of facing a suit for damages resulting from remarks and/or efforts allegedly made by you or a member of your staff while harassing one or more key company members or while attempting to discredit the customer company with other members of the trade, bankers, credit report companies, industry groups, etc.

The number of legal options available to collect your company's money are too numerous to allow yourself to slip into any illegal practices. The following are some examples of legal collection methods:

- Your own efforts and the efforts of staff members
- The efforts of a commercial collection agency
- The use of an attorney who is a collection specialist

Never let an obligation become a bad-debt item because you failed to use every legitimate tool to collect the receivables balance, but *do not* fall into the trap of allowing your zeal to cross into the area of illegal collection practices.

If you use every conventional collection procedure that is presented and discussed in this book, including obtaining a judgment against assets that cannot be found or may no longer exist, then you have confirmed that it is a bad-debt account. Put it in the category of a learning experience. Charge the account balance against the *Bad Debt Reserve* and get on with managing your other accounts.

The Absence of Malice

There is no room in the collection effort for any action or statement that might be interpreted as the product of malice or of malicious intent. The legal definition of *malice*, as given in Webster's *Encyclopedic Unabridged Dictionary of the English Language*, says it is "evil intent on the part of one who commits a wrongful act injurious to others." That definition, plus the potential for legal action based upon a "wrongful act injurious to others" should be more than enough incentive to keep collection people on the legal path.

Malice has no place in any technique for collecting accounts receivable balances. It is so out of "synch" with the reality of an appropriate collection procedure that any person who taints a collection effort by using it should be barred from engaging in that type of work. You may not like a customer because of what the customer has successfully imposed upon your company—chronic past-due balances, broken payment promises, frequent and unjustified claims for credits based upon prices that were never quoted, etc.—but the dislike that you have for the customer cannot be allowed to interject itself into the way the collection effort is conducted.

It is true that you should lean heavier on those accounts whose payment problems are chronic, whose financial problems seem to be increasing, whose management and key support personnel seem to be leaving, and whose market area share has lost much of its early momentum and potential. But when you are working to collect the types and categories of accounts just mentioned, remember that many of those accounts—with adequate monitoring, can probably be sold successfully for a long period of time.

Malice is the driving force in the following: "It is not the obligation of this company to sell product(s) to a customer whose unfamiliarity with ethical business practice has been channeled into a pricing policy that is calculated to force reputable firms to close their doors. Quite the contrary. Our obligation is to the ethical members of this industry, and this industry will be well served when your company is unable to get product(s) it needs to continue to make a shambles of your regional marketplace."

This is certainly not an acceptable letter. The threat to get other suppliers to join with this supplier and withhold product(s) is strongly implied, which may then cause severe mental stress or mental anguish for a debtor whose business may not deserve to survive but who is protected by law from acts motivated by malice or threats of extortion, libel, involuntary bankruptcy, harassment, coercion, criminal prosecution, etc. The recipient of a letter that contains remarks such as the above is looking at the ingredients for a suit for damages that could add a criminal liability to the civil liability.

The Right to Privacy

The interpretation of *the right to privacy* does not have a uniform national standard. Although facts regarding a specific creditor/debtor situation may be published, great care must be taken to ensure that there is no suggestion of insolvency or impropriety; this may be but is not necessarily a defense against libel. The right of privacy is a different matter and may be considered to have been violated when publicity is given to the debts of another. Not every state accepts *the right to privacy* as an actionable cause (a basis for a lawsuit), but there is enough support nationwide for it to be a very dangerous area for a creditor's collection effort to find itself.

A suit to defend the right to privacy, or a suit for damages as the result of what is alleged to have been an invasion of privacy, may use a set of facts that is the same or similar to facts that could form the basis of other suits; in that context we speak of slander, libel, false imprisonment, etc. Malice, along with whether the debt was due and actually owed, once again lifts its head as a factor in determining whether the creditor violated the debtor's right to privacy. In the process of establishing liability, the many jurisdictions whose laws recognize the right to privacy do not consider that *motive* is of any consequence in establishing whether there is liability. The creditor, for whatever reason, may have violated the right to privacy of the debtor. In jurisdictions whose laws support the right to privacy, a court will move on to the process of establishing liability.

Harassing a debtor is one of the more common and one of the more expensive mistakes made by overly zealous collectors. It is unacceptable to push a debtor—whether a partnership, a sole proprietorship, or a company—with telephone calls that are too frequent or harassing in their content, letters that are threatening in tone and may be available or made available to third parties, and one or more of a litany of tactics that may seek to collect a debt but use a process that reeks of harassment. This tactic returns the collection effort/procedure to the point where the debtor is subject to unacceptable consequences: mental anguish, embarrassment, injury to the reputation of a company or an individual, damage to the ability of the business or company to compete effectively in the marketplace, etc.

Although claims of invasion of privacy may be asserted in a lawsuit, if the circumstances fit the criteria for an action that might be successfully litigated, this does not mean that creditors cannot collect their company's money while successfully defending the company against a formal charge of invasion of privacy. The law and the courts have in recent years seemed to tip the scales in favor of debtors more frequently than they have recognized the rights of creditors.

Decide whether the right of privacy—defined in National Association of Credit Management's (NACM) Credit Manual of Commercial Laws as "the giving of publicity to the private affairs, including debts, of another"—is or is not violated in the following example:

The credit manager of the creditor company writes a letter to the controller of the debtor company in which:

1. A demand is made for payment of the past-due balance.

2. A statement is made that questions the honesty of the debtor firm.

3. Included is a threat to initiate an involuntary petition in bankruptcy if the account is not paid immediately. Copies of the letter are then sent to other suppliers of the debtor, and separate copies are mailed to three of the debtor's major customers.

Is there a violation of privacy in the above? Is there more than one violation? What about any visible sign of malice?

If the example occurs in one of the many jurisdictions that recognize a right to privacy, numbers one through three of the example are in violation of that right. And copies of the letter sent to three of the debtor's major customers? I think we can agree that the items listed in the example contain enough raw malice to bury each statement under a thick layer of it!

Interchange of Information Among Creditors

The complete title of this section should be "The Interchange of Information Among Creditors Having Mutual Interests in an Account." Fortunately for those of us in the credit profession, the interchange of such information is not only legal but an essential part of the credit and collections process.

Within an organization such as the NACM, members of an industry group may meet once a month to discuss their common account problems; this includes accounts which may be a problem for one, two or several of the 20 or 25 companies represented at the meeting. At the end of the luncheon, each credit manager is given the opportunity to *go around the table* with the names of one-to-four accounts that are, for his or her company: a collection problem, have never been a collection problem but are sliding deeper into a pattern of past-due balances, are applying for a credit line, or some other problem of mutual interest that relates to a specific account or class of accounts.

It is legal to exchange information among creditors (suppliers, banks, credit reporting agencies, etc.) when there is no collusion among suppliers to stop selling product(s) or service(s) to a customer. There must be truth in the reporting of experience and data between companies of like interest. No company should purposely downgrade the payment performance of a customer—not for any reason. When an honest mistake is made and subsequently discovered, it should be corrected immediately. The uncorrected version is not only an unfair report of the customer's record with your company but it could cause another supplier to withhold merchandise, to impose a lower credit line, or to insist on COD payment from a customer whose record with your company warrants a higher level of trust.

Example: The credit manager of Company A remembers that at the last month's industry credit meeting, company B's credit manager reported that company Z had slid from payments that were within terms to an increasing number of balances 30 and 40 days past due.

Company A picks up the phone, gets through to Company B's credit manager, tells her his problem with Company Z (balances from current to 40 days past due), and asks how Company Z is paying its account with Company B. Company B's credit manager checks her current accounts receivable aged trial balance report and tells Company A's credit manager that Company Z is running 20 to 30 days slow—but she has gone beyond that record. She has verified that Company Z has taken on a new major product line; to obtain the new line, Company Z had to agree to pay invoices within terms for the first six months. This gives Company A's credit manager the assurance he needs to continue a controlled program of credit sales to Company Z while he works with the company to reduce past-due balances.

The exchange of credit information (whether over the telephone, at a one-on-one lunch, at a credit group meeting, etc.), requires that parties involved observe certain rules of conduct. Those rules include ensuring that what should be a simple exchange of experience data and/or information does not become something that takes on elements of restraint of trade. There can be no *group agreement* (explicit or implied) to withhold goods from a customer(s) whose account is delinquent with some or all members of the group, or whose account has been placed on cash or COD terms. Credit managers will be influenced by the combination of their own knowledge and experience and that of other credit managers in the same trade group, and that is fine. Individual judgment made on the basis of the best and widest base of information available to the credit manager should determine decisions. Nowhere in the scenario of a decision that has been reached independently is there a shred of restraint of trade.

Competitors or members of a trade group may not set or maintain uniform prices, discounts, or terms or conditions of sale. Practices of this nature fall under the jurisdiction of the Fair Trade Act and carry the potential for some very heavy fines. Your credit group must also recognize the potential for trouble if a qualified applicant is refused membership in the group. Questions arising regarding the integrity of the applicant and whether the applicant could be expected to adhere to the rules of confidentiality (as it relates to information shared at meetings with all or some members of the group), is a relevant concern when considering an application for membership. The rule of confidentiality is the cornerstone upon which every exchange of information pertaining to customers or potential customers is based. No person who seeks information from other credit managers regarding the payment habits, reputation, etc., of a customer or prospective customer should repeat any of that information to the subject. Credit managers must know they can trust other credit managers, as individual managers or as members of a credit group, to protect the confidentiality of information and the sources of information.

Remember that lists of delinquent accounts, which are frequently exchanged or discussed at credit group meetings, must not include persons, businesses, or companies whose normal payment pattern is within terms or on an acceptable basis, and whose only current problems may be a disputed charge or charges. These customers do not belong on a list of past-due or delinquent accounts, and any negative or disparaging remarks about a charge or a balance that the customer views as a valid problem is totally out of line.

The confidentiality that members of a credit group agree to maintain as group members and as individual credit professionals is applicable also to credit reports available to members from commercial credit reporting organizations such as Dun & Bradstreet, the National Association of Credit Management, etc. Reports offered by these organizations are compiled from data furnished voluntarily by subscribers, nonsubscribers, members, and nonmembers. Reports issued to a subscriber on request are considered to be privileged information. If, however, these reports are given general circulation, any negative or defamatory information must be verified before the report is issued. Can credit groups revoke the membership privilege of a group member? If there is a provision in the bylaws that relates to specific situations, membership can be revoked for a violation of that bylaw. the key to the legality of the provision is that it must be applied uniformly.

When there is an alleged violation of antitrust laws, there must be provable or demonstrable evidence to substantiate the allegation. The plaintiff must be able to prove that an agreement existed among group members before the subject information was shared either orally or in written form. What about a group acting in unison? The allegation must have legs on which to stand.

Postal Laws

Postal laws address themselves to the rights of creditors and debtors, and both parties must be especially careful to avoid straying into an area that could be punishable by a fine and/or a prison sentence. Because any violation of a postal law is a federal offense, a misstep at this level is not to be taken lightly or carelessly.

The following paragraph from the United States Code (1976) addresses itself to what is and is not legal under this Code. It covers the use of the mails as they can or might be used to defraud and the penalties for failing to operate within the Code's parameters:

> Whoever, having devised or intending to devise any scheme or artifice to defraud, or for obtaining money or property by means of false or fraudulent pretenses, representations, or promises ... for the purpose of executing such scheme or artifice or attempting to do so, places in any post office or authorized depository for mail matter, any matter or thing whatever to be sent or delivered by the Postal Service, or takes or receives therefrom, any such matter or thing, or knowingly causes to be delivered by mail according to the direction thereon, or at a place at which it is directed to be delivered by the person to whom it is addressed, any such matter or thing, shall be fined not more than $1,000 or imprisoned not more than five years, or both.

The United States Code states also that it is illegal to use the United States mails to transmit a false financial statement, either to a corporation or to a particular individual. This is a powerful tool when a major collection problem develops with an account and it can be proven that the financial statement(s) was instrumental in persuading the creditor to sell product(s) or service(s) to the debtor on credit terms. The Code does not differentiate between the sending by a person or company of a financial statement that was successful in the attempt to defraud and a similar act that was not successful. The presence of the elements of a fraud—a plan or a scheme to defraud, an actual or an attempted fraud, and the use of the mails in connection with the execution or attempted execution of the fraud—is all that is necessary for the offense to be real under the Code.

To prove that the financial statement was materially false, several elements must be present. If there is no proof—or if the proof is not conclusive—it will not be possible to prove that the alleged offense did occur.

Proof of the offense can be substantiated if the following can be established:

1. The statement is materially false and to the degree that a prudent business person would not, had the true facts been known, in the normal course of business, have extended credit upon the strength of the statement.

2. It must be shown that the statement was made or used for the purpose of obtaining credit from the individual or company/business to whom it was mailed.

3. The statement submitted to the company or individual as a document that the creditor company could rely upon.

4. And the key requirement in the process of proving that the mails were used with the intent to defraud: that the statement was sent to the creditor through the United States mails.

It can be extremely difficult to prove the above-listed requirements for proving intent to defraud, but proving that the financial statement was materially false is the most difficult. Statements prepared from a combination of figures that are real and others that are estimates can be given legitimacy by an accused as something that was prepared quickly because the supplier wanted it. Was there an intent to defraud the supplier? The supplier may be sure there was, but how is the supplier company going to prove it?

When your company receives a financial statement from an applicant or a customer—one other than with whom your company has a long and a satisfactory relationship—take the envelope in which the financial statement arrived and put it in the customer file. Why do that? It provides proof via the postmark date that the financial statement was sent to your company through the United States mails. When you are sure there has been fraud, the envelope becomes a starting point from which you may develop a case of using the mails to defraud.

Intent to Defraud as Perceived by Law

The effort to prove that a financial statement is a fraud requires a level of proof that meets the test of being "beyond the shadow of a doubt." This can be an almost impossible task because to prove that the financial statement is false requires an item by item verification of the statement. To do this successfully, it is necessary to first convince a prosecuting attorney that the facts that point to a fraudulent financial statement are strong enough to give him or her a good chance to convince a judge or a jury. The prosecuting attorney must have facts upon which to base the case; nothing can be done if what he or she is shown is *opinion* or *estimation*. An analysis of the items on a financial statement will either give a prosecuting attorney the material necessary (a) to proceed with a charge of fraud, or (b) decline to prosecute because the evidence is not strong enough to prove charges of fraud.

An investigation of the items on a financial statement that are relevant to a possible prosecution of the maker of the statement on a charge of intent to defraud will usually include the following items:

1. *Cash on hand and in the bank:* Cash in the bank is easily verified by the records of the maker's bank. Cash on hand must be proven by the debtor's own records.

2. *Accounts receivable:* These can be verified by the receivables records of the maker.

3. *Inventory:* The investigator must ascertain from the maker whether inventory is valued at cost or market value, and determine how seasonal merchandise is depreciated versus original cost.

4. *Fixed assets:* These should be carried at their depreciated value but may reflect opinion as to their worth, rather than fact.

5. *Accounts payable* (past due and not due): These are verified by the records of the maker of the financial statement. If the information is not available from the maker, creditors must be contracted.

6. *Taxes:* These can be verified from tax records, tax accruals, and from general ledger entries if not carried as an item in the financial statement.

7. *Mortgages* (land and buildings): Financial statement figures can be checked against public records.

8. *Owing to banks, finance companies, or others:* This category can be verified against official public records.

Proof that a financial statement is materially false is all the criteria that is required for a prosecutor to prove that the maker—the person or company who furnished it to the creditor as an inducement to extend credit—had *intent to defraud*.

It should be mentioned also that most states have enacted a statute that establishes the criteria for prosecuting people who use a false/fraudulent financial statement to obtain property (goods, etc.). These statutes, which are known as the *false pretense statutes*, provide prosecutors with a legal foundation for proceeding against makers of false financial statements. The statutes spell out the conditions that must be present, such as a maker who knowingly makes or causes to be made a false written statement regarding the financial condition of the business for the purpose of obtaining credit, a loan, merchandise, personal property, etc.

The two examples that follow offer circumstances under which (1) a creditor takes what appears to be a fraudulent financial statement to the prosecutor for the filing of charges, which the prosecutor is unable to do. Example 2 involves circumstances upon which the prosecutor can base a case of *intent to defraud* against the debtor.

Example 1: A creditor goes to the office of the prosecuting attorney with a financial statement which he or she now believes to be materially false. It was the key or persuasive document that led to the granting of a substantial line of credit, most of which was used and is now 60 to 90 days past due. No effort is being made to reduce the balance and the debtor is buying product(s) similar to those sold by the creditor from another supplier—and for cash.

The owner of the business states that the figures used for the challenged statement were compiled quickly to meet the creditor's request for a currently applicable report, included estimates and opinions, and was an unaudited, internally prepared statement. He contends that in hindsight the financial statement may have had significant inaccuracies but it was not possible to know about them given the conditions—creditor's pressure to deliver a statement, the absence of hard figures, the use of estimates and opinions—under which the statement was prepared.

Although there are strong indications in a report prepared by a credit reporting agency that the debtor company is not truthful in its relationships with most suppliers, the body of evidence is not strong enough for the prosecuting attorney to charge the maker/debtor with *intent to defraud*. The financial statement fails to meet the criteria for a level of proof that is "beyond the shadow of a doubt." There are too many ambiguities that might or might not be the product of an intent to defraud, and any proof of *intent* cannot be separated from the ambiguities.

Example 2: The financial statement in this example is one that could prove to be the basis for charges of *intent to defraud* because it has the creditor in the position of obtaining from one source or another—the debtor's bank, a credit reporting agency, another creditor, etc.—a copy of a true financial statement for the business covering virtually the same time frame as the one involving figures thought to be fraudulent. When an item-by-item comparison of the two statements reveals errors that could only have been committed with the intent to deceive and to defraud, the prosecutor will have no problem proceeding with charges against the maker of the fraudulent statement.

Proof—being able to prove that there was intent to defraud—is the key to whether there is an actionable cause for filing charges, or whether a prosecutor has the hard proof he or she needs to prevail with a judge or jury. It is a bitter pill when indications of intent to defraud are quite strong but there is no hard, provable evidence of that intent. Debtors who obtain credit through deceit and fraud may eventually slip and find themselves facing charges, however, it will be no help to those creditors who were defrauded earlier and were unable to prove it.

4

Illegal Collection Methods to Avoid

A credit person who is responsible for collecting past-due accounts receivable balances must be very careful that what may appear to be nothing more threatening than a good, aggressive collection effort does not stray from that narrow corridor into the sometimes gray areas of harassment or threats.

Ambiguity is in any area where you cannot clearly draw lines, but it is especially frustrating to walk a tightrope of ethical collection conduct when you know that the person or company with whom you are dealing is addicted to devious thinking and behavior. When the situation is extreme, the benefits of the law tip in favor of the unscrupulous. The law is meant to be equitable for all parties, and it is legally and morally correct to protect a debtor against threats and harassment, but the law does sometimes lose sight of where justice begins and ends. The obvious becomes blatant when the one who allegedly needs the protection is busily engaged in trying to take advantage of his/her creditors, and often to a degree that involves fraud. At that point, the law's protective umbrella can be somewhat less than equitable.

Never stray from a collection procedure that is totally ethical and legal or your debtors might counter your efforts with a suit alleging that your actions have been detrimental to their business reputation, and also injurious to their mental health. In that same context, never use the services of a commercial collection agency whose reputation for ethical practices is not well-known; your company could incur liability because of the actions of an authorized representative. Problems of this nature can get very complicated and suddenly quite expensive if a suit becomes a jury trial and the jury is persuaded that your actions have heaped wrongs upon the head of your former customer. Some collection actions are so heavy-handed as to provide a legitimate basis for a suit alleging damages. Such behavior is reprehensible and has no place in credit management. Many legal options are available for attempting to collect your money. Your own efforts, the efforts of a commercial collection agency, and the use of an attorney. If you have tried all of them, including obtaining a judgment against assets that cannot be found or do not exist, then you have confirmed that this is a bad-debt account. Put it in the category of a learning experience. Charge the account balance against the Bad-Debt Reserve, and get on with managing your other accounts.

Harassment

This is one of the most dangerous and volatile of the illegal collection techniques. When it surfaces in one of its less flagrant applications, it is not always easy to label. As it progresses into the more persistent, disturbing and damaging aspects of the tactic, there can be no question as to the quality and the intent. Taken to a high level of intensity and persistence, it can have an eroding effect on the physical and mental health of the person(s) upon which it is being practiced.

Webster's *Encyclopedic Unabridged Dictionary* defines *harass* as "to disturb persistently; to torment, as with troubles, cares, etc.; pester, persecute." *Harassment* is more of the same: to disturb or irritate persistently; to wear out; to exhaust."

These defining key words—persecute, torment, disturb persistently, wear out, exhaust—are the foundation material used by federal and state lawmakers to define the parameters for what constitutes an illegal collection tactic or procedure. No collection effort can incorporate any of these tactics and expect to escape punitive action. Think about the word *persecute* and picture yourself in the position of a debtor who is being hounded relentlessly (telephone calls day and night to your home and business) by a creditor who has lost all perspective. This is a creditor who is so vindictive that he or she has lost sight of the parameters within which a legal collection process must be conducted.

Does the person in this hypothetical situation recognize the limitations imposed by the United States Criminal Code or by statutes enacted by the various states? This is not a person who is willing to recognize and abide by federal and state statutes—and that can add up to some expensive problems for the company or business represented by this individual.

A debtor cannot be subjected to home and business telephone calls that, by their frequency and time frame, are intended to torment, persecute, and harass. Civil and punitive damages, in addition to the penalties of federal and state statutes for illegal collection tactics, are the natural results of a debtor who has been persecuted to the point where his or her mental and physical health has been damaged. Can you wear down and exhaust the debtor with an endless barrage of mean-spirited telephone calls? Can you disturb and disrupt the routine of a person at all hours of the day or night, beyond all rights and options created by the past-due obligation? Absolutely not! You cannot retaliate with collection tactics that are unconscionable and illegal.

Postal Laws

The following are examples of violations of the postal laws which might, in some of the examples, provide the basis for a suit for damages. Evidence is based upon libelous statements or material upon the outside cover of a letter, in or on a postal card, etc.

a. The definition of nonmailable matter is covered in the United States Criminal Code.

b. Penalties of up to one year in prison, a fine of not more than $1000—or both—may be imposed if the sender is convicted of a Code offense.

c. Postal cards which indicate that the addressee is being contacted for payment of past-due account are nonmailable under the U.S. Criminal Code.

d. Postal cards which threaten any form of legal action are illegal under the Code.

e. Postal cards that request payment or note when an account will be due are not prohibited by the Code, *but* all such card requests must be in language that is respectful and nonthreatening.

It is a common sense collection practice to avoid the use of postal cards. The language used in collection letters should never be so strong that it goes over the line into an area that is illegal; but why bother to try to walk the language line on something that has the high visibility of a postal card? The simple fact is that a postal card is not a good collection tool; at times it is a dangerous one.

False or Damaging Statements

The use of false and damaging statements about a person or business either spoken, or sent through the United States mails during the course of trying to collect a past-due account balance, is neither proper nor an ethical collection technique. It is, in fact, a very dangerous technique that can backfire into an enormously expensive experience. It is neither legal nor appropriate to speak or to write false or damaging statements about an individual, a business, or a company. Suppose you are unhappy with the individual or the company because you feel that statements and promises were made by the customer/debtor not in good faith, but as a ploy to get your company to release more product? Your suspicions may be 100 percent correct but unless you have irrefutable evidence of these actions—dates, witnesses, locations, etc.—you cannot say anything that might be interpreted as a false or a damaging statement.

The potential is great for trouble for you and/or your company if you make false or damaging statements in a setting that includes a person or persons other than the person to whom you are speaking. It is improper as a collection technique and could be the basis for the debtor bringing a civil suit for damages. One must also be cautious about what is said in a letter addressed to a debtor. Remember that a letter sent to a company or a business, even when directed to the owner or proprietor, may be read by one or more other people before it reaches the person to whom it is addressed; such a letter never succeeds in becoming a private communication between the addressor and addressee. Third persons, either in the course of their work or because they might see the letter on the addressee's desk, could read it and become aware of your false and damaging statements. Your statements have become the knowledge of a person or persons for whom the letter was not intended—but you cannot escape the liability for those false and damaging statements or for putting them in a format accessible to parties other than the addressee.

A creditor cannot say to a debtor while standing or sitting within the hearing range of other people: "Your business is built on lies and deceit. There isn't a supplier in our industry who hasn't been cheated or lied to by you and your company." This statement is probably false, is certainly very damaging, and is quite vicious. Put the same statements in a letter sent through the United States mails and you have what was discussed in the proceeding paragraph: a piece of correspondence read by parties other than the addressee, and that activates the potential for a suit for civil damages.

A debtor is not required to stand quietly while a disgruntled supplier trashes his or her personal and business reputation within the hearing or sight of one or more third persons. It is irrelevant to this scenario that the debtor may in the past have made some false and/or questionable statements to one or more of the company's suppliers. The bottom line is that a creditor cannot trash a reputation— personal, business or company—with false and damaging statements which are spoken or stated in a format that makes it possible for those statements to become the knowledge of a third party.

Statements that are false or damaging have no goal or purpose other than a desire to demean, belittle, and/or destroy the reputation of the person, business, or company to whom it is directed. Such a heavy load of baggage brings with it an equally heavy load of irresponsibility and recklessness, and this then becomes the personal and potentially the financial burden of the person who launched the unconscionable attack. Never allow yourself to be angered to the point where your tongue does a quick release before the material it releases has received a clearance from your brain. The consequences could be personally and financially devastating.

Periodically, credit reporting agencies request suppliers to provide information regarding their payment experience with a specific account. Unless the person who prepares the information does an honest and a conscientious job, a customer whose payment record is acceptable could be reported in such a manner as to diminish the quality of the account and to influence the relationship other or prospective suppliers might have with the account. False or damaging statements to a credit reporting agency (a bank or another supplier) are as unacceptable as the types of false and damaging statements discussed in the preceding part of this section. They all carry the potential to damage and to destroy, and that is never an acceptable option in any area of credit and collections.

Provable Intent to Damage the Customer's Reputation

"Damaging the customer's reputation" can be a double-edged sword that attacks both reputations—the personal reputation of an owner/manager and the reputation of his or her company or business. Many statements are so blatantly anticustomer that there can be no question regarding their intent to damage; the way in which language is used, whether in a letter or in a conversation, may provide irrefutable evidence of intent. No creditor is going to make flagrantly damaging statements pertaining to the customer's business unless there is intent. Substantiating provable intent with a background of other statements or incidents that reflect a similar pattern will provide evidence conclusive of intent to damage the customer/debtor's reputation.

Can you visualize yourself (the creditor) saying any of the following statements to a debtor? Can you visualize yourself saying these things in the presence, or within the hearing, of a third party or parties? Should any of the following statements be spoken or be allowed to find their way into a letter that might opened and/or read by a person other than the addressee?

1. I don't know what you think your company is going to gain from us with what has been a long pattern of lies and broken promises, but I can tell you what is going to happen. When we get through spreading the word, there won't be a supplier or a potential customer in the industry who won't know what an unreliable company you and your fellow jackals are running.

2. We are not interested in promises that are broken immediately after they are made. We are also not interested in lies and double talk that rolls out of your mouth on cue.

3. Why should this company accept your word on anything? Based upon what you have fed us over the past six or eight months, your personal and business integrity is worthless.

4. My opinion regarding you and your company is something that I have been happy to volunteer to other suppliers and to credit reporting agencies. There is—and never has been—any evidence of honesty or integrity in your conduct toward this company. In the spirit of helping to clean up the industry, we are happy to offer our experience and our opinion regarding your shoddy standards of personal and business ethics.

To include any of the preceding four examples in a letter to a customer would provide that customer with plenty of ammunition to prove intent to damage the personal and the business reputation of that customer. If you were to verbalize any of these four statements to a customer in any environment in which the statements might be overheard by a third party, the potential for claiming willful intent to damage the personal and business reputation of the customer would be overwhelmingly positive.

Any intent to damage the reputation of a customer/debtor, whether provable or not provable, is not conduct that is acceptable. There can be no justification for any business person—credit and collections or some other area of business life—to indulge in such a personally demeaning level of conduct. Not only is it illegal under the law, it is also unethical, improper, and can lead to a civil suit that has as its result a *big dollars* judgment for the plaintiff (customer/debtor).

General and Punitive Damages

A civil suit initiated by a debtor/plaintiff against a creditor in which the plaintiff charges *intent to damage the plaintiff's reputation* will be based upon certain acts and/or statements made by the creditor/defendant. The debtor/plaintiff will attempt to prove that what was done and/or stated by the creditor/defendant damaged the debtor's business and inflicted unconscionable amounts of stress upon the plaintiff, which led in turn to physical damage. It is the debtor/plaintiff's hope to prove these two charges, and thus ask the judge (or jury) to award general and punitive damages in amounts specified in the suit.

Whether the court will find in favor of the plaintiff, or find for the plaintiff at the monetary levels requested, cannot be foretold. If, however, the plaintiff has a strong case—plenty of documented episodes of *intent to damage*—the odds are good that the plaintiff will win a judgment for damages, both general and punitive.

General Damages

This category of damages may be assessed by a judge or a jury when there is a provable loss of business and/or business income caused by the illegal act(s) of a creditor. If the finding of the judge or jury is in favor of the debtor/plaintiff (the creditor is guilty as charged), a judgment for general damages set by the judge or jury will be entered into the record. The amount may or may not be what the plaintiff requested in the suit but if the court finds for the plaintiff, the amount of the judgment will favorably address the loss of business income caused by the creditor's illegal actions.

Punitive Damages

Although it may not have been the creditor's intent to inflict stress on the debtor to the point where it resulted in physical damage, the fact that it did occur places the responsibility (if proven to the satisfaction of the court) squarely on the back of the creditor. Punitive damages may be assessed by the judge or jury to compensate the plaintiff for being subjected to unconscionable levels of stress and for physical damage resulting from that stress.

Fear is a dangerous tool for a creditor to use. When it is used improperly, a debtor/plaintiff with provable charges of malice, extortion, libel, harassment, or any other overtly aggressive or illegal acts, stands an excellent chance of being awarded a judgment for a memorable amount of money.

Libel

Of the many actionable causes that may arise from a collection effort that is alleged to be illegal, none is more virulent than a charge of libel. It probably receives more attention from the courts than any of the other categories of illegal collection tactics or methods. A libelous statement made by the creditor about a customer/debtor is an unsolicited invitation for the debtor to take a charge of special damage or special injury to the civil courts in the form of a suit for damages. Whether a statement(s) that appears to have been libelous (tends to disgrace or degrade or holds the customer/debtor up to public hatred, contempt, or ridicule) does in fact meet the legal test for libelous statements or remarks is something that will be decided in court by a judge or a jury.

A person or a company must be careful to avoid any statements or remarks that might be interpreted as libelous. You would not want to charge another company or individual with fraud or dishonesty, not even if you have proof that in court it might be used to successfully refute any charge that you or your company had libeled the customer/debtor. Is the debtor a swindler, or a person who makes false representations with intent to deceive? Combine either of these statements to a man, woman, business or company with the person or company who is responsible for the statements (still unproven allegations) and the ingredients for a suit for damages have come together.

There is never a justification for one company or individual to make libelous statements about another. It is such a volatile area and can become such an expensive experience that nothing remotely resembling a libelous statement should be allowed to surface. If you have strong justification for feeling that a customer/debtor has handled the account relationship with your company in a deceitful manner, do not vocalize those feelings or allow them to insert themselves in any other manner into a format that might be construed as libelous or otherwise injurious to the debtor.

Defamation

Defamation is a charge brought frequently in law suits that result from published credit information that indicates dishonesty. The basis for a suit is the publication of information which might cause suppliers to withhold credit while it also subjects the customer to the probability of public ridicule, hatred, and contempt. Defamation is a fertile area for customer/debtors and attorneys to expand upon the amount of damage done, and the potential for additional damage. One of the more important cautions is in the use of words: words which may say nothing more than the truth but because of the manner in which they are published, may attribute insolvency of the debtor, a pending bankruptcy, or an inability to get credit. Taken in the context of their publication, the *words of truth* may become the basis for a civil court in which the debtor seeks damages from the creditor.

Extortion

This is a word that can create a variety of scenarios in the minds of people. Some will associate it with news stories of mob pressure and violence; others might relate it to one person's threat against another to reveal some terrible secret if certain payments are not made as the price for silence. Extortion comes in many forms. Some are more blatant than others and may only indirectly involve the process of collecting a past-due account.

The legal Webster's definition of "extortion" is "the crime of obtaining money or some other thing of value under color of office, when none or not so much is due, or before it is due." It is also defined as "oppressive or illegal extraction, as of excessive price or interest." Choose your poison, but it is essentially an attempt by threat to collect money (or other value) which is not legally due. Remember, however, that if there is an attempt to collect by collection letter a balance which is legally due *but* the letter uses language intended to coerce or harass the debtor into paying the account or claim, the creditor may have committed an act that is actionable by the customer/debtor.

There is a fine line between a creditor's legal right to collect a debt and whether the creditor implements that legal right through the use of language and methods inappropriate for the collection situation. For example, it is legal for a creditor to sue a debtor to collect a past-due balance—and generally without fear of liability—but it is not legal for the creditor to threaten the debtor with bankruptcy, an unfavorable report to other suppliers and credit reporting agencies, or any of several other actions which might be defined in a court of law as attempting to coerce (or extort) payment from the debtor.

Some collection efforts stray into the illegal when a deceptive simulation of the legal process is used in the hope that it will frighten the customer/debtor into paying what is owed. It is a process that is illegal in every state and is a punishable offense in all states. Deceptive simulation sent to a debtor include:

- Any communication that might be confused with a legal document.
- Any notice that resembles a summons.
- Any notice that is printed in a legal format, including type and print style of a court-initiated document.
- Anything having the appearance of a court-initiated order directing that debtor (person(s) or company) to pay the debt.

It is inconceivable that any person whose job it is to collect accounts receivables balances would allow a collection effort to get so far out of control as to use tactics that any person in such a position should recognize immediately as extortion. The law is justifiably uncharitable when given strong evidence to support a charge that the creditor pushed the collection process beyond the boundaries of a legal collection effort and into the minefield of extortion.

Unconscionable, unethical, and illegal: either one of the first two should offer enough to dissuade a person or a company from using practices that result in either of these judgments. If, however, conscience and ethics are not strong personal and company attributes—and as a consequence do not appear in the creditor's collection practices—it must then be obvious to even the most insensitive person or company that federal and state governments impose legal limitations beyond which a creditor cannot go under penalty of criminal and/or civil law.

Collection procedures must be constructed to stay within the spirit and letter of the law. Anything less than compliance based upon a knowledge of the boundaries for a legal collection effort is unacceptable behavior, and is conduct inappropriate for a credit professional.

Inappropriate Collection Letter

To categorize the following as an *inappropriate letter* is to understate the truth by light years. Read this scathing piece and decide how many unforgivable comments there are in it—comments that range from calculated nastiness to statements that are intentionally and/or inadvertently damaging to the subject business, company, partnership, sole proprietorship, or individual. How much of it is illegal? Does the letter offer any grounds that are actionable as a suit for damages? Do the terms *slander* and *defamation of character*, in addition to a few others, come to mind?

4.1   [date]

Attention: Accounts Payable Department

Gentlemen:

Don't you people have any business integrity? Are you programmed to give a request for payment of past-due invoices whatever response you think will buy your company some additional time? Are you, in fact, nothing more than a group of con artists who are doing a disservice to this industry by staying in business?

Unless payment for past due invoices in the amount of $_____ reaches this office by _____, it will be my pleasure to contact others of your suppliers and suggest that we withhold all product lines. A second part of the program will be to contact all known customers of your company and suggest that they would be better served with another supplier. Between the two approaches, I believe we can rid the industry of a real loser.

I have discussed your account with our attorney and although he suggested that I might want to rewrite this letter, I am not persuaded by his suggestion. It is my opinion that predator companies such as yours do not deserve the level of treatment guaranteed to common thieves.

It will come as an enormous surprise if we receive a check prior to the stated payment deadline. In fact, I look forward to being able to deal with your company in the manner outlined in preceding paragraphs. It should prove to be beneficial therapy for others who might consider following in the footsteps of your company.

Sincerely,

Credit Manager

See Letter 4.1. Well? Do you have enough friends who might lend you their fingers and toes to count the ways this credit manager is hanging his company out to dry? Let me state at the outset that any credit management person who would consider writing such a blatantly damaging letter—or anything that might remotely resemble it—has no place in the credit profession.

Can the errors be narrowed to specifics? Here are some.

1. From word one, the viciously confrontational approach of the letter is totally unacceptable. In the context of what is legal to write or to say, it is a disaster.

2. The use of "Gentlemen" as a salutation is not appropriate usage; use Mr., Ms., Mrs., etc.

3. The first paragraph is defamatory, slanderous, abusive, demeaning, and represents almost everything that is bad.

4. Paragraph two is vindictive (expresses the desire to harm the business, to force it to close), talks openly and with gusto of attempting to initiate acts of collusion and restraint of trade with other suppliers. This paragraph provides the basic fuel for an enormous damages lawsuit. When it is combined with other threats and statements, it effectively puts the writer's company on the path toward a major, if not a terminal, financial disaster.

To summarize: Under no circumstances would you write such a letter. You would not allow any piece of correspondence to leave your department or your company that is not written in language that is civil and does not meet the legal parameters for an acceptable document. Be direct, be forceful, be concise, and state in straightforward language exactly what you expect from the customer and what your company is prepared to do to collect receivables balances. You must *never*, however, stray into areas of implied or real threats, abusive or vindictive language, harassment, threats of collusion, defamation of a company or individuals, actions that constitute an attempt to—or the threat to—restrain trade, or any other illegal act or action.

Every phase of your company's collection effort must be within a framework that is acceptable under the law and under the dictates of good conscience. There is no room in modern business for a standard that does not meet that criteria.

5

Effective Collection Letters: Techniques and Ingredients

No experienced collection professional would spend time and effort preparing and mailing letters that had, on previous occasions, failed to motivate customers to pay or to respond with an explanation for not paying. Remember, however, that because a collection letter does not work with one customer doesn't mean that the letter will not be effective with another; but when a basic letter has been personalized, has been sent to several customers, and still fails to motivate a reasonable number of those customers to respond with money or an explanation, the letter should be reworked or dropped.

Collection letters come in assorted lengths and strengths. It may be a letter that fills the better part of a page—and if it does, it had better be packed with material to grab and hold the recipient's attention. It may be a format that is shorter, or short (short is usually better); this is particularly true when the nature of the collection problem lends itself to a direct, no-nonsense message that can be delivered in the compact format.

Never belabor a point. Remember that the customer whose account is past due to 30, 45, or 60 days is probably honest and is aware that he or she has a past-due problem with your company. There will have been telephone calls that preceded the letter(s) so we are not talking about something that requires detailed or repetitive explanations. Allow your long, short, or mid-length collection letters to present your company's views and requirements in a context that offers a feasible solution (a monthly payment plan coupled to some releases of products, more frequent small payments and subsequent smaller releases of products, etc.). Your collection letters must motivate the customer to want to bring receivables totals back into an aging area that is acceptable to your company.

One of the best and most productive motivational situations for a credit person is when the creditor company is one of the customer's major suppliers—and the customer cannot do business without your product(s) or service(s). If your company is not one of the customer's major suppliers, or the supplier of a key product or ingredient, then this is not as good a position as that of a key supplier, but your company is not without some leverage. Suppliers are asked frequently for their payment experience with various accounts by credit reporting organizations such as Dun & Bradstreet, other suppliers, banks, landlords, and various types of service businesses and companies. The customer company should be reminded that cooperation in working with a supplier(s) to reduce past-due balances is viewed with favor by most current or prospective creditors.

Customers get themselves into financial difficulties for a variety of reasons, many of which are unexpected and beyond the customer's control. Your company should want to do whatever is helpful and reasonable to assist a good customer, or to assist a customer with good management and strong potential, to recover from what should be a temporary cashflow problem. The customer cannot make the larger payments that you have proposed but is willing to make payments that are smaller and more frequent? If the time frame for the payment program proposed by the customer is not significantly out of phase with your company's proposal, you should accommodate the customer's request.

Evaluate carefully any payment program that would extend the reduction of receivables balances beyond a time frame that can be accepted as realistic in the hard light of the customer company's own receivables and cashflow problems. Is the customer on a fast-moving downward spiral that might cause it to file for protection under Chapter 11 of the Bankruptcy Act? Does your company view the customer as a strong, or potentially strong, presence in a market area that has no significant competition? Has the customer's image been damaged (and perhaps that of your company) because cashflow problems have not allowed it to fulfill appropriately its obligations to customers? And lastly—is your company's comfort zone with this customer at a point where it is willing to carry larger balances for longer periods of time than it can afford to do for most of its other customers? If the answer to these questions is "Yes," then this account must be the beneficiary of a collection effort that is softer and more nurturing than with other accounts whose receivables aging is similar.

Should you be innovative? Absolutely. Should you use a gimmick to grab and hold the debtor's attention? Why not? The customer knows already that his or her company owes a past-due balance to your company. Anything you might do or say to focus the customer's attention on your account—all within the limits of a legal collection procedure—is a big plus. If the customer's attention remains focused on your account for a reasonable period of time, it is possible that your account balance will be moved to the top of the accounts payable list. Although a check might not be mailed immediately to your company (cashflow could be so slow that very little is being paid), you might get a telephone call acknowledging your letter, an explanation of what is happening at the customer company, and a date when some or all of the past-due account will be paid.

There is nothing wrong with a format that is straightforward in asking for payment of an account balance. A written request for payment can create its own problem, however, when the customer opens the collection letter and begins to read something so stereotyped that he or she could close their eyes and quote it almost to dotted i's, commas, and frayed old cliches.

I don't suggest that you open a letter with something irrelevant or inappropriate for the subject of your letter, but use your imagination! What might grab *your* attention if the flow of collection correspondence were reversed? Would you be willing to accept the fact that this customer has waited too long and that the customer is making his or her pitch for payment in a direct but nonthreatening manner? Of course your reaction will be more favorable and longer-lasting to this out-of-the ordinary letter. Surely there is reason to hope that people who are responsible for collecting their company's receivables dollars can be goaded into reaching for more innovative techniques, more attention-getting phrases in their collection letters. Who knows? Perhaps a positive might arise from the ashes of monotony and the endless monotony of pedestrian prose. It is possible that customer/debtors might become so depressed with the mundane quality of collection letters that they will be stimulated to pay on time in order to avoid receiving them? A hopeful thought but probably not one steeped in practicality.

Having said the above, let me hasten to add that there are only so many ways a person or a company can ask for money. A letter is about money that is past due; about money that you would like to have, and, yes, yesterday would have been just fine. But of course you did not receive it yesterday so the push—what you hope will be attention-getting and response-triggering—is on to collect the open balance before too many tomorrows add more aging to it.

Collection letters should be as uncomplicated as the creditor-customer/debtor relationship will permit. You do not want the letter to be misunderstood or misinterpreted, and always do exactly what and when you tell the customer you are going to do it.

Key Words and Phrases

There are words and phrases whose power add focus, strength, and persuasion to a collection letter. These are words whose impact is so positive that a debtor cannot fail to acknowledge, if not act upon, the message they convey. The debtor's cashflow is a trickle, the credit line has been drawn down, and a big payment from a major customer has been held up because your materials were incorrectly installed by the customer. Your company has been advised of the problem and of the three or four weeks it will take to undo the mistake. Do you sit quietly and wait? You do not. The size of the past-due balance demands that you persuade the customer to divert some of the diminished cashflow to your company.

The following are phrases that indicate to a customer that you do want to be paid but that you understand and are supportive of the customer's efforts to stabilize the company's financial position:

What can we do to help?

Please call me.

Your good credit rating ...

We want to be fair.

A payment program is acceptable.

Cordial relations ...

Reciprocate.

Trust ...

Confidence ...

These are words and phrases that are positive in what they project and in how they are perceived by a debtor. You might open a letter relating to the problem outlined above with something similar to the following:

> We can empathize with the problem of getting payment from your customer because one of your people installed our product incorrectly. What can we do to help?

> or

> We know all about the impact on cashflow when a major customer withholds payment until a faulty product or a faulty installation has been corrected. A payment on account would be appreciated but we are not about to make an issue of it. In fact, what can we do to help?

> or

> My thanks for the telephone call. A problem such as the one you described yesterday afternoon is not going to disturb your good credit rating with us. There is always a need for money but we can live with the past-due aging until your customer releases your money.

Negative Words and Phrases

When a credit applicant submits information that does not allow your company to grant the requested credit line, your response should be phrased so that it does not accentuate the fact that you cannot offer a credit line for the amount requested. The ideal response is to point to a short-term reason for granting a lower line of credit (company is too new, expansion into new territory has put a severe financial strain on the company, etc.) but close by implying that your company hopes to increase the line in the near future.

The words and phrases that follow have a built-in negativism; they do nothing positive for the attitudes of creditors or debtors. Many debtors who might otherwise be receptive to some form of payment program program will stiffen their backs when a creditor laces his or her collection letters with some form of the following:

We must have	Disregard
Overdue	Intemperate remarks
Ill-advised	Your refusal
Arrears	Resent
Refute	Protest
Deceive	Dispute
Uncooperative attitude	Ignore
Require	Argue
Unconscionable	

The majority of debtors are not deadbeats and they resent any implication that their intentions toward the creditor are anything but honorable. Creditors cannot quarrel with this attitude because in a similar situation, that attitude would be theirs. But in the absence of a thinking man's approach to collection letters, decide what your reaction would be to the following:

Your refusal to comply with the payment schedule that was included in our letter of March 29 has narrowed our options for avoiding a third-party collection assignment.

or

We have been more than patient with your company, but our patience has failed to generate a payment. We cannot continue this charade. Payment in full must be in this office by the last day of the current month or the account will be assigned to a collection agency.

When a creditor has tried diligently to work with a debtor and every effort to accommodate the debtor has been met with double talk, evasion, broken promises, and an obvious lack of integrity, a letter that includes a tailored version of the two proceeding paragraphs is justified. You no longer have any interest in salvaging a customer; your only interest is in recovering the dollars in accounts receivable. You will not refer to the customer (individual, partnership, business, or company) in any of the actionable terms cited in Chaps. 2 and 3, but you may state in language that is both plain and forceful that your company is unwilling to devote additional time to the account. It is third-party collection time, and you want the customer/debtor to know it.

Debtors will occasionally make the commercial equivalent of a deathbed confession by coming forward immediately with a check for some portion of the account to a collection service. A debtor whose problems probably involve several suppliers, does not want those other suppliers to hear of a collection assignment. When the dominoes begin to fall, debtors know that suppliers will become more insistent in their demands for payment and much more restrictive when asked to extend new credit.

Set an Appropriate Tone

In the high percentage of collection situations the goal is to collect the past-due balance(s): use creditor, bank, and reporting agency data to establish that the customer is not on a downslide, and return the account to the status of an active customer as rapidly as possible.

It is not the function of the credit department to close the door to any customer whose prospects for survival are somewhat better than terminal. To paraphrase a remark used by crime fighters, it is the goal of credit and collection people to help a customer company to rehabilitate itself and its image with this and other creditors. Any business or company whose management is conscientious, hard working, knowledgeable, and shows integrity in its dealings with suppliers, is going to get the quality of help that will allow it to *rehabilitate its image*.

When you are called upon to collect a balance that is more than a few days past due (and you must collect it from an account whose record has been good over a period of several years), the tone and content of your letters and telephone conversations will be helpful, conciliatory, and will show concern for the company and its employees. Your questions will relate to the restricted cashflow and how long the customer thinks it might be before it will again meet the company's requirements. Your interest will also extend to whether the problem is the result of expansion into a new territory; a down turn in the national or area economy; a new product or product technology that is making it difficult for the customer to maintain market share; or the retirement, death, or buy-out of a key man, partnership insurance, etc. to ensure a transition not compromised by a sudden shortage of cash. When the relationship has been a good one and has extended over one, two, five, or more years, your objective is to help the customer get past-due balances out of the way and move forward. This is a customer who needs and receives your support.

Near the opposite end of the spectrum is another customer whose relationship with your company covers a period of 14 or 15 months, and during that period of time has gone from one collection problem to another. Your early observation regarding the absence of any discernible effort to bring the company's expenditures into line with cashflow has been confirmed by recent events. Money has been spent in areas and on projects that seem to offer almost no chance for success. Unless there is a turnaround in the company's financial controls, the company may soon be in deep trouble.

The example in Letter 5.1, sets the tone for what your company might do to help a good customer.

Would you offer the same level of help to the other customer: the one whose constant problems over the 14 or 15 months of your relationship have been a disproportionate drain on your time and patience? You would not. This is not a customer who has potential for developing into a good, long-term account. As Letter 5.2 indicates, your course of action is to push to get your company's money from the customer/debtor before the downslide becomes a voluntary (or an involuntary) filing of a petition for the protection of the bankruptcy court.

And what should your company be willing to do for the customer whose normal payment pattern is consistently near the median average for all of the company's credit accounts, but whose payment pattern has suddenly become much slower than usual? You will first attempt to determine the cause of the problem (a telephone call to the credit manager, the controller, or the financial officer should do it), and if it has not been triggered by gross mismanagement, you will offer to help the faltering customer make its way through an unfamiliar and a potentially dangerous period. (See Letter 5.3.)

5.1   [date]

Dear Mr. Johnson:

I had a conversation earlier this week with Franklin Oliveri, our sales rep who calls on your company. He told me that the economy in your market area has taken a downturn, and that is never good news. We know what an unstable economy can do to a sales projection that under normal circumstances would be right on target.

The relationship between your company and ours has always been excellent, so we want to help you in whatever ways we can. If you need some extra time to pay invoices, it can be arranged; you'll also need a normal flow of product(s) during this period, and that too can be arranged.

Give me a call at your earliest convenience. We're ready to help you move past this momentary problem.

Sincerely,

5.2   [date]

Dear Mr. Weathers:

We are sorry to hear that your hopes for improvement in cashflow have experienced another setback. As you stated during our conversation earlier today, it does not help your relationship with suppliers when payment promises are not met.

Our company operates within parameters that reflect our attitude toward strong financial controls. We do not ask our suppliers to wait for their money more than a few days past terms, and we do not expect our customers to assume arbitrarily that we expect anything less of them.

Please adjust your payables projection for the coming week to accommodate the release of a check for the past due account balance of $_____.

Sincerely,

5.3   [date]

Dear Ms. Canfield:

I greatly appreciate the candor with which you addressed your company's cashflow problem when we talked on the telephone earlier today. It has given me a clear picture of the problem your company is currently facing, how it occurred, and what is being done to work through it.

Your assessment of the cashflow problem as a temporary one seems realistic. We can empathize with the dismay that comes when other problems begin to appear as the flow of payments from a major supplier begins to decrease. The adjustments that must be made—temporary though they may be—can be unexpected and unwelcome.

The attached payment schedule for the next three months is based upon our telephone conversation earlier today. If you see any problem with it, or if we can help in any other area, please do not hesitate to call me.

Sincerely,

There is mutual benefit when a creditor who will be affected by a problem involving cash flow—a problem which will impact payments to the creditor—is notified by the customer immediately after the problem has been confirmed. When there is prompt and full disclosure of a problem, the creditor is much more favorably persuaded to give the customer additional time to clear older receivables balances—and to continue to buy product from the creditor. A tool that enables creditor and customer to bring what both parties accept as a temporary situation is a payment plan: one in which payments are smaller, are extended over a longer period of time, and in which the dollar amount has been decreased. It works in many situations. Try it.

Extended or Special Terms

A customer may occasionally be put in a situation where it becomes necessary to ask for credit on terms other than standard if the company is going to be able to handle a particularly large piece of business.

Example: When a smaller floor covering contractor makes a request for extended/special terms from a manufacturer or distributor, it is usually because the product(s) of the manufacturer/distributor have been specified by the architect. The job is much larger, and requires more cashflow, than the smaller floor covering contractor deals with in the normal course of business.

If the customer is already established, you will find a way to accommodate it while carefully protecting the interest of your own company. A filing under the Uniform Commercial Code (and other protective actions) will give your company the extra protection it should have. Because the customer will be operating at a level that (1) taxes the firm's financial capabilities and (2) may dangerously stretch job management and supervisory depth, you should watch for problems.

It is, however, a good piece of business for your company, and because your customer is the successful bidder, you will help the customer. In that context, the following sample letters are indicative of what a helpful and innovative supplier might do to help the customer's cashflow stretch to cover what has become a much broader base of requirements.

5.4   [date]

Name of Company
Street Address (or P.O. Box Number)
City, State, Zip Code

Dear Mr./Ms. _____:

Congratulations! I was delighted to hear that your company's bid was selected to install floor tile and cove base in the new county agriculture department building. As you suggest, the size of the job will put pressure on your cashflow, and we are very willing to do what we can to ease the pressure.

In line with suggestions that were made during yesterday's telephone conversation, let me suggest the following extended payment plan for materials that will be shipped directly to the job site and which will simplify any problem of control that might arise if job materials were commingled with other materials in your warehouse (storage area).

1. Payment for the first one-fourth of the order ($21,500 of an order total of $86,000) to be made within 45 days from your job-start date:

2. Payment for the second one-fourth of the order ($21,500 of an order total of $86,000) is to be made within 45 days from date of the first payment.

3. Payment for the third one-fourth of the order ($21,500 of an order total of $86,000) is to be made within 45 days from date of the second payment.

4. Payment for the fourth (and final) one-fourth of the order ($21,500 of an order total of $86,000) is to be made within 45 days from date of the third payment.

If you agree that this payment program is something your company can live with, please sign, date and return this copy to my attention. Call me if there is anything else I can do.

Best wishes,

Credit Manager

5.5   [date]

Name of Company
Street Address (or P.O. Box Number)
City, State, Zip Code

Dear Mr./Ms. _____:

The contract to install resilient flooring products in the new county agriculture building is a major breakthrough for your company! But as you mentioned during our telephone conversation yesterday, it does impose some problems in the areas of cashflow and job supervision.

Our feeling is that your company will handle the problems of job supervision with the required level of professionalism; our commitment, moreover, will be to help you to ease the cashflow problem presented by a job of this size.

In line with what we discussed yesterday, I have prepared the following extended payment program. It should help to solve the problem of cashflow:

1. All floor covering products supplied to this job by our company will be delivered at job site.

2. Payment for the first 25 percent of the total order ($21,500 of $86,000) will be paid within 45 days of your job start date.

3. Second, third, and fourth payments of $21,500 each will be made 90 days after your company's job start date, 135 days after your company's job start date, and 180 days after your company's job start date.

If this sounds like something your company can handle, please sign, date, and return this original copy to my attention; the second copy is for your records.

Your company was overdue for this recognition. Please contact me if there is anything further we can do to help in this or other job situations.

Sincerely,

Credit Manager

5.6

[date]

Name of Company
Street Address (or P.O. Box Number)
City, State, Zip Code

Dear Mr./Ms. _____:

Congratulations on your successful bid for the West Cameron Center for the Performing Arts. As you said yesterday, it represents a significant step in the growth of your company.

I have put the following payment program together for the materials you will need from us. I think this is in line with what we discussed yesterday but if it needs more fine tuning, give me a call and we'll work it out.

First payment—$38,500 (due within 40 days after your company starts to install the seats)

Second payment—$42,000 (due within 40 days of the first payment)

Third payment—$42,000 (due within 40 days of the second payment)

(All floor covering materials will be delivered to the job site. Payment in full is to be received by this supplier within 150 days after your job start date.)

We wish you a clean and trouble-free job. Please call me as you get into the job if there is anything more we can do.

Sincerely,

Credit Manager

5.7   [date]

Name of Company
Street Address (or P.O. Box Number)
City, State, Zip Code

Dear Mr./Ms. _____:

Thank you for calling me yesterday afternoon. I am sorry to hear that the temporary cashflow problem of one of your best customers is doing the same to your company, but those things will happen from time to time.

We have no problem with your request for a restructuring of due dates for products of ours that your firm used on the Washington Manor project. Because your cashflow from other job sources is adequate to meet other payment commitments, and because we have had a long and successful relationship, it is very easy to say "yes."

As you suggested, spread the payments for the Washington Manor project over the next 120 days. Pay 25 percent of the $588,000 total ($147,000) within 30 days from this date, then follow with three more payments of $147,000 each at intervals of 30 days—the $588,000 total to be paid in full within 120 days from this date.

I'm glad we were able to help. Don't hesitate to call if there should be a future problem.

Regards,

Credit Manager

There are times when something as straightforward as a sales promotion can backfire and cause the credit department to find itself in the middle of a collection problem: For instance, one problem could occur when an announcement letter omits or fails to state correctly how the customer can earn a special promotional credit on net invoiced purchases above a specific purchase figure.

The following exchange of information between the supplier's credit manager and the owner of the Parnell Company is indicative of what can happen when a letter omits one or more key pieces of information. In this example, the credit manager was able to respond to the customer's inquiry with the missing and key piece of information.

5.8   [date]

Name of Company
Street Address (or P.O. Box Number)
City, State, Zip Code

Dear Mr./Ms. _____:

Many thanks for your call. After our conversation this afternoon, I reviewed the problem with Ted Pilson, the company's sales manager.

Ted's May 8 letter to our dealers did indeed state that an additional promotional credit of three percent (3%) could be earned on net invoices on all purchases above stated figures during the period April 1 through July 31, 19XX. Your Company's base figure upon which the promotional credit could be built was $131,418.00.

Unfortunately, Mr. Pilson inadvertently omitted from the May 8 letter the information that our company will prepare credits for each dealer account. Sales figures for the subject period will be the basis for determining credit amounts and should pose no computation or reconciliation problem for our dealers.

The inconvenience is regrettable but we must ask you to continue to pay invoices in the normal manner, applying the promotional credit only after the specific figure has been received from us.

Sincerely,

Credit Manager

5.9   [date]

Name of Company
Street Address (or P.O. Box Number)
City, State, Zip Code

Dear Mr./Ms. _____:

Thank you for your two recent letters. I have taken to heart your letter of August 17 and will proceed to pay invoices taking only my 3 percent. I place my additional three percent in your capable hands. How's that for blind faith?

Enclosed is a check for invoice 4891, less 3 percent. I understand that our most recent shipment has been found in the wilds of North Carolina so you will have more checks in the near future.

It is very reassuring to know that your company has a competent credit department working for its business success and the success of its customers as well.

Sincerely,

Henry Parnell
President

5.10   [date]

Name of Company
Street Address (or P.O. Box Number)
City, State, Zip Code

Dear Mr./Ms. _____:

You will want to compare the attached application of payments against the notations that were on your Company's checks 1261 and 1262.

A second 3 percent discount was deducted from certain of the invoices listed on your checks. Because it was not an applicable deduction (only one 3 percent discount is allowable), it was necessary to adjust the amount of money applied and change the mix of invoices involved.

I hope the attached detail sheet will give you the information necessary to adjust your records, and that it does not impose an unreasonable burden.

Sincerely,

Credit Manager

Avoid the Look of *Canned* or *Mass Mailer*

Form letters should be personalized to reflect the patterns of language and style that reflect the person or company that initiates them. Unless a form letter is a rare glove fit for a particular collection situation, the collection effort will usually be best served if form letters are fine-tuned to reflect the attitudes and the business philosophy of the creditor company.

A credit manager should never hesitate to change a word or a phrase to give form letters a more personal touch. No person can be comfortable with a collection letter that does not address the problem of past-due payment(s) with clarity, compassion, perseverance, and an understanding of the problem(s) that may be strangling the debtor company.

A *canned* letter—one that is used to cover specific collection situations—is a valid piece of correspondence when it communicates in language that is pertinent to the collection problem or situation of the company to which it is being addressed. Minor changes in the format of good canned collection letters will allow the creditor company to give a letter the appearance of tailored correspondence. The same letter (the same format) can be used many times and in many different ways; it is not necessary to reinvent the wheel every time it becomes necessary to send out a collection letter.

No piece of correspondence that has the appearance of a *mass mailer* can hope to deliver an effective message. It will not project the urgency of a letter that appears to have been tailored to fit a specific collection situation. In the context of the *most persuasive* collection letter sent to a delinquent account by two or more creditors, the one that defines most effectively the need for immediate payment of past-due balances is usually the one that receives priority attention. Would you feel a sense of urgency if the letter requesting payment had no more focus than a public announcement for a warehouse clearance sale? Of course you wouldn't—and neither would I.

Form letters (such as the ones in this book) can be very effective when they are used selectively, are adjusted to accommodate a specific collection effort, and are produced on a high-tech processor (word processor, computer with laser printer, etc.) that delivers a *look* far removed from that of many *canned* or *mass mailer* products. Whether form letters have been written to be used as individual letters or as part of a series of two or more, you will find that they are interchangeable: After some very minor adjustments, letters in this book can be coupled to form a fresh approach to your company's collection problems.

The collection letters in this and subsequent chapters represent some of the most innovative and effective pieces of corporate and retail collection correspondence being used today. How do you freshen a favorite letter? Change the construction of a paragraph or give one or two key phrases a quarter or a half turn. These are simple adjustments that can magnify the effectiveness of your company's collection program, and that will bring a good percentage of those slow receivables dollars back into the company's cashflow!

Sample Letters

A temptation during the writing of this book has been to categorize the many letters in these chapters as *sample letters* rather than *form letters*. The fact that no change has been made does not eliminate the possibility that semantics may be jiggled and *sample letter* emerges as the preferred term of reference.

Any sample letter is an indicator of what can be said to embellish a specific format. If the sample letter is good, it opens the subject to the possibility of other letters expanding on the same approach or moving off in other directions. Sample letters should be gateways to many variations on the sample: to variations that offer an interesting and an informative read while holding the attention of the reader.

This book chooses to overlook minor differences in the dictionary definitions of *sample letter* and *form letter* and considers one to be a synonym of the other. *The American Heritage Dictionary* offers the following: A *sample* is "a portion, piece, or segment representative of a whole"; a *form* is, among other definitions, "the contour and structure of something."

Not all letters generated in the credit department ask for money. Some answer questions, provide information, or serve as cover letters. Sample letters from the previous program and one following fulfill some of these categories.

5.11   [date]

Name of Company
Street Address (or P.O. Box Number)
City, State, Zip Code

Dear Mr./Ms. _____:

We have no desire to project the image of a whining, complaining or ungrateful supplier. Our customers are much too important for us to slide into any of those unpleasant behavioral attitudes. This is meant only to be a mutual self-help suggestion, and if it works for you it will automatically work for us.

When you receive an invoice that lists a quantity of product that does not agree with the quantity you received, please do not change the invoice and pay what you calculate to be the correct amount. It may be correct, but call us with the information so we can promptly issue a credit, mail it to you, and protect your discount on the specific invoice for 10 days beyond the normal discount period. Issuing the credit simplifies our bookkeeping and should also simplify yours if for one reason or another we calculate two different amounts for the goods billed but not received.

Are there errors or questions regarding the price quoted to you and the price billed? Please contact this department as soon as you notice the discrepancy—and before the invoice is input for payment. We'll either promptly correct the problem with a credit for the difference or have our sales representative call you to discuss or clarify any misunderstanding that might have occurred.

We can do our best job for you when your telephone call puts the matter of correcting our mistake or problem exactly where it belongs—in our lap.

Many thanks for your cooperation.

Sincerely,

Henry Bonner
Credit Manager

Controversy: Statements That Provoke or Sustain It

Controversy between a creditor/supplier and a customer is never healthy; it becomes increasingly unhealthy when the shadow cast over the relationship by the controversy begins to create an atmosphere that is filled with acrimony and mistrust. The parties may become so distracted that they lose their perspective for what seemed a promising relationship between the two firms.

Example 1: If my company is a customer of yours, it cannot make claims of faulty product shipments as a ploy for withholding payment for product which your company's quality control people insists exceeds specifications for acceptable quality. If my company is having a cashflow problem, it should approach your company with honesty and not diminish the integrity of my company with claims that are not true. Given a background relationship based upon reason and integrity, the attitude of your company toward a legitimate problem of my company is far more likely to generate a favorable reaction. My company should handle all areas of its business in an honest and straightforward manner: no double-talk, no double-dealing, no games, no ploys, and definitely no lies.

Example 2: A creditor has become increasingly frustrated because it has been unable to collect balances that are 30, 60, and 90 days past due. The situation has been exacerbated because the customer/debtor has had no regard for the truth, stacking broken promises one on top of the other until any respect the creditor may have had for the debtor has been eroded. Nothing is left to form a basis upon which to build a meaningful future relationship—one that might be expected to withstand the problems of growth because each has respect for the honesty and integrity of the other.

Examples of controversial statements made by a customer to a supplier:

1. Your company has failed to live up to the promises it made when we began to buy your products. (What promises? Why should a supplier/creditor make promises that are not standard for all of the company's customers? And if, as it should be, there is one standard for all customers, it is reasonable to assume that all customers routinely receive the same consideration.)

2. We are not going to pay for anything on invoices 6593 and 6599 until a credit is received for a $3.26 pricing error on invoice 6593 and a $5.55 error because one unit was missing on invoice 6599. (There is no justification for withholding payment for items other than the ones mentioned if credit memos are issued within a reasonable time frame. The supplier/creditor should not accept a flagrant abuse of credit terms based solely upon two incidents of minor importance.)

3. Our company has been in business for 28 years, and we have done business with your company for the last 11 of those years. We would consider it a breach of our supplier/customer relationship if you should decide to sell your products to our upstart competitor. (In the absence of an exclusive agreement between supplier and customer for a specific area or territory, the supplier company is within its rights to sell products to the upstart competitor or any other customer in the area. This doesn't mean that the supplier should not feel loyalty toward the good customer, but competition and sales is what business is all about.)

4. We know you've been selling to the Wellington Company for a long time but we're looking for some price breaks. We need some help from your company to get our foot in the door in this territory. (There are special and limited circumstances for price breaks, and placing orders of routine size to "get a foot

in the door" doesn't qualify as special and limited circumstances. Your company has had a long and profitable relationship with the Wellington Company; you are not going to participate in any arrangement that is less than ethical and would inevitably damage the relationship.)

Ambiguity and Innuendo

This chapter is loaded with topics and categories that, if allowed to become a part of the creditor/debtor relationship, will succeed in pulling it down to the shoe-tops of the participants. *Ambiguity* (Webster says doubtful, uncertain, capable of being interpreted in more than one way), and *innuendo* (Webster defines it as an indirect, subtle, usually derogatory insinuation) is a straight-line path to misunderstandings, resentments, withdrawal, and anger. Nowhere in this list do you see growth in respect for an individual or a company.

Ambiguity

A collection letter (or a collection telephone call), misses the mark if it does not clearly define the message you wish to convey. The customer should never be uncertain regarding the meaning of a letter, or any part of the letter. The customer is 30 to 60 days past due and you want a specific number of dollars by a specific date? Say it, and say it in language that is polite but leaves no room for misinterpretation. Say nothing that is ambiguous, and never say anything like the following:

"It is difficult for the credit department to release current orders when the account has balances that are 30 and 60 days past due. (That line is acceptable; watch out for what follows.) Of course there is a possibility that if we were to receive a partial payment within the next 7 to 10 days, we might be able to work around the credit barrier. I really cannot be more definite until we see how much money you send, when it is received, and whether we feel comfortable with new credit exposure." (This doesn't tell the customer what is expected or what can be expected as the result of a payment. Name figures, set payment dates, then tell the customer what your company is prepared to do.)

Your customer may not be thrilled with a set of requirements that spells out what you want and when you want it, but there can be no question regarding what must be done. Ambiguity should not appear in any phase of credit or collections.

Innuendo

This is another in the category of words whose meaning is either not clear enough or can evolve into an insinuation that is all too clear. Once again, there is no credibility to a collection letter that does not state clearly what the creditor requires of the customer, does not state by what date it is required, and, if there is any possibility for negotiation, by what date the customer must contact the creditor to initiate those negotiations.

It is difficult to understand why someone who hopes to collect money from a past-due account will use expressions or terms that are not direct (indirect or subtle), or use an insinuation that is derogatory. Earlier in this chapter we ruled out *defamatory* as an acceptable area for printed or spoken statements, and *derogatory* is in the same bag. It is an 800-pound monster whose presence in a letter, in a telephone conversation, or in a face-to-face confrontation—one that might be overheard by a third party—is an invitation for the debtor to sue in numbers compatible with the 800-pound derogatory statement or remark. No sensible person would use language that brings with it such heavy elements of risk.

Do not try to be subtle or indirect when the situation calls for *direct*; and never, *never fall into the trap of using a derogatory insinuation.*

6

First Collection Letters

The objective of a first collection letter is to get the debtor's money without further fuss or effort. One letter—well constructed and personalized to appeal effectively to the customer/debtor's sense of obligation and fair play—is the goal of every collection effort. There is never an unlimited amount of time to spend on the account of one customer. The person who has responsibility for collecting past-due balances must minimize the number of lengthy collection experiences while maximizing results from as many short-term collection efforts as possible.

The format for the *first collection letter* may not be the same for all customers. A customer who is a chronic past due—one who never sends a check until the supplier's credit department has sent more than one letter and made at least one telephone call—does not receive the same first collection letter as the company whose account balance is rarely more than five or ten days past due. The first example represents a collection effort that from one month to the next does not stop. As the balance for one month is paid, the balance for a subsequent month becomes past due and unless the second or subsequent balance is paid quickly, the *subsequent balance* will be eligible for the collector's attention.

A first collection letter may be written in language that expresses no doubt that failure to send the payment is an oversight and that the customer will send it upon receipt of the supplier's letter. A second version of the first collection letter may address the past-due balance as something that must be paid before a more current balance becomes past due. There are customers who, because their account is always past due, would never see the reminder version of the first collection letter. These are accounts that can be sold profitably but because they do not pay until varying time-consuming degrees of pressure have been exerted, do not deliver the same margin of profit as accounts that require nothing more than a reminder (extra collection effort plus extra days on the accounts receivable aged trial balance report equals less rapid internally generated cashflow—and very possibly more bank borrowing to supplement occasional shortages of internally generated cashflow.

The first group of letters that follow offer examples of the softest type of first collection letter. These are nothing more than friendly reminders to customers who may occasionally slide a few days past credit terms but who are so conscious of their obligations to suppliers and of their good credit record that they will respond almost immediately to this level of collection letter. Accounts in this category should never be subjected to a letter that exerts pressure. A soft first letter should be sent to accounts known to be conscientious in their desire and their belief that bills should be paid within terms or as close to terms as is humanly possible. There is no other way when you are dealing with people of integrity and good conscience.

6.1   [date]

Name of Company
Street Address (or P.O. Box Number)
City, State, Zip Code

Dear Mr./Ms. _____:

The [month] balance of [amount] is only _____ days past due but it is so uncharacteristic of your company not to pay every invoice within terms that I know you did not receive our invoice or it has inadvertently fallen through one of those cracks we all have experienced.

Please input the attached invoice for payment with the next regular cycle of invoices. It isn't necessary to give this item special handling to protect your good credit rating with us.

Sincerely,

Credit Manager

6.2   [date]

Name of Company
Street Address (or P.O. Box Number)
City, State, Zip Code

Attention: [name and title]

Dear Mr./Ms. _____:

This is one of those rare occasions when your account has an invoice that has not been cleared within terms.

The obvious question is whether you have a copy of invoice #_____ in the amount of $_____. To eliminate the need for an answer, I have attached a copy to this letter. If you can process it with the next batch of payables, it will return your account to its normal "within terms" payment status.

Sincerely,

Credit Manager

6.3   [date]

Name of Company
Street Address (or P.O. Box Number)
City, State, Zip Code

Attention: [name and title]

Dear Mr./Ms. _____:

Our payment records do not show that we have received your check for [month and year] invoices in the amount of $_____.

If our records do not agree, please contact the undersigned so we can go over our respective records, locate the problem, and make whatever adjustment(s) may be necessary. If our records do agree, prompt payment of the above-listed balance will be appreciated.

Sincerely,

Credit Manager

6.4   [date]

Name of Company
Street Address (or P.O. Box Number)
City, State, Zip Code

Attention: [name and title]

Dear Mr./Ms. _____:

We have applied your check No. _____ to the invoice (invoices) listed on the remittance section of the check. Unfortunately, the deduction(s) taken on invoice __ (invoices numbered _____ and _____) is/are not allowable on the basis of information in our files.

If you can provide us with information that will substantiate the deduction (these deductions), we shall be happy to adjust our records. If that is not possible, please forward your check in the amount of $_____ to cover the unauthorized deduction(s).

Sincerely,

Credit Manager

6.5   [date]

Name of Company
Street Address ((or P.O. Box Number)
City, State, Zip Code

Attention: [name and title]

Dear Mr./Ms. _____:

We are sending this note to thank you for being one of the companies whose account never needs collection-type telephone calls or correspondence.

We appreciate our good customers. We thought you might like to know that we do.

Sincerely,

Credit Manager

6.6   [date]

Name of Company
Street Address (or P.O. Box Number)
City, State, Zip Code

Attention: [name and title]

Dear Mr./Ms. _____:

It may be an exaggeration to say that we do not need a calendar to tell us when the date is the 10th of the month but your check arrives with such regularity that without looking at the calendar, we know it must be the 10th!

But we lost a day this month. Your check did not arrive, which tells me that the invoice covering the purchase you made last month either got lost between our company and yours, or it slipped through a crack during the processing for payment.

It is not a problem. I have attached a copy of the invoice but we ask that you do not give it special handling. If you can input it with the next regular run of payables items, the check will get to us soon enough.

Sincerely,

Credit Manager

6.7   [date]

Name of Company
Street Address (or P.O. Box Number)
City, State, Zip Code

Attention: [name and title]

Dear Mr./Ms. _____:

Our appreciation level for customers who pay within terms is always high—and we know who they are.

Your company is one of our regulars in that category, which has made it easy for us to notice that your "like clockwork" check in payment for last month's purchases has not arrived.

My guess is that the winter flu bug has hit your payables department as hard as it has ours and that your people are struggling to keep up. Whatever the reason, we know the check will be along shortly—and that gives us a chance to close by thanking you for consistently being one of our *good customers*.

Sincerely,

Credit Manager

6.8   [date]

Name of Company
Street Address (or P.O. Box Number)
City, State, Zip Code

Attention: [name and title]

Dear Mr./Ms. _____:

I hope the following information is adequate for you to investigate the payment status of the listed invoices, and process payment for us.

P.O. Number	Invoice No.	Invoice Date	Invoice Amt.

Your prompt assistance is greatly appreciated.

Sincerely yours,

Credit Manager

6.9   [date]

Name of Company
Street Address (or P.O. Box Number)
City, State, Zip Code

Attention: [name and title]

Dear Mr./Ms. _____:

Our payment records do not show that we have received your check for _____ and _____ invoices in the amounts of $_____ and $_____.

If our records do not agree, please contact the undersigned so we may go over our respective records, locate the problem, and make whatever adjustment(s) may be necessary. If you find that our records do agree, prompt payment of the items listed above will be appreciated.

Sincerely,

Credit Manager

6.10   [date]

Name of Company
Street Address (or P.O. Box Number)
City, State, Zip Code

Attention: [name and title]

Dear Mr./Ms. _____:

We are unable to allow the discount(s) taken on your check _____ and applicable to invoice(s) _____.

The deduction was taken after the discount period has expired, so we must ask that you include the disallowed amount of $_____ as a part of your next account payment.

Sincerely,

Credit Manager

6.11   [date]

Name of Company
Street Address (or P.O. Box Number)
City, State, Zip Code

Attention: [name and title]

Dear Mr./Ms. _____:

Thank you for letting us know that you did not receive a copy of invoice number _____ (and date) in the amount of $_____.

If the attached copy leaves anything unanswered, please contact me at your earliest convenience.

Sincerely,

Credit Manager

6.12   [date]

Name of Company
Street Address (or P.O. Box Number)
City, State, Zip Code

Attention: [name and title]

Dear Mr./Ms. _____:

Our auditors tell me they have not received a response to their request for confirmation of the balance owed to this company on September 30, 19XX.

The figure they are asking you to confirm is $_____. If that figure does not agree with your records, please note in the space provided at the bottom of this letter. Your prompt "yes" or "no" will enable the auditors to complete their year-end work for us.

Many thanks for your cooperation.

Sincerely,

Credit Manager

____ The above figure is correct.

Our records show a 9/30/XX balance due of $_____.

_____   _____
Date   Signature and Title

6.13   [date]

Name of Company
Street Address (or P.O. Box Number)
City, State, Zip Code

Attention: [name and title]

Dear Mr./Ms. _____:

Our thanks for the check covering invoices for five purchases made during the preceding billing period.

Attached to this letter is a copy of our invoice [date] in the amount of $_____. I suspect that it went astray somewhere between our company and yours. If, however, you are unable to locate a receiver for the merchandise, please call me and I shall have one forwarded to you.

We appreciate our good customers—and your company is one of our oldest and best.

Sincerely,

Credit Manager

Statements and comments in the preceding several letters are uniformly cordial, supportive, helpful, and express gratitude for the quality of the relationship. Each letter affirms the tone of the relationship which emanates from the supplier/creditor to the customer. The recipients of these letters are among the supplier's best customers and the tone that pervades the letters confirms the esteem in which the customer is held. Such letters are an easy read because it is obvious to the recipient that the sender did not consider the writing of the letter to be an unpleasant chore. Pleasure radiates from each of these letters, letters which have more than a small amount of therapeutic value for the writer as well as the hoped-for level of appreciation for the recipient.

Some other first collection letters are somewhat more formal in their tone and in their approach. In many instances, however, they may not represent a major deviation from the preceding *reminder* format. Letters in this section of first collection letters are designed for the eyes of customers whose payment pattern is less frequently within credit terms than it is 10, 15, or 20 days past due. Are these problem accounts? Only in the sense that they require more attention, more monitoring, than the people with whom we have just been dealing. Accounts in this area of the *first collection letter* picture are a bit more casual about respecting credit terms, about considering the cashflow problems and requirements of their suppliers, and about how this more casual approach to payables downgrades the account from Excellent or Very good to what we might categorize as *Good, but—*. These are accounts that will rarely find their way into your bad debt write-offs but they can cause you to devote a disproportionate amount of your time to keeping their account balances in line with your company's needs and objectives.

What follows are some examples of first collection letters you might write to this type of account: the *Good, but*— account whose proclivity for being less than diligent in clearing payables might not cause you to send a first collection letter every month, but you will send one too many months out of the possible of 12.

The letters in the sections of this book give you a multitude of options: use them as a guideline; use them to personalize; use them to fit specific situations; use them almost verbatim, but do use them.

6.14   [date]

Name of Company
Street Address (or P.O. Box Number)
City, State, Zip Code

Attention: [name and title]

Dear Mr./Ms. _____:

A past-due balance is not unusual in our business but it becomes a matter of special concern when our experience with a good customer has always been *within terms* or *near terms*.

If there is a problem that we should discuss—a temporary cashflow problem, personnel changes, a missing invoice, etc.—please contact me at your earliest convenience. If none of the above is applicable, your payment will undoubtedly arrive within the coming week.

Sincerely,

Credit Manager

6.15 [date]

Name of Company
Street Address (or P.O. Box Number)
City, State, Zip Code

Attention: [name and title]

Dear Mr./Ms. _____:

I am always reluctant to contact a good customer regarding a past-due balance but there are times when it proves to be mutually beneficial.

Please check your records for the payment status of (date and invoice number) in the amount of $_____. If you do not have a copy, call me and one will be mailed promptly. If the check has been mailed or is being processed, please accept our appreciation for mailing it in time for the post office to deliver it during the coming week.

Sincerely,

Credit Manager

6.16 [date]

Name of Company
Street Address (or P.O. Box Number)
City, State, Zip Code

Attention: [name and title]

Dear Mr./Ms. _____:

I have just noticed something very unusual on our accounts receivable aging report. The breakdown of open items on your company's account includes an invoice (number and date) for $_____, that, if our report is correct, is _____ days past due.

The balance could be the result of an invoice that went astray between our office and your payables department, or it could be any of several other reasons. It is important, however, that we get the balance off of your account so I have attached an invoice copy.

Many thanks for your help in clearing this odd item.

Sincerely,

Credit Manager

6.17   [date]

Name of Company
Street Address (or P.O. Box Number)
City, State, Zip Code

Attention: [name and title]

Dear Mr./Ms. _____:

The attached copy (copies) of invoice (invoices) _____ (and _____)
is/are being forwarded as you requested during our telephone conversation on [date].

This information should enable you to verify the accuracy of these invoice balances
and expedite the processing of payment.

Sincerely,

Credit Manager

6.18   [date]

Name of Company
Street Address (or P.O. Box Number)
City, State, Zip Code

Attention: [name and title]

Dear Mr./Ms. _____:

Attached is a copy of invoice _____ dated _____ in the amount of
$_____. This invoice is _____ days past due and is unfavorably impacting the
aging of your account.

Please contact me if there is a problem with the merchandise. If there is no problem,
your payment response by _____ will be greatly appreciated.

Sincerely,

Credit Manager

6.19   [date]

Name of Company
Street Address (or P.O. Box Number)
City, State, Zip Code

Attention: [name and title]

Dear Mr./Ms. _____:

With some of our accounts, past-due balances are a way of life; with others, a past-due balance is a rare occurrence.

During the _____ years since your company first became one of our valued customers, account balances have almost always been paid within or near terms. When there is a rare deviation from that payment pattern, as in the current past due balance of $_____, you can understand our surprise.

If the problem stems from a temporary decrease in the flow of cash, call me. We can very quickly work out a solution that will ensure an adequate program of payments and an uninterrupted supply of product(s). If the problem might be more serious than temporary, then it is even more imperative that we talk before past-due balances impact unfavorably on our good relationship.

Please give me a call. We are anxious to help.

Sincerely,

Credit Manager

6.20   [date]

Name of Company
Street Address (or P.O. Box Number)
City, State, Zip Code

Attention: [name and title]

Dear Mr./Ms. _____:

Our receivables records indicate that payment(s) has/have not been received for [month or months] invoicing in the amount of $_____.

Please verify promptly and clear this/these balance(s) which is/are several days past our net 30 terms.

Sincerely,

Credit Manager

Every collection letter should include the type and level of stimulation the creditor's experience with the account tells him or her is necessary to get a check for the requested amount. Whether the approach is in the context of a friendly reminder—so soft and pliable that the recipient actually feels good about receiving it—or one of several progressively more persuasive and/or insistent payment requests, the goal is always the same: every collection effort is geared toward motivating the debtor to send a check—and the sooner the better!

At no point in the collection process is it ever appropriate to send correspondence or to make verbal statements that are not accurate or not presented in a polite manner. *Polite* does not mean, however, that you cannot make your point in a direct and/or a forceful manner. The nature of your past experience with the account will dictate the tone, but it can be done in language that enables an honest, conscientious customer to come through the experience without loss of reputation or face (credibility, etc.).

The process of collecting money frequently puts the creditor and customer/ debtor in a mutually uncomfortable position. Your company must have its money to sustain a reasonable level of internally generated cashflow. Your customer probably wants to pay, may be in a temporary cashflow bind, and is reluctant to call you to explain the problem. Fortunately, when you have a long relationship with the person in the customer company who handles payments, it is easier for one of you to pick up the telephone and say "We have a temporary problem," or "Do you have a problem?" Communication between the two companies is the key to minimizing problems at all levels and in all areas, and it is especially important when the specific agenda is the collecting of accounts receivable.

It is a rare business or company that does not at some time experience a problem of such financial magnitude that it must request the help of understanding suppliers. A good account deserves that level of courtesy and concern; a good supplier/creditor will be there to help a good customer when help is appropriate.

Only a small section of your company's arsenal of collection letters should be in the category of *reminders*. The letters that follow fit the criterion for what a first collection letter should include, although a few *remind* more than they *request*. They vary in the intensity of their request for money but none of them relates to a prior unsuccessful first letter or first telephone call. Optimism regarding the debtor's resolve to pay the past-due balance(s) remains the key ingredient in the approach taken at this time.

There is an almost indiscernible line between some of the first letters that follow and some in preceding pages. Select letters that your experience tells you match specific accounts. Your good judgment and familiarity with accounts will tell you when, where, and how much should be personalized.

6.21   [date]

Name of Company
Street Address (or P.O. Box Number)
City, State, Zip Code

Attention: [name and title]

Dear Mr./Ms. _____:

Our payment records do not show that we have received your check for [date(s) and number(s)] in the amount of $_____.

If our records do not agree, please contact the undersigned so we may go over our respective records, locate the problem, and make whatever adjustment(s) may be necessary.

If our records do agree, prompt payment of the above-listed balance will be appreciated.

Sincerely,

6.22   [date]

Name of Company
Street Address (or P.O. Box Number)
City, State, Zip Code

Attention: [name and title]

Dear Mr./Ms. _____:

Attached to this letter is a copy of invoice _____ dated _____ in the amount of $_____. The invoice is _____ days past due and is at a point where it is beginning to unfavorably impact the aging of your account.

Please contact me if there is a problem with the merchandise, a temporary decrease in the flow of cash, or any other situation that may be impacting your ability to pay closer to terms. We understand how an unexpected problem or event can make it difficult for a company to maintain normal patterns, and we are willing to help.

Sincerely,

6.23   [date]

Name of Company
Street Address (or P.O. Box Number)
City, State, Zip Code

Attention: [name and title]

Dear Mr./Ms. _____:

A review of our current accounts receivable aging report indicates that we have not received payment for the listed invoices.

Invoice No.	Invoice Date	Invoice Amt.

Some of these invoices are a considerable number of days past our terms. If there is any problem with the paper work (an invoice missing, a pricing error, etc.), please call me so we can eliminate the problem. If a temporary cashflow problem is the reason for the unpaid invoices, we can work out a payment program that will reduce some of the pressure on cashflow.

There are two orders in-house that I am unable to release until your check arrives or we have had a chance to talk. We are anxious to help, so please do not hesitate to call.

Sincerely,

Credit Manager

6.24   [date]

Name of Company
Street Address (or P.O. Box Number)
City, State, Zip Code

Attention: [name and title]

Dear Mr./Ms. _____:

When a good account such as yours surprises us by allowing a balance to remain open several days beyond the due date, we begin to feel that it is a candidate for the "slipped through the crack" category.

Please check your payables records for the payment status of the listed item.

Invoice Date	Invoice No.	P.O. Number	Invoice Amt.

If your records agree that some or all of the listed items are unpaid, please forward a check for the unpaid items that you are able to identify. The attached invoice copies should be helpful in identifying others on the list whose original invoice could have been lost between your company and ours.

Please call me if you need any additional information.

Sincerely,

Credit Manager

6.25   [date]

Name of Company
Street Address (or P.O. Box Number)
City, State, Zip Code

Attention: [name and title]

Dear Mr./Ms. _____:

Our receivables records indicate that payment(s) has/have not been received for [month or months] invoicing in the amount of $_____.

Please verify promptly and clear this/these balance(s) which is/are several days past our Net 30 terms.

Sincerely,

Credit Manager

6.26   [date]

Name of Company
Street Address (or P.O. Box Number)
City, State, Zip Code

Attention: [name and title]

Dear Mr./Ms. _____:

Attached is a copy of invoice _____, dated_____, in the amount of $_____. This invoice is __days past due and is unfavorably impacting the aging of your account.

Please contact me if there is a problem with the merchandise. If there is no problem, your payment response by _____ will be greatly appreciated.

Sincerely,

Credit Manager

6.27   [date]

Name of Company
Street Address (or P.O. Box Number)
City, State, Zip Code

Attention: [name and title]

Dear Mr./Ms. _____:

Our payment records do not show that we have received your check for _____ and _____ invoices in the amounts of $_____ and $_____.

If our records do not agree, please contact the undersigned so we may go over our respective records, locate the problem, and make whatever adjustment(s) may be necessary. If you find that our records do agree, prompt payment of the items listed above will be appreciated.

Sincerely,

Credit Manager

6.28   [date]

Name of Company
Street Address (or P.O. Box Number)
City, State, Zip Code

Attention: [name and title]

Dear Mr./Ms. _____:

The attached copy (copies) of invoice (invoices) _____ (and _____) is/are being forwarded as you requested during our telephone conversation on _____.

This information should enable you to verify the accuracy of these invoice balances and expedite the processing of payment.

Sincerely,

Credit Manager

6.29   [date]

Name of Company
Street Address (or P.O. Box Number)
City, State, Zip Code

Attention: [name and title]

Dear Mr./Ms. _____:

Our sales representative for your territory just told me that the [color, dye lot, quantity, etc.] of the order we delivered to your warehouse on [date and invoice number] was not what you had ordered (was defective, wrong color, wrong size(s), wrong quantity, etc.).

Please—never hesitate to call and tell us about the problem. We now understand why your account appears to be _____ days past due.

The replacement order left our plant yesterday and should be delivered today or tomorrow.

If there is a repeat of this problem—or a future problem of any kind—please contact us immediately, pay for product that is not a part of the problem order, and know that we will take steps immediately to correct the problem.

Sincerely,

Credit Manager

6.30   [date]

Name of Company
Street Address (or P.O. Box Number)
City, State, Zip Code

Attention: [name and title]

Dear Mr./Ms. _____:

Our records do not indicate that the listed invoices have been paid, nor are we able to give our auditors a reason for the nonpayment.

P.O. Number	Invoice No.	Invoice Date	Invoice Amt.

Copies of the listed invoices are attached to simplify the process of checking your payables records. A check covering invoices that have not been paid will be appreciated.

If there is a problem with any of the product covered by these invoices—quality, quantity, color, price, etc.—give me a call. Your payment record should not be unfavorably impacted because of a problem over which you had no control.

Your cooperation is appreciated.

Sincerely,

Credit Manager

6.31   [date]

Name of Company
Street Address (or P.O. Box Number)
City, State, Zip Code

Attention: [name and title]

Dear Mr./Ms. _____:

Our records indicate that payment has not been received for the listed invoices.

Invoice No.	Invoice Date	P.O. Number	Invoice Amt.

These invoices vary from several-to-many days past our sales terms of net 30 days. Such unfavorable aging inevitably raises a question regarding the continuation of our open-account relationship.

Prompt payment of the above items will certainly be a key factor in our decision regarding future sales terms for your account.

Sincerely,

Manager

6.32   [date]

Name of Company
Street Address (or P.O. Box Number)
City, State, Zip Code

Attention: [name and title]

Dear Mr./Ms. _____:

Thank you for the prompt response to the question I voiced during our first telephone conversation today. I have attached copies of the two invoices that were lost somewhere between our two companies.

Your company's excellent payment record made it obvious that the past-due balance had to be the result of a missing invoice, a pricing error, or an overdue credit memo. Because the post office has not been infallible, it was easy to eliminate *pricing error* and *overdue credit memo*.

Many thanks for your help. We appreciate it.

Sincerely,

Credit Manager

6.33   [date]

Name of Company
Street Address (or P.O. Box Number)
City, State, Zip Code

Attention: [name and title]

Dear Mr./Ms. _____:

I appreciate your call earlier today regarding the past-due balance of $_____.

Your suggestion that two checks in the amount of $_____ will be mailed on the [date] and [date] of this month is very satisfactory.

Life would be much easier if more of our customers would be as conscientious about their credit relationships as your company. Please contact me if there is anything further that we can do to help you over this temporary cashflow shortage.

Sincerely,

Credit Manager

6.34   [date]

Name of Company
Street Address (or P.O. Box Number)
City, State, Zip Code

Attention: [name and title]

Dear Mr./Ms. _____:

Thank you for the telephone call this morning. It was a good way to start the day.

As I said this morning, we have no problem with your request for an additional 10 days in which to make the third (and final) payment on our special payment program.

You're a good customer and we appreciate your business.

Sincerely,

Credit Manager

6.35   [date]

Name of Company
Street Address (or P.O. Box Number)
City, State, Zip Code

Attention: [name and title]

Dear Mr./Ms. _____:

Some of the worst scams in the history of modern commerce have involved merchants who overcharged for shoddy goods or customers who took the quality merchandise of an honest merchant and refused to honor the obligation to pay.

We are very grateful that our relationship has worked—and continues to work—in the following manner: We supply your company with quality merchandise for the dollars spent with us, and you honor faithfully the obligation to pay us when due for that merchandise.

Not all of our customers are as dependable as you are. We thought it might be a good idea if we let you know how we feel about our relationship.

Sincerely,

Credit Manager

6.36   [date]

Name of Company
Street Address (or P.O. Box Number)
City, State, Zip Code

Attention: [name and title]

Dear Mr./Ms. _____:

The *color of money* is green: the color of a check offered in payment of a bill or an account can be almost any color.

We are gathering and processing checks from customers whose account has one or more past-due balances. Every color in the rainbow is welcome but we are certainly not prejudiced against white.

Please send your money in the color of your choice and in the amount shown at the bottom of this letter.

Sincerely,

Credit Manager

6.37   [date]

Name of Company
Street Address (or P.O. Box Number)
City, State, Zip Code

Attention: [name and title]

Dear Mr./Ms. _____:

The [month] past-due balance of $_____ is so uncharacteristic of your company that I know it represents an oversight or a missing invoice.

A photocopy of the invoice is attached for your convenience in processing payment.

Sincerely,

Credit Manager

6.38   [date]

Name of Company
Street Address (or P.O. Box Number)
City, State, Zip Code

Attention: [name and title]

Dear Mr./Ms. _____:

Our payment records do not indicate that we have received your check for [invoice number(s) and date(s)] in the total amount of $_____. During our telephone conversation on _____, it was promised that payment would be in this office by _____.

We anticipate that you will promptly honor our agreement so this office can consider lifting the current hold on product shipment to your company.

Sincerely,

Credit Manager

6.39   [date]

Name of Company
Street Address (or P.O. Box Number)
City, State, Zip Code

Attention: [name and title]

Dear Mr./Ms. _____:

Our payment records do not indicate that we have received your check for [invoice number and date] in the amount of $_____.

If this data does not agree with your records, please contact the undersigned so we may compare our records, locate the problem, and make any necessary adjustment(s).

If our records agree, then we'll appreciate your prompt payment of the invoice balance.

Sincerely,

Credit Manager

6.40   [date]

Name of Company
Street Address (or P.O. Box Number)
City, State, Zip Code

Attention: [name and title]

Dear Mr./Ms. _____:

Our accounts receivable records do not indicate that we have received your payment for the listed invoices.

P.O. Number	Invoice Date	Invoice No.	Invoice Amt.

If there is a reason why payment cannot be processed promptly, please contact the undersigned.

Sincerely,

Credit Manager

6.41   [date]

Name of Company
Street Address (or P.O. Box Number)
City, State, Zip Code

Attention: [name and title]

Dear Mr./Ms. _____:

We have received payment for several invoices more current than [invoice number/date/amount], so I know it is either an oversight or the original copy went astray between our company and yours.

If your records show that it has been paid, please send the payment information to my attention and I'll see that it is cleared from your account record. If it has not been paid, routine payment processing will be fine.

Sincerely,

Credit Manager

6.42   [date]

Name of Company
Street Address (or P.O. Box Number)
City, State, Zip Code

Attention: [name and title]

Dear Mr./Ms. _____:

Memorandum to Our Customers

Invoice errors in the pricing of product units or in the quantity of product units listed on the invoice versus the quantity of product units received by the customer can be a problem. Unless the customer has gone through it once before, there is an inclination to adjust the price and remit the correct figure, or in the instance of a quantity error, pay on the basis of product units received rather than the number listed on the invoice.

It is our experience that these problems occur infrequently but when they do occur, we ask that the customer notify us as soon as the error is discovered. We will issue immediately a credit memo for the difference between the incorrect invoice and the correct total, mail the customer a copy of the credit memo, and ask that the customer pay on the basis of the adjusted invoice total.

Customers who worry that their good credit standing may be jeopardized if they do not pay the invoice before a credit memo has been received should not be concerned. When the customer notifies us of the error, any delay in getting a credit memo to the customer is our responsibility.

I hope these answers will be helpful should your company encounter a future pricing or quantity error.

_____   _____
Credit Manager   Date

Collecting your company's past-due accounts receivable is serious business. You should not, however, be afraid to move away from collection letters and techniques that were conceived and used effectively more than a decade ago. These letters and techniques do nothing to grab the customer's attention or to motivate him or her to find a way to fit a payment to your company into a cashflow that is much closer to cash trickle.

The occasional use of one of the following lines might be justified because of the special nature of a problem or of the relationship between the creditor/supplier and the customer/debtor. Use them sparingly, if at all. Time has left them tired, worn, and ineffective.

1. A review of your account indicates that we have not received your check for...

2. We have made every effort to work with your company but...

3. Our company cannot spend more time trying to collect the past-due...

4. Every reasonable effort has been made to get your company to pay...

5. Letters and telephone calls have not been successful in...

6. Our current accounts receivable aging report indicates that your account is...

Whether or not you would send a payment in response to a letter that included one of the above opening statements is a matter of personal reaction and company conscience. It is not possible to motivate debtors with run-of-the-mill, absence-of-imagination collection letters. Too many creditors are competing for what is frequently a limited number of debtor dollars. Your company cannot afford to send out collection letters that do or say nothing to set them apart from the others.

Remember, too, that all companies do not project the same image. If your company is an old-line, well-established business or company whose roots in the community can be traced back farther than the current generation of officers or principals, the preferred style of correspondence might be more formal. If, however, management and the firm itself is anxious to project an image that is contemporary—one of a friendly, outgoing company whose officers and employees are anxious to develop close business relationships with their customers—the correspondence will reflect the general attitude of informality.

What is appropriate and effective for one company might not get the job done for a company whose attitude and image are different, and perhaps more contemporary. The following is a comparison of two different styles of correspondence whose messages to the customer/debtor are the same but presented in dissimilar language and format.

[date]

Name of Company
Street Address (or P.O. Box Number)
City, State, Zip Code

Attention: [name and title]

Dear Mr./Ms. _____:

We appreciate the concern that was expressed when Ms._____ called earlier today regarding invoice [name/date/amount], now _____ days past due.

Or if your customer's approach is less formal:

[date]

Name of Company
Street Address (or P.O. Box Number)
City, State, Zip Code

Dear Mr./Ms. _____:

Your call this morning was a real jump-start for me. We had noticed yesterday that invoice [number and date] is past due more than a few days and we didn't have a clue as to the reason.

The first introduction points out the more structured format of the company's correspondence. The second introduction tells us that informality is the company's style. All areas of each company or business will be expected to project an image that is in "synch" with the one projected by the company.

[date]

Name of Company
Street Address (or P.O. Box Number)
City, State, Zip Code

Attention: [name and title]

Dear Mr./Ms. _____:

We regret any inconvenience that may have been caused because of our error in the count of product shipped versus the quantity that was billed. It is an uncommon error but one we do not dismiss lightly.

Or if your customer's approach is less formal:

[date]

Name of Company
Street Address (or P.O. Box Number)
City, State, Zip Code

Attention: [name and title]

Dear Mr./Ms. _____:

Thanks for contacting me regarding the short count in product shipped versus the quantity billed. Our apologies for blowing this one. The number of units shorted is going out to you today via overnight delivery.

6.43   [date]

Name of Company
Street Address (or P.O. Box Number)
City, State, Zip Code

Attention: [name and title]

Dear Mr./Ms. _____:

The attached copies of invoices _____ and _____ are being forwarded in response to your telephone call yesterday afternoon.

We appreciate the call. It explains the past-due status of these two invoices versus your company's traditional *on time* handling of invoice payments.

Sincerely,

Credit Manager

6.44   [date]

Name of Company
Street Address (or P.O. Box Number)
City, State, Zip Code

Attention: [name and title]

Dear Mr./Ms. _____:

We were not aware that the attached invoice [date/number/purchase order/amount] was still open until it appeared on our latest accounts receivable aging report.

I have to assume that there is nothing in your payables records to identify it as an open item or if it was received at your office at all. Where has it been for the past 46 days? We wish we knew, but the one thing we can confirm is that it is an unpaid item.

It's our fault that an invoice copy was not forwarded when the shipment was made. This one does not deserve any special handling. Please input it with your next regular batch of payables items and we'll watch the mail for a check.

Sincerely,

Credit Manager

The first collection letter should confine itself to a statement of what is owed and do it in language that infers or states the belief that the balance is unpaid because of oversight, a lost invoice, a personnel problem on the payables desk, etc. This letter is almost always supportive, helpful, conciliatory, and expresses confidence that the oversight, or a problem caused because a key invoice or credit memo is missing, will now be eliminated. At no point in most of these letters will you find the creditor inferring or making a statement which indicates a level of concern higher than slight.

The first collection letters that represent a departure from the above-described format do not include a lot of praise regarding past payment performance. These letters go to customers whose monthly payment pattern is chronically slow; not generally so slow as to cause concern regarding the safety of accounts receivable dollars, but slow in the context of consistently abusing the creditor/supplier's credit terms.

Accounts in this second category frequently require more attention than just the first collection letter. There may be a follow-up telephone call, possibly a second telephone call, and if that level of attention has not caused the debtor/customer to mail a check, the customer will get a second collection letter: one that addresses the problem clearly and directly. Unless the customer is in dire financial straits, the check will be mailed.

A customer whose cashflow forces a pattern of payments that each month is slow more than a few days will try generally to avoid pushing key suppliers to the point where they suggest the possibility of suspending the customer's open account privilege. No business or company can operate successfully if one or more of its major suppliers is refusing to sell on terms other than COD, and no company whose cashflow is not in crisis will allow the account to remain unpaid.

Consignment agreements are an effective tool for many companies to get their products into the hands of distributors and dealers who might otherwise be unable to stock enough of a selection of the supplier's products to make it a mutually successful relationship. When a major supplier consummates an agreement with a customer, it can be the difference between a customer accepting the risks of expanding into a new area or territory, or enlarging the capability of the customer to more effectively service the present marketplace area. And when the creditor/supplier is protected with an appropriate filing under the Uniform Commercial Code, risk is minimized.

There is always the possibility that problems will develop as the parties get into the agreement. If the customer's cashflow is tight, consigned product might be sold from inventory and not reported (via invoice copy, etc.) to the cosigner. Although the consignment agreement may call for the consignor to do a quarterly inventory to verify the consignee's figures, a gap of three months between inventories could add up to a discrepancy of several thousand dollars. A monthly inventory could be a burden, but it might be a necessity.

The letters that follow are examples of collection-related correspondence that a supplier's credit manager might initiate to cope with certain situations and problems. There is always the possibility of loss, but diligent monitoring of the agreement—payments and inventory controls within parameters of the agreement—should minimize that possibility.

6.45   [date]

Name of Company
Street Address (or P.O. Box Number)
City, State, Zip Code

Attention: [name and title]

Dear Mr./Ms. _____:

Good news. We're glad that the consignment agreement we negotiated six months ago when you were about to go into the new territory is working as well for your company as it is for ours.

If I may repeat something that I said during our telephone conversation yesterday afternoon, I again want to thank you for the on-time monthly payments for consigned product(s) sold to your customers during a calendar month. Checks have arrived within the agreed time frame, and the quarterly inventories that our representative conducted at three and six months were virtually on the mark—and the few minor differences were quickly adjusted.

It was especially good to hear that your company is off to a better start in the new territory than had been projected. Any time the results are that positive, you can be very pleased with the decision to assume the risks of expansion.

If there is anything further we can do to ease the burden—or to expand the joy—of successful growth, please give me a call.

Sincerely,

Credit Manager

6.46   [date]

Name of Company
Street Address (or P.O. Box Number)
City, State, Zip Code

Attention: [name and title]

Dear Mr./Ms. _____:

Our consignment agreement is not working as well as we had anticipated.

When our representative conducted the first inventory 10 days ago—and six months after the effective date of the agreement—there were discrepancies in the count that we assumed could be readily adjusted. This has not been the situation. After a careful recheck, including a second warehouse count of major items, the total discrepancy between your inventory figures and ours comes to a total of $_____.

This represents a discrepancy of _____ percent of the total value of the products we have shipped to you during the first six months of the consignment agreement. Obviously we cannot accept controls over our merchandise that with the first six months, has led to this level of discrepancy. Control is an area of concern that we are currently addressing, and one that we will be taking up with you when our marketing manager, [name], and I meet with you [day and date].

Meanwhile, our two companies agree that the difference between your inventory figure and ours is the amount listed above. Your suggestion that a check for half of the amount will be mailed on [date] and the second half on [date] is, as I said earlier, acceptable to us.

We should have no problem getting the agreement—and the control of inventory—back on track when we meet next week.

Sincerely,

Credit Manager

6.47   [date]

Name of Company
Street Address (or P.O. Box Number)
City, State, Zip Code

Attention: [name and title]

Dear Mr./Ms. _____:

I have just had an opportunity to compare the figures from your inventory and the inventory taken by our area rep a week ago.

My first thought was—or could have been—that one of the reports was a photocopy of the other. The figures in each of the product categories were either exactly the same or were so close that it did nothing but confirm the conscientious attitude brought to the agreement by your company.

To say that we are delighted is to understate the fact. Not only is the inventory itself being monitored carefully but the checks for product sold during the six calendar months that the agreement has been in force have all been on time. Any differences between product(s) in inventory at the end of the first six months and product(s) sold during the same period are within parameters that can only be defined as excellent.

If there is anything further we can do to help ease your company's path to successful growth, please give us a call.

Sincerely,

Credit Manager

6.48   [date]

Name of Company
Street Address (or P.O. Box Number)
City, State, Zip Code

Attention: [name and title]

Dear Mr./Ms. _____:

Our feeling is that the consignment agreement we negotiated six months ago is not doing a job that is effective for us.

During the six months since the agreement's effective date, we have supplied your company with a full inventory of products and have replaced inventory as it has been reported sold. Unfortunately, the inventory count that our people took last week indicates a major discrepancy between your figures and ours in several of our product lines: a discrepancy that at the end of the first six months' totals $_____.

Monthly payments for product sold have not, with the exception of the first two, been within parameters set in the consignment agreement. I was surprised to see that payment for goods sold during the fifth month was _____ days past the agreement date, and payment for goods sold during the sixth month was _____ days overdue.

The problem was addressed during our telephone conversation yesterday afternoon. I told you at that time what must happen if the agreement is to continue. Of immediate concern is a check for $_____ by the [date] of this month, which will clear the discrepancy between inventory, reported sales, and unreported sales. Of equal importance is a set of requirements for tighter inventory control, including a monthly inventory by an outside firm of our choice.

We should get together at your office within the next week or ten days to be sure the attached list of changes has been implemented, and is working successfully. I'll call within the next four or five days to set up a mutually convenient time for the meeting.

Sincerely,

Credit Manager

6.49   [date]

Name of Company
Street Address (or P.O. Box Number)
City, State, Zip Code

Attention: [name and title]

Dear Mr./Ms. _____:

Your telephone call and request for a special payment program that will enable your company to reduce past-due balances while still being able to buy our company's products is a reasonable one.

A payment program that meets our requirements—and one that would allow you to make current purchases within levels that have been normal in preceding months—is set out below. I believe it is a program that stays within the constraints of your current cashflow crunch, will reduce past-due balances at an acceptable rate of speed, will prevent the creation of new past-due problems, and will address your ongoing need for our products.

Invoice Date	Invoice No.	P.O. Number	Payment Amt.	Due Date

Please review this plan carefully. If your company can handle it, keep the original copy; sign, date and return the second copy to my attention. If there is a problem with any one of the amounts or payment dates, call me and we will try to accommodate an appropriate change.

Sincerely,

Credit Manager

Collection Aids

It is essential that people who have the responsibility for collecting past-due receivables balances should maintain simple but effective records of their activities—past, current and ongoing—with these accounts. The forms that follow meet the criteria for simplicity, relevant areas of information, past and current problems, and what evolved from the various discussions with the customer-debtor.

Customer Call Sheet

Used to record collection calls to a customer, who was contacted, what was said, and what follow-up is projected. A copy of this form should be in the file folder of every customer whose past-due balances(s) necessitate collection calls, letters or visits. Everything relevant to the various conversations between the supplier and the customer should be recapped on this sheet. A notation is made subsequently on the Daily Follow-Up Schedule and the Past-Due Balances report.

Daily Follow-Up Schedule

It covers a period of 10 days. Its purpose is to indicate when a follow-up call should be made if a check is not received by the date specified in a letter or a telephone call.

Past-Due Balances–Calls as Listed

This recaps the payment commitments made by customers as the result of telephone calls, letters, and office visits. It can be used also as a report from Credit and Collections to the company's financial officer, owner/manager, COO, or CEO.

Customer Call Sheet

Owner _____ Company Name _____

Contact _____ Phone _____

Date	Contact	Subject/Comments	Follow-Up

6.51   **Customer Call Log Sheet**

Customer: _____ Phone _____

_____ Time Dif._____

Date Called   Call Details

_____   _____

_____

_____

_____

_____   _____

_____

_____

_____

_____   _____

_____

_____

_____

_____   _____

_____

_____

_____

_____   _____

_____

_____

_____

6.52   **Daily Follow-Up Schedule**

Mon.	Tues.	Wed.	Thurs.	Fri.	Mon.	Tues.	Wed.	Thurs.	Fri.

6.53   **Past-Due Balances–Calls as Listed**

Acct. #	Customer Name/Location	Date Called	Payment Promised		Date Promised	Date and Amt. Rec'd.
			Invoices	Amount		

Collection Strategies

Collecting money from many past-due accounts is not a simple matter of sending a reminder letter, or making a telephone call, then sitting back and waiting for the check to come in. It involves making choices: reviewing collection strategies and selecting the collection tools that seem most appropriate for the target company or situation.

Many collection efforts will not be as productive as the creditor had anticipated because there is no collection strategy, or because the collection strategy has not been tailored to the individual account. There is no substitute for a collection effort that pays off rapidly and in full, and there is in many cases little hope for such a return on the investment of time and energy if there is no tailored collection strategy. Know the customer's strengths, weaknesses and needs—and take full advantage of that knowledge to pattern your collection strategy.

The following questions are relevant to the strength and the thrust of strategies for individual companies:

1. Is what you sell to the customer important (a key) in the product or service that the customer manufactures, assembles, or provides in its service to others?

2. Would it be difficult for the customer to find a substitute material or product that would be as effective as the product or material purchased from your company?

3. Is your product—a component, a material or a *stand-alone* product—frequently specified by architects, planners, builders, etc.?

4. If the customer has no acceptable alternative to what your company is supplying, why allow the Payables Department (or the Controller) to play games with your invoices?

5. Have you been letting your appreciation for a customer's buying habits (frequency and quantity) get in the way of your thinking regarding the appropriate handling of a slow-pay, contentious, time-consuming, and profits-eroding account?

6. Why should you allow your company's money to be held hostage by the Payables Department, the Controller, or some person in finance?

One of the most successful strategies for a major creditor/supplier—one whose material(s) or product(s) is of key importance to the customer/debtor—is to carry the collection effort one level beyond the usual one. At the bottom of your letter to the Accounts Payable Supervisor or the Controller, include the following one-or-two liner:

cc: [name], Purchasing Manager

and/or

cc: [name], Manufacturing Manager

To personalize the above, I have over the decades had some great payment breakthroughs because I let the Purchasing and Manufacturing Managers know that payables was playing a dangerous game with an important/key supplier. Most people in payables, accounting, and finance have no idea where the material(s), product(s), or service(s) provided by your company fit into the manufacturing or services scheme of their company. When it is their own Manufacturing or Purchasing Manager—albeit an irate one—who provides the enlightenment, the effect can be lasting and very beneficial for the creditor/supplier. It has not been unusual, in fact, for me to receive a call from either the Purchasing or the Manufacturing Manager to advise me that he or she has contacted payables (or the controller or financial officer), and that a check for the past-due balance will be released during the current week—this plus assurances that future payments will be released much closer to sales terms.

Many accounts will respond to a reminder letter; some will require one or two telephone calls plus a second letter before a check finds its way to your desk. There are accounts whose payment pattern is so slow or so unpredictable that a *collection strategy* would seem a waste of time. Not true with a large majority of accounts. You enhance the chances of a short and successful collection effort if you know the account and exploit that knowledge into a tailored collection strategy. Nothing is effective every time but you will spend less time collecting more money from more accounts than you will if there is no advance thought or planning.

Payment Plans

A knotty collection problem can be solved frequently with a payment plan that enables the creditor to generate some cash from the account while it enables the customer to continue buying some of the creditor's products. This can be a "best of both worlds" situation in that it combines collecting past-due balances with the sales of more product(s). Where all else has failed, it can be the tool that effects an agreement between the two parties.

A payment plan might be proposed by a creditor who has been unsuccessful in other attempts to collect past-due balances and perceives the creditor to be sliding into a terminal position (an imminent or an eventual filing for protection under provisions of the bankruptcy code). It is obvious that in this situation, any creditor company wants its money as rapidly as the customer's precarious financial condition will allow. Under circumstances that are not so grim, a payment plan may be used as a prop to help a customer who has what both parties recognize as a cashflow crunch; but should not extend beyond a period of four-to-six months. A payment program is in this situation an appropriate solution for both the supplier and the customer.

One somewhat flexible format will cover most situations where a payment plan is a reasonable solution. The content of individual payment plans will vary, however, with the dollar amount of past-due balances, the aging of those balances, and the financial capability of the customer. A payment program is never used unless the customer's cashflow is somewhere between *restricted* and a *trickle*. When a plan is devised to fit within those parameters, it should have an excellent chance of accomplishing its purpose.

6.54   [date]

Name of Company
Street Address (or P.O. Box Number)
City, State, Zip Code

Attention: [name and title]

Dear Mr./Ms. _____:

I appreciate the candor with which you addressed your company's cashflow problem when we talked earlier today. If more customers would pick up the telephone and lay out the problem, misunderstandings would be reduced by a whopping percentage.

After you outlined the extent and the probable duration of the company's cashflow crunch, I went to the drawing board and put a payment plan together that seems to have what it takes to work within your tight cashflow. It reduces past-due balances at a rate that is acceptable and also allows for ongoing purchases of our products.

Payment Date	Payment Amt.	Invoice Date	Invoice No.	P.O. Number

Payments are spaced _____ weeks apart. The amount of each payment has been set at a figure calculated to minimize the demand on your company's cashflow while it meets our expectations for a debt-reduction plan. Any suggestions for change should be minor to ensure that it does the job for which it has been designed.

Please keep the original copy; sign, date and return the second copy to my attention.

Sincerely,

Credit Manager

6.55   [date]

Name of Company
Street Address (or P.O. Box Number)
City, State, Zip Code

Attention: [name and title]

Dear Mr./Ms. _____:

We know that your company is going through a difficult cashflow experience but, as I said when we talked earlier today, we must have money on a regular basis to reduce past-due balances if we are to continue supplying you with product.

I believe the following payment program is a fit for the level of cashflow you described to me. It will reduce the past-due balances and allow enough space for a slightly reduced level of open account purchases.

Payment Date	Payment Amt.	Invoice Date	Invoice No.	P.O. Number

If there are any suggestions for changes in the program, they should be minor to ensure that the payment plan does the job for which it has been created.

Please keep the original copy; sign, date and return the second copy to my attention.

Sincerely,

Credit Manager

7

Second Collection Letters

When a collection effort moves to the point where a second letter is about to be sent, it usually means that a considerable amount of time has already been spent on the account. Although the sequence of collection steps may be varied from one account to another, the sending of a second letter means that there has been a first collection letter, probably one or two telephone calls to the debtor firm's accounts payable supervisor, and possibly a telephone call to the company's controller or financial officer. By the time a second letter has been mailed, creditor and debtor are well aware that a serious effort is being made to collect the past-due balance.

Is there a right or a wrong format for the sequence of a mix and match collection effort? Not at all. Different companies and different individuals respond in different ways. Some might respond more readily to a telephone call than to a letter. Others might not acknowledge that the creditor is serious about collecting the past-due balance until the request for payment has been made in a letter. A creditor must use some form of trial and error in almost every collection situation. There is no way to predetermine whether a letter might be more effective if it is preceded by one or more telephone calls or if one or two telephone calls might eliminate the need for a letter.

The goal of every collection effort should be to collect the company's money with a minimal expenditure of time. The goal should include establishing an effective and efficient collection program geared to those accounts whose performance is solidly in the category of *slow or slower*. A key part of such a collection program is the collection letters with which a collection person can be comfortable and that can offer the best chance to motivate the customer to send a check.

If the customer resists requests for payment, the problem can be one or more of the following: the customer does not have the money to pay the past-due balance; the customer is stalling and has no intention of making the payment; or the mix and match of letters and telephone calls may not be a motivational fit for that customer. Remember the importance of selecting the right collection letter or the right format for a telephone call. The scripted telephone call (or format) that works with one customer may have to be changed to be effective with another. Each account presents a separate challenge, and many of the challenges are unique. Try to match something from your inventory of letters and scripted telephone calls to what you know regarding the personality and quality of the debtor company and continue to fine tune or change the material you use until the results meet your expectations.

The second collection letter must emphasize the need for prompt payment of the past-due balance. Unless no telephone conversations have occurred between the first and second letters, there is no place for the face-saving devices that were sprinkled liberally throughout the group of first collection letters. If after receiving the first collection letter or telephone call, the customer claimed a pricing error or a missing invoice, it should have been given immediate attention. If nothing was said about either of these problems in the first letter or during a first or second telephone call, then this is the type of clerical problem that should be cleared up front, with the first letter or telephone call. It takes very little time to attach a photo copy of an unpaid invoice to a first collection letter; and it takes seconds to inquire of a payables person whether the customer received a copy of the unpaid invoice. Tidy up the clerical problems promptly because they can come back to slow your collection effort and have an adverse impact on your cashflow.

Examples of Second Letters

The letters that follow are examples of the format for second collection letters. They are less easy going and pliable in their approach to the past-due balance. There is more push, more of an edge, and a consciously diminished effort to give the customer a face-saving *out*. The creditor/supplier has not given up on the debt-or/customer as a future customer, but the priority is to collect from the customer a past-due balance that is not being given the proper attention or respect. Creditors whose account balances are not given the proper level of respect by their customers begin to lean consciously toward a concern regarding the fate of future accounts receivable balances.

Whether the customer is experiencing short- or long-term payment difficulties, any problem that might impact the capability of a customer to make payments of appropriate size should surface with the first collection letter or collection telephone call. It is in the customer's interest to protect the company's credit standing, but the customer has to be candid about the problem(s). For a customer to know of a problem, to purposely conceal it, then to *discover* it at a moment when the creditor is expressing concern over the past-due balance—and the future direction of the relationship—does not speak well for the customer's ethics.

Give the customer some additional latitude when the file indicates that the first letter is the only contact your company has had regarding payment of the past-due balance. It is always possible for a first letter to go astray and if your second letter—sent with no telephone calls between the two letters—does not recognize the possibility that the first letter was not received, it could be unjustly assumed that the customer was deliberately trying to avoid a response.

No second letter should be blunt, strident, assertive, or dogmatic. When there has been telephone contact and the information given to you indicates that the customer is caught up in a potentially serious but hopefully temporary cash crunch, understanding and cooperation are still very much a part of your collection technique. Customers are almost never so plentiful that a supplier, or a member of a service industry, can afford to trash a relationship with a customer whose ongoing problems may cause extra work but whose monthly level of purchases is well within the profit zone.

Be understanding when it is obvious that the customer is doing what he or she can to cooperate with your request; do not, however, allow *understanding* to become a substitute for a payment program (reasonable amounts at reasonable intervals). Unless a customer's predicament is serious, both the creditor and customer should work to reduce old balances while keeping the product supply line open as wide as prudent credit management will allow.

Here are some second letters that address the problem of past-due balances in language that delivers the message but does not do it in a callous or an offensive manner.

7.1   [date]

Name of Company
Street Address (or P.O. Box Number)
City, State, Zip Code

Attention: [name and title]

Dear Mr./Ms. _____:

Thank you for letting us know that you did not receive a copy of [invoice number and date] in the amount of $_____.

If the attached copy leaves anything unanswered, please contact me at your earliest convenience.

Sincerely,

Credit Manager

7.2   [date]

Name of Company
Street Address (or P.O. Box Number)
City, State, Zip Code

Attention: [name and title]

Dear Mr./Ms. _____:

We are unable to allow the discounts taken on your check [number] and applicable to invoices _____.

The deduction was taken after the discount period had expired so we must ask that you include the disallowed amount ($_____) as a part of your next account payment.

Sincerely,

Credit Manager

7.3   [date]

Name of Company
Street Address (or P.O. Box Number)
City, State, Zip Code

Attention: [name and title]

Dear Mr./Ms. _____:

Over the period of the past five months, there has been a major change in the way your company has handled its account obligations. Invoice payments that were invariably within discount or prompt terms have deteriorated to 20, 30, and 40 days past due, and that is not acceptable.

The following list of invoices includes a date by which each must be paid. During the period covered by this payment list, product will not be released in an amount that exceeds $1 for every $2 in payments received.

I am aware that this is inconvenient for you as it is for us, but there can be no change until the payment pattern is again within acceptable parameters.

Invoice No.	Invoice Date	Invoice Amt.	Payment By This Date

Your cooperation is appreciated.

Sincerely,

Credit Manager

7.4

[date]

Name of Company
Street Address (or P.O. Box Number)
City, State, Zip Code

Attention: [name and title]

Dear Mr./Ms. _____:

The call sheet for your account indicates that telephone calls to your office on [date] and [date] were not successful in obtaining a payment commitment for the past-due balances. Copies of the two invoices were mailed almost two weeks ago, and there has been no indication that the merchandise failed to arrive on time and in good condition.

Customers are very important people but the continuing success of our company demands a solid reciprocal with our customers: we provide you with good merchandise and good service at a fair price, and we expect payment within (or near) sales terms. Anything less—on our part or yours—erodes the relationship to the point where there no longer is mutual confidence.

Your check for $_____ (invoices _____ and _____) in our office by [date] is the confidence builder we need to continue the past level of open-account sales.

Sincerely,

Credit Manager

7.5   [date]

Name of Company
Street Address (or P.O. Box Number)
City, State, Zip Code

Attention: [name and title]

Dear Mr./Ms. _____:

Our company takes pride in developing strong customer relationships. The majority of our customers have been with us for several years which is, I guess, one of the positive results from what we try to do in support of our customers.

Not every customer can discount invoices, pay within terms, or even pay a few days past terms. We accept those facts when account data is evaluated and a credit line is assigned to a customer. From that point forward it becomes a matter of developing a rapport with the customer: a rapport that will enable both of us to address any problem that may arise before it can become a contentious issue.

Our relationship has, however, slid to a point where there is an unanticipated problem—and no rapport. Your account is [days] past due, we need $_____ yesterday, and the promises made during telephone conversations have brought no money.

Orders will be held until we have your check for $_____. The check must arrive prior to [date] to avoid having the current *hold order* status eventually give way to COD sales, and nothing on open account terms.

Your prompt payment response will get us back on track.

Sincerely,

Credit Manager

7.6   [date]

Name of Company
Street Address (or P.O. Box Number)
City, State, Zip Code

Attention: [name and title]

Dear Mr./Ms. _____:

Your company has an in-house order that cannot be released until payment has been received for past-due invoices _____ and _____ in the amounts of $_____ and $_____.

We dislike having to do this but a letter and two telephone calls—all within the past _____ days—have not produced a check; our only realistic alternative is to hold your order until the check is received. If the check arrives within the next _____ days, your order will be shipped immediately.

Your money is all it takes to get our product(s).

Sincerely,

Credit Manager

7.7   [date]

Name of Company
Street Address (or P.O. Box Number)
City, State, Zip Code

Attention: [name and title]

Dear Mr./Ms. _____:

Calling or writing to customers regarding past-due balances has to be the least favorite activity of most credit people. But because it goes with the territory, and because our company's need for a strong cashflow depends on accounts receivable that turn over rapidly, we do what we must to collect from our accounts.

The file folder for your account contains one letter and recap of two telephone calls, all dated during the past two weeks. Obviously they did not solve our problem: the past-due balance is still open; it is getting older by the day; and it is about to be joined by invoices for purchases made last month.

Two things have resulted from this situation: we cannot allow the unpaid balances to get older and we cannot sell any product(s) to your company until payment has been received.

The following payment plan offers the best opportunity for your company to continue to receive a reasonable percentage of your normal monthly product requirement.

Payment Due Date   Amount   Release Product ($)

Please sign, date, and return the second copy to my attention.

Sincerely,

Credit Manager

7.8   [date]

Name of Company
Street Address (or P.O. Box Number)
City, State, Zip Code

Attention: [name and title]

Dear Mr./Ms. _____:

Current notes pertaining to conversations with your office regarding a payment release date for invoices [number/amount] and [number/amount] indicate payment was to be in this office by [date]. It is now _____ days past the scheduled arrival date and we don't have a check.

The success or failure of relationships between people and companies is often decided on the presence or the absence of credibility: the fact that one party makes a commitment to the second party, and that commitment is honored. If it cannot be honored, the party who made the commitment is obligated to notify the second party of that fact in advance of the commitment date.

The check you were to mail on [date] should be rescheduled as a *must mail* on [date]. If we receive the check within five days of that date, the failure to release the check on [date] will go into the account record as an oversight.

Sincerely,

Credit Manager

7.9   [date]

Name of Company
Street Address (or P.O. Box Number)
City, State, Zip Code

Attention: [name and title]

Dear Mr./Ms. _____:

Two telephone calls to your office within the past 12 days have failed to relieve the problem of past-due invoices in the total amount of $_____.

Invoice Date	Invoice No.	P.O Number	Invoice Amt.

Your check by [date] will allow us to release three in-house orders currently on hold. Whether we can avoid the mutual inconvenience of holding future orders is in your hands.

A return to an acceptable payment pattern—and an acceptable aging of account invoices—will solve our problem.

Sincerely,

Credit Manager

7.10   [date]

Name of Company
Street Address (or P.O. Box Number)
City, State, Zip Code

Attention: [name and title]

Dear Mr./Ms. _____:

The payment commitment that you made during our telephone conversation earlier today will ease the strain put on the account by the past-due aging of four invoices.

Your commitment is to send a check in the amount of $_____ in time for it to arrive in this office by [date]. Our commitment is that when the check for $_____ is received here, three in-house orders totaling $_____ will be released immediately.

We are looking forward to resuming what has been a strong relationship.

Sincerely,

Credit Manager

7.11   [date]

Name of Company
Street Address (or P.O. Box Number)
City, State, Zip Code

Attention: [name and title]

Dear Mr./Ms. _____:

Please check your notes pertaining to the release of a check for past-due invoices in the amount of $_____. When we talked on [date], you agreed to release it on [date].

Your purchasing department has just placed two orders, which we are unable to release until the check is received.

Sincerely,

Credit Manager

7.12   [date]

Name of Company
Street Address (or P.O. Box Number)
City, State, Zip Code

Attention: [name and title]

Dear Mr./Ms. _____:

One letter, two telephone calls, and a promise of payment—now five days past the date when the payment was to arrive—has left this department with the obvious question and no obvious answer.

What must be answered immediately and with a payment check, is the past-due balance of $_____, referred to in the first paragraph of this letter. How you structure the other names on your payables list is your business, but a check for $_____ must arrive in this office by [date]. The aging of the past-due invoices does not allow for any further delay in getting a check to us.

No product can be shipped until the problem of past-due invoices has been solved. Be assured, however, that if the payment arrives by [date], some in-house orders will be released on open account.

Sincerely,

Credit Manager

7.13   [date]

Name of Company
Street Address (or P.O. Box Number)
City, State, Zip Code

Attention: [name and title]

Dear Mr./Ms. _____:

I have just reviewed the payment pattern of your account over the past six months versus the payment pattern for the preceding six months. Frankly, it looks like two different accounts, and if what I am seeing now (restricted cashflow, loss of momentum in your new territory, etc.) is a different company from what it was 6 or 12 months ago, we need to talk.

Because the aging of accounts receivable has deteriorated so rapidly, I have put a hold on the release of product(s) until (1) past-due balances have been cleared and (2) we have had a chance to discuss in depth the nature of your company's problem(s). If the problem of $_____ in past-due invoices can be resolved with one or several payments (a payment plan), and your company's problems are temporary, I would hope for a quick return to our past program of open-account sales.

A telephone call to you tomorrow may provide the answers we need but the problem of past-due invoices is, from our viewpoint, sufficiently compelling for me to put our concerns on paper. We should both have this record as a prelude to subsequent discussions and explanations.

Sincerely,

Credit Manager

Collection guidelines, criteria, and variations on both are being offered throughout this book to help you and your company deal with the ploys, smoke screens, and the legitimate problems of your customers. There is, as I have stated before, no single *best way* to collect past-due balances from your customers. You must be willing to try anything that is within the scope of a legal collection effort, and whatever might give your company an edge in the ongoing struggle to get your money from a customer's restricted flow of cash.

One of the more consistently effective collection techniques is an expression or an attitude of surprise when the customer has not responded to a previous letter or telephone call. Your acting skills do not need to be of professional quality but when you call the customer and express surprise that payment has not been received, we want *surprise* to sound authentic! Forget *surprise*, however, if the account is a chronic slow-pay offender; it is not an effective collection tool with accounts of this type.

Any tactic that your judgment and experience tells you might work with a specific customer is worth the effort. Is the customer an old-line company whose reputation for good service, top quality products, and timely payment of its obligations have always been a matter of company policy and pride? When your customer fits this mold, a letter or a telephone call expressing *surprise* that a previous reminder has not brought a check could be the tactic that moves the account balance into the check-writing process.

Perhaps the payables supervisor of another company promised that payment for one or more past-due invoices would be mailed on a specific date; it is now five or six days past the date when the check should have been mailed, your company is no more than *second day* mail delivery away, and there is no check. Unless this account is one whose payment promises have been meaningless (will say anything to buy time, etc.) then you have reason to call and express *surprise* that payment was apparently not mailed as promised. (Be careful to use the phrase "apparently not mailed." We all know that strange things can happen when something is committed to the tender mercies of the postal service.)

Unless the integrity of the company or individual is virtually nonexistent, you should be able to get a commitment for an *immediate* payment release based upon the embarrassing (hopefully) failure of the customer to send the check when promised. Suppose the reason for not sending the check was the failure of an expected check to arrive from one of the customer's customers? It can happen, and unless your company is uncommonly lucky, it has had the same experience. So you can understand the problem but you cannot accept the failure to contact you or your department. You also cannot accept the customer's failure to send a partial payment from other funds, although you do not make an issue of that point. If money is tight, settle for an immediate partial payment with the balance to be paid over two or three intervals of seven-to-ten days. This time frame depends on the aging of past-due invoices and the customer's realistic expectations for receiving money from its customers.

The following is a partial list of reasons used by customers who fail to meet a payment commitment, or who do their utmost to delay making a payment.

1. Check from the customer's customer failed to arrive.

2. Vacations and/or sickness in the payables section.

3. Former payables person quit—new employee is trying to "straighten out the mess."

4. Waiting for a credit memo (to adjust pricing error or error in shipped versus received count).

5. Owner/manager has been sick—no authorized signature was/is available to sign the check.

6. We thought your driver would pick it up.

7. We thought we would have our new bank credit line in place before the promised date.

The letters that follow are guidelines for dealing with situations that involve customers whose survival is not in question—or certainly not considered a short-term problem. These customers may, however, have seasonal or other periods when cashflow is inconsistent: periods when they have temporary difficulty meeting supplier and other obligations within parameters that are acceptable to these creditors. Give these customers latitude during periods of financial stress but do not allow these variances to become flagrant.

7.14   [date]

Name of Company
Street Address (or P.O. Box Number)
City, State, Zip Code

Attention: [name and title]

Dear Mr./Ms. _____:

Our telephone conversation on [date] was a satisfactory follow-up to the problem of past-due invoices addressed in my letter dated _____.

Your commitment to put a check for $_____ in the mail by [date] is satisfactory. As I stated during our telephone conversation, we will be unable to release any product until the check for $_____ has been received.

Sincerely,

Credit Manager

7.15   [date]

Name of Company
Street Address (or P.O. Box Number)
City, State, Zip Code

Attention: [name and title]

Dear Mr./Ms. _____:

I appreciate your call in response to my letter of [date]. Renovating an office or an administrative area—with desks, files, and people in inconvenient and unfamiliar locations—can turn working conditions into a struggle for survival.

We'll look for your check for $_____ between the [date] and the [date] of this month. It will eliminate the past-due balance and return account aging to its customary position on our *on time* roster of accounts.

Sincerely,

Credit Manager

7.16   [date]

Name of Company
Street Address (or P.O. Box Number)
City, State, Zip Code

Attention: [name and title]

Dear Mr./Ms. _____:

Second collection letters usually follow a pattern that includes one or two telephone calls. Your telephone call earlier today has lifted this letter from the category of *collection* and put it in the category of *thank you*.

Payment for the past-due items ($_____) by the [date] of this month is satisfactory. We understand the meaning of *temporary cashflow problem* and appreciate your candor in telling us about it.

Sincerely,

Credit Manager

7.17   [date]

Name of Company
Street Address (or P.O. Box Number)
City, State, Zip Code

Attention: [name and title]

Dear Mr./Ms. _____:

The downside of a failure to communicate effectively can lead to the erosion of a supplier/customer relationship that may have taken years to attain. We are not allowing "erosion" to enter our relationship at this point, but we do not understand your failure to respond to our letter of [date] and telephone calls on [date] and [date].

The second most important thing you can do (the first being to send a $_____ check to cover past-due balances) is to pick up the phone, call me, tell me the scope and projected duration of your cashflow problem, and tell me what we can do to help you work through it. Yes, we will need some money but the amount and the frequency of payments is something that can be put together within the framework of your total obligations.

Let's talk before the [date] of this month. Your stock of our products must be dropping to a level that is causing some concern when you try to fill customer orders.

Sincerely,

Credit Manager

7.18   [date]

Name of Company
Street Address (or P.O. Box Number)
City, State, Zip Code

Attention: [name and title]

Dear Mr./Ms. _____:

No two companies handle their communications with creditors/suppliers in the same way when cashflow begins to get tight. Some make promises they know they cannot keep while others try to curl up into a tight ball and pull their problems in with them.

Our relationship is still good but we want you to uncurl a little bit. Let us know the severity of your cashflow problem, how long you expect it to last, and what we can do to help you through it.

Money? We do need some on a regularly scheduled basis, but we can help and we want to do what we can to help. Isn't that what friends are for?

Give me a call by [date]. I know we can help you.

Sincerely,

Credit Manager

7.19   [date]

Name of Company
Street Address (or P.O. Box Number)
City, State, Zip Code

Attention: [name and title]

Dear Mr./Ms. _____:

How many times during the years of our relationship have you looked at your monthly payables list and found us to be one of the majors? Probably almost every one of the years your company has been in business, because that's about how long we have been one of your major suppliers.

Credit and collections is never free of dilemmas, and our *dilemma of the moment* centers in trying to understand why our letter of [date] and telephone calls on [date] and [date] have failed to generate a check or an explanation. A check for $_____ will clear past-due invoices but we are interested also in the scope and the projected length of the cashflow problem.

It is imperative that you contact me before [date]. If we are still being asked to guess at what is happening beyond [date], our willingness to consider a return to open account sales will have been seriously compromised.

Sincerely,

Credit Manager

7.20   [date]

Name of Company
Street Address (or P.O. Box Number)
City, State, Zip Code

Attention: [name and title]

Dear Mr./Ms. _____:

When your company has cashflow problems that affect its ability to pay us for our merchandise, we are very interested in what is going on. Our interest becomes even more focused when a payment commitment is not honored and no explanation is given for failing to send a check.

Our relationship has had its share of these types of experiences. I cannot, however, think of a past problem or situation that reached a point where communication was much less than acceptable. Money has at times been slow to come by, but candor has helped us over several rough spots.

Let's reopen those lines of communication. We are anxious to work with your company in every way that we can, but payments—at a reasonable dollar and frequency level—must be made to reduce past-due balances. Until we have an acceptable amount of money and a formal payment plan, we cannot release any product(s).

Call me by the [date] of this month. It is very important that we resolve this problem promptly.

Sincerely,

Credit Manager

7.21   [date]

Name of Company
Street Address (or P.O. Box Number)
City, State, Zip Code

Attention: [name and title]

Dear Mr./Ms. _____:

One letter and two telephone calls is usually enough to convince a customer that we are interested in what is going on at the customer company. It is also usually enough to make the point that we are very interested in getting paid—and promptly—for past-due invoices.

If the cashflow problem that we discussed during the [date] telephone call has not eased, we need to talk about it in much greater depth. A payment arrangement can be worked out that is acceptable to both companies, but we must hear from you by [date].

Let's not allow the relationship to continue to erode.

Sincerely,

Credit Manager

7.22   [date]

Name of Company
Street Address (or P.O. Box Number)
City, State, Zip Code

Attention: [name and title]

Dear Mr./Ms. _____:

Nobody likes to talk to a creditor about money, especially when the demand for it exceeds the supply.

Unfortunately, not talking about it does not solve a thing; in fact, it adds to the problem. Our earlier letter [date] and [date] telephone call asked for payment by a specific date. Payment has not been received, no reason for nonpayment has been received, and time is running out.

When handling obligations in a straightforward manner, the reputation you save could be that of your own company. Do us both a favor and send a check ($_____) or call me prior to [date].

Sincerely,

Credit Manager

7.23 [date]

Name of Company
Street Address (or P.O. Box Number)
City, State, Zip Code

Attention: [name and title]

Dear Mr./Ms. _____:

The letter containing your check #_____ for $_____ arrived today. It was postmarked on the date you said you mailed it, but where it has been for the past _____ days is anybody's guess!

However, the point is that we have the payment and your two orders should be delivered to your warehouse tomorrow before noon.

Sincerely,

Credit Manager

7.24 [date]

Name of Company
Street Address (or P.O. Box Number)
City, State, Zip Code

Attention: [name and title]

Dear Mr./Ms. _____:

Your check #_____ in the amount of $_____ arrived today. We appreciate it but it is much less than the commitment you made to me on [date].

We are assuming that a second check for $_____ (the difference between the check received today and the payment commitment of $_____) will follow in a day or two. Because a commitment (payment or other) puts the credibility of a company or an individual on the line, I feel that the assumption of a second check arriving during the current week is a valid one.

Should assumptions made in the preceding paragraph prove to be incorrect, our relationship will drop to a low we have not previously experienced. There will also be no alternative to an immediate and a complete explanation.

Expect my telephone call at [hour] on [date].

Sincerely,

Credit Manager

7.25   [date]

Name of Company
Street Address (or P.O. Box Number)
City, State, Zip Code

Attention: [name and title]

Dear Mr./Ms. _____:

Collection letters—especially second ones—are not popular with suppliers or their customers. They invariably discuss past-due balances that both parties know are due and conclude with some reference to holding orders (or a COD relationship) until a certain sum of money has been received.

This letter is, unfortunately, in the exact center of that pattern. Because of unpaid past-due balances, we cannot release any product(s) to your company until we receive $_____ for the invoices listed in collection letter dated _____.

It is important that we have your check for $_____ by the [date] of this month. Our willingness to return the account to open-account status is tied directly to whether you do or do not meet the payment date.

I'm sorry we have to be so unbending about this, but the first letter and two telephone calls got us no feedback, and no money. Your check will solve our problem.

Sincerely,

Credit Manager

    None of the preceding letters or those that follow begin with a stereotype phrase such as "Our records show that your company has not ...," or "A review of our accounts payable records indicates ...." The purpose of a collection letter is to (1) get the attention of the customer/debtor, (2) get the customer/debtor to focus on the problem, and (3) motivate the customer/debtor to pay the past-due balance(s). Would "A review of ...," or "Our records show ..." get your attention, focus your attention, or motivate you to pay? I don't think so. I suspect that one of these stereotype openings would lose you in the middle of the first sentence.

    Use some imagination. Be innovative. Go with something that the customer hasn't seen or heard before. If the customer's cashflow is tight, you may still have the problem of motivating him or her to move your company higher on the to-be-paid list, but you will, however, have succeeded in getting the customer to focus on the problem and will have motivated him or her to do something about it.

7.26   [date]

Name of Company
Street Address (or P.O. Box Number)
City, State, Zip Code

Attention: [name and title]

Dear Mr./Ms. _____:

One of the hardest things for most of us is to face up to a difficult problem and commit to working out an equitable solution. The process often is not easy but more times than not, it can be done!

Our two companies have a long and a solid relationship. We're willing to help but we need to hear from you what is needed.

Please call at your earliest convenience.

Sincerely,

Credit Manager

7.27   [date]

Name of Company
Street Address (or P.O. Box Number)
City, State, Zip Code

Attention: [name and title]

Dear Mr./Ms. _____:

I don't recall ever being the beneficiary of a spontaneous, light-up-the-sky revelation—and this is certainly not one of them—but have you noticed that although the competition for customers is fierce, the competition for the customer's dollars is even worse?

I know that cash is seldom plentiful but as I said in my letter dated _____, we must have our share of yours, and we must have it close enough to our sales terms so there is no unfavorable impact on our cashflow.

We'll expect your check for $_____ by the [date] of this month. I refuse to deal in negatives, but at risk here is the danger of permanently forfeiting the open-account privilege—and neither your company nor ours wants a COD relationship.

Sincerely,

Credit Manager

7.28   [date]

Name of Company
Street Address (or P.O. Box Number)
City, State, Zip Code

Attention: [name and title]

Dear Mr./Ms. _____:

What would I do if my company had $10,000 in available cash, we owed our major supplier $11,000, and three of our less important suppliers a total of $6,000? I would apportion it fairly, giving the biggest percentage to the major supplier and adequate payments to the supporting suppliers.

Your approach to the problem of distributing available cash may differ from ours but the end result has to be the same. Whether the customer is a major supplier or a supporting player in a cast of several, they all must be paid, and as near to terms as possible.

Our company? We probably qualify as a *featured player* on your list of suppliers, and that's ideal for us. We do, however, need more rapid payments to avoid the kind of past-due balance we're addressing now.

Your check for $_____ by the [date] will clear the oldest of the past-due items. A second check for $_____ by the [date] will clear the remaining past-due items and open your credit line for the busy months ahead.

Sincerely,

Credit Manager

7.29   [date]

Name of Company
Street Address (or P.O. Box Number)
City, State, Zip Code

Attention: [name and title]

Dear Mr./Ms. _____:

Our company takes pride in the knowledge that our products are an important part of the service your company provides for customers in your market area. And to properly service old, new, and future customers, you need to maintain a complete line of those products.

The bad news first? We cannot release any of your orders until the check for $_____ (requested in my letter of [date]) is in this office. Past-due balances have been getting larger, and we cannot allow it to continue.

The good news? Put the check for $_____ in the mail so we get it by the [date] and the orders we are currently holding will go out the same afternoon. What can be better than a normal relationship with uninterrupted shipments of product(s)?

Sincerely,

Credit Manager

7.30   [date]

Name of Company
Street Address (or P.O. Box Number)
City, State, Zip Code

Attention: [name and title]

Dear Mr./Ms. _____:

I can't think of a single reason how a supplier could derive pleasure from holding shipments to a customer. It is an inconvenience to the customer, and the supplier makes no money!

But when past-due balances begin to climb, strong measures become necessary when more flexible ones have failed. That is why receipt of your check for $_____ (invoices _____ and _____) is the key to whether our open-account relationship can get back on track—a move that will give you the full line of merchandise you need to properly service your customers.

You have my word. The day the check arrives is the day your orders will leave our freight dock.

Sincerely,

Credit Manager

7.31   [date]

Name of Company
Street Address (or P.O. Box Number)
City, State, Zip Code

Attention: [name and title]

Dear Mr./Ms. _____:

If you had a friend who, quite uncharacteristically, began suddenly to disregard your letters and telephone calls, you would understand the concern we feel over your failure to respond to ours.

Let's face it. We cannot disregard the past-due balances. They can only become a bigger and a more threatening barrier to an open-account relationship between our two companies if they are not treated with the respect and urgency that their aging demands.

Give me a call before the [date] of this month so we can get a payment program started; a payment program that will allow us to get back to a more mutually helpful and advantageous atmosphere.

Your check for $_____ by [date] will get us started in the right direction. The amount and timing of subsequent payments can be worked out in a telephone call.

Sincerely,

Credit Manager

7.32   [date]

Name of Company
Street Address (or P.O. Box Number)
City, State, Zip Code

Attention: [name and title]

Dear Mr./Ms. _____:

We forwarded a credit memo via cover letter dated _____ and requested that you send a check for $_____ to cover the past-due portion of the referenced invoice. The past-due balance was to be cleared by [date], but it was either not sent or it went astray in the mails.

This balance is much too old and, frankly, it is doing our relationship more than a small amount of damage. Get rid of it. Send us a check for $_____ by the [date] of this month and—from this end—we'll do our best to get the relationship back on track.

Sincerely,

Credit Manager

7.33   [date]

Name of Company
Street Address (or P.O. Box Number)
City, State, Zip Code

Attention: [name and title]

Dear Mr./Ms. _____:

Although we do not have a long relationship, it has been our experience that your company is not one to make promises it does not intend to keep. Because of that observation, we are assuming that something unexpected caused you to miss your commitment for a $_____ payment by the [date] of this month.

All is not lost. There is still enough time before the end of the month to get the check to us. It will eliminate any question that might arise regarding our willingness to work through a problem with your company and subsequently return the relationship to a mutually acceptable level.

If the problem is cashflow, and you have been reluctant to discuss it, please call me immediately. I know of very few companies who over the years have not had to deal with that very problem, including our own. We can put together a payment program that will satisfy your need to reduce account aging while it allows your company to have some open-account credit during the period of reduced cashflow.

There is no insurmountable problem, unless it is one you do not give us a chance to address.

Sincerely,

Credit Manager

7.34   [date]

Name of Company
Street Address (or P.O. Box Number)
City, State, Zip Code

Attention: [name and title]

Dear Mr./Ms. _____:

The book on collection people is that we "lurk" or "lie in hiding"—that we move stealthily as we scheme to devise ways to tap into the customer's mother lode of cashflow.

Well, it isn't true—certainly not true of every one of us. What we must do, and try to do as painlessly as possible, is to collect past-due balances for our company from customers who usually are doing what they can to stretch a tight cashflow to cover as many creditors as they can.

The reputation of your company is one of the best in the industry, and that certainly includes your relationship with our company. Our current problem, recapped in my letter of [date] and telephone call of [date], is one that should, however, be resolved promptly. If past-due balances in the amount of $_____ are paid by [date], this one problem will have no influence on the relationship between our two companies.

This is really one of those priority payment situations. We do expect your check before the end of this month, and that will allow us to ship your in-house orders the day the check arrives.

Sincerely,

Credit Manager

7.35   [date]

Name of Company
Street Address (or P.O. Box Number)
City, State, Zip Code

Attention: [name and title]

Dear Mr./Ms. _____:

Very few of our customers are thanked for a payment before it is in our hands. On the other hand, your company has never been a routine name on our list of customers.

Credit memo #_____ in the amount of $_____ is attached. This corrects the pricing error on invoice _____ and clears the way for you to send us a check for the net unpaid balance.

Sincerely,

Credit Manager

7.36   [date]

Name of Company
Street Address (or P.O. Box Number)
City, State, Zip Code

Attention: [name and title]

Dear Mr./Ms. _____:

This is a follow-up to my letter dated _____ and my telephone call on [date] regarding the past-due balance of $_____.

We are not your major supplier but the strong acceptance of our products by the people in your marketplace area is a dollars and cents incentive for you to move us at or near the top of the payables priority list.

These are the invoices that must be paid before we can resume product shipments to your company.

Invoice Date	Invoice No.	P.O. Number	Invoice Amt.

If the check is mailed a day or two after you receive this letter, orders will be shipped the day the check arrives.

Sincerely,

Credit Manager

7.37   [date]

Name of Company
Street Address (or P.O. Box Number)
City, State, Zip Code

Attention: [name and title]

Dear Mr./Ms. _____:

I would be suprised if you were not aware that our products have played a key role in the growth of your company, and continue to do so.

It's wonderful, but from this growth a separate problem has sprung. Past-due balances (my letter of [date] and telephone call of [date]) have not been paid and the aging of those balances is at a point where we cannot ship more product(s) until we have a check for $_____.

Don't risk losing the momentum that your company has worked so hard to build. Get the check to this office within the next seven days—while your stock of our product(s) is still high—and the orders that are currently on hold will be shipped the day the check arrives.

Sincerely,

Credit Manager

7.38   [date]

Name of Company
Street Address (or P.O. Box Number)
City, State, Zip Code

Attention: [name and title]

Dear Mr./Ms. _____:

I can think of very few companies whose early relationship with our company was more positive than yours. Payments were within terms for several of those early months, followed by a few months of within terms to 15, 20, and 25 days past due. Now the receivables aging report puts the payment pattern somewhere between 30 and 40 days past due—and still sliding. This is a troubling experience, and one that does not encourage us to continue selling the account at the current credit limit.

Past-due invoices, which are listed below, must be paid on a schedule that recognizes the integrity of our credit terms. Any deviation from the date when payment for individual invoices must be in this office—listed under "Payment By This Date"—is not an acceptable alternative.

Invoice No.	Date	Amount	Payment By This Date

The payment response will be evaluated 30 days from this date. If past-due invoices have been paid prior to the dates listed on this payment schedule, the undersigned will be happy to favorably consider a continuation of the current credit line and credit terms.

Sincerely yours,

Credit Manager

The letter that follows is a hypothetical one that may never occur in your company—or most other companies. It is the most complete form of control: a combination of a red hot product, more orders than plant capacity can accommodate, and no plans to expand production and distribution capabilities. Your company is in total control! You are in a position to call each and every shot! But is it really "Welcome to Utopia"?

7.39   [date]

Name of Company
Street Address (or P.O. Box Number)
City, State, Zip Code

Attention: [name and title]

Dear Mr./Ms. _____:

There is a first time for everything but we are amazed that for the first time our company is in a position where demand for our products is exceeding our capacity to produce them! And will you believe something even more amazing? We are not doing a thing to increase our production capability!

This surprising level of product acceptance has brought us the right—really the necessity—to insist that our customers pay for products within terms. That's right. We are minimizing our credit problems and maximizing our cashflow by weeding out those customers who do not pay within an acceptable time frame.

My letter of [date] asked that you forward payment for past-due invoices ($_____) by the [date] of this month. It is _____ days past the above date, which means that orders are being held while we wait for your check and decide whether we can afford to continue an open-account relationship with your company.

The demands on our cashflow do not give us the latitude to carry past-due balances. With regret, we must have your check for $_____ by [date] or we can no longer offer your company our line of products.

I hope you are able to adjust your payables to handle our account on a *within terms* basis. The future of our relationship is tied to payment within our sales terms.

Sincerely,

Credit Manager

A collection procedure that involves a first collection letter, one or two telephone calls, and a second collection letter should, as I have stated before, take you as far down the collection road as you need to go to collect your company's money. Any effort beyond these steps—especially if it is more than a one-time occurrence—is indicative of a customer whose cashflow is inadequate to pay the obligation within a time frame compatible with the requirements of your own cashflow.

Your customer may give *inadequate or restricted cashflow* as the reason for not paying within or close to terms, but is it a situation that can be improved? Of course it can. If your company has the leverage of one or more of the following (a major supplier, a hot product, product(s) that have little or no competition, a constant level of sales, etc.), there is every reason to expect that you can get the customer to move your company to a position at-or-near the top of the payables list. If your product(s) sells well and is a money maker for the customer, then it is your responsibility to insist that the customer company recognize the importance of its obligation to your company.

The expression "you scratch my back and I'll scratch yours" may have disappeared from the vernacular of twentieth century business but it is a reciprocal philosophy that is still very much in the mainstream of commerce. The two "backscratchers" of commerce are goods and payment for those goods; and if it takes more than gentle persuasion to get your company's share of the customer's monthly supply of cash, then it isn't just your right to get it—it is your *duty* to get it!

8

Third Collection Letters

When a customer/creditor relationship has reached the point where a third collection letter is being considered, the collection process is sliding into deep trouble, if it hasn't arrived already.

A third collection letter means that two earlier letters—and one, two, or three telephone calls—have not resolved the problem. Perhaps a first or a second collection letter was successful in setting up a payment program that broke down after one or two payments; the third collection letter could be an attempt to get the customer to resume payments on a revised schedule.

In a *worst case* scenario, a third collection letter indicates that nothing has been successful to date; not one dollar of the past-due balance has been collected. A slightly more encouraging scenario might be when the customer responded to one of the telephone calls or one of the first two letters with a partial payment of the amount requested, but there has been no payment subsequent to the partial. And what is happening during this period of time to the financial condition of the customer/debtor? It may be deteriorating so rapidly that the customer is not responding to any request for money unless it comes from the one or two major suppliers. For other suppliers of products or services, however, key people are impossible to reach by telephone, do not return calls, and do not respond to letters.

It is not a healthy sign when a creditor has sent two collection letters, has talked with payables or financial people on two or three occasions, has received a firm or a tentative promise of payment, and then comes up empty. When a company, a business, or an individual has the money, a reminder letter or one or two telephone calls will usually generate a check. Nobody likes to be reminded again and again that they owe money and if they do not send a specific sum by a specific date, orders will be held, the account will be put on COD terms, suit will be filed in small claims court, etc. The annoyance, the hassle, and the inconvenience is more than any rational person should be willing to experience if money is available to pay what is due.

By the time your company is faced with the reality of sending a third collection letter to an account whose payment performance has become so poor that it has put some of your accounts receivable dollars beyond normal risk, your primary consideration may no longer be to retain the customer or the customer's goodwill. Your primary consideration, at this point, is to collect your company's money as rapidly as you can. Don't worry about future open-account sales. You will cross that bridge after the account has done what two collection letters and one or more collection calls have failed to accomplish. No credit executive whose company has experienced an absence of cooperation such as I have just described should be easily persuaded, after finally collecting a past-due balance, to release more product(s) on open-account terms.

So you have finally succeeded in extricating the company's receivables dollars from an account whose cashflow problem is clearly worsening. Why then, after more time and effort than one such account should command, would you put more of the company's dollars at greater risk than you would experience with the great majority of your other accounts? At this point, the customer must level with you: facts and figures to substantiate any claim that restricted or diminished cashflow is a temporary situation. You want to know how long it will last—and you want facts, not romance!

The relationship that your company had with the debtor prior to the current impasse will determine the strength and/or the finality of the third letter. The third letter is not usually a formal *final demand* but it may signify to the customer that in-house collection options are about at an end. Your company may have had prior difficulties with an account when cashflow was not strong, but if your company and the customer company worked through the problem, your company will want to do anything within reason before going to small claims court, assigning the account to a collection agency, or taking any of the other options available to it.

At the opposite end of the spectrum is the customer with whom your company has had a relatively short-term relationship (less than a year or not more than two), and several episodes of very slow pay. This is a customer whose business does not seem to be growing. In fact, a comparison of credit reports covering the period of the past 12 months (Dun & Bradstreet or National Association of Credit Management) indicates that the sales figure has not moved upward during the past six months, and trade payments have slowed and are getting slower.

Collect your company's past-due balance, and do not sell this account or any other whose situation is similar. Protect your company's receivables dollars; and the best way to do it is to avoid accounts whose documented performance with your company and with others offers (1) too many risk factors, and (2) too great an investment of time versus areas where it can be invested more productively and profitably.

Failed Payment Schedules

One of the more successful solutions to a collections problem is a payment schedule. It is tailored to achieve two things: it must reduce the past-due balance(s), and provide also for the release of enough product(s) or material to accommodate the requirements of the *customer's customers*. But when you have negotiated a payment schedule with a customer and that customer fails to deliver a check by one of the schedule payment dates, you must deal with it promptly and firmly.

When a payment schedule is in place, the customer is obligated to send a check on the scheduled dates: It is a matter of company integrity that the customer follows through on what it has agreed to do. When the customer fails to meet a scheduled payment, let the customer know how seriously your company views any deviation from the commitment. At that point, make one more attempt to push the customer into compliance with the payment agreement.

In the situations for which the following letters have been crafted, the customer has in some examples not only failed to send the scheduled payment(s) but has failed to offer an explanation to the creditor. This is not responsible or acceptable behavior from a customer whose business has benefited from the trust your company placed in it. You should not hesitate to take whatever action your experience with this and other accounts tells you is appropriate to protect your company's interest.

8.1   [date]

Name of Company
Street Address (or P.O. Box Number)
City, State, Zip Code

Attention: [name and title]

Dear Mr./Ms. _____:

This letter will confirm the payment schedule that we worked out during our telephone conversation on [date].

First Payment—Check for ($2000) to arrive at this office by [date].

Second Payment—Check for ($2000) to arrive at this office by [date].

Third Payment—Check for ($1651.42) to arrive at this office by [date].

As each payment is received within the time frame set by this schedule, orders will be released to a cumulative total of $500. If the payment schedule is not maintained, no product will be released until the past-due total ($_____) has been paid.

Sincerely,

Credit Manager

8.2   [date]

Name of Company
Street Address (or P.O. Box Number)
City, State, Zip Code

Attention: [name and title]

Dear Mr./Ms. _____:

This company's commitment to strong customer relationships has occasionally put us out on a limb, and in some of those situations we have wondered if the silence that followed meant that we had been abandoned by the other party to the commitment.

I hope the fact that we have not received the first $2000 of three scheduled payments—the first $2000 due by [date]—does not indicate that we are in one of those "abandonment" situations. You can understand that when the signs begin to become indicative of a unilateral commitment—ours alone—the primary objective becomes the protection of our receivables dollars.

Please forward your company's check for $2000 by express mail or delivery to the attention of the undersigned. If the check arrives in this office by [date], it will be considered an oversight and will not impact the integrity of the payment schedule.

Sincerely,

Credit Manager

8.3   [date]

Name of Company
Street Address (or P.O. Box Number)
City, State, Zip Code

Attention: [name and title]

Dear Mr./Ms. _____:

The payment schedule that we worked out during our telephone conversation on [date], then forwarded to your attention on [date], has failed to pass the payment test.

A check in the amount of $2000 was scheduled to arrive at this office by [date]; it has not arrived through this date and the second $2000 check is scheduled to arrive by [date]. The failure to meet the first commitment does not give us confidence that a check for $4000 will be here by [date].

This company is committed to working with our customers whenever it is possible; it is, however, a commitment that to be effective must be a shared one. The payment schedule states that product cannot be released if the schedule is not maintained as agreed; so orders will be held until a check for $4000 by [date] restores the integrity of the schedule.

Sincerely,

Credit Manager

8.4   [date]

Name of Company
Street Address (or P.O. Box Number)
City, State, Zip Code

Attention: [name and title]

Dear Mr./Ms. _____:

The call sheet for your account indicates that telephone calls to your office on [date] and [date] were not successful in obtaining a payment commitment for past-due balances. Copies of the subject invoices were mailed almost two weeks ago, and there has been no indication that the merchandise failed to arrive on time or in good condition.

Customers are very important people but the continuing success of our company demands a solid reciprocal with our customers: we give you good merchandise and good service at a fair price and we expect payment within (or near) sales terms. Anything less—on your part or ours—erodes the relationship to the point where there no longer is mutual confidence.

Your check for $_____ (invoices _____ and_____) in our offices by [date] is the confidence builder we need to consider future open-account sales.

Sincerely,

Credit Manager

8.5   [date]

Name of Company
Street Address (or P.O. Box Number)
City, State, Zip Code

Attention: [name and title]

Dear Mr./Ms. _____:

Our company takes great pride in developing good customer relationships. Most of our customers have been with us for a number of years, which I guess is one of the positive results from what we try to do to support our customers.

Not every customer can discount invoices, pay within terms, or even pay a few days past terms. We accept that fact when account data is evaluated and a credit line assigned to a customer. From that point forward it becomes a matter of developing a rapport with the customer: a rapport that will enable both of us to address any problem that may arise before it can become a contentious issue.

We have slid to a point with your account where there is an unanticipated problem, and no rapport. Your account is _____ days past due, we need $_____ yesterday, and the promises made during telephone conversations have brought no money.

I must now hold orders until we have your check for $_____ which must arrive prior to [date]. The hold also includes any COD orders that have not been released.

Sincerely,

Credit Manager

8.6   [date]

Name of Company
Street Address (or P.O. Box Number)
City, State, Zip Code

Attention: [name and title]

Dear Mr./Ms. _____:

What happened? The second of four scheduled payments was due to arrive by [date]. To date we have not received the payment or an explanation from your office.

The payment schedule that our respective companies agreed was equitable helps your company in two major areas: it reduces the past-due balance(s) and provides for the release of enough of our product(s) to accommodate the requirements of your customers. What could be fairer than that? And of course we do expect your company to honor it.

Orders will be released when the check arrives if the check arrives by [date]. After that date, no product(s) will be released on any basis until the entire past-due balance has been paid.

Sincerely,

Credit Manager

8.7   [date]

Name of Company
Street Address (or P.O. Box Number)
City, State, Zip Code

Attention: [name and title]

Dear Mr./Ms. _____:

It is __days past the date when the second of four scheduled payments was due to arrive.

I am cautiously optimistic that the postal service is at fault and that this does not represent a breakdown in a very fair and helpful payment arrangement. We couldn't do it any other way. If we had no effective schedule for reducing past-due balances, continuing to supply your company with our product(s) would be impossible; impossible until all past-due balances had been paid.

No payment schedule is easy but the benefits that accrue from this one far outweigh any temporary pressure it may be imposing upon your cashflow.

Sincerely,

Credit Manager

8.8   [date]

Name of Company
Street Address (or P.O. Box Number)
City, State, Zip Code

Attention: [name and title]

Dear Mr./Ms. _____:

This is disappointing. When we talked on [date], you assured me that a check for the past-due balance ($_____) would be released by your office in time to arrive at this office by [date]. Because it has not arrived, I must now do something that is a negative for both companies.

Effective today, we will be unable to supply your company with product(s) until the past-due balance ($_____) has been paid. When it has been paid, the option to sell your account on terms other than COD will be reviewed.

We value our customer relationships but it would be unwise if we were to continue to offer credit terms to a customer when the signals between the customer and ourselves continue to be unclear.

Our hope is that this situation can be corrected to the mutual benefit of our respective companies.

Sincerely,

Credit Manager

The following is recognition of the customer's need to make a minor adjustment in the payment schedule, and a word of appreciation for the manner in which the change has been handled.

8.9   [date]

Name of Company
Street Address (or P.O. Box Number)
City, State, Zip Code

Attention: [name and title]

Dear Mr./Ms. _____:

I could not let my appreciation for your call earlier today be confined to a few words in a telephone conversation.

If the more universal approach taken by customers was the one you took today—advising us by telephone that collections from your receivables have been slower than anticipated and that the $_____ payment promised for [date] will be released five days later than the date agreed upon earlier—relationships between suppliers and customers would take on new levels of commitment and respect.

Again, my thanks for your call. The new release date for the payment is satisfactory.

Sincerely,

Credit Manager

Another response to a customer who has failed to keep the first of three payment commitments should leave no doubt in the mind of the recipient as to how seriously your company views this breech of the commitment. Unlike the preceding letter, this customer has not contacted the supplier to offer an explanation for failing to send the scheduled payment or to offer a new release date for it.

8.10   [date]

Name of Company
Street Address (or P.O. Box Number)
City, State, Zip Code

Attention: [name and title]

Dear Mr./Ms. _____:

This company's commitment to strong customer relationships has occasionally put us out on a limb; and in some of those situations, the silence that followed has meant that we were abandoned by the other party to the commitment.

I hope this is not the case with your company but the fact that we have not received the first of three $_____ payments—the first due on [date]—is not a favorable sign. The protection of our receivables dollars becomes the primary concern when it becomes obvious that the commitment is ours alone. In the current situation, our protective action will take this form: payment in the amount of $_____ is to be in this office by [date of second scheduled payment] or the account will be referred immediately to a third party collection service.

Your prompt recognition of this payment responsibility will enable us to avoid this mutually unsatisfactory step. However, at this late date in the past-due relationship, I must say it is an action that is not open to further discussion.

Sincerely,

Credit Manager

The third collection letter is not a time for optimism. You have already sent two collection letters, made no less than two telephone calls, and the customer has not forwarded a check—or a check for the right amount. But there is still a chance that the customer/debtor is not willing to push the problem beyond *crunch time*, and the third collection letter is definitely that. If the debtor has not sent an acceptable payment within the time frame stated in the third letter, the customer company knows that it can say "goodbye" to your product line and "hello" to a new and hard-nosed collection effort.

Most debtors are not looking to escalate the aggravation that is theirs when the aging of a past-due balance has been pushed too far. At this point, something has to give. The customer's business and financial condition will either support a program to pay past-due balances or these problems may eventually overwhelm a debtor company to the point where it seeks protection under the Bankruptcy Code.

The letters that follow will help your company motivate a debtor/customer to realize it is *crunch time*.

8.11   [date]

Name of Company
Street Address (or P.O. Box Number)
City, State, Zip Code

Attention: [name and title]

Dear Mr./Ms. _____:

Requests for payment of the listed invoices, which were made by telephone on [date] and [date], have failed to bring the promised payment response.

Invoice No.	Invoice Date	P.O Number	Invoice Amt.

The past-due aging of these invoices has made it necessary for me to notify you in writing that the need for payment is *immediate*. There is no longer a buffer zone of days that can be used as a framework within which payment can be negotiated. The time for payment is NOW.

The check must be released so it will arrive in this office within ten days from the date of this letter. Orders will be held until the check has been received.

Sincerely,

Credit Manager

8.12 [date]

Name of Company
Street Address (or P.O. Box Number)
City, State, Zip Code

Attention: [name and title]

Dear Mr./Ms. _____:

We do our best to think and act as a customer-oriented company should but, unfortunately, it is a philosophy that does have limitations.

Accounts whose balances range consistently from current through _____ days past due go well beyond what we are willing to accept from our customers. The impact on our cashflow of allowing customer accounts to slide into a pattern of past-due balances is something that we cannot accept.

Your check in the amount of $_____ by [date] will enable us to release product(s) on a "$1 of product for each $2 of payment" until past-due balances have been paid. At that time the account will be reviewed to determine whether a new credit line can be assigned.

Sincerely,

Credit Manager

8.13   [date]

Name of Company
Street Address (or P.O. Box Number)
City, State, Zip Code

Attention: [name and title]

Dear Mr./Ms. _____:

We have a major problem. The payment program that two weeks ago we agreed was the solution to clearing past-due balances from your account is already out of synch. It is _____ days past the date we were to receive the first payment of $_____, a check has not arrived, and we have heard nothing from you.

The customers to whom we give an opportunity to enter into a payment program—one that provides for a limited release of product(s)—are customers we think will make it work. Your company is in that category and although the present situation represents a setback, we are not persuaded that our decision to offer your company a payment program was not the right one.

If an unexpected problem has complicated your best intentions, silence can only exacerbate it. Get on the telephone and tell us about it. We'll do our best to accommodate any short-term changes that seem appropriate.

Sincerely,

Credit Manager

8.14   [date]

Name of Company
Street Address (or P.O. Box Number)
City, State, Zip Code

Attention: [name and title]

Dear Mr./Ms. _____:

Past-due balances are a problem but there is no reason why they should interfere with our attempts to get through to your office to discuss them.

I can understand your reluctance to talk about the reasons for the recent failure of the payment program, but not talking about it will not get our products to your customers or get our money for products sold to you weeks ago. These problems have to be discussed, and they must be resolved without further delay.

Expect my telephone call at [time] on [date]. We have never had difficulty resolving prior past-due problems and there is no reason why we can't do it again this time.

Sincerely,

Credit Manager

8.15   [date]

Name of Company
Street Address (or P.O. Box Number)
City, State, Zip Code

Attention: [name and title]

Dear Mr./Ms. _____:

We sent you photo copies of invoices _____ and _____ on the [date] of [month]. A second request for the $_____ payment followed on [date], but to date we have not received your check.

At _____ and _____ days past due, these items have been on our aging report far too long. The current hold on your orders is mutually inconvenient but the longer-lasting problem centers around the question of our willingness to consider a return to open-account status after past-due balances have been cleared.

The choice is yours. We need a check for $_____ by [date] or the best terms we can offer on future sales is COD.

Sincerely,

Credit Manager

8.16   [date]

Name of Company
Street Address (or P.O. Box Number)
City, State, Zip Code

Attention: [name and title]

Dear Mr./Ms. _____:

Any time we have to send three collection letters, make two or more telephone calls, and still fail to motivate a customer to pay the past-due balance(s), a not-very-subtle change occurs in how we regard the account. At that point we move the account from the category of *customer* to that of *debtor*, and with that simple move we begin a new and mutually less rewarding relationship.

No company is more responsive to the problems and needs of customers than we are but there is a time limit beyond which we cannot carry past-due balances. The motivation is self interest. Our own cashflow could be jeopardized if we did not insist that customers handle account payments in a fair and a reasonable manner.

A check for your company's past-due balance of $_____ must be in this office by [date]. The regrettable alternative would be permanent termination of open-account privileges. We are currently holding orders but that is a minor inconvenience when it is compared with never being able to buy on terms more favorable than COD.

Send your check for $_____ so that it arrives at this office by [date]. Our product(s) have been moneymakers for you. Don't allow the current problem to cause your company to lose the competitive edge they give you.

Sincerely,

Credit Manager

8.17   [date]

Name of Company
Street Address (or P.O. Box Number)
City, State, Zip Code

Attention: [name and title]

Dear Mr./Ms. _____:

Come on, now! Since when has it been necessary for us to flood your office with collection letters and telephone calls to get a check for past-due balances? And the most disturbing thing is that we still have not received a check!

Our telephone conversation on [date] ended with your commitment of a check for $_____ by the _____ of this month. If something has happened to derail your cashflow projection, not talking about it is not going to help the situation.

Give me a call and let's discuss any new problem. When a problem is reasonable, we can be too.

Sincerely,

Credit Manager

8.18   [date]

Name of Company
Street Address (or P.O. Box Number)
City, State, Zip Code

Attention: [name and title]

Dear Mr./Ms. _____:

After our conversation on [date], I breathed the proverbial sigh of relief. We had worked out a mutually acceptable payment plan and the problem of past-due balances would soon be under control.

My reaction was apparently somewhat premature. The first payment of $_____ was due [date] but it has not arrived through this date. And because the first one has not arrived, what does that do to the prospects for the timely arrival of payments two, three, and four?

This is a serious, "must do" payment program. If it does not work, we will be unable to offer your company a future line of open credit—and neither of our companies is interested in a COD relationship.

If there is a temporary problem, call me. If not, send the first check now and the others on the scheduled dates.

Sincerely,

Credit Manager

The person who must collect accounts receivable balances is in a much more favorable position when the person to whom he or she addresses collection calls and letters is someone with whom the person has spoken frequently, or has had one or more business-related lunches. In such a situation, the chances of negotiating an acceptable payment or putting together an acceptable payment program are better than average.

There is more than a little to be said for the "let's do lunch the next time I'm in town" type of a relationship with the controller or financial officer of the company from which you must collect money that is past due. In the best of all relationships, you will have helped the customer with extended terms or another helpful turn or two. A relationship of this type can greatly improve your company's chances of establishing an effective payment program. But even a strong relationship will not be good enough if the customer's cashflow is not strong enough to support the payment commitment.

The next several collection letters recognize that the customer is in trouble. Use any business/social relationship you have at the company: the controller, director of finance, or any of the officers or partners. Use the relationship—shamelessly if you must—to get the type of inside leverage you need to get as much money for your company as you possibly can.

8.19　　[date]

Name of Company
Street Address (or P.O. Box Number)
City, State, Zip Code

Attention: [name and title]

Dear Mr./Ms. _____:

When a payment for past-due invoices fails to arrive from a customer who has promised to send it on a specific date—and on not one but two occasions—faith in that customer drops out of sight and hope for a future relationship slides almost below the horizon.

This is not good. We discussed your cashflow problems on [date] and [date], and both were alleged to be so manageable that you committed to mail a specific amount on a specific date. The first time it did not arrive, we could accept the possibility that the post office had done something indecent to it. But the second time? Our reaction was—and is—that it was not mailed.

Although we are almost at the point where we decide that enough of this department's time has been spent trying to accommodate your company, there is still time to keep the account out of the hands of a commercial collection agency. That would, of course, be the end of any access to our product(s)—certainly until all past due and current balances have been paid—with only the mutually unsatisfactory prospect of doing any future business on COD terms.

It is no secret that our products are important to your customer base. They do a good job for your customers at a price and quality level that is second to none. And what other product(s) do you handle that deliver a higher percentage of net profit?

Do both of our companies a favor. Send a check for $_____ by the _____ of this month.

Sincerely,

Credit Manager

Third collection letters should alert the customer to the probability that the failure to send a check for a stated sum of money by a specific date, whether it was or was not promised, can lead to one or more of a number of collection alternatives. These do not at this point need to be enumerated to the customer: They are, however, listed below for your information.

1. No product to be released until all open balances (past due and current) have been paid.

2. Payment of the stated amount by the stated date or no future credit line.

3. All sales to be on COD terms after past and current balances have been paid.

4. Account to be assigned to a commercial collection agency (or an attorney specialist) if past-due balances are not paid by the date stated.

5. Sue in small claims court (if applicable). Obtain judgment and seek to levy on goods, property, etc.

6. Proceed with a civil suit and obtain judgment for amount of the debt.

7. Remind customer that filings (legal actions of all types) are picked up by credit reporting agencies who make them (a) the subject of a special report, and/or (b) incorporate them into an update of the regular report (Dun & Bradstreet, National Association of Credit Management, etc.). This information can have a negative impact on current suppliers and others who might be approached.

8. Account experience is routinely exchanged among suppliers within an industry or a geographic area of that industry. Monthly credit association meetings cover the problems members are having collecting money from accounts serviced by other members of the same group (floor covering, electrical, florists, etc.).

The *third collection letters* that follow address the fact that the customer is standing at the edge of a precipice. You are telling the customer that if there is no payment by the date specified in the letter, the creditor/supplier will move the collection procedure into one or a combination of formal collection accounts as was just mentioned.

This is a customer who has had several opportunities to do the right thing. There may have been one or two encouraging starts (paid the first payment of a payment program, etc.), but they quickly came to a halt. After numerous letters and telephone calls (at least five in the combination), there is no evidence to support a thought that the customer's commitment to getting the account back to a current status is sincere; or if it is sincere, that the cashflow is available to implement it.

8.20   [date]

Name of Company
Street Address (or P.O. Box Number)
City, State, Zip Code

Attention: [name and title]

Dear Mr./Ms. _____:

I could have sworn that the metallic sound I heard a few days ago was the sound of a street corner mailbox being opened as a check addressed to this company was dropped into it; that would be the check that was to get here in time to meet your commitment date. Obviously I was wrong—but so were you.

When a company gives us a commitment to pay a past-due balance by a specific date, we assume that following through on the commitment is not something that is taken lightly. The check fails to arrive as promised—or at all—and we do not get an explanation for that failure. It certainly diminishes the faith we place in any future promise, commitment, or agreement we might otherwise be persuaded to make with that company.

I do not believe this is the image your company intends to project. A good reason for it not to be the image of choice is that it will definitely not wear well with creditors and suppliers.

Your check for $_____ by [date] will put this episode into a more favorable framework.

Sincerely,

Credit Manager

8.21   [date]

Name of Company
Street Address (or P.O. Box Number)
City, State, Zip Code

Attention: [name and title]

Dear Mr./Ms. _____:

Of the several collection letters and telephone calls that have gone to your company over the past _____ weeks, none of them seem to have pushed the magic button that would have produced a check.

No payment response to any of the letters and telephone calls tells us that we should move on to a more formal collection procedure. To avoid that procedure, your check for $_____ is to be in this office no later than [date].

Sincerely,

Credit Manager

8.22   [date]

Name of Company
Street Address (or P.O. Box Number)
City, State, Zip Code

Attention: [name and title]

Dear Mr./Ms. _____:

Your check for $_____ was scheduled to arrive by the [date] of this month. It is now [date], we do not have the check, and there has been no explanation for the delay.

At this point in our relationship, *delay* is not a good word. Frankly, there is no more latitude for it. Past-due aging of _____ to _____ days is unacceptable, and it becomes increasingly unacceptable as time adds more aging to the receivables balance.

The payment deadline is [date]. If your check for $_____ has not arrived, the collection process will be escalated to a more formal procedure.

Sincerely,

Credit Manager

8.23   [date]

Name of Company
Street Address (or P.O. Box Number)
City, State, Zip Code

Attention: [name and title]

Dear Mr./Ms. _____:

Our collection effort has to date been fair, patient, and unproductive. _____ collection letters, _____ telephone calls, _____ promise(s) of a payment by a specific date, and _____ attempt(s) to work out a payment program add up to more than a reasonable attempt to salvage this supplier/customer relationship.

Our mutual interests will be best served if your check for $_____ is in this office by [date]. If balances are not cleared by that date, we will activate one or more of the several formal collection options available to us.

Sincerely,

Credit Manager

8.24   [date]

Name of Company
Street Address (or P.O. Box Number)
City, State, Zip Code

Attention: [name and title]

Dear Mr./Ms. _____:

When a customer commits to a payment for a past-due balance, my reaction has always been one of relief; relief for ourselves and for the customer. It means generally that the customer's cashflow is still a positive factor and that the customer is willing to put some of that cashflow behind those good payment intentions.

Something has happened between our letters and telephone calls, your good intentions, your payment commitment, and the check that should have arrived in this office by [date]. We have no check and no word of explanation from your office; and when we are talking about a balance that is _____ to _____ days past due, our faith begins to wear thin.

Do both of our companies a favor: call me by [date] if there is an acceptable explanation. If there is no acceptable explanation, your check for $_____ by [date] is what we must have to avoid escalating this into a formal collection procedure.

Sincerely,

Credit Manager

8.25   [date]

Name of Company
Street Address (or P.O. Box Number)
City, State, Zip Code

Attention: [name and title]

Dear Mr./Ms. _____:

I hope there is a good reason why your company did not send the check for
$_____ that was due to arrive by [date]; and that you will share that reason
with us.

The aging of your account is so poor that we do not expect your company to deviate
from the payment program worked out on [date]. Unilateral changes are never
acceptable and there is no reason for this office to be wondering what is going on at
your company.

We worked out the payment program, and you committed to it for your company.
Two payments totaling $_____ are due in this office no later than [date].

Sincerely,

Credit Manager

8.26   [date]

Name of Company
Street Address (or P.O. Box Number)
City, State, Zip Code

Attention: [name and title]

Dear Mr./Ms. _____:

We seem to be at a point in our relationship where my instincts would normally tell me to write a *final demand* letter. Because a *final demand* is usually the prelude to the end of a relationship, and because our relationship was for many years a good one, that letter has been put on hold.

The aging of past-due balances has increased as the flow of payments has decreased. _____ payment programs have not been successful and the current one—designated as the *must do* program—is already in serious trouble.

There is no alternative to receiving your company's check for $_____ by [date]. This will get the payment program back on track and will enable us to continue to help your company to work out the problem. I cannot stress too strongly that, at this point in our relationship, there is no substitute for sending us the payments as scheduled in the current agreement.

A *final demand* letter is not something that we send unless cooperation between ourselves and the customer no longer exists. I really don't think we are at that point, but this is the moment when we find out whether we are or we are not.

Sincerely,

Credit Manager

8.27   [date]

Name of Company
Street Address (or P.O. Box Number)
City, State, Zip Code

Attention: [name and title]

Dear Mr./Ms. _____:

I don't like to think in terms that are negative but after looking at your account, my impression is that the wheels are coming off of the wagon. What [number] weeks ago seemed to be a mutual desire to eliminate past-due balances and get back to the wonderful world of open-account sales, now gives every indication of having deteriorated into a unilateral desire for that result.

Take a look at my letter of [date]; it contains the payment schedule we negotiated in a telephone call earlier that day. The $_____ payment that was due on [date] has not arrived and a second payment for the same amount is due to get here by [date]. What is at least as disturbing as the failure to send a check, is the fact that there has been no telephone call to offer an explanation.

We have gone beyond the point where there can be any more negotiating. You agreed to the payment program; we agreed to the payment program. The aging of past-due balances has moved us beyond the point where the payment program can be changed.

Send a check for the first two payments ($_____) by [date]. If the payment does not arrive on time, we will be unable to favorably consider any future request for a credit line.

Sincerely,

Credit Manager

8.28   [date]

Name of Company
Street Address (or P.O. Box Number)
City, State, Zip Code

Attention: [name and title]

Dear Mr./Ms. _____:

The payment program got off to a great start (the first two of six payments arrived on time), but it seems to have struck a snag. Payment three should have been here by [date] and we are only _____ days away from expecting payment number four.

There has obviously been an unanticipated problem but because the past-due aging of these balances has elevated the payment program to priority status, we want to know about any of your company's problems that might jeopardize scheduled payment dates and amounts.

We will have talked before you receive this letter but I did not want this episode to escalate into a more complex problem than we have now without advising your company, in writing, of our feelings and intentions.

Your check for $_____ to cover the third and fourth payments must be released so it will get here before [date].

Sincerely,

Credit Manager

8.29   [date]

Name of Company
Street Address (or P.O. Box Number)
City, State, Zip Code

Attention: [name and title]

Dear Mr./Ms. _____:

This is the second consecutive month that we have not received the scheduled payment by the payment date.

My statement to you last month is applicable to each of the six scheduled payments: Past-due balances are at unacceptable levels of aging and the only way to correct the problem is to make monthly payments by their scheduled dates. No other solution will guarantee that balances are reduced on a regular, rather than a sporadic basis.

Get the [date] payment to us by [date].

Sincerely,

Credit Manager

8.30   [date]

Name of Company
Street Address (or P.O. Box Number)
City, State, Zip Code

Attention: [name and title]

Dear Mr./Ms. _____:

I don't know how you react to such things, but I get very uncomfortable when an agreement that seemed to be working well begins suddenly to stumble and falter.

Payment [number] of our [number] payment program arrived _____ days after the due date, causing nothing more serious than a mild ripple. The second payment is another matter because it was due by [date] and we have not received it yet.

The aging of past-due balances is not acceptable. This payment program has to work if the account is to have any chance to rejoin accounts who have the credit privilege. COD sales is not something that is acceptable for your company or ours.

Get us out of this situation with a check for $_____ by [date].

Sincerely,

Credit Manager

8.31   [date]

Name of Company
Street Address (or P.O. Box Number)
City, State, Zip Code

Attention: [name and title]

Dear Mr./Ms. _____:

The response of our company to customer payment problems is as varied as the causes of those problems. We try to be as understanding and as helpful as good business practice and the cashflow requirements of our company will permit; but we are not always successful in working with a customer to bridge a problem. Are we successful with your company? I think that's something you will have to tell me.

The payment program that we worked out on [date] has been successful until the current payment, which was due on [date]. It has not arrived, but what is even more surprising is that there has been no call to explain why the check was not mailed. This is not a confidence builder. If you did mail the check for $_____ and it has gone astray in the mails, please stop payment on it and send a replacement. If the check was not mailed, there is still time to get it in the mail in time to arrive by [date]. I understand that this compresses the period of time between payments number _____ and _____, but it will protect the integrity of our agreement and confirm your company's commitment to that agreement.

As a tangible indication of our appreciation for getting the payment program back on track, the [number] orders that are in-house and on hold will be released on open-account terms when we receive your check for schedule payments _____ and ___ in the total amount of $_____.

This should improve your warehouse stock of our products to the point where customer orders can be filled promptly.

Sincerely,

Credit Manager

8.32   [date]

Name of Company
Street Address (or P.O. Box Number)
City, State, Zip Code

Attention: [name and title]

Dear Mr./Ms. _____:

Not many of our customers get a third collection letter after two earlier letters, two or three telephone calls, and a payment program that has gone out of synch. But we have not given up on your company. We think there is a relationship that can be salvaged in addition to past-due balances that must be collected.

The payment program that we agreed on [date] was mutually acceptable, is not so far behind the scheduled payment dates that it cannot be brought up-to-date. Your company's check for $_____ by [date] will do it—and it will bring us closer to the date when we can consider assigning a new credit line.

We can work our way through the current tight money and come out of it with a relationship that is stronger because the commitment to succeed was a mutual one.

Sincerely,

Credit Manager

8.33   [date]

Name of Company
Street Address (or P.O. Box Number)
City, State, Zip Code

Attention: [name and title]

Dear Mr./Ms. _____:

It isn't often that we devote this much time to one account (three collection letters, three telephone calls, and an ongoing attempt to restructure a payment program), but our relationship has had more than a short period of success. We think we can help you get back to the point where it can be successful again.

I know money is tight, but this is very important. A check for $_____ by [date] will get the payment program back on track. It will also enable us to release the $_____ worth of product (material) your company needs to complete the [name] job.

Sincerely,

Credit Manager

8.34   [date]

Name of Company
Street Address (or P.O. Box Number)
City, State, Zip Code

Attention: [name and title]

Dear Mr./Ms. _____:

You know what a rumor mill our industry is, and the hottest current rumor has your company about to be acquired by [name of company].

We are not looking for back-door information: We can wait with the rest of our industry for the formal announcement of the marriage. What we do need now—and we need it whether you are or are not negotiating—is a check for $_____ to pick up the payment that we agreed was to arrive by [date].

Our only concern at this point is to maintain the integrity of the payment schedule, which means that we expect the above-mentioned check to arrive by [date] and the four checks still on the schedule to arrive by their scheduled dates.

We hope that the culmination of current negotiations will result in a major benefit for your company, your customers, and to the community in which the company is headquartered. The possibility of acquiring *deep pockets* is not an end in itself, but in a total package it can be an enormously attractive *plus*.

Sincerely,

Credit Manager

8.35   [date]

Name of Company
Street Address (or P.O. Box Number)
City, State, Zip Code

Attention: [name and title]

Dear Mr./Ms. _____:

No company tries harder than ours to help a customer over a rough spot. We stay with a customer beyond the point where many suppliers throw up their hands, collect their money, and move on to a replacement customer. That has never been our style—and we have no plans to change.

What we do need from your company, however, is a check or an explanation. A payment of $_____ was due to arrive in this office by [date]. We have not received the payment and there has been no explanation from your office.

When on the _____ of [month] we arrived at a mutually acceptable payment program, I told you that there was no more latitude for change; following this payment program was to be a firm commitment. Nothing has changed. It remains as inflexible as it was when we agreed that it was acceptable and workable.

Your company's check for $_____ must be in this office by [date].

Sincerely,

Credit Manager

8.36   [date]

Name of Company
Street Address (or P.O. Box Number)
City, State, Zip Code

Attention: [name and title]

Dear Mr./Ms. _____:

Some days are better than others but it is never a good day when one of our customers is having problems that impact our relationship. And it is especially bad when our best efforts to work out a program to clear past-due balances while supplying the customer with some product do not seem to come together.

Past-due balances must be cleared and the best way to do it is to follow the payment schedule we worked out on [date]. You knew it would not be easy, but it is a schedule that can and must be maintained.

Your check for $_____ by the _____ of [month] will put the payment program back on schedule. It is imperative that the check is in this office by that date.

Sincerely,

Credit Manager

As the sample letters illustrate, third collection letters should not be weak or tentative. They should reflect the resolve that your company has demonstrated while it has attempted to work with the customer/debtor (a payment program, $2 for $1 of product, etc.). And because a third collection letter may be the last your company sends before it takes more formal collection action (there may not be a *final demand* letter), there must be no doubt in the mind of the recipient that this is it: a check for a specific amount in the mail by a specified date or there is the probability that the collection procedure will become very formal and very hard-nosed.

When there has been no response to the first two letters and/or two or three telephone calls that may have raised hopes but failed ultimately to meet expectations, it is time to do whatever is necessary (and legal) to get your company's money before moving on to other customers. It is not wise to continue to invest disproportionate amounts of your time on a collection effort that is going nowhere. What about the conventional appeals of "Protect your credit rating"; "Nobody can do business on COD terms"; or "We must have $_____ by _____ or ... "? By the third letter, the chances are slim that you have not already pressed all of the buttons. When you have pressed them all and it has become obvious that there is no *magic button* among them, it is time to assign the account to a commercial collection agency and focus on other accounts.

The overwhelming majority of customers want to pay for their product(s) or material(s), and although they would prefer to do it within terms, it is not always possible. If you have screened your accounts thoroughly before assigning a credit line, you will know going into the relationship which of these accounts does not pay other suppliers within terms. When you know that an account pays an average of several or many days past due, you enter the relationship knowing that there might be an occasional collection problem, but that the account is basically solid. It is your judgment call and it should come as no surprise when an account with a slow pay record with other suppliers settles into the same pattern with your company.

When an account does not respond to your in-house collection effort, do not talk yourself into staying with it longer than you should. If the customer would like to pay but promises of payment invariably fail because cashflow is not strong enough to do it, insist that the customer/debtor pay something against past-due balances each month (an amount acceptable to your company).

Maximize your collection successes with well-matched combinations of collection letters or collection letters and telephone calls. Select prototypes from the broad selection in this book; personalize them with comments and data relevant to the aging, payments, or some phase of the business experience or collection effort. When you are working from a selection of letters that cover the gamut of collection-oriented possibilities, the job of collecting your company's past-due accounts receivable will never be the proverbial "piece of cake." But it will be an easier and a more successful process.

A collection technique that works well with one account may not work with the next one, or it may not be as effective as the circumstance requires. Try a different verbal approach, or if the focus of the collection effort has involved a series of collection letters, make any adjustments in the format that your experience with the account indicates might be helpful in resolving the past-due problem. Be flexible in your approach to specific accounts. After a certain period of time, you should begin to read accounts well enough that you will be able to adjust your collection effort to fit the attitudes and the individual business patterns of specific problem accounts.

9

Series Collection Letters

A well-crafted series of collection letters can be very effective and can save the creditor an impressive amount of time. Letters for use in a series are either prewritten to meet specific types of past-due situations or they may be selected from a broad range of prototype letters to fit a specific collection problem (or a specific company image or personality).

No single series of letters can be bent, twisted, or shoved into a form that will give them universal appeal. It is not possible. The failure rate would exceed acceptable parameters. What must be avoided is a letter—or a series of letters—that look and sound *canned*; an ordinary, lifeless, dogmatic, no-imagination approach to the problem of extracting money from an account whose mail is probably already checkered with ordinary, lifeless, dogmatic, no-imagination approaches for payment from other creditors. Yours must be a *grabber*. The opening sentence must grab the reader's attention so that what follows has a better than average chance of being read, and a better than slim chance of generating a payment response.

The letters in Chaps. 6, 7, and 8 illustrate what is meant—in the context of a collection letter—by the expression *a grabber*. It should not be an explosive statement or observation, and it should not be inflammatory. It might be a statement or a question—one that perhaps appears to be unrelated or only indirectly related to the subject of past-due balances.

Keep the customer/debtor off balance. When your letter arrives, there is a preconceived idea of what it says and how it says it. "O.K., so you want money. I'm up to here with the 'your account is 35 days past due and unless you ...' approach." So be different. Let the customer know that your company's approach to collecting past-due balances is a little different. It doesn't mean that you aren't as dedicated to collecting your company's money as the other creditors; it does mean that your company tries to avoid the dogmatic and the confrontational.

Let the customer know that your company doesn't see itself as the frontier blacksmith, bent over an anvil beating a shoe into shape, then trying to nail the shoe (perhaps a payment program or an attempt to breathe new life into one that has gone off track) onto the foot of a balky customer. Let your customer/debtors know that you expect to receive your money, but do it in a way that takes your company out of the "I know what the letter is going to say" or "He (or she) won't say anything I haven't heard a hundred times before from other companies" mode.

If a collection letter doesn't give the recipient a good and a personally tailored read, why should he or she be expected to reach for the checkbook and write a check? The opening line (and the opening paragraph) should have a flavor and a style designed to reach the reader. Leave the stereotype phrases to the other creditor companies. Give the customer/debtor the message but do not let it stand naked on the page. Embellish it: say something positive; and if saying something positive is a stretch with some accounts, put it in anyway. It can't do any harm and it might motivate your customer/debtor to move in your direction.

The Advantages of Series Letters

Series letters offer a level of continuity that is not always present when letters have not been planned (or formatted) in advance. Your goal is to motivate the customer to write the requested check or to commit to a debt-reduction program and series of checks on specific dates. Your series letters should build one upon the other. If the first one does not cause a check to be mailed, the second letter should acknowledge the *no payment response* to the first letter and escalate the need for payment(s)—lump sum, schedule, etc.—to be started by a specific date. There is an increase in the level of urgency, a sense that a good relationship (if indeed it was) is slipping away. Unless the debtor is racing toward bankruptcy, motivating a customer/debtor to pay promptly can be advantageous for both companies. This is especially true when your company is a key or a major supplier.

The third in a series of three collection letters should be set up so that with minor adjustment, it can become the *final demand* letter. It should advise the customer/debtor that payment for a specific amount is to arrive by a specified date or the account will be referred to a collection service or to an attorney who specializes in collection matters. Assure the customer that you are not looking forward to taking this step, but the aging of past-due balances is at the point where the options are a check or third-party collection action. Your past and current experience with the account plus the recent-to-current experience of other suppliers will determine whether letter three is the final demand or whether the final demand is made with a fourth letter.

The five sets of letters that follow are examples of how each letter in a collection series should make its own payment statement, with subsequent letters reinforcing the theme that delay serves no purpose other than to escalate the need and the time frame in which payment *must* be made.

9.1   **"Slipped Through the Crack" Series (1 of 5)**

[date]

Name of Company
Street Address (or P.O. Box Number)
City, State, Zip Code

Attention: [name and title]

Dear Mr./Ms. _____:

The expression "slipped through the crack" is no stranger to our company as I am sure it is no stranger to yours.

Your company's payment pattern is so delightfully predictable that the unpaid [month or invoice] balance of $_____ must have found one of those cracks. Sometimes the "crack" is an invoice that did not arrive, so I am attaching a copy of [invoice number] to compare with your payables records.

Many thanks for expediting the processing of this $_____ item.

Sincerely,

Credit Manager

9.2   **"Slipped Through the Crack" Series (2 of 5)**

[date]

Name of Company
Street Address (or P.O. Box Number)
City, State, Zip Code

Attention: [name and title]

Dear Mr./Ms. _____:

An unpaid invoice that is ___ days past due? I checked the last two years of our receivables records for your account and I haven't come up with a parallel situation. Your company invariably pays on time, or no worse than five or ten days past due—but this time it did neither.

The subject of a temporary cashflow problem has never come up but if there is one, please give me a call. We can work through it with you and continue to supply product(s) in quantities adequate to meet the requirements of your customers.

Cashflow isn't the problem? Your check for $_____ by [date] will put the incident behind us.

Sincerely,

Credit Manager

[date]

Name of Company
Street Address (or P.O. Box Number)
City, State, Zip Code

Attention: [name and title]

Dear Mr./Ms. _____:

Many thanks for the telephone call on [date]. This has been an especially difficult summer for us too what with vacations [or sickness] and more absenteeism than we usually experience. Some of our departments have had difficulty keeping up with the work load, and I'm not at all sure they have succeeded.

The check for $_____ arrived this morning. It was good of you to follow up on our request so quickly.

Sincerely,

Credit Manager

[date]

Name of Company
Street Address (or P.O. Box Number)
City, State, Zip Code

Attention: [name and title]

Dear Mr./Ms. _____:

I guess it's a good thing I'm not a betting man. If someone had wanted to bet me that your company would not have paid the $_____ past-due balance within 10 days after I sent the second reminder letter, I would have bet heavily that you would pay—and would now be standing here in my shorts. I would have bet the farm that there would be no reason to write this third letter!

We do not have a check and there has been no telephone call to tell us why. We must now consider the possibility that the problem is more than a temporary cashflow crunch—and that does bother us. It is one thing to try to guess what is going on when there is a base of information, but it is quite another when there is no information.

The aging of receivables is important and the [number] days past-due status of your account is unacceptable. Further delay is not possible. Your company's check for $_____ must be here before [date].

Sincerely,

Credit Manager

[date]

Name of Company
Street Address (or P.O. Box Number)
City, State, Zip Code

Attention: [name and title]

Dear Mr./Ms. _____:

This has been a collection experience that I would not have anticipated with your company. Three letters and two telephone calls have failed to get your company to release a check for $_____ to clear past-due invoice(s) _____ (and _____). Based upon the experience we had with your company prior to this problem, I would not have expected this to become a third-party collection item.

But as of today, it does become a third-party collection item. The collection procedure and all relevant letters and telephone calls will be initiated, handled, and processed by [name of collection agency] located at [street, number, and city]. Our involvement will be limited to information relayed to us by the collection agency.

There is still time to avoid a formal collection procedure. If your check for $_____ arrives in this office, or the office of the collection agency listed above, within 10 days from the current date, that action will terminate the collection assignment. No formal collection action will be initiated by the collection agency until the 10-day period has expired.

Payment within the next ten days will help to protect your company from the unfavorable reaction of suppliers and other creditors when legal notices are picked up by credit reporting agencies and made a part of their report. Whenever a collection problem goes to a collection agency and there is a formal collection procedure, we both lose.

Sincerely,

Credit Manager

9.6 **Reminder Letter Series (1 of 3)**

[date]

Name of Company
Street Address (or P.O. Box Number)
City, State, Zip Code

Attention: [name and title]

Dear Mr./Ms. _____:

It surprises us that we haven't received your check for the [month] invoices (or specific invoices). If there is a temporary cashflow problem, please give me a call so we can help you work through it. A simple oversight? Our company has its share of those, but we will appreciate a check at your earliest convenience.

Incidentally, there is a big difference between one of our reminder letters and a collection letter. This is a reminder letter.

Sincerely,

Credit Manager

9.7 **Reminder Letter Series (2 of 3)**

[date]

Name of Company
Street Address (or P.O. Box Number)
City, State, Zip Code

Attention: [name and title]

Dear Mr./Ms. _____:

This letter is still a reminder but, frankly, it is closing in on the category of *collection*.

We haven't heard from you so we do not know whether the problem is a temporary cashflow crunch or something more serious. We do know, however, that it is not a simple oversight or the earlier letter would have brought a response before now.

Mutually satisfactory relationships are hard to come by. Your company can protect the one it has with us by mailing a check for $_____ in time for it to be in our office by [date]. Beyond that date an evaluation of our relationship will have to place the major emphasis on what we are experiencing currently with far less emphasis on our earlier experience.

We'll be looking for your check.

Sincerely,

Credit Manager

[date]

Name of Company
Street Address (or P.O. Box Number)
City, State, Zip Code

Attention: [name and title]

Dear Mr./Ms. _____:

It should interest you to know that we are no longer in the category of reminder letters. This is letter number three—and it is solidly in the category of collection.

Silence may be golden, but not when your company is sitting on our money. We have asked several times for a check ($_____) to clear past-due balances. To this date there has been no check and no explanation. To continue what has to date been an unsuccessful attempt to rejuvenate a once-good relationship is not good management of available time.

There is no more latitude for delay. Payment is due in this office no later than [date] or the account will be assigned to our commercial agency for whatever action may be appropriate.

If your company is interested in saving a mutually profitable relationship, now is the time to do it.

Sincerely,

Credit Manager

[date]

Name of Company
Street Address (or P.O. Box Number)
City, State, Zip Code

Attention: [name and title]

Dear Mr./Ms. _____:

One of the qualities that has always set your company apart from many of our other customers is the fact that invoices are almost always paid within terms, and never more than five or ten days past.

Because of this established payment pattern, I was surprised to see a lone invoice begin to wander across our receivables aging report and into a past-due area that has been foreign to your account. A missing invoice seems the most logical reason for it to be unpaid so I have attached a photocopy to this letter.

There is always the possibility that the problem is something other than a missing invoice. If it is something else, please give me a call and we'll help in whatever ways we can.

Sincerely,

Credit Manager

[date]

Name of Company
Street Address (or P.O. Box Number)
City, State, Zip Code

Attention: [name and title]

Dear Mr./Ms. _____:

Life is not without its surprises. It is 10 days since my letter dated _____ (with invoice copy attached), but there has been no payment and no explanation for the past-due balance.

Before the aging of invoice _____ begins to have an adverse impact on our good relationship, verify that it is an unpaid item and set it up for prompt payment. Our feeling is that the invoice has escaped somehow from the mainstream of your payables items. This reminder should focus enough attention on it to move it into the payment pipeline.

Your check for $_____ will restore the good payment performance that we appreciate and have come to expect from your company.

Sincerely,

Credit Manager

[date]

Name of Company
Street Address (or P.O. Box Number)
City, State, Zip Code

Attention: [name and title]

Dear Mr./Ms. _____:

Whether the "third letter is the charm" depends on your current approach to past-due payables items.

When I wrote the first letter regarding invoice _____ on [date], I did not think it would fail to bring a response. The second letter? I am still not over the surprise of hearing nothing after the second letter was received. We all know that conditions within a business or company can worsen unexpectedly but such a complete 180-degree turn from your usual attitude of cooperation and communication is difficult for us to understand.

A telephone call to your office on [date] was unproductive. The person who made the call was apparently unable to speak with anyone who could give an explanation for the payment problem. And as you should understand, at _____ days past due, it has become a problem.

Before this invoice and the rather large sum of money it represents takes on a relationship-destroying life of its own, I am going to stop by your office and see if it can't be pushed through the payables system. I'll be in [city] on the _____ of [month] but will set up an appointment before I leave here.

I look forward to getting this resolved and returning to our old—and very good—relationship.

Sincerely,

Credit Manager

[date]

Name of Company
Street Address (or P.O. Box Number)
City, State, Zip Code

Attention: [name and title]

Dear Mr./Ms. _____:

A consistent pattern of past-due balances is not something we like to see on a customer's account. An occasional one? Yes. A monthly pattern? No.

Our supplier/customer relationship is only seven months old and at this point is still going through a period of adjustment. The credit line of $_____, assigned five months ago, is being monitored constantly. The experience we are having with receivables payments is being monitored constantly. Putting the two together, if we find that the credit line is putting dollars into receivables that are not clearing as promptly as we think they should, the credit line may be reduced and the customer asked to hold balances closer to terms.

It is our intent to cooperate with our customers as closely as good business practice and the requirements of our own cashflow will allow. In that spirit we ask for prompt payment of the $_____ balance for purchases made in the month of _____. Purchases made during the current billing month should be paid by the _____ of [month].

If there is any problem—permanent or temporary—that is impacting cashflow to the point where you are unable to pay invoices closer to terms, let us hear about it. When we know about problems, we are better able to offer our customers some meaningful help in working with and/or through a problem.

Sincerely,

Credit Manager

[date]

Name of Company
Street Address (or P.O. Box Number)
City, State, Zip Code

Attention: [name and title]

Dear Mr./Ms. _____:

I appreciate your call regarding my letter of [date], but what you suggest is not possible. There can be no adjustment in our terms that would give your company a preference (or preferential treatment) over what we offer to and/or do for our other customers. It is one of the most volatile and self-destructive business practices and an area that we would never touch.

My suggestion is the following: We will reduce your line of credit from $_____ to $_____ until past-due balances have been paid and monthly account balances are being paid within terms—or not more than 10 days past terms. Based upon your monthly requirement for our products, we shall then increase the line by increments of $_____ per month until purchases and payments are in acceptable balance.

The problem that we discussed—restricted cashflow due to the rapid growth and expansion of your business—is a common one. It is also a problem that we as suppliers and you as an entrepreneur must monitor carefully to ensure that growth does not accelerate so rapidly that it exceeds the ability and capabilities of the company to cope. At that point, everybody is in jeopardy.

We'll expect your check for $_____ by the _____ of this month.

Sincerely,

Credit Manager

[date]

Name of Company
Street Address (or P.O. Box Number)
City, State, Zip Code

Attention: [name and title]

Dear Mr./Ms. _____:

Your check in the amount of $_____ arrived today. I want to thank you for it and respond in more detail to yesterday afternoon's telephone conversation.

We are looking constantly for customers whose potential for growth is well-grounded in sound business practices, enough cashflow and bank support to adequately fund a program of growth, and the personnel to manage a level of growth that might become more rapid than was anticipated. Your company is young but all signs point to strong management, good current progress, and a well-conceived plan for the future.

Our feeling is that you are on the right track—and a fairly fast track. If there is any mental reservation, it is that no company can successfully prepare for growth that comes too fast. Can you grow rapidly but not so rapidly that the gap between growth and cashflow becomes too wide? We think you can.

During our conversation yesterday, I mentioned the Uniform Commercial Code and the fact that we want to be protected under Division 9 (Secured Transactions) of the Code. I have attached copies of a Security Agreement for Accounts Receivable which I ask you to sign and date. Keep the bottom copy for your records, return the original and second copy to me, and we will file the original as a financing statement to perfect our security interest.

We see this as having the potential for a long and a mutually profitable association.

Sincerely,

Credit Manager

9.15   **Errors on Invoice Series (1 of 3)**

[date]

Name of Company
Street Address (or P.O. Box Number)
City, State, Zip Code

Attention: [name and title]

Dear Mr./Ms. _____:

We apologize for the errors in both the price and quantity of two products on
invoices _____ and _____. It is unusual for our people to make an error
in one of these categories but errors of the same type on two invoices is at least one
set of errors too many.

The attached credit memorandums correct price and quantity errors on both
invoices. Please apply them to the respective invoices and remit the net difference.

If there is a future problem in this or any other area, do not hesitate to contact me.

Sincerely,

Credit Manager

9.16   **Errors on Invoice Series (2 of 3)**

[date]

Name of Company
Street Address (or P.O. Box Number)
City, State, Zip Code

Attention: [name and title]

Dear Mr./Ms. _____:

Approximately two weeks have passed since my letter to you of [date], and to which
I attached credit memorandums applicable to invoices _____ and _____.

The price and quantity errors were ours. Now that you have our credits for those
errors, it would be counter-productive to allow the invoices to slide into an
unacceptable area of past-due aging.

Your check for $_____ by the _____ of [month] will put this behind us.

Sincerely,

Credit Manager

[date]

Name of Company
Street Address (or P.O. Box Number)
City, State, Zip Code

Attention: [name and title]

Dear Mr./Ms. _____:

Invoices _____ and _____ have slipped to _____ days past due and are becoming a bigger problem as the days go by.

A telephone call to your office on [date] indicated that data for the two invoices had been input for the next payables run. If checks had been mailed shortly thereafter, ours for $_____ should have arrived two or three days ago.

If the problem is cashflow, it should have been mentioned during the telephone conversation on [date]. In the absence of any such information, we have no alternative but to insist that the check arrive here by [date], or orders will be held until the problem has been cleared.

Past due aging of _____ days is not in line with what is acceptable for accounts such as yours; an account in which our faith in your company has allowed us to assign a strong credit line. When account performance does not meet the criteria for a strong credit line, we must reevaluate the account, the circumstances of the situation, and whether we can continue the present credit line on into the future.

Our products are important to you and your customers; your business and your customers are important to us. Let us get this behind us and move on to areas that are more rewarding.

Sincerely,

Credit Manager

The Disadvantages of Series Collection Letters

Unless series collection letters are crafted carefully, there is the potential for slipping into a *canned* or a *mass mailer* mode. Because series letters are an all-purpose, prepared-in-advance type of correspondence that is set up to be easily adapted to a variety of collection situations, the spontaneity essential to grabbing the attention of the recipient could be missing from one or more of the letters. The return address on the envelope tells the recipient that the contents pertain to the company's past-due balance(s), but how you address the problem—opening lines, possible solution, incentive(s) to pay, etc.—is the key to the level and intensity of the read that your letter(s) will receive.

It seems ridiculous now, but I remember a series of collection letters several decades ago that was so well crafted—the review was "amusing, satirical, and nonthreatening"—that three customers admitted later to the writer/sender that they had purposely delayed paying their past-due balance just so they would receive additional letters! Any credit manager whose collection letters wander that far from their intended focal point had better make some adjustments in form and content. Remember the objective: you are writing letters to collect past-due receivables for your company. If you want to develop a cult following for your writings, aim them in another direction. I know I learned my lesson.

Some of the more glaring disadvantages of series letters are listed below.

1. The quality (spontaneity, appeal, etc.) of some letters in a collection series is not comparable with *first letters* that were not written as a part of a series.

2. Letters that are part of a series should build upon the preceding letter(s): Number two must escalate from number one (urgency, etc.); number three must escalate from number two.

3. Some series collection letters look and sound like form letters; nonmotivational words in form and content that could be applicable to any company—but to no specific company.

4. Letters are not personalized to give the customer/debtor the feeling that the supplier/creditor wants to be paid but is interested also in helping the customer to work through the problem(s).

5. Series collection letters should not be used in a situation so unique or having such an unusual degree of sensitivity that the fit is less than a totally personalized one.

6. The customer/debtor may not feel the same sense of urgency that is conveyed in a mix of one or two nonseries letters and one or two telephone calls.

7. When the customer's business and financial situation is precarious, those problems cannot be addressed effectively in a conventional series of letters.

Some series collection letters are fatally flawed as motivational forces for collecting past-due balances. If they do not progressively and successfully escalate the urgency for the customer to pay—adding new and stronger reasons as the collection process progresses—the customer who is under payment pressure from several suppliers will pay the major suppliers first, the secondary suppliers next, and the occasional supplier last.

Expressions such as the following have no place in a collection effort. They are weak, indicate indecision, and generally present a collection effort that is destined to take much longer than it should—and perhaps require the services of an outside collection service to get the job done.

1. "You really shouldn't do this to us ...." (When did you last rush to respond to a whiny request for anything? Nobody likes a whiner, and nobody goes out of their way to accommodate a whiner.)

2. "We don't really know how to go about solving this problem ...." (If a creditor uses a version of this in any of his or her collection letters or telephone calls, I would be amazed if the customer/debtor paid. You should never project such a directionless attitude. By the second or third letters, you should be telling the customer how much, where it's to be paid, and when.)

3. "I don't like to hold orders but if we don't get your check by ...." (No supplier likes to hold orders, and the customer doesn't jump for joy either. The point is you tell the customer, flatly and unemotionally, what the payment deadline is if the customer is to avoid having orders held. If payment does not come by the date specified, you do exactly what you said you would do: you hold orders!)

4. "There hasn't been a reply to my letter of [date] or my telephone call on [date], but I'm sure you mailed the check and it has been delayed in the mails." (When there has been no payment satisfaction from one letter and one or two telephone calls, there is no reason to assume that the customer/debtor has mailed the check. It is more reasonable to assume that the customer did not mail the check. It is also reasonable to assume that if the customer continues to receive tepid little payment requests, the customer will not pay until immediately before the account is scheduled to be assigned to a commercial collection agency, or at some point *after* the account has been assigned.)

5. "Has our invoice fallen through a crack or is it ...?" (Every supplier should give the customer a face-saving escape route from an embarrassing payment situation, but not *this* after a letter and telephone calls!)

The Comfort Zone

You should be most comfortable with collection letters that reflect your own thoughts, opinions, and/or the philosophy of your company. This is true of any business correspondence. Use terms, expressions, and speech patterns with which you are comfortable, but use them only if they deliver the type and quality of message that you are attempting to convey to the customer/debtor.

Example: You are a person who has lived and worked in one of the regions of this country where there is a distinctive speech pattern, an accent, etc. You are from Brooklyn, New Jersey, Texas, Georgia, Arkansas, Tennessee, Louisiana, or perhaps you are from California where trendy talk is a way of life. Certain speech patterns, accents, and expressions are distinctive and recognizable. Would you not draw upon those qualities which are a part of the culture of your area—a part of your roots—to impart the flavor of your area, your personality, and that of your company to the pieces of material in this book? The format and content is in this book; adding appropriate touches of personal and regional flavor can only enhance the strength of the material that you choose to use.

Whether it is a letter, a telephone call, a personal collection call, or a fax message, material to fit almost any collection situation is in this book. How you choose to use it will have an enormous affect on the degree to which it is successful.

Consider this. How embarrassing would it be to you, and how confusing to your customer, if, when the two of you met, your speech pattern (expressions, content, etc.) bore no resemblance to the relaxed, semistructured, or structured format of the letters and telephone conversations you will have shared with this customer over a period of months or years? Your goal is to get the customer to pay, and to pay in the shortest period of time: Good business form plus some special and innovative touches can be enormously helpful as you strive to achieve that goal.

Every letter and conversation in this book can be modified to reflect your own speech or writing pattern, your business philosophy, or the business philosophy of your company. If expressions that are common to you, your region, or your industry fit the format of a collection letter or a collection call, use them! Use the material in this book but "to your own self be true," and be true also to the financial requirements and philosophy of your business or company.

The following are examples of what you should not say and how you should not say it.

Things you should not do or say in the *first* collection letter:

1. Come on too strong in what should be a reminder letter only.

2. Burden the reminder letter with a recap of the collection problems you may have had with this customer in the past.

3. Refer to the customer/debtor in a derogatory or a demeaning manner.

4. Suggest or infer that you have low expectations for the success of a reminder letter to this customer/debtor.

5. Say or do anything that the customer might construe as something less than the expectation that payment will be mailed immediately.

6. Offer to do anything for the customer that might weaken your position if the reminder letter does not do the job.

Things you should not do or say in the *second* collection letter:

1. Automatically give the customer/debtor the benefit of several excuses for why the check has not arrived. This is especially true if the customer is a chronic offender.

2. Write your second letter in a tone that seems to reflect a position or a feeling of weakness.

3. Leave no doubt in the mind of your customer that your company views the past-due balance as a serious threat to the supplier-customer relationship.

4. Let the customer delay the processing and release of a payment when you sent invoice copies or a credit memo with the first letter.

5. Send your letter to someone with whom you have had no prior contact. (Contact the financial officer, a partner, the sole proprietor; preferably someone in authority with whom you are on a first-name basis.)

6. Relinquish the position of strength, although it should not be used in a belligerent, an aggressive, or a confrontational manner.

Things you should not do or say in the *third* collection letter:

1. Be less than civil when you make it clear that you (your company) are not accepting the customer/debtor's failure to send money.

2. Let the customer know that access to your company's product line(s) has been cut off, and if payment is not made by a specific date, the cut-off could become permanent.

3. Give the customer the benefit of *any* doubt. Two collection letters and one or two telephone calls have given the customer ample opportunity to respond. The customer either pays the required amount by a specific date or you assign the account to a collection agency.

4. Let the customer see anything less than the determination to collect your company's money.

5. Fail to take advantage of an opportunity to force (pressure) the customer to make a payment against past-due balances to get product(s) or material(s) to complete a project, a job, service the customer base, etc. (If the customer files for protection under the Bankruptcy Code within the following 30 or 60 days, your pressure-collected money should not be interpreted as a preference by the bankruptcy court since you gave the customer something in return—albeit a *something* of lesser dollar value.)

6. Let a customer who is about to receive a third collection letter have a dollars worth of anything until (a) a payment plan is in place—and your company is receiving payments as promised or (b) you have received a check from the customer for the amount specified in your second letter or a subsequent telephone conversation.

When your objective is to collect a past-due balance, a good tactic is to offer the customer some level of access to your company's product(s) or material(s), but not on a one dollar cash for one dollar of product basis. The yardstick to which you should hold these customers is two dollars for one dollar of product. If the customer claims an acute but temporary shortage of cash, and your knowledge of the company and faith in the person with whom you are working is such that you know it is the truth, a three dollars for two dollars of product is about as generous as you can afford to be.

When the cashflow problem has been caused by something that is beyond the control of your customer, should be corrected or cured within a short period of time (maximum of six months), and there is every reason to expect that the relationship will return to a payment basis that is satisfactory to your company, then it is reasonable to assume that some mutually acceptable payment plan will be worked out to cover the period of cashflow shortage. This plan can allow product to be shipped as past-due balances are reduced.

Collection-Related Problems That Are Inexcusable

The second or third letter—or the second or third telephone call—is not the time to be exploring the possibility that the customer has not received an invoice, or that a credit memo, one that should have been issued weeks ago, has still not been sent to the customer.

By the time a receivables balance has become past due and the first reminder telephone call or letter contact has been made with the customer, problems such as missing invoices, disallowed discounts, deductions from invoices when a credit is pending, and problems of a similar nature should no longer be part of the payment problem. These are problems that must be addressed early in the collection procedure. It will be productive to remember that your company should be no less aggressive in its effort to eliminate problems of this type, as it is to collect past-due balances that might be attributable to one or more of these problems.

When your company has been doing business with a company for a period of time, the pattern of payments usually becomes quite routine. Most companies pay at a specific time each month; other companies never seem to pay at the same time of the month and, for those accounts, the *no pattern* is really their *payment pattern*. Trying to project when accounts in the *no payment pattern* category will send checks is much less than an ideal scenario. You will begin to see, however, that many of these accounts pay within a fairly broad time frame; a time frame whose parameters may not allow you to pinpoint the week when payment will arrive but should allow you to project it as a *floater*—one that almost unfailingly arrives within a predictable time frame.

The effectiveness of your collection letters—series and other—will be enhanced when the problem between your company and the customer company is narrowed to one of money. Allow nothing else to interfere with the collection effort.

10

Mix and Match

Modern business is much too complex for any one collection procedure or technique to be the all-inclusive, sure-fire solution to the problem of collecting past-due receivables balances. Some customers are motivated to pay after one or two telephone calls; others do not see it as a serious collection effort until telephone calls have been replaced by one or two collection letters. There is a third group: a group that feels no motivation to pay until telephone calls and collection letters have been combined into what this book chooses to call the *mix and match* technique.

Those who respond more readily to *mix and match* than to the individual techniques of telephone calls and collection letters are, unfortunately, no easier to identify than accounts that respond to the individual techniques. And if you find that for a specific account, *mix and match* is the technique of choice, the next relevant decision is the sequence and the mix of telephone calls and letters. So, do you start the collection procedure with a telephone call or a letter? If the first contact is a telephone call and the collector elicits a promise or an indication from the debtor that payment will be made by a specific date, what is step number two (another phone call or the first letter) if the payment does not arrive? If the decision is to make the second contact the first collection letter (are we still together?), then, because the first collection letter was preceded by a telephone call, the first letter is elevated from the status of a reminder letter to a collection letter. Why not a reminder? First letters are reminders only when the customer has not been put on notice with an earlier telephone call.

The question of whether to begin a *mix and match* collection series with a first letter, follow it with a telephone call, make a second telephone call, send a second letter, and finally send the customer/debtor a third letter, is all tied up in the mechanics of collecting past-due receivables dollars. At some point in the sequence of collection steps, you are hoping that the customer/debtor halts the process by forwarding a check for the past-due balance. This could come at any point in the chain of letters and telephone calls, and the sooner it happens the better it will be for the creditor. A drawn-out collection effort uses additional time, effort, and money to successfully conclude the process. There is a very real incentive to collect the past-due balance as quickly as possible and move on to other problem accounts.

What follows is an illustration of how *mix and match* can be used to overcome the payment resistance of a customer/debtor. To broaden the scope of this illustration, we are assuming that the supplier/creditor is forced to go through several steps in the collection procedure before the check is mailed.

If there is one word to describe the process that follows, it is *flexibility*. It is the key guideline to which all other facets of the collection procedure is attached.

Telephone Call 1: The creditor's in-house collection person has decided to open this collection procedure with a call to the debtor company's accounts payable supervisor.

Operator at the debtor company: This is the [customer] company. May I help you?

Frank Beatty, Collector: This is Frank Beatty with the [supplier] corporation. I'd like to speak with Mary Wiloby in Accounts Payable, please.

Operator: I'll connect you, Mr. Beatty.

Beatty: Thank you.

There is a short pause, then ...

Mary Welby: This is Mary Welby.

Beatty: Mary, this is Frank Beatty with the [supplier] corporation. How are you this morning?

Welby: I'm fine, thank you, Mr. Beatty. What can I do for you?

Beatty: One of the invoices on your accounts has slid into the past-due column and I'm wondering if you have an invoice copy.

Welby: Do you have the purchase order number, the invoice number, and the amount of the invoice?

Beatty: Yes, Mary, it's—uh—P.O. 35191, invoice 4631, and the amount is $28,945.62.

Welby: P.O. 35191, invoice 4631, and $28,945.62. If you'll give me your telephone number, I'll get back to you later today or tomorrow forenoon.

Beatty: That will be fine. My number is, Area Code 463 555 3249.

Welby: I'll have the invoice checked and get back to you.

Beatty: I appreciate it. Goodbye.

Welby: Goodbye.

At this point, no payment has been requested and none has been promised, but a dialogue has been opened between the two companies. If Mary Welby finds that her department has a copy of invoice 4631, she should call Frank Beatty, tell him that the invoice was missing but has been found (or it is missing and she will ask him to send a photo copy—or a fax copy), and that the invoice is being input for payment on the payables run on the coming Friday.

Two days go by and Frank Beatty has not received the information promised for the preceding day by Mary Welby. He picks up the phone and dials the number of the customer/debtor company.

Telephone Call 2:

Operator at the debtor company: This is the [customer] company. May I help you?

Beatty: This is Frank Beatty at the [supplier] corporation. I'd like to speak with Mary Welby in Accounts Payable, please.

Operator: I'm sorry, Mr. Beatty. Ms. Welby is out of town for the rest of the week.

Beatty: Oh? (This is Wednesday.) She will be back on Monday?

Operator: Yes, Mr. Beatty. Would you care to speak with any other person in Accounts Payable?

Beatty: No—no, I think I'll wait and talk with her on Monday. Thanks. Goodbye.

Operator: Goodbye, Mr. Beatty.

Beatty has come up against a delay he had not anticipated when he talked with Mary Welby on Monday. A full week will go by before he is able to get the answer to his question regarding a copy of invoice 4631. Does he do nothing about it until the following Monday? He does not. Frank writes a letter to which he attaches a photo copy of invoice 4631. (See Letter 10.1 on page 221.)

When Frank Beatty mailed the above letter to Mary Welby, it was the start of his collection effort. The two telephone calls that preceded the first letter were not collection calls; they were fact-finding in their content and intent. Now, however, Beatty has turned the collection procedure (and the collection effort) up a notch to compensate for Mary Welby's failure to keep her commitment regarding information pertaining to invoice 4631. It is not a time for Frank Beatty to sit back and wait for something positive to happen. Mary Welby's failure to follow through has presented Beatty with the potential for a collection problem that should be terminated as soon as possible.

To this point in the collection procedure, Frank Beatty has called Accounts Payable Supervisor Mary Welby twice and has sent her one letter. What has been the result of these contacts? There has been no contact with Mary Welby since the first telephone call and no indication or commitment regarding a payment date for the past-due balance.

Ten days after Frank mailed the first letter, there has been no acknowledgment of it. As an alternative to sending a second letter and taking the risk of no response, Frank elects to make a third telephone call.

Telephone Call 3: The telephone operator identifies the customer/debtor company.

Frank: Frank Beatty at the [supplier] corporation. Mary Welby in Accounts Payable, please.

Operator: Let me see if she's available, Mr. Beatty.

Frank: It's important that I speak with her, operator.

Operator: I'll try to get her for you.

Frank: Thank you.

After a short pause ...

Mary: Mr. Beatty, Mary Welby here.

Frank: Good morning, Ms. Welby. Did you receive my [date] letter and the photo copy of invoice 4631?

Mary: Yes, I did—and you were right. We were not able to find the original copy of the invoice.

Frank: Then that solves our problem? You'll be able to release a check for $____ _____ so it will get here by the _____ of [month]?

Mary: I'm reasonably optimistic that we can do it.

Frank: (Thinking to himself, she's "reasonably optimistic that it can be done?" Not good enough.) I'm afraid *reasonably optimistic* isn't good enough, Ms. Welby. If we're going to continue to release product(s) to your company, I need a firm payment commitment.

Mary: I don't know. We are having a temporary cashflow problem. I would like to tell you that I can release the check in time for it to get to your company by [date] but I can't be that positive.

Frank: Then let's do it this way. Send me a check for $_____ (50 percent of the past-due total) by [date] and the second $_____ by [date] (two weeks after the first 50 percent). That should ease the pressure on your cashflow and give us a payment arrangement we can live with.

Mary: O.K. I'll commit to 50 percent by [date] and the second 50 percent by [date]. Will you continue to release product(s) to us?

Frank: When we receive the first check for 50 percent, I'll release product(s) up to a total of $_____. The same payment-versus-product release program will apply when the second $_____ payment arrives.

Mary: That sounds fair enough. Thank you.

Frank: Thank you—and we'll talk again.

Mary: Goodbye.

Frank: Goodbye.

[date]

Name of Company
Street Address (or P.O. Box Number)
City, State, Zip Code

Attention: [name and title]

Dear Mr./Ms. _____:

After our telephone conversation on Monday, I decided that the follow-up call you were going to make to me regarding our invoice 4631 (your P.O. 35191) would probably reveal that the invoice copy is not to be found.

To avoid putting any additional aging on the invoice, I have attached a copy of invoice 4631 to this letter. Please enter it into the payables cycle in time for it to clear our accounts receivable aging report prior to the [day] of [month].

If there is any other problem, please contact me at your earliest convenience.

Sincerely,

Frank Beatty
Credit Manager

This reads very well, but is it a *done deal*? An agreement has been created and now all that remains is for Mary Welby and her company to fulfill that agreement. Did I say *all* that remains? The *all* is merely the heart of the attempt by Frank Beatty to resolve the past-due problem. Until Beatty's corporation receives that first check for $_____, the *agreement* is nothing more than a verbal exercise—perhaps an exercise in "I'll say or agree to anything if it will buy my company some additional time" type of reaction. Money is the only voice in this arrangement, and until Frank Beatty hears the sound of that voice in the form of a check, he will monitor the situation *very* closely.

So, does Mary Welby release the check for $_____ by [date]? (We can go two ways with this hypothetical situation. If Mary releases the check for $_____, the immediate pressure for payment is off of the account. Some pressure will continue until the second $_____ check has been received, but the arrival of the first check is the key. It is indicative of a strong desire on Mary's part to honor the commitment she made on behalf of her company to Frank Beatty and his corporation. If, however, the first check for $_____ does not arrive, Frank will be obliged to accelerate the collection effort.)

The date specified for the arrival of the $_____ check has come and gone. Mary Welby did not call to give an explanation for failing to send the check. Frank reviews his collection effort to date; three telephone calls, one letter, one failed payment commitment, and one failed commitment for information. He decides to write a second letter, which is also a final demand. This time, however, he addresses it to the Vice President-Finance, with copies to the Vice President-Sales and Accounts Payable Supervisor Mary Welby. Why the change in strategy? It is to alert the Finance and Sales Departments that their company is about to lose a money-making line of products.

[date]

Name of Company
Street Address (or P.O. Box Number)
City, State, Zip Code

Attention: Alvin Cambrey, Vice President-Finance

Dear Mr. Cambrey:

Our association with your company has not been a long one but in those two years
our products have enjoyed rapid acceptance in your marketplace area—and a
mutually profitable sales growth.

Unfortunately, that relationship is about to come to an end, and primarily because
we are unable to get payment for Invoice 4631 dated _____ in the amount of
$28,945.62. Not a lot of money? True, but we view any failure to handle our invoices
and sales terms with appropriate respect as a serious beach of the supplier-customer
relationship. When a payment commitment is made, is not kept, and there is no prior
or subsequent explanation, it is difficult to maintain a confidence level appropriate to
that which is necessary for a credit relationship to operate successfully.

We are certainly not anxious to lose good growth-oriented customers but this situation
does represent something of a crossroads in our relationship. But if you, Mr. Cambrey,
will commit your company to payments of $_____ and $_____ by the
respective dates of _____ and _____, the relationship between our
two companies will miss doing a full 360 degree turn by no more than a few degrees.

Sincerely,

Frank Beatty
Credit Manager

cc: Wilburn Cole, Vice President-Sales
    Mary Welby, Supervisor-Accounts Payable

    Addressing the second collection letter to the Vice President-Finance and
covering the Vice President-Sales with a copy, enabled Frank Beatty to (1) improve
the chances that the debtor company would pay within the dates specified in his
letter, and (2) could salvage a customer whose efforts on behalf of his corporation's
products had been very impressive. Aggressive merchandisers who know how to
present and promote a product to customers in their marketplace area are not
plentiful and should be given as much consideration as the circumstances will
allow.

Four days after Frank sent the second collection letter to the customer/debtor company's Alvin Cambrey, that gentleman placed a call to Frank.

Cambrey: Mr. Beatty, this is Alvin Cambrey, V.P.-Finance at the (customer) company.

Beatty: Yes, Mr. Cambrey. You got my letter.

Cambrey: I did indeed—and you made your point. I have discussed your products and our cashflow with Wilburn Cole, our V.P.-Sales, and he supports your position one hundred percent.

Beatty: You mean that balances should not be allowed to stretch out and cause a problem such as the current one.

Cambrey: Certainly that too, but Will Cole agrees with your point that your products are strong items for us. (Cambrey chuckled.) He assures me that the easiest way for me to incur the wrath of my fellow executives is to—as he put it—screw up with your company.

Beatty: It sounds to me as though we're in synch on every facet of the relationship.

Cambrey: Depend on it, Mr.—uh—could we make it Alvin and Frank?

Beatty: It Makes good sense to me, Alvin.

Cambrey: Good. The first $_____ check will be cut tomorrow and mailed the following day. The second check will be cut next Wednesday or Thursday and mailed not later than Friday.

Beatty: That's great, but you don't have to accelerate the release date of the second check by that many days.

Cambrey: No, we owe it to you, Frank—and in more ways than the one. I don't want receivables aging to be a problem in our relationship. We're growing, we need your long-term support, and the best way for us to get it is to earn it.

Beatty: I'm a happy man, Alvin. Many thanks for your cooperation, and we'll talk again soon.

Cambrey: My pleasure. I'll look forward to meeting you the next time you're in our area.

Beatty: Fair enough. Goodbye, Alvin.

Cambrey: Goodbye, Frank.

Frank Beatty's performance was exemplary. He took a relationship that was coming apart rapidly, changed the thrust of his collection effort, resolved the problem of a past-due balance, and moved the two companies to a better understanding and the beginning of a stronger relationship than had existed before. The change in Frank's tactics also opened a revolving door through which the customer company's Alvin Cambrey could ride in on his white horse, take the account out of Mary Welby's hands, make the payment(s) that she had been unable to make because of guidelines for conserving cash that had come from the office of—guess who?—Vice President-Finance Alvin Cambrey.

Not every reader is willing to buy into the neat little arrangement—and the first-name relationship—that evolved so rapidly between Frank Beatty and Alvin

Cambrey. There are also those among you who may not accept the picture of Alvin Cambrey agreeing so readily to the payment requirement of Frank Beatty. These are valid doubts and valid concerns, and the best way to eliminate them is to deal with them on a conventional basis.

There is always the strong probability that the second collection letter is persuasive enough to force a check but reasons for nonpayment extend far beyond the control of the financial officer. If Frank Beatty's second letter does not do the job, a third letter must be written. A deadline for payment will be set after which the account will be assigned to a commercial collection agency. (Any action that changes the collection effort from in-house to a commercial collection agency or to an attorney collection specialist is doubly unfortunate: the supplier/creditor must pay the collection agency a percentage of the assigned balance: usually 25 to 40 percent of the assigned amount, and the business relationship between the supplier/creditor and the customer/debtor is frequently damaged beyond repair.)

So let us assume that, instead of the amiable agreement that resulted from the telephone call that Vice President-Finance Alvin Cambrey placed to Frank Beatty, there was no telephone contact, no letter response, and no money. After a week or 10 days of waiting for a response from the customer company, Frank has no alternative other than to write a third letter: a formal demand for payment by a specific date or the account will be assigned to a collection agency.

10.3   Additional Follow-Up to V.P.-Finance (3 of 4)

[date]

Attention: Alvin Cambrey, Vice President-Finance

Dear Mr. Cambrey:

This is a letter that I write very rarely, and one that gives me no pleasure. However, when the collection effort includes three telephone calls, two letters, a broken commitment or two—and no money—then I have no alternative.

The deadline for payment of the $_____ past-due balance is [date]. If the check is not in our hands by that date, the account will be referred immediately to a commercial collection agency.

It is unfortunate that your company will no longer be able to offer customers our line of products; a line that, as we are both aware, has made a strong contribution to the growth and success of your company.

Sincerely,

Frank Beatty
Credit Manager

[date]

Name of Company
Street Address (or P.O. Box Number)
City, State, Zip Code

Attention: Alvin Cambrey, Vice President-Finance

Dear Mr. Cambrey:

A promising relationship has taken a dismal turn, and your company is the only one with the power to restore it.

It would be unfortunate if there is thinking at your company that we are less than serious about collecting the past-due balance of $_____. Certainly the number and frequency of our telephone calls and letters would give no credibility to that thought.

This is a letter that I write very rarely, Mr. Cambrey, and one that gives me no pleasure. The deadline for payment of the past-due balance of $_____ is [date]. If the check is not in our hands by that date, the account will be referred immediately to a commercial collection agency.

It is unfortunate that our products will no longer be available to your customers. As we are both aware, our product line has made a strong contribution to the growth and success of your company.

Sincerely,

Frank Beatty
Credit Manager

The hypothetical situation of Frank Beatty's effort to collect a past-due balance of $28,945.62 from the customer company offers the reader a variety of variables. The customer company might have paid the $28,945.62 after Beatty's first telephone call to Accounts Payable Supervisor Mary Welby, which would have terminated the collection procedure and eliminated the time-consuming necessity for two additional telephone calls and three collection letters. If the customer company had paid after the second telephone call, the third call, or even after the first letter, payment would have saved a considerable amount of time and money that could have been channeled more productively into other problems of the credit and collection department.

Because the hypothetical case was brought down to a second letter (and the agreement between the customer company's Vice President-Finance and Frank Beatty) and the third letter (which was necessitated because telephone calls and two earlier letters had accomplished nothing), the reader has the opportunity to review the full spectrum of a collection effort that (1) could have been terminated at any stage by the payment of the past-due balance, and (2) was assigned ultimately to a collection agency because too much in-house time and effort had come up with a nonproductive result.

Almost any of the letters and telephone conversations in this book can be used to create a *mix and match* series that will represent the attitude and the wishes of your own company. Whether the nature of your relationship with certain accounts causes you to move more-or-less rapidly from an initial reminder call or letter to a formal demand for payment is a decision that the letters and telephone guidance in this book will help you to make. The possibilities for effective combinations of letters, phone calls, and fax messages (an explanation of fax appears later in this chapter and in Chap. 13) is virtually limitless. And if one combination proves to be less effective than you had anticipated? Be innovative! Change the focus of *mix and match* until you come up with a combination that is most effective with a specific account, a specific type of situation, or a personality that is unique to a specific company or individual.

Fax Machines

Mix telephone calls and letters with the immediacy of documents and letters that have been transmitted—and received—on a fax machine. Every major company and many smaller companies and businesses have fax machines. They have found that the cost of the machine and the service is not only affordable, it has become almost mandatory. The potential for transmitting, in seconds or minutes, a document or a message has introduced a new level of communication to the business world.

As this is being written, companies such as Sharp, Brother, Panasonic, and many domestic manufacturers offer a variety of machines whose potential is geared to various levels of speed and activity. There are affordable units that offer 40-, 50-, 100-, and 118-number speed dial memories; 10-, 15-, 20-, and 50-page document feeders, page cutter, and a fax/telephone switch. Prices for the three units cited as examples of what the marketplace is offering currently range from approximately $400 to $1595. Domestic manufacturers are also actively offering units of comparable price, quality, and features.

I never recommend one unit of *any* piece of electronic equipment over the units of competing manufacturers. Oh, I am seldom without an opinion but I do not express that opinion because I do not know the conditions under which the unit of my choice—or any of the others—will be asked to perform. Is the unit to operate in a high-volume situation? What are the short- and long-term plans for growth, and which of the available units is best qualified to work well today and accommodate tomorrow's growth? If price is the main criteria, a unit that is priced moderately offers the speed dial memory, document feeder capacity, and other features adequate for the volume of work it will be expected to handle. There is no reason to spend an additional several hundred dollars for capabilities and features that are not relevant to the current and near-future needs of your company.

Having said that, let me add a few words of caution. If your company is in a strong growth mode, a more expensive machine (one with more capacity, capabilities, and features) might be the most inexpensive (cost effective) in the long term. If yours is a growth company, consider buying something that has the capability to cope with the additional demands of growth. This will almost surely not be the least expensive fax machine, or the least expensive of any other category of electronic equipment. Buy for today, but as you are buying for today, try to accommodate some of tomorrow's needs. Do not buy something because it is cheap and will do an acceptable job today; spend a few more dollars to get something that will serve your company well into the next phase of its growth.

Personal Visits

A personal visit by a Credit Manager or a Collection Supervisor to the customer/debtor can be one of the most effective tactics of the collection tools. It is shock therapy for most debtors when they see a supplier's Credit Manager or Collection Supervisor standing at their reception desk. The reaction is frequently a badly handled attempt to explain away the broken promises, the telephone calls that were never returned, and the letters that were not answered.

Faced with the necessity to improvise believable lies, most fail the test by an embarrassing margin. They get caught up in the attempt to turn blame away from themselves and assign it to others, and the attempt almost invariably falls short of being convincing. The sudden appearance of the creditor he or she has been dodging for weeks or months is an unsettling experience: one that makes the "artful dodger" blink when standing eye-to-eye with the creditor's representative.

A personal visit to a customer/debtor is a good tactic when the past-due balance is large enough (thousands of dollars, or hundreds if the business is small). It is also a tactic that makes sense when there are two or more smaller past-due accounts in the same town, city, or immediate geographic area. Maximizing the potential benefit from a collection-related trip is a worthy objective, one that should be applauded by the supplier-creditor's financial management.

The following is representative of dialogue that might take place between a Credit Manager (or a Collection Supervisor) and the Financial Officer/Manager, owner, or partner of a customer/debtor.

(Aubrey Williamson is the Credit Manager of Fieldcrust Systems, Inc. He has driven 80 miles to the office and warehouse of Bigger Brothers, one of Fieldcrust System's newer accounts and one that (11 months before) had seemed destined to become a major success story as a wholesale dealer for Fieldcrust Systems, Inc. But the bloom had barely started to come to the relationship before there were major changes in Bigger Brothers' payment pattern. *Within terms* payments slid quickly into 10 and 15 days past due, then 30 to 40 days past, and finally 45 to 60 days past due.)

Williamson pushed open the glass door and stepped into the lobby of Bigger Brothers. He glanced around, then walked to the reception desk.

A young woman looked up from the desk.

"May I help you?"

"I hope so." Williamson smiled. "I'm here to see Carl Fielding, your V.P.-Finance."

"Do you have an appointment with Mr. Fielding?"

"No," Williamson took a card from his pocket, "but it is quite urgent that I see him. Tell him Aubrey Williamson with Fieldcrust Systems is here to see him"

"And your title is—"

"I'm the corporate Credit Manager."

"Oh." She looked at the card. "I'll tell him you're here, Mr. Williamson."

"Thank you."

Seconds after the woman indicated to Williamson that Fielding would be right out, he was.

"Aubrey Williamson?"

"That's right, Mr. Fielding."

Fielding grabbed Williamson's hand and began to pump it.

"Good to meet you, Aubrey. I've been meaning to call you but you know how difficult it is to find the time to do all the things that should be done."

Williamson shook his head.

"I'm afraid I don't understand, Mr. Fielding. When I or one of my people take the time to make three telephone calls, send one or two collection letters, and in return we get one or two broken payment promises, I am unable to empathize with that level of unconcern."

"Oh, we are concerned—we really are!" Fielding's head bobbed up and down. "It's just that our cashflow has been very slow the last three months and we haven't been able to take care of some of our suppliers the way we should."

Williamson nodded.

"I know. My company has been in that category." He put his briefcase on the counter. "You have been making monthly payments to some of your suppliers?"

"Oh, yes. Our key suppliers have been getting the bulk of our money and our attention."

"We are a key supplier, Mr. Fielding, and we have not been getting your attention or your money." As Fielding's mouth opened in surprise, Williamson continued. "The products that your firm buys from us have been instrumental in your success." He shook his head. "I don't see you being as successful in the future if our product line is not available to your company or to the company's customers."

"Absolutely, Mr. Williamson, your product line is very important to us!" He turned toward the woman at the desk. "Get me Linda in accounts payable." Fielding looked at Williamson. "I'll get to the bottom of this right now." The telephone receiver was deposited in his outstretched hand. "Linda—Carl Fielding. Aubrey Williamson, Fieldcrust System's Credit Manager is here about a $42,000 check that I told you to release last week." (Oh, really? The oldest ploy in the business. Blame it on the payables person because she can't tell her boss how two-faced he is without running the risk of losing her job.) She apparently gave it a shot, however, because Fielding's face turned pink. "Alright, alright! Get the check, put it in an envelope, and bring it to me at the reception desk." A brief pause, then—"That is correct. We are releasing the check—now!"

Not every visit ends with the Credit Manager or the collection person walking out of the office with a check for the past-due balance. It is, in fact, unrealistic to expect that every such visit will result in a check being cut on the spot and handed to the supplier/creditor's representative. The best you can expect from most surprise visits is a dose of shock therapy which should lead to nothing less than a firm promise that a check for all of the past-due balance (or whatever amount you can negotiate or impose realistically upon the customer's finance director) will be released by a specific date—but never later than five working days after you have appeared in the customer's office. Longer than five days could activate the *weasel factor* (the more time that elapses between your visit and the agreement to send money, the greater the possibility that the financial director will attempt to *weasel out* of the agreement to send a specific sum of money by a specific date.)

A second version of the above visit to the customer's office has Aubrey Williamson pitching *immediate payment* to a Carl Fielding who has major cashflow problems (temporary, he insists) and seems reluctant to reapportion money scheduled to be paid to Bigger's other suppliers so some can be applied to reduce the past-due balance owed to Fieldcrust Systems. What Fielding either does not know or is attempting to ignore is Williamson's two telephone calls the preceding day to the Director of Purchasing and to the Vice President-Sales. Both had expressed concern that the past-due balance had not been paid and had been adamant in their support of Fieldcrust's products and of their importance to the Bigger Brothers' marketing strategy.

Fielding shook his head.

"I know we owe you $42,000 and I know it's past due, but our cash position is such that I can't do anything about it this month."

"Think about it, Mr. Fielding. If you have money to pay some of your creditors, you are definitely in a position to prorate that money over all of the accounts to whom you owe money. I don't like to put it this bluntly, Carl, but we get a payment or your customers are not going to be buying our products from your company."

"Now wait a minute! We need your product line!"

"That's almost exactly what your Director of Purchasing and your Vice President-Sales said when I talked with them yesterday."

"They know that we owe Fieldcrust a past-due balance?"

Williamson nodded.

"I felt that the mutual interest of our companies would be better served if they were aware of the problem." Williamson's expression did not change. "You aren't going to tell me that at least one of them hasn't told you that I called?"

"No. Our Vice President-Sales called me this morning. He made it clear that my colleagues in senior management would not be pleased if we lost your product line."

Williamson nodded.

"So the sensible way out of this is to give me a check for $14,000 now, send another $14,000 two weeks from today, and a final $14,000 four weeks from today. Those three payments will eliminate the past-due balance and will allow us to maintain your inventory of our products."

Fielding hesitated briefly, then he nodded.

"Alright. I'll have payables cut a check for $14,000." He glanced at his watch. "Give me 15 or 20 minutes and I'll have it for you."

"Good. I'll be happy to wait."

Of course it would be satisfying to get the $42,000 past-due balance in one payment but the financial facts have to be faced. Bigger Brothers is having severe cashflow problems and although Aubrey Williamson wants to get his company's money as rapidly as possible, he doesn't want to take too large a percentage of available cash. Other creditors could begin to turn their accounts over to a collection service—or even worse—they might decide that Bigger's cashflow problem is not temporary and push so hard for their money that Bigger is forced to file for protection under the Bankruptcy Act. Williamson will take the check for $14,000, and if the second or third checks do not arrive when due, he will follow up immediately with a telephone call. The check must arrive within five days of the telephone call or Williamson will place calls to the Director of Purchasing and the Vice President-Sales, asking for their assistance to get a check released for $14,000. Because they need Fieldcrust's product line, they will lean heavily on Carl Fielding to ensure that he expedites release of the check.

Collection visits to the place of business of a customer whose balance, or part of it, is past due should be reserved for special collection situations and/or certain problem accounts. It is not a tactic that should be incorporated routinely into a collection procedure. It should be regarded as a tactic of last resort or a tactic that can be used when telephone calls and letters have failed and the next formal collection step (after the visit) is assignment of the account to a collection agency. The amount of the account receivable versus its importance to the supplier/creditor company will determine whether a personal visit to the customer/debtor is worth the time, travel, and expense. If it can be combined with a credit meeting or other business in the same general area, so much the better. Prorating travel expenses over three or four company-related activities reduces the cost of collecting the account balance and the cost of calls and business meetings unrelated to the collection item.

When your company is not a major or a key supplier of the customer/debtor, your leverage is considerably less than when your company's products are important to the customer's marketing strategy. Customers do not mistreat suppliers whose products are essential to the customer's success. Other suppliers may have to call several times or write two or more letters before they receive their money, but not the major and/or key supplier(s). Unless the customer's cashflow has dried up to the point where even the major creditors cannot be paid in a timely fashion, there is reason to hope that the customer will not slide into bankruptcy.

The practicality of a *mix and match* collection procedure has its foundation in the well-documented notion that a customer whose account is past due will respond much more readily to letters and telephone calls whose message is delivered in a nonroutine manner. It's alright to say the same old things but say them in a way that has not been done to the point where they induce nausea. Most customers know or can find out very quickly, what they owe, how old the balance is, and why they have not paid it. Your job is to motivate them to move on, to write the check that puts the money in your company's cashflow. There are any number of ways for a creditor to ask a customer for money, so why don't we see or hear more requests for payment that are motivational?

Collection letters, telephone calls, fax messages, and visits to the office of customers must bring the message to the customer/debtor in a format that sets it apart from the general run of payment requests. If we can proceed on the assumption that the debtor has some payment capability, it follows that the major and key suppliers will be paid first regardless of whether there is or is not motivational content in collection letters and telephone conversations. But when the payment request is presented in a different wrapping—one that romances or carrot sticks the debtor—the chances for an early resolution of the problem are much better than they would be if *general run* is the best that can be said for the collection effort.

11

Collection Calls (Scripted)

There has been a gradual change during the past two or three decades from a collection effort that depended almost totally upon collection letters to one that currently employs a strong mix of telephone calls and letters. The decrease in long-distance rates plus a business climate that, in the age of electronics moves much more rapidly and demands more information and tighter control, has caused a sharp increase in the number and frequency of telephone calls to collect past-due accounts.

Labor costs have increased dramatically the cost of a personalized letter. The same well-organized person can make several telephone calls, get answers from the majority of the people called, and get on to other work before the person who elects to personalize several letters has gotten more than halfway into the task. Letters do, however, continue to play an important role, and especially when a first or second telephone call is unproductive. A letter can state the case for immediate payment while creating a record of facts—or facts as related and interpreted by the letter writer—that can serve as a point of reference during future conversations or exchanges of letters.

Telephone calls enable a creditor to get his or her message to a key person or department in a matter of minutes, and to get a response from the person called. What about the people who never seem to be in when you call? There will always be those who have their telephone calls screened to avoid—or to delay as long as possible—taking a call from a creditor. Inevitably, however, the person who is "out of the office" or is "unavailable but will get back to you as soon as possible" is only delaying the inevitable connection with the creditor. If you persist (and you must) you will get through or you will get your collection message through. When you or your message have gotten through, it should force the hand of the customer/ debtor whose approach to dealing with creditors is much less than straightforward.

If you have ever met or talked with a person under circumstances other than a previous collection call, you are in an excellent position to read that person's voice. Tension will often creep into the voice of a person who, because of unsatisfactory or deteriorating business circumstances, is forced to put the best face on the situation. It is in the tone of the voice; the inability of a normally fluent person to say what they want to say; a hesitant, less than forthright recitation of what is alleged to be the problem, or an attempt to dismiss as unimportant something that obviously poses a problem, with the potential to cause a major disruption to the customer/debtor's business. When your read of a conversation tells you that one or more of these signs is present, there is good reason to dig much deeper than the level being offered to you by the customer-debtor.

Telephone Calls and the Collection Procedure

The following is an accounts receivable collection procedure that features the use of telephone calls. It does not exclude collection letters but the primary thrust of the collection effort is through telephone calls.

1. When customer balances become 10 days past due, a first collection call should be made.

2. When customer balances become 20 days past due, a second collection call should be made.

3. When customer balances become 30 days past due, a collection letter should be sent to the customer. It should be a letter that reminds the customer of the two telephone calls that have preceded it and direct the customer's attention to the past-due aging.

4. Variations on the above (the spacing of letters and telephone calls) may also be based upon the following criteria of priority and/or urgency:
   a. When balances are in two or more columns of the accounts receivable aged trial balance report, the urgency is based upon the combination of dollars and aging. (All balances are past due or open balances are a combination of current and past due.)
   b. Past experience with the account plus the past and current experience of other suppliers. If report data is not current (Dun & Bradstreet or National Association of Credit Management), those reports should be updated.
   c. The quality of the customer's response to the first letter or telephone call. (Key person not available, not return telephone call, etc.)
   d. Whether there appears to be a downward trend in the customer's business.
   e. Whether cashflow seems to have been impacted by any single factor or a combination of extremely rapid growth, management that has not kept pace with growth, the loss of a key person or key personnel, or the loss of what may have been a long-standing advantage in the marketplace.
   f. Product-related litigation that might involve the potential for a damaging financial settlement or impact product sales.

These are some of the factors that influence the timing and the amount of effort that should go into collecting past-due balances. They are some of the factors that dictate how much time and effort company credit department personnel should expend on an account before the account is assigned to an outside collection agency.

There is no inflexible criteria for handling most credit and collection problems. The primary criteria is the company's credit policy which sets the parameters of latitude and flexibility. There is a need to deal fairly and honestly with the company's credit customers, and the phrase *company's credit customers* will probably include almost every customer who buys on a regular basis.

Department staff with account responsibility should monitor all accounts on an ongoing basis: prorating time and energy to focus first on major customers with an account or a payment problem, and second on accounts with a lower dollar volume and some new or recurring payment problems, and then focus an increasingly diminishing amount of time on the lower-to-lowest dollar volume accounts.

You should not expect to lose a single dollar in bad debt write-offs that could have been avoided with solid, diligent monitoring and collecting procedure. The customer is king, but his or her crown diminishes in size and importance as it relates to the payment performance of the account.

The Leverage of Holding Orders

Holding orders is not a collection technique that should be abused. It should be used only when there has been a strong effort—telephone calls, letters, fax, personal visits, etc.—to collect past-due balances from a customer who has demonstrated an unwillingness to respond to less restrictive tactics.

Example: When I was the corporate Credit Manager for a Silicon Valley manufacturer of semiconductor products, we began to sell to a major electronics company with headquarters in Chicago. Within four months after the first sale, our receivables experience had become unsatisfactory: invoices slipped right on through our sales terms of 2%/Net 30 and went right on into the 30 days and 60 days past-due columns.

Telephone calls to the accounts payable person who handled our account brought promises but no money; subsequent calls to the controller were equally unproductive. Past-due balances were climbing, and our cashflow was being impacted adversely. The situation demanded drastic action—so I took it.

I called the customer's controller in Chicago and told him that I had just put a hold on all of his company's orders until a specific dollar total of past-due invoices had been paid.

There were several seconds of silence followed by a stammered and an incredulous reaction.

"You, you're doing *what*?! No supplier has *ever* held our orders!"

"That's quite possible," I replied, "but I don't seem to have a choice. We've exhausted a conventional, nondisruptive approach that did not succeed in getting your company to pay our invoices." I paused. "I'm sorry to have to do this, but we are holding orders until the specified payment has been received."

Another stunned silence was followed by a sharp intake of breath.

"I don't believe this. I—I'll get back to you."

The controller did not get back to me but within the hour, I had a call from the Vice President-Finance at the company's Chicago headquarters.

"Mr. Bond, this is Herbert Simpson, Vice President-Finance at Acme Electronics."

"Yes, Mr. Simpson."

"Our controller tells me that you…" had I been in his Chicago office, I'm sure I would have seen Herbert Simpson's eyeballs roll skyward "… that you are holding our orders."

"That is true, Mr. Simpson. I don't know if the controller briefed you regarding the aging and amounts of the past-due balances, but conventional calls and letters have been ineffective."

"But no one has ever held our orders, or no one had ever held them before today."

"We're in a growth mode, Mr. Simpson, and internally generated cashflow is an important part of our financial picture." I paused just long enough to change the angle of focus. "We appreciate the business that your company has been giving us, and I believe we've been doing a good job for you."

"I understand that you have. I am somewhat surprised that we haven't kept your account at a more current aging."

"That would certainly solve our problem. As you know, there are accounts whose payment pattern is so unstable that something like this is part of the pattern of doing business—but not your company."

"I agree. How about this. Will you accept my word that a check for the required amount will be processed and mailed to your attention by the end of tomorrow's business day?"

"Certainly. And, on that basis, I'll immediately release the hold on your orders."

"Fair enough." Simpson chuckled. "I'll tell you this, Mr. Bond, you've succeeded in shaking us up. I'll pass the word to our controller that he's to take better care of your account."

"I'll appreciate it, Mr. Simpson. And incidentally," it was my turn to chuckle, "we really do appreciate your company's business."

"I know. Goodbye, Mr. Bond."

"Goodbye, Mr. Simpson."

A Company *Out of Control*

An example of the dilemma that can immobilize a credit manager is the scenario of a hypothetical company—Celebrity Games, Inc. Founded by three men who left other companies in a related industry, Celebrity Games received 42 percent of its start-up and support funding from a firm of venture capitalists. The company product incorporates various elements of advanced technology, has been aggressively promoted in the media, and has enjoyed strong early market appeal. So what is Celebrity Games' most obvious and self-destructive problem? The company did not go into the marketplace battleground with a credit manager. In fact, they did not hire one until accounts receivable had reached eight million dollars, with more than half of that total ranging from 45 to 90 days past due!

Fred Fuller is an experienced credit manager who has come to Celebrity Games from a semiconductor company that has sales in excess of 100 million dollars. His first day at Celebrity is a shocker. There are only 17 credit files on the 132 active receivables accounts. Perhaps the most startling fact is that past-due accounts—some of which have past-due balances of $100,000 to $250,000—are still being sold on open-account terms despite the fact that no payment has been received for weeks! Has anyone been attempting to contact these accounts for payments? And why hasn't someone had the good sense to stop open-account shipments to these accounts until (1) a substantial payment has been received, and (2) credit references (bank and supplier) have been received and evaluated? The answer is that management has placed the lowest priority possible on the quality of customer accounts (accounts receivable) and the highest priority on increasing sales and shipments.

After two days of evaluating the situation—trying to get a handle on what is in the files versus the enormous amount of essential bank, supplier, and credit reporting agency information that isn't there—Fred picks up his yellow-ruled pad and takes his problems to Bill Sharp, Vice President of Finance.

"Bill," Fred tapped his forefinger on several pages of notes. "This is a disaster. This is the most out of control operation I've ever seen!"

Sharp had known Fred when the two were in the semiconductor industry. He leaned back in his chair.

"Come on, Fred. You've only been here two days." He shook his head. "That isn't enough time to brand us an out-of-control company."

"Oh, I differ with you on that one, Bill." Fred turned several pages, glancing at the notes on each. "I've been able to find 17 file folders out of a possible active account total of 132." He looked up. "Seventeen file folders, Bill, and not one of them has anything in it that pertains to the evaluation of the account as a good or a poor credit risk."

Sharp leaned forward.

"That's why you're here, Fred. We need to get a handle on these accounts to help prepare us for a public offering of the company's stock."

"How can you be thinking of a public offering when the biggest chunk of the company's assets are in such terrible shape?" Fred shook his head. "I didn't have to be here more than an hour to know that you aren't generating more than a trickle of the company's monthly cashflow requirement from these receivables."

"We have seven million dollars from the venture capitalists that we're using to help us in that area." Sharp nodded. "But you're right about the monthly contribution from accounts receivable."

Fred put the note pad on Sharp's desk.

"I want to put a hold on shipments to accounts that are past due 30 days and over, or at least until we can get some credit data from suppliers, banks, and a credit reporting agency."

"I don't think we subscribe to a credit report service."

"No, and I want to subscribe to one today, preferably to both D & B (Dun and Bradstreet) and NACM (National Association of Credit Management)."

Bill nodded.

"I don't have a problem with that. Order what you feel is necessary." He paused. "A hold on past-due open accounts is something else—something I'll have to clear with the CEO."

Fred's eyes widened.

"There aren't any acceptable alternatives, Bill! If we don't hold orders, or go to a $2 for $1 or a $3 for $2 *cash versus merchandise* formula for reducing past-due balances, those balances are going to get bigger and older."

"I hear what you're saying but approval for anything that would slow the company's rate of quarterly sales growth is beyond my authority." Sharp glanced at his watch. "I've got a meeting in five minutes, Bill. I'll get back to you later today or tomorrow on the accounts receivable problem."

Fred stood up.

"I don't like to put it this way, Bill, but I need the backing of the company to do the job that I was hired to do." He turned toward the door. "If I'm to be denied the authority necessary to apply the most basic controls to the management of the company's credit accounts, then the company is wasting its money on me—and I'm sitting here spinning my wheels."

Bill nodded.

"We'll work it out, Fred."

It is obvious that Fred Fuller must have the support and the authority to do his job. The question that immediately arises is how far down the road toward financial gridlock has Celebrity Games gone? If there is full-and-accurate disclosure regarding the state of the company's receivables, will the SEC approve a public offering? If there is no approval for a public offering, how long can Celebrity Games continue the charade of a strong and a healthy growth pattern when it is based upon sales to customers who provide receivables of limited liquidity? And how long can Fred Fuller accept a situation in which solid principles of credit management are questioned, or even unacceptable, to the very executives who should be most responsive to his recommendations?

Unless Celebrity Games, Inc. reverses its philosophy suddenly and dramatically, it is inevitable that the company will peak quickly, then slide into a pattern of declining sales and increasingly strong pressure from creditors. There will be an increase in past-due balances, a continuing decrease in the liquidity of accounts receivable, and the inevitability of a Chapter 11, a buy-out of a badly faltering company—and the potential for substantial investor losses. Too bad.

Entrepreneurs should be rewarded for their willingness to take risks, but creditors and investors should not be put in the position of losing their money because owners and venture capitalists are unwilling to shackle greed and build instead a company based on sound business principles, not excluding personal and corporate integrity. In situations of this type, the credit manager is destined to be ineffective; a helpless pawn in a game that is driven by a syndrome of questionable personal and corporate ethics. Fortunately, the majority of entrepreneurs, managers, and corporate CEOs are working to build their companies, not to put them on the road to self-destruction. In that conventional environment, the credit manager (small business, entrepreneur, large company) can make strong and meaningful contributions to the success of the business or company.

Scripted Telephone Collection Calls

The following scripted telephone calls have been segregated into three categories: Reminder, Follow-up, and Precollection Assignment. Each call is structured to stand alone or to be combined with one of the collection letters in Chaps. 6 through 10. Unless an account balance is paid within a few days of a reminder telephone call, you will want to put together a *mix and match* package that includes all of the in-house collection tools available to you.

Reminder Calls

Telephone Call 1: The Carpenter Company is a good, well-established company and a long-time customer of Lindquist Products, Inc. Occasionally, however, Carpenter's payables people fail to pay balances within terms or as close to terms as they usually do. When that occurs, Cliff Weston, Credit Manager for Lindquist Products, gets on the phone to The Carpenter Company.

Operator: This is The Carpenter Company. May I help you?

Weston: This is Cliff Weston, Credit Manager at Lindquist Products. I'd like to speak to Susan Foxworth in Accounts Payable, please.

Operator: I'll ring her extension for you, Mr. Weston.

Weston: Thank you, operator.

The operator connects Weston with Susan Foxworth.

Foxworth: This is Susan Foxworth.

Weston: Cliff Weston at Lindquist Products, Susan.

Foxworth: Oh, don't tell me! Didn't we put your check in the mail?

Weston: I'm afraid not, Susan—or if you did, we haven't seen it.

Foxworth: Hold on a minute, Cliff. Let me take a look at the check run we did the day before yesterday.

Weston: Thanks, Susan.

Susan is back on the phone in a couple of minutes.

Foxworth: I'm sorry, Cliff. We didn't get you on the run we did Tuesday (the call is being made on Thursday), but we do have you on the list for tomorrow's check run.

Weston: That's great. Does that mean the check will be mailed tomorrow or the fore part of next week?

Foxworth: What we run tomorrow, we mail tomorrow.

Weston: That takes care of it. Thanks again, Susan.

Foxworth: You're welcome, Cliff.

Telephone Call 2: For this call, let us assume that The Carpenter Company does not pay as close to terms as was stated in Call 1. For this reminder call, the script calls for a payment performance that is rarely closer to terms than 15 to 20 days past due, and occasionally the account is slow to 30 and 35 days past due. Cliff Weston calls Susan Foxworth (Accounts Payable person who handles the Lindquist Products account) almost every month, and frequently twice before the check is mailed.

Operator: This is The Carpenter Company. May I help you?

Weston: This is Cliff Weston, Credit Manager at Lindquist Products. I'd like to speak to Susan Foxworth in Accounts Payable, please.

Operator: Certainly, Mr. Weston. I'll ring her extension for you.

Weston: Thanks, operator.

Seconds later, Susan Foxworth is on the phone.

Foxworth: Accounts Payable—Susan Foxworth speaking.

Weston: This is Cliff Weston, Susan. Our aging sheet tells me that Lindquist Products needs a check for $_____ to clear three invoices past due 15 to 20 days.

Foxworth: I know we didn't process anything for you this week, Cliff. I feel quite sure we can cut a check for you about this time next week (call is being made on a Thursday).

Weston: I'm surprised you didn't get something to us this week; as a minimum, payment for the oldest of the three invoices.

Foxworth: Cashflow was tight this week—*very* tight. The best I could do was to send some money to our three major suppliers.

Weston: But you think you have some good money coming in the fore part of next week?

Foxworth: That's what I'm told. If it doesn't come in, Accounts Payable is going to have to put on some extra telephone operators to handle the complaints!

Weston: Alright, Susan. I'll call next Thursday to be sure we're on the list of companies that are getting a check.

Foxworth: Unless something really unexpected happens, your check should be mailed next Friday.

Weston: Thanks, Susan. I know you're doing the best you can for us.

Foxworth: No problem, Cliff. We have copies of the three invoices. If we get the money, we'll pay them.

Weston: Good. I'll talk with you later.

Foxworth: I hope I'll have good news for you.

The first (or reminder) collection call could be the first you have ever made to a company, or it could be another in a parade of tiresome monthly episodes with a specific account or accounts. When a customer's cashflow begins to become restricted, and regardless of whether it is projected to be a short- or a long-term situation, the relationship must inevitably experience an increasing amount of strain. Calls that might have been routine reminders in preceding months may begin to suffer a tone and an attitude that ranges between defensive and belligerent. Few people like to be reminded that they owe money; nobody likes to be reminded of it when there isn't enough money coming in to properly service the company's monthly debt.

What, for an indefinite period of time may have been a cordial, open relationship, may suddenly become a much less congenial and/or cooperative relationship. There are one- and two-word responses to questions that call for a more helpful and a more definitive response.

If the accounts payable person has been instructed to release nothing unless it has been cleared by the controller or finance director, then your access to what is going on in The Carpenter Company, for example, and access to projected timeframe for improved cashflow becomes blocked.

Telephone Call 3: The background for this call involves the same two companies but in this scenario, The Carpenter Company has (1) a different payables person handling the Lindquist Products account, and (2) The Carpenter Company's payment record with Lindquist has, over the past six or eight months, deteriorated at an alarming rate. Efforts by Cliff Weston to get ongoing information from The Carpenter Company have become more and more difficult with most of the information coming from other suppliers (their account experience and what their sales/marketing people are picking up) and from credit reporting agencies such as Dun & Bradstreet and National Association of Credit Management. Lindquist's own people have been contributing any information they pick up from the field but there is not enough for a meaningful evaluation of Carpenter's internal and external problems.

Operator: This is The Carpenter Company. May I help you?

Weston: Cliff Weston, Credit Manager at Lindquist Products. I'd like to speak with Susan Foxworth in Accounts Payable.

Operator: I'm sorry, Mr. Weston. Susan has transferred to another department.

Weston: She has? Can you connect me with the person who has taken her place?

Operator: Let me check for you.

After a wait of three or four minutes ...

Courtney: This is Ann Courtney. Can I help you?

Weston: Ms. Courtney, this is Cliff Weston, Credit Manager at Lindquist Products. Have you been assigned payment responsibility for the accounts that were Susan Foxworth's?

Courtney: That's right.

Weston: I don't know how familiar you are with our account, but payments have slowed over the past few months to the point where it has been taking two or three telephone calls for us to get our money.

Courtney: I haven't been here long enough to know how long it takes to release some checks.

Weston: I understand. I do hear, however, that your controller holds checks until suppliers are about to cut you off.

Courtney: I can't answer that but it does seem that our suppliers are being paid a lot slower than they were six or eight months ago.

Weston: I'm calling about a check for two invoices—$__ to be exact—that are almost 40 days past due. Can you tell me if the check was cut this week, if it was released, and if not, when?

Courtney: I think it was on the check run we did three days ago. Let me try to find out what happened to it.

Weston: Thank you.

Ann Courtney is gone four or five minutes.

Courtney: Mr. Weston?

Weston: Yes?

Courtney: The check was cut but the controller is still holding it. I called his office but they couldn't give me a release date.

Weston: Thanks, Ann. Can you have the operator transfer me to Bill Warburton's office?

Courtney: That's our controller's office.

Weston: I know. Mr. Warburton and I have been through this sort of thing before.

Courtney: Hold on. I'll have the operator transfer you.

Weston: Thanks, Ann.

Telephone Call 4:   We pause only long enough for me to break the continuity between Call 3 and Call 4. This call—to Controller Bill Warburton—could be to the Vice President-Finance, the sole proprietor, one of two partners, or to any one in the business or corporation who has control over the release of payments to suppliers of services, products, or materials. If you have a good relationship with someone at the corporate officer level, don't abuse it. But don't fail to use it when it appears that all other avenues are closed or posted with signs indicating a detour or a lengthy delay.

Warton: Bill Warburton here.

Weston: Cliff Weston, Credit Manager at Lindquist Products.

Warton: Oh, yes. What can I do for you, Cliff?

Weston: You're holding a $_____ check for two invoices that are 40 days past due. That check represents the difference between your company's orders being held and a limited amount of product(s) released on open-account terms.

Warton: I know there is a past-due problem but I don't think I can release your check until the latter part of next week. Cashflow has been so slow that ...

Weston: Tell me something new, Bill. It has been getting slow for the past several months, but that is your problem. Your company needs our products to stay alive. We have four in-house orders right now but until the past-due aging is down to a maximum of 15 days—not one day more—the two smallest of the four orders are the only ones that I'll release.

Warton: You're playing hardball, aren't you? We need your products for current and future jobs!

Weston: I know you do. I know also that we are not being paid for our products in proportion to the amount of money your customers have been paying you for them.

Warton: Well, we've had to spread the money around. Our internally generated cashflow isn't coming in fast enough to meet our monthly requirement, and the bank line doesn't give us enough help to pick up the slack.

Weston: If other suppliers are willing to go along with past-due balances that are out of line, that's their problem. From this point forward, Bill, I expect that our account will never exceed 15 days past due.

Warton: And if it goes beyond 15 days?

Weston: I'll hold all shipments until none of our money is over 10 days past due. We are not one of your two or three major suppliers but we are your key supplier. You must have our products and the only way we can see that you have them as you need them is if your company maintains account aging within the parameters of current to 10 or 15 days past due. Do we have an understanding on this?

Warton: You don't leave me a choice.

Weston: That's right. I don't leave you a choice because for both of us, I don't want it to be the wrong one. You will release the check for $_____ today?

Warton: I'll try to get it out.

Weston: Today, Bill. Nothing moves out of our warehouse until we receive the check. Other checks should follow promptly to reduce past-due balances to a maximum of 15 days. When that happens, we can release some more product(s) on open account.

Warton: Alright. I'll release the $_____ check today. I'll have Ann Courtney pull the invoices that are past due 15 days and over and get them ready for the next check run.

Weston: I appreciate your cooperation. I'll be monitoring the account myself so expect to hear from me if there is a payment problem.

Warton: I'll do what I can to steer us away from a more serious problem.

Weston: Good. Thanks again, Bill.

Warton: Goodbye, Cliff.

Telephone Call 5. This is a *first ever* reminder call from Lindquist Products' Credit Manager, Cliff Weston, to the relatively new account (four months) of George Parnell Associates. Parnell Associates has been in business for six months and Weston is noting signs that the account has gone from "within terms" to an average of "10 to 15 days past due" with all of its suppliers. Because the company is too new to have established a trend, it is not possible for Weston to know whether what has been happening is just a momentary hesitation before the firm moves on to the next growth plateau, or whether the increase in the number of past-due days is indicative of a major problem in its earliest stage.

Operator: George Parnell Associates.

Weston: Cliff Weston, Credit Manager, Lindquist Products. I'd like to speak with someone in Accounts Payable, please.

Operator: I'll transfer you to payables.

Weston: Thank you.

Barnes: Accounts Payable. Janet Barnes speaking.

Weston: I'm Cliff Weston, Ms. Barnes, Credit Manager for Lindquist Products. Do you handle the payments for our account?

Barnes: Yes, I do.

Weston: For the first time since your company became one of our customers, we have a balance that's 10 days past due. Could you tell me if the check has been processed, released, or is about to be processed?

Barnes: Good timing, Mr. Weston.

Weston: Oh?

Barnes: I was just starting to prepare a list of items for tomorrow's check run.

Weston: And we're on the list?

Barnes: That's right. The check total will be $_____.

Weston: That's the amount I'm looking for. If the data is input tomorrow, when will you be doing the check run—and when will the check be released?

Barnes: Checks will be run tomorrow, verified tomorrow, and released the day after tomorrow.

Weston: Great. Thanks for the information, Janet.

Barnes: You're very welcome.

Another version—although it uses the same basic set of facts as those in Call 5—changes one major premise. In Call 6, Parnell Associates has been a customer of Lindquist Products for approximately two years (not the 4 months cited in the background to Call 5), and Cliff has called accounts payable two or three times.

Telephone Call 6:   The operator identifies the Parnell Company. Cliff Weston identifies himself and his company, then he asks to be transferred to Accounts Payable. The call is transferred.

Barnes: Accounts Payable. This is Janet Barnes.

Weston: Janet, this is Cliff Weston, Credit Manager at Lindquist Products.

Barnes: Yes, Mr. Weston. I haven't talked to you in a long time.

Weston: That speaks well for the job you've been doing on our account, Janet.

Barnes: Thank you. But this call must mean that we've missed something.

Weston: Yes, but it certainly isn't serious. Payment for last month's invoices is 10 to 15 days past due and because your company almost always pays within terms, I thought an invoice or two might have gone astray.

Barnes: Let me see what we show as unpaid invoices.

Weston: Thanks.

Barnes: (Comes back on the phone) You're right. We show three past-due invoices that total $_____. I'm looking at yesterday's check run and they were not on it.

Weston: When is your next check run, Janet?

Barnes: We'll have one on Thursday: the day after tomorrow.

Weston: Can you get our three invoices on that run?

Barnes: Absolutely. I'm sorry about this. I don't have an explanation for how I overlooked these invoices.

Weston: No problem, Janet. If all of our customers paid as close to terms as these invoices are, my job would be a walk in the park.

Barnes: I'm glad. You can count on a check for $____ going out on Friday of this week.

Weston: I appreciate it, Janet.

Barnes: You're welcome.

Follow-Up Calls

The second series of collection calls is a follow-up to what was said and/or agreed during the first (or reminder) call. If the person to whom you (Cliff Weston) talked during Call 1 has followed up on what he or she agreed to do, then there might be no second telephone call, unless the call is to acknowledge receipt of a check and to thank the person for putting it in the mail as promised. No check has been received and there has been no telephone call to explain why? If the receivables balance was past due when you made the first call, it is now several additional days past due, and that is all the motivation you should need to make that second collection telephone call.

Telephone Call 1 (of second series of calls):   This is a follow-up to Call 1 (the reminder series). The premise of Call 1 depicted The Carpenter Company as a well-established, long-time customer of Lindquist Products. Although Carpenter usually pays within terms, there is an occasional lapse of a few days. Your stand-in (Cliff Weston) talked with Susan Foxworth and Susan promised that the check would be mailed the day after Cliff's call. Did she mail the check? She did, and Cliff is calling to thank her.

Operator: The Carpenter Company.

Weston: Cliff Weston, Credit Manager for Lindquist Products. Susan Foxworth in Accounts Payable, please.

Operator: I'll connect you, Mr. Weston.

Weston: Thanks, operator.

The transfer takes no more than a few seconds.

Foxworth: Accounts Payable. Susan Foxworth speaking.

Weston: Susan, this is Cliff Weston at Lindquist Products.

Foxworth: Yes, Cliff, (Her laugh is mixed with surprise.) The check is not only in the mail, you should have it by now!

Weston: That's right—we have it. I just called to thank you for getting it to us so fast.

Foxworth: I told you I would.

Weston: I know, and I appreciate the fact that you are a woman whose promise is as good as a done deed.

Foxworth: Well, thank you. Anything else?

Weston: That's it.

Foxworth: I really appreciate the call, Cliff.

Weston: You're welcome. I wish I could make more of these calls to more of our customers but ....

Foxworth: I know. I'm sure our credit people have the same problem with some of our customers.

Weston: It's really a shame and it doesn't build much of a relationship. Oh, well. Talk with you again, Susan.

Foxworth: Goodbye, Cliff.

Call 2 (of second series of calls): The payment pattern of The Carpenter Company was changed for Call 2 (the reminder series) to a fairly constant past due of 15 to 20 days with balances occasionally going to 30 and 35 days. Cliff Weston's conversation with Susan Foxworth had involved some persuasion before she committed tentatively to mailing a check on the Friday following their telephone conversation. Why "tentatively"? Because the release of the check to Lindquist Products would depend upon some checks that The Carpenter Company was expecting from its customers.

Did the check arrive from The Carpenter Company? It did not, but Susan Foxworth called Cliff Weston on Friday—the day she had hoped to release the check.

Weston: Cliff Weston.

Foxworth: Cliff, this is Susan Foxworth in Accounts Payable at The Carpenter Company.

Weston: Yes, Susan. What's going on?

Foxworth: Not as much as I had hoped for when we talked last week.

Weston: You didn't get the checks you were expecting?

Foxworth: No, and that means I won't be able to release your check today. However, our credit department is picking up a big check from one of our past-due customers this coming Monday, so I should be able to release your check on Tuesday.

Weston: I can live with that, and I appreciate the call. Not too many people realize what a difference something like your call can make in a relationship between two companies.

Foxworth: I wanted you to know why the check won't be mailed today, and to know also that it will go out on Tuesday.

Weston: I'll be looking for it. Thanks, Susan.

Foxworth: You're welcome, Cliff.

Telephone Call 3 (of second series of calls):   This call assumed that cashflow has continued to deteriorate, that there is another accounts payable person handling the Lindquist Products account, and that there is some apprehension throughout the ranks of The Carpenter Company's suppliers regarding the increasing slowness of accounts payments.

The gist of Call 3 (the reminder series) was that Ann Courtney did not have the authority to release the Lindquist Products check. All check releases, Cliff was told, are coming from Controller Bill Warburton's office—and it is to Controller Warburton's office that Cliff has Ann Courtney transfer his call.

Call 4 (the reminder series) developed into a force play with Cliff Weston telling Bill Warburton that no product(s) would move from Lindquist's warehouse until the check for $_____ was in Cliff's hands. Warton agreed to release the subject check and at Cliff's insistence, agreed also to reduce other past-due balances to a maximum of 15 days past due. Did Warburton release the $_____ check? He did. Did he release another check during the following week to bring aging within the "maximum of 15 days past due" that Cliff had imposed during their telephone conversation? He had not, although Warburton had tried to reach Weston when Cliff was out of town for the day.

Telephone Call 4 (of second series of calls):   Cliff is back in the office the day after Warton tried to reach him. He returns Bill Warburton's call.

Operator: The Carpenter Company.

Weston: Cliff Weston at Lindquist Products. I'm returning Bill Warburton's call.

Operator: I'll connect you, Mr. Weston.

Weston: Thank you, operator.

Several seconds later ...

Warburton: This is Bill Warburton.

Weston: Cliff Weston, Bill. You tried to reach me yesterday.

Warburton: Yes, Cliff, I did. I need to talk to you about the 15 day maximum on past-due invoices—and the hold you have on our orders.

Weston: We discussed this at length the other day, Bill, and you agreed that you could reduce past-due aging to 15 days, right?

Warburton: That's right, but cashflow isn't cooperating. We're having a devil of a time collecting money from two of our biggest customers and I'm not sure we're going to see a rapid improvement in their pattern of payments.

Weston: You're not just blowing smoke, are you? We're talking about a cash crunch that has the potential to be survival-threatening.

Warburton: I don't know if I'd characterize it as survival-threatening—at least not yet—but if it continues, we'll have a major problem.

Weston: You need our products and we need a reasonable flow of money. Somewhere in here we have to come up with a payment program that your company can live up to and a program that will enable my company to release enough product(s) to satisfy the ongoing needs of your customers.

Warburton: I'm willing to do as much for your company as our cashflow will allow.

Weston: We're currently holding Carpenter Company orders in the total amount of $_____, but I'm sure not every order is a priority one.

Warburton: That's right. Sales tells me that two of the purchase orders—number _____ and _____ totaling $_____—are needed now. The other three are either to rebuild our stock of certain items or are for a specific job and won't be needed for four to six weeks.

Weston: Can you handle a $2 payment for every $1 of product that we release?

Warburton: I can't give up that much cash to one company, Cliff.

Weston: I understand, but under the present circumstances of your company's past-due balance and its deteriorating cashflow, the best I can do is $2 worth of product for every $3 payment.

Warburton: I should be able to handle those figures.

Weston: Purchase orders 388 and 416 total $15,682. Can you send me a check today or tomorrow for $23,523 ($3 in cash for every $2 worth of product(s) released)?

Warburton: We need the products on those two P.O.s. Yes, I can send you a check today.

Weston: For $23,523?

Warburton: That's right.

Weston: Excellent. We've got a deal, Bill. The products on P.O.s 388 and 416 will be shipped the day we receive The Carpenter Company's check for $23,523.

Warburton: Good! Our sales people will be pleased.

Weston: About the other three P.O.s and any others that come in from today forward: the arrangement is $3 cash for $2 of product. You or your people can designate which P.O.—or combination of P.O.s—you want us to release.

Warburton: To minimize the number of calls to your office, I'll have that information routed through my office.

Weston: I appreciate it. So you'll get a check for the $23,523 on its way today or tomorrow?

Warburton: You'll have it in two days—three at the latest.

Weston: I'll be staying in touch, Bill.

Warburton: Fine—and thanks for your help.

Call 5 (in the reminder series) changed the name of the customer/debtor to George Parnell Associates, a relatively new account to which Cliff Weston was about to make his first-ever reminder call. The four-month relationship with

Parnell Associates had gone from an initial "within terms" payment relationship to one that had deteriorated rapidly into an average of 10 to 15 days past due. Other suppliers reported the same experience, or worse.

Telephone Call 5 (of second series of calls): Janet Baines, in Parnell Associates Accounts Payable section, had told Cliff in Call 5 of the reminder series that a check would be cut the day after his call and mailed the day following. Did the check arrive? It did not. Three days past the projected arrival date, Cliff is on the telephone to Janet Baines.

Operator: George Parnell Associates.

Weston: Cliff Weston with Lindquist Products. Janet Baines in Accounts Payable, please.

Operator: I'm sorry, Mr. Weston. Janet Baines has left the company.

Weston: Really? Can you connect me with the person who took her place in the department?

Operator: That would be Ms. Egan—Patricia Egan. I'll connect you, Mr. Weston.

Weston: Thank you.

A few seconds later …

Egan: Accounts Payable. This is Patricia Egan.

Weston: Cliff Weston, Ms. Egan. I'm Lindquist Products' Credit Manager.

Egan: Yes, Mr. Weston. I've seen your account on our list of payables items.

Weston: That's encouraging. Actually, I'm not looking so much for encouragement as I am for a check—a check for $_____ that Janet Baines was going to mail two days after I talked with her on [date]. Can you tell me if the check has been mailed, and if not, what is the release date?

Egan: It's no secret. Our cashflow has been so slow recently that some checks are being held that were cut six or seven days ago.

Weston: The check for Lindquist Products should have been cut five days ago. Is it among the items being held?

Egan: I have the list right here and—yes—it is being held. Oh, good news! Yours is one of the checks I've been given permission to release this week.

Weston: We're already looking at several days past the date it was promised. Do you think you can release it tomorrow for us?

Egan: Yes, I can do that. Yours was promised before some of the others so it's only fair that it should be released as early as possible.

Weston: I appreciate it—may I call you Patricia?

Egan: Please do.

Weston: And I don't answer to Mr. Weston, so please call me Cliff.

Egan: Cliff it is.

Weston: Thanks again, Patricia.

Egan: It will go out tomorrow, Mr.—uh—Cliff.

Almost any well-coordinated collection program will intermingle letters with telephone calls. The sequence is a matter of choice. There is no right or wrong way to do it but a carefully thought-out mix of the collection tools available to you—or a mix that might have been selected for a specific account or type of account—is generally the most effective way to handle the problem of collecting past-due balances.

Precollection Assignment

This chapter has offered examples of Reminder Calls and Follow-Up Calls. From the broad spectrum of letters in this book, you will have selected and used a letter between the reminder call and the follow-up call, between the follow-up call and a third (precollection) call, or perhaps two letters following the reminder and follow-up calls. The effectiveness of *mix and match*, which also includes fax messages and visits to the customer/debtor's place of business, is a variable that should be used from one collection challenge to the next. When one tactic or procedure is not getting the job done, be innovative; emphasize one or more of the other tools in your kit of collection aids.

The category of the Precollection Call may be the one that tells your customer/debtor that his or her company is about to be turned over to a collection agency. It is near the end of the in-house collection procedure. Your company cannot afford to have its credit department spending disproportionate amounts of time trying to collect from one, two, or a few past-due accounts at the expense of an appropriate level of attention to other accounts whose balances might be sliding into a new and deeper area of past due. Do not concentrate your collection effort on one or two accounts; spread it over the entire spectrum of your accounts receivable aged trial balance report (your receivables aging report).

The third series of collection calls is the final act—or part of the final act—in the sequence of an in-house collection effort. I suggest that it might be part of the final act in that a third collection, or precollection, call to a customer/debtor could be followed immediately by a letter making a final demand, which might recap what was said in the telephone call. It will also make the point—in writing—that the account will be assigned to a third-party collection agency if the required payment is not received by a specific date. Final demand, the final third collection call and/or the collection letter that follows it, must be structured to do the job.

What is said in a precollection telephone call—a part of a collection effort that may have included one or two collection letters in lieu of one or two telephone calls—is another key to a successful collection effort. What can be said by the creditor company at such a late date in the collection effort that might motivate the debtor company to pay? What can be said when *payment resolve* may have produced one or two partial payments, a payment that was insignificant and/or insulting, or no payment at all? There is always the possibility that a debtor company might try to stave off the stigma of a collection assignment to prevent other creditors from coming down harder than they have been, and possibly forcing the customer-debtor to move one or two steps closer to a voluntary filing for protection under the bankruptcy code. Even worse is the possibility that creditors might move to put the customer/debtor in a position of involuntary bankruptcy (see more on bankruptcy in Chap. 14).

Excerpts from the third series of collection calls categorized earlier as precollection assignment:

Weston: As a courtesy to your company, I've allowed this collection procedure to drag on much longer than was necessary. Now there is no more time. A check for $_____ must arrive at my company by [date] or the account will be assigned to a collection agency (Dun & Bradstreet, National Association of Credit Management, etc.).

Debtor: If you do that, it will be on reports prepared by credit reporting agencies and our other suppliers will increase their pressure.

Weston: That's your problem. I've given you plenty of time and opportunities to take care of our account. This is it. A check for $_____ in this office by [date] or your problem magnifies.

Debtor: You couldn't give me another ten days?

Weston: No.

Debtor: Well—I'll see what I can do.

Weston: It's your choice. No check by [date] and the account will go the following day to either D & B's collection service or NACM's collection division.

or

The debtor has promised payment twice during the preceding 15 days and both times there was no check and no call to offer an explanation. This is not the quality of attitude that encourages a supplier/creditor to make a lot of concessions to a customer/debtor.

The debtor has just told Weston that he did not mail the promised check.

Weston: I know you didn't send it. If you had, I wouldn't be sitting here expressing my frustration because there was no check and no telephone call to explain why you failed to send it. Understand me: I much prefer a check that has been promised—especially when it has been promised twice—but my patience gets very short when the check doesn't arrive and there is no attempt to explain why it wasn't mailed.

Debtor: I know, but when we didn't get enough money to release your check by the date I promised, I didn't call because I thought it might come in the next day, or the day after that. Unfortunately, it's five days past the day I was supposed to release the check and the money to cover it still isn't here.

Weston: Are you waiting for one check or a combination of several smaller ones?

Debtor: We've got one major account that is sending us a check for $_____ to cover invoices 30 to 50 days past due.

Weston: If the account is that many days past due, what makes you think they're about to release the $_____ check?

Debtor: Because I'm giving them the same level of pressure that you're giving me! I've told the customer that we either have the check in our hands by Thursday (it is Monday) or Friday morning I'm assigning the account to a collection agency.

Weston: It sounds like you're making the moves that the situation is forcing you to make. I called to tell you that if I don't have the check for $_____ by [date] the account will go to our collection service. But because of what you've just told me, I'll delay the collection assignment until noon Friday.

Debtor: That's a big help, Cliff.

Weston: Remember. If you don't call Friday to tell me that the check will be released that day, I'll assign the account to the collection service without any more conversation.

Debtor: Our customer has promised that we'll have the payment by Thursday. As soon as it comes in I'll call you—and if it doesn't come in, I'll call you.

Weston: Alright. I'll expect your call Friday.

Special Telephone Calls

The following example is the only one that I shall personalize. I developed this relationship while I was a corporate Credit Manager in the floor-covering industry and it spanned the 14 years I was in that industry. It is an excellent example of rapport at its finest between a corporate Credit Manager (myself) and an owner whose integrity was as sustaining to me as my willingness to work with him was for his company—and for him. Remember that strong customer relationships can enable you to deal with potential problems before they have a chance to move beyond the embryo stage. Develop good relationships with key people in your customer companies. Many relationships will be confined to telephone conversations or an occasional meeting at an industry function. Others will involve a lunch now and then, not only because you have business to discuss but because there is genuine pleasure in getting together. It couldn't be better for you or your company!

The Telephone Call

I received a telephone call from the president and owner of a 26-year-old firm (floor covering contractor and retailer) with whom my company had done an ever-increasing level of business. At this point in the relationship, our annual sales to this company are about $450,000. The conversation is as follows:

"This is Cecil Bond."

"Cec, this is Harvey Shaw. How are you?"

The call came in on my direct outside line. Harvey usually does not use that line.

"I'm fine, Harvey. This call is a surprise. What's doing?"

"I've got a problem, Cec, and it could be a big one."

"Oh? What is it?"

"One of my major customers has filed a Chapter 11 and I don't think they can come up with a reorganization plan that the creditors will buy."

"Are you secured, Harvey?" (referring to accounts receivable balances protected by a Uniform Commercial Code filing).

"Probably 40 percent of our account is in with the general creditors. I've done business with these people for 16 years. I never thought their account would be a problem."

"If you think that highly of them, probably most of their other creditors do too. It's possible you can work out a plan that's acceptable to them."

"I suppose there's a chance. Meanwhile, we won't be getting the $82,000 check that they were going to mail this week. The absence of that check puts our cashflow in a real vise."

"What about scaling back your payments to suppliers? Tell the others what you've just told me. Tell them you'll prorate payments on a percentage basis for two or three months, then you'll increase the payment amounts until you're back on a normal payment schedule."

"That schedule would give us some breathing room."

"What do you think, Harvey? Can you work your way out of the cash bind in four to six months?"

"Oh, sure. The account is a major one but we're in good long-term shape. We can close the gap within six months and move forward."

"Good. Harvey, use my name and our conversation if it'll help you with some of your other suppliers. If anybody hesitates, have them give me a call."

"I appreciate it, Cec. Are you going to be in the area later this month?"

"Yes, I think I'll be down there—here it is—on the 24th, 25th, and 26th."

"Pick a day and let me buy lunch."

"You're on. What about the 26th? I'll confirm with your office when I get in on the 24th."

"Great! See you on the 26th—and thanks again, Cec."

"No problem, Harvey."

There is one priceless ingredient in a genuinely strong customer relationship—a relationship in which the years of your association with an owner or a partner give you total confidence in the personal and business integrity of that person. Do your best to generate those same feelings of confidence and integrity in others by your actions and deeds. A relationship of that quality can return business and personal dividends beyond any expectations.

Not every collection call will fulfill your expectation of a resolution to the past-due payments problem. Customers exist whose credibility and use of time-buying ploys will test your patience to the maximum. Following a particularly unsatisfactory string of collection calls, you might lean toward the thought that your customer list has too many people who seem to want to trash the supplier-customer relationship. You will move that thought out of your mind very quickly because the overwhelming majority of your customers, if you selected them wisely, are people of integrity who will give your company the kind of treatment they expect for themselves. It is unpleasant, however, when you start to recap a conversation on your call sheet and find that the customer cast his or her commitment not in stone but in Silly Putty.

You do not want your collection calls to become adversarial. When a customer whose account is totally out of phase with payment terms persists in trying to turn payment problems back onto your prices (too high, not competitive), your products (inconsistent quality, etc.), or your delivery time ("You don't deliver on time and that costs me money!"), do not say what you are justified in thinking. You must convince problem accounts such as the one just described that credit sales are unacceptable until account balances are close to payment terms, or you should put some constraints on the when and how of product releases. Is the account past due? Really past due? Then don't release any product or perform any services until aging and balances are in line with your company's credit policy. Is the customer unhappy? You have been unhappy with the account's payment performance much longer than the customer has been unhappy. The only thing that should change this relationship is the customer's money: at the time and in the amount requested.

It is frequently necessary to follow one or two collection calls with a letter referencing those calls, including whether or not you were able to get through to the person in authority, summarizing what was discussed if there was a completed call, and noting whether or not there was a payment commitment. This is not generally a point where you would go immediately to a final demand letter; not unless the payment record of the customer is so uneven as to cause concern regarding the prognosis for the firm's survival.

11.1   [date]

Name of Company
Street Address (or P.O. Box Number)
City, State, Zip Code

Attention: [name and title]

Dear Mr./Ms. _____:

Our efforts to contact you by telephone on [date] and [date] were not successful, and there is no record here of a return call from you.

It is imperative that we have your check for $_____ by the [day] of [month]. The relationship between our two companies has deteriorated to the point where we are currently holding orders. I hope that the situation does not worsen to the point where stronger and more formal collection actions become necessary.

Call me when you receive this letter.

Sincerely,

Credit Manager

11.2   [date]

Name of Company
Street Address (or P.O. Box Number)
City, State, Zip Code

Attention: [name and title]

Dear Mr./Ms. _____:

The call sheet for your account indicates that telephone calls to your office on [date] and [date] were not successful in obtaining a payment commitment for past-due balances. Copies of the subject invoices were mailed almost two weeks ago, and there has been no indication that the merchandise failed to arrive on time or in good condition.

Customers are very important people but the continuing success of our company demands a solid reciprocal with our customers: we give you good merchandise and good service at a fair price and we expect payment within (or near) sales terms. Anything less—on your part or ours—erodes the relationship to the point where there no longer is mutual confidence.

Your check for $_____ (Invoices _____ and _____) in our offices by [date] is the confidence builder we need to consider future open-account sales.

Sincerely,

Credit Manager

Date _____

Account No.	Amt. Owing	Current	Past Due 1-30 Days	Past Due 31-60 Days	Past Due 61-90 Days	Past Due Over 90

12

Collection Visits (Scripted)

A collection visit to the place of business of a customer/debtor is not something for which a guideline criteria can be set. It is a discretionary tactic, one that might, under specific sets of circumstances, be used with equal success by the person who handles credit and collection duties for a small company or business and by the credit manager of a large company who is equally anxious to collect his or her proportionately larger past-due balance.

Customers whose past-due account balances have become a collection problem generally do not start out fabricating a story that is based upon half-truths, misleading statements, and clear-cut lies. Any customer base that has more than half a dozen of these types is an example of a new account screening procedure that is not doing the job for which it was intended. I know what you're about to say: Good accounts can deteriorate gradually or they can go bad suddenly—and that is why we constantly monitor our accounts receivable so we can minimize the danger of that sort of thing.

Most customers will attempt to put the best face on their problem(s)—and no one can fault that—but it is the customer who is willing to tell you anything in order to buy time that is your biggest collection problem. It is one thing to have an account that has a problem but it is an entirely new and far more dangerous problem when the customer adds distortion and lies. And how can you believe the word of a man or a woman who may already have run the gamut of excuses for failing to meet payment promises? Your company's money is on the line and you cannot continue to accept excuses and delays when it has become obvious that the customer/debtor has no basis for promises that are made too frequently and too glibly.

When the telephone conversations between yourself and a *no credibility debtor* have reached the point where what you are hearing on the telephone is more of what has been unproductive for some period of time, it is time to consider a collection visit to the customer/debtor. But first there are factors to be considered before you rush to prepare for the visit.

1. What is the amount of the past-due receivable?

2. Is the amount of the past-due balance large enough to warrant a special trip (if out of your city or area) to collect it?

3. If the collection visit cannot be tied to other business in the customer/debtor's area, review question 2.

4. How long will you have to be away from your company's office?

5. If the customer/debtor is in another city, state, or region, is the combination of time and travel expenses justified by the amount of the past-due receivable?

6. The element of surprise is good but you do not want to travel half-way across the country to find that the person you want to see is (a) away on business, (b) on vacation, (c) heard you were coming and left instructions that you were to be given excuses (a) or (b).

The size of your company and the size of the credit and collection department will be a major factor in determining when you can use this tactic to pressure a customer/debtor. If your company has not moved deeply enough into the modern era to realize that credit managers—even the best ones—are usually only as effective as the options available to them, then the constraints imposed by such an archaic attitude will adversely impact results. Suppose the credit manager has no other reason to travel half-way across the country than to drop in on a customer who owes the company a bundle of money? Why should the credit manager need another reason? Before the account is assigned to a collection agency, and before the agency goes to work on what should be a collection fee ranging from 20 percent to 40 percent of the assigned total, isn't it worth one more try—a collection visit to the customer/debtor's place of business before the account is assigned to a collection service? Of course it is. Those among you who have never used the tactic of a collection visit to the office(s) of the debtor company should try it; select an appropriate problem account, get the necessary travel and expense authorization (if your credit department budget does not include money for that type of activity), and accomplish a double positive—collect the past-due balance and save the fee that would have been paid to the collection service if you had assigned the account.

Scripted Visit–Examples

The collection of scripted visits that follows offers a variety of company situations, past-due situations, and characters. What these scripted visits do not pretend to do is to offer the reader something that should be taken from these pages and used verbatim. It is not necessary, however, for the credit person to change the format of these scripted visits when care has been taken to select one that is appropriate to the circumstances of the supplier-customer situation. When the proper format has been selected for the visit, the way to make it effective is to personalize the script so that it fits all areas and nuances of the specific collection problem.

Let me again remind you that this is guideline material only. You should try to impart your individual flavor to all facets of the collection procedure; and a personal collection visit to the office of a customer/debtor is about as personal as a collection effort can get. Language that is used in the examples may not be appropriate for your personal speech pattern or be compatible with the dialect of your particular area or region. The format (or structure) of these visits can be used almost without change(s); it is how you change the process of *fleshing out* these formats to accommodate your thoughts, speech, and the requirements of your company that translates into the level of success you will attain when you use them.

Collection Visit 1

Your company is less than five years old and although annual growth has been consistent (it has been keeping pace with projections in the business plan), cash-flow has not reached the point where it is not necessary to support internally generated cashflow with funds borrowed from the bank. The company is making good progress but growth is costly, and in that situation, cashflow lags consistently behind.

One major customer has allowed balances to become 10 to 25 days past due from day one of the supplier-customer relationship. (Is that a factual statement? It is not. As the person in charge of collecting accounts receivable, it is *you* who has allowed the customer to get away with this abuse of the company's credit policy.) Now, however, the abuse has grown and past-due aging has increased to 30 to 40 days, the customer does not fulfill payment commitments, letters and telephone calls are often disregarded, and there is concern in the trade that this two-year-old company may be slipping into serious financial trouble.

You decide that this account fits the criteria (amount of money owing to your company, age of the past-due balance, distance from your office, trip expenses, and time away from your office) for a collection visit. Without indicating to the finance director's secretary, controller, or payables supervisor that you intend to visit the company, you are able to verify that the person you want to see will be in the office the following day.

The following day you drive the 110 miles to the offices of the customer/debtor. As you, Frances Walsh, walk into the reception area of the small office building, the receptionist looks up from her desk.

Receptionist: May I help you?

Walsh: Yes. I'm Frances Walsh, Credit Manager for the Beardsley-Hines Company. I'd like to see the Finance Director, David Barton.

Receptionist: Do you have an appointment, Ms. Walsh?

Walsh: No, but I'm sure he will recognize the name of my company if he doesn't recognize mine.

Receptionist: Let me ring his office for you.

Walsh: Thank you.

After three or four minutes, Barton appears.

Barton: I'm David Barton.

Walsh: Frances Walsh, Mr. Barton. I'm the Credit Manager for Beardsley-Hines Company.

Barton: Yes, Ms. Walsh. Your company isn't one of our major suppliers but it certainly is a key supplier.

Walsh: That's what our Sales Manager has been telling me, Mr. Barton. I guess we might say that on the basis of our importance to your company and to your customers a prolonged period without our products would be more than a minor inconvenience.

Barton: I don't think I follow you, Ms. Walsh.

Walsh: I think you do, Mr. Barton. I'm talking about a prolonged period of time during which my company holds orders—plus the possibility that we'll pull the product line from your company if we don't have your check for $_____ by [date].

Barton: Is our past-due balance that high?

Walsh: It's that high and far too many days past due, Mr. Barton.

Barton: We need your company's products, Ms. Walsh. I could probably get $_ _____ (approx. half of amount requested by Walsh) together by [above date] but I couldn't do any better than that. Cashflow has been very slow the past three months and …

Walsh: I'm sure it has been, but that doesn't help our account balance and it is no incentive for us to allow it to continue.

Barton: If you don't sell to us, Ms. Walsh, your company is going to lose a lot of customers. Your products sell well in our area and if we don't continue to carry them for you, who will?

Walsh: There are other dealers in and around your area who could satisfy the requirements of your customers in your area—but our goal isn't to take the line away from your company. Our goal is to eliminate your past-due balance and improve our own cashflow.

Barton: Well, will you settle for $_____ now (half of what Walsh has asked for) and the second $_____ in 45 days?

Walsh: We'll take $_____ now (half of the total past-due balance), $_____ in two weeks (one-fourth of the total), and the final $_____ (one-fourth of the total) 30-days from today. I really can't do any better than that.

Barton: And what about product releases? Will you release the orders that you're holding when you get the check for $_____ (half of the total)?

Walsh: If you get a check for $_____ (half of the total) to me within the next 48 hours, I'll release up to $_____ (half of check total) worth of product. As each of the three checks arrive, I'll release new orders to a total of 50 percent of the amount of each check.

Barton: It's going to be hard on our cashflow. You can't stretch the payments over a period longer than 30 days?

Walsh: I'm sorry, Mr. Barton. When past-due balances reach a point that we consider to be unacceptable, I have to put the interest of my company ahead of any other considerations.

Barton: Alright. I'll mail a check for $_____ (half of the total) tomorrow.

Walsh: And checks for $_____ (each to be one-quarter of the total) 15 and 30 days from today?

Barton: Yes—we'll do that.

Walsh: I appreciate your time and your cooperation, Mr. Barton. Follow through on these payment commitments and we'll take care of our part of the bargain.

Barton: We don't have too much choice. Your products are important to us so we'll do what has to be done.

Walsh: Good. I'll send you a letter tomorrow confirming what we have agreed to do.

Barton: Have a safe trip home.

Walsh: Thank you. Goodbye, Mr. Barton.

Barton: Goodbye, Ms. Walsh.

Gender is interchangeable in virtually every example in this book. Whether you are a man or a woman, the objective is to collect past-due accounts receivable balances for your company. When that is your assigned task—and it should be a key one when you are a member of a credit department or in some other capacity have a collection responsibility—no person should differentiate between a goal (or a standard) set for a man or one set for a woman. The quality of work should be comparable; the results should be comparable; and the pay should be comparable.

Collection Visit 2

The same characters as in Visit 1, but a different direction from the point in Visit 1 where David Barton suggests to Frances Walsh that her company will lose customers if Baron's company loses the Beardsley-Hines line of products.

Walsh: You know our products. There are three or four companies who would do a very good job for us in this area. We haven't given them our products because we wanted to see if your company could give us the type of representation we'd like to have here.

Barton: From my knowledge of our sales totals, we have been doing a very strong job for your company's products.

Walsh: That isn't the problem. You have been using money collected from the sale of our products to take care of other suppliers and expenses. We do not want the money that you owe us for our products to come off of the bottom; we want it to come off of the top.

Barton: Well, sometimes there are account or other financial problems that force us to move our cashflow in a pattern that doesn't please everybody.

Walsh: We aren't concerned about everybody, Mr. Barton. Our primary concern is that the Beardsley-Hines Company gets paid promptly. No more 30 or 40 days past due. We are not bankers and we are not interested in subsidizing any part of your operation with money that should be paid promptly to us.

Barton: You don't mince words, Ms. Walsh.

Walsh: I hope that in a similar situation, you don't either. This is the way our management likes to operate the business, Mr. Barton, and I am here to be sure you understand what we require from your company if it is to continue to represent us in this area.

Barton: You've made your point. It will take a major job of restructuring our payables but I think we can work off the past-due balance over the next three or four months.

Walsh: No, no. The past due balance of $_____ is to be paid in three installments of $_____ each. The first check for $_____ must arrive at my company by [date]; the second check must arrive within 20 days of the first check, and the third check within 20 days of the second.

Barton: That's too much! I can't commit to a schedule that gives me no flexibility.

Walsh: There isn't room for flexibility; you used it all during the past three months. Make the payments on the schedule I've just given to you and we'll release orders for product up to 50 percent of the amount of each check.

Barton: And if we don't meet the payment schedule?

Walsh: I won't have any choice. No product will be released and the account will be assigned to a collection service. Incidentally, that means also that no product would be sold on a COD basis.

Barton: What can I say? We have no choice. We must have your products, so we'll try to give you what you want.

Additional Benefits

Before we move on to Collection Visit 3, it should be noted that there are benefits from a collection visit in addition to a face-to-face meeting with the person who has control over the customer's cashflow. What may be essentially a visit to make the position and the resolve of your company very clear to the customer can also be used as a fact-finding mission. Get the person you are "visiting" to give you a quick tour of the office, warehouse, manufacturing area, etc., or have that person assign another to take you around. Some examples of what you should look for include the following:

1. What is the condition of the warehouse? Is the layout consistent with an efficient operation? Is maintenance appropriate for the type and volume of the operation?

2. Do stock of product(s) (yours and those of other suppliers) seem to be low, adequate, or too high?

3. If stocks of certain products seem too low, make a mental note to contact the Credit Manager at the supplier company for a comment on how the account is handling payments. Also, over the past year, has the volume of shipments declined, remained constant, or grown?

4. Does plant machinery and equipment appear to be maintained properly?

5. Are production lines running at what is said by your guide to be 50, 75, 90, or what percent of capacity? If one or more of the production lines is not operating, and there is no evidence that it has been shut down for repairs or maintenance, try to find out why it is not operating, how long it has not been operating, and when it is expected to be activated.

6. Does the company seem to be changing to an appropriate level of high-tech office, manufacturing, and order processing equipment, as the budget for new and/or improved equipment will allow?

7. Finally, does this look like a company that has peaked, one that is still following a well-controlled pattern of growth, or one that is beginning to falter and lose momentum?

You can take these observations back to your office, integrate and compare them with data from other suppliers and reporting agencies such as D&B or NACM, analyze what should be a rather impressive amount of data from a variety of sources, and arrive at some helpful conclusions regarding the short- and long-term prognosis for this customer/debtor.

Of course there are things you cannot know—things that go on in the board room, in top management meetings, and in the minds of those who make the corporate decisions and chart the corporate course—but you can be as well informed regarding the condition of the customer as it is possible for an outsider to be.

Collection Visit 3

The same characters (Frances Walsh and David Barton) as in Collection Visit 1, but the major change in this visit is in the amount of leverage that Frances Walsh brings to the visit. In Collection Visits 1 and 2, the Beardsley-Hines Company's line of products was a key product line for David Barton's company. She does not have that leverage in Visit 3. The Beardsley-Hines line of products is purchased frequently and is always in stock, but there are competing lines that might be substituted if that source were shut off to David Barton's company.

It is obvious that when the leverage of being a *key supplier* is removed from the scenario, Frances Walsh is not in a position to dictate what David Barton's company must do based upon her company's position as the logical (or sole) source of products offered by Beardsley-Hines. She must now offer more options, be more receptive to a less-rigid payment plan or arrangement, and exhibit much more flexibility in her discussion with David Barton.

Walsh: Are you projecting a near-term improvement in cashflow?

Barton: It should improve somewhat over the next two or three months. Our problem is that growth has been so much more rapid than we had anticipated. We're encountering any number of growth-related expenditures that we didn't expect to see for at least a year, and possibly two.

Walsh: So at this point you aren't projecting much real improvement in your company's pattern of paying its suppliers and other creditors?

Barton: That's right. The best we can do for the foreseeable future is to take care of our major suppliers on an *as close to terms as possible* basis. Suppliers such as your company—people from whom we don't buy in quantity every month—will continue to be paid no closer to terms than 30 to 40 days past due.

Walsh: The payment pattern of your company's account with us is currently 25 to 40 days past due. Is past-due aging going to get worse before it gets better or do you see the company staying within those figures and eventually beginning to move closer to terms?

Barton: I can't make any promises but, realistically, it could get slower before there's improvement.

Walsh: That would make it very, very difficult for us to continue to sell to your company. Anything slower than an occasional 30 to 40 days past due isn't something that we're willing to live with. We have our own cashflow to think about and carrying accounts past terms too far and too long would not work to our advantage.

Barton: Are you saying that we won't be able to buy your products if the aging of our account is consistently 35 or 40 days past due?

Walsh: I'm saying that aging of 35 or 40 days is the absolute maximum, and we really are not eager to lock ourselves into account aging that's so out of phase with our terms. My company's credit policy makes no provision for supplying customers whose accounts are consistently more than 30 days past due—and that is based upon our desire to minimize bank borrowing to supplement our internally generated cashflow.

Barton: I understand the rationale but you people should consider also that we are a company that is growing fast. If you continue to ride with us as we grow, the amount of business we do with Beardsley-Hines will increase proportionately.

Walsh: That might work quite well for some companies but, for mine, it isn't a persuasive argument. My reason for being here is not to talk about future sales but to let you know that we must have a check for $_____ by the [date] (three or four days from this date). Until the check arrives, I can't release either of the two in-house orders or any other order.

Barton: You're holding our orders now?

Walsh: Yes, but it shouldn't come as a surprise.

Barton: Why?

Walsh: In my letter of [date], which was sent to your attention, I stated that no product(s) would be released after [date] unless we received a check for $_____ _____ prior to that date.

Barton: I don't remember seeing the letter.

Walsh: Sorry, but I sent it. If you didn't see it, it has to be a breakdown between your company's mailroom and your office, or within your office. We would like to continue the relationship but we can't do it if the ground rules include something that would impose past-due aging of 30 to 40 days upon us. Once in a while we might live with it; but as a regular pattern—not at all.

Barton: It is not possible for me to get a check for $_____ to your company by [date]. I could come up with one-third or one-half of it but not the total amount.

Walsh: Try this. If you can give us $_____ (one half of the total) by [date stated above], $_____ (one quarter of the total) by [date], and the final $_____ ___ (one quarter of the total) by the _____ of [month], I can O.K. the release of enough of our products to take care of your normal requirements.

Barton: What's the criteria for releasing product?

Walsh: As I receive each of the three checks for past-due balances, I'll release new product to a maximum of 50 percent of the check. Two for one; for every two dollars we receive, we'll ship one dollar's worth of a new order.

Barton: It might work for a while but if we continue to grow as rapidly as we have been, it won't be long before we won't have enough product to supply our customers.

Walsh: Why don't you work on the past-due balance, we'll ship new product as we can, and by the time you've grown to the point where we need to rethink this arrangement, we should come up with something that we both can live with on into the next plateau of growth.

Barton: Our people do like your products. Alright—we'll try it!

Collection Visit 4

This customer visit involves an entirely different set of characters. The cast of characters is You, He (the owner or the financial officer of the customer company), and She (the bookkeeper or accounts payable person). Again, this is a hypothetical that can be applied to companies and businesses of all sizes—large, medium, and small—and is as demeaning to the She in a small company as it would be to a person in a similar situation in a company of medium or large size.

As we pick up the dialogue, you have already introduced yourself to the owner and the accounts payable person. This is a small company and the conversation is being held in the office-reception area of a building of modest size. You are standing on one side of a counter, He (the owner) is standing on the other side, and She (the payables person) is seated at a desk 6 or 8 feet behind the counter.

You: (Addressing the owner) This has been an experience I wouldn't want to repeat. I've sent two letters, had two telephone conversations with you, and nothing has come from any of them, including the payment commitment that was due to arrive at my company four or five days ago.

He: (The owner's eyes widen in a good imitation of surprise) You didn't get a check? (He turns toward the payables person) I told you to mail a check to [name of company] last week! What's the matter with you?!

She: (If looks could kill, he would be cold on the floor. He is trying to stick Her with the blame, and all three of them know it) I'm sorry, Mr. _____. It must have slipped my mind when I got involved with the quarterly payroll tax report.

He: Well, get with it! This lady (or gentleman) doesn't want to stand around here all day waiting for a check!

She: Yes, sir. I'll get it ready right away.

He: (Directing his attention to You) Boy! Things really slip through the cracks around here. This is embarrassing to me personally and to my company.

You: (You don't bother to remind him that his account is always past due and always a collection problem. This time, however, it happens to be more of a problem than usual) That's alright. I have a meeting in downtown L.A. in about an hour and a half, but I have enough time.

He: Business has been a little slow lately. A couple of our long-time contractor customers have moved to another part of the L.A. Basin, so we don't get any business from them anymore.

You: Your cashflow isn't strong enough to maintain the company at the reduced level of business?

He: Well, some of our accounts haven't paid the way they should so some months we don't come close to generating enough cashflow from our receivables.

You: (This is interesting—and not very comforting) So you are doing quite a bit of bank borrowing?

He: We go to the well quite often.

She: (Brings check to the counter) Here you are, Mr. _____.

He: (Signs check, hands it to you) I apologize for the inconvenience. (He glances at payables person) I'll try to see that it doesn't happen again. (Payables person glares at him)

You: (Putting the check in your briefcase) I too hope we don't have any further problem with payments. (You look at the payables person) I was once in a similar position so I know you're doing the best you can.

He: What is this? I'm the bad guy here?

You: No, but you really shouldn't shift the blame onto someone who doesn't have the authority to act on her own. (You turn and walk toward the door) Thank you for the check.

He: Oh, sure—you're welcome.

Collection Visit 5

You are about to visit an account whose payment performance over the three years of your association with it has been a parade of past-due balances, orders held until checks for amounts specifically requested have been sent, and a pattern of broken payment promises. The customer is in constant payment trouble with other suppliers of goods and services, has made very little progress toward establishing a loyal customer base in its marketplace area, is considered by the trade to be making no headway, and is an increasingly high-risk account.

Your company is owed a sum of money that is significant by the standard of your average account receivable, and 80 percent of the past-due balance ranges from 10 to 45 days past due. You have been holding orders for seven days—since a promised check for 25 percent of the past-due balance failed to arrive—and both your company's Sales Manager and the Vice President-Finance have been supportive of the need for a collection visit. They are supportive also of whatever action you may elect to take, including one which might sidetrack any thoughts of a continuing supplier-customer relationship. The customer company's Finance Director is your primary target. If he is not in—and when you called yesterday it was unclear whether he would be—then the company's Controller (or the Accounts Payable Supervisor) are next in the line of preference. And who are you? You are Francis (with an *i* or an *e*) Campbell, Credit Manager for Wimbley Products, Inc., and you are targeting Larry Zampher, Finance Director of Hammersley-Fields Company, your past-due customer.

The lobby area of Hammersley-Fields is large and well furnished. Several people are waiting as you walk to the counter. A smiling receptionist/telephone operator greets you.

Operator: Good morning. May I help you?

Campbell: Yes. I'm Francis Campbell, Credit Manager for Wimbley Products. I'd like to see your Finance Director, Larry Zampher.

Operator: Do you have an appointment with Mr. Zampher?

Campbell: No, but my reason for seeing him is so important to both of our companies that I decided to take a chance that he might be in.

Operator: I'm not sure if he's in today, but let me ring his office for you.

Campbell: Thank you.

The operator punches an extension number and converses briefly with someone. A few seconds later, she is pointing to a door leading to an inner office.

Operator: Mr. Zampher can see you. Go through that door and his office is the second door on the right.

Campbell: (Thanks the operator, picks up briefcase, and goes through the door. The second door on the right is open—and Larry Zampher stands behind his desk and extends his hand.)

Zampher: I'm Larry Zampher. (Glances at his watch.) I have a meeting in 20 minutes, but 15 of them are yours.

Campbell: Francis Campbell, Mr. Zampher, and I appreciate the opportunity to see you. (Campbell opens his briefcase and removes an accounts receivable aging report on Hammersley-Fields. He puts it on Zampher's desk.) During the three years of our supplier-customer relationship, past-due problems have been the rule rather than the exception, but what we've been seeing the past three or four months has pushed the boundaries of what we will accept to the limit and beyond.

Zampher: (Glances at aging report, then looks at Campbell.) What can I tell you, Mr. Campbell? We've been going through a period of slower cashflow than we had anticipated. The result, unfortunately, has been an increase in the past-due aging of most of our accounts payable.

Campbell: With three years of business experience behind you, our analysis leads us to the conclusion that you should be in a much better position with us—and with the rest of your creditors—than you are now. In a nutshell, Mr. Zampher, what can you do in the next six months to improve your business and financial condition that you shouldn't have been doing for the last year or more?

Zamphor: There are several reasons for our problems but suffice to say that it took longer to establish a customer base than we had anticipated and the economy in this areas hasn't been as strong as we had projected.

Campbell: Those are serious flaws in planning—flaws that cannot have failed to impact the integrity of your business plan.

Zampher: Of course we've had to make some adjustments but those setbacks haven't changed our goals for the long term.

Campbell: Possibly—but one of the more important things your adjustments have done is to make the *long term* an even more distant goal than it was at the beginning.

Zampher: I don't follow you.

Campbell: If Hammersley-Field doesn't begin to generate more business—and more cashflow—the company won't be around to experience the *long term*.

Zampher: We aren't having any really serious supplier problems. Oh, we get some calls for money—the same as any other company—and now and then somebody holds an order, but nothing serious.

Campbell: Then our company is the exception. We are not going to continue to supply products while payments get slower and slower. And Mr. Zampher, I've talked with some of your other suppliers. They aren't any more tolerant of this type of risk-taking than we are.

At this point, if there is any kind of a distribution agreement between your company (as manufacturer and/or wholesaler) and the customer (as a wholesaler and/or retailer), the customer is probably in violation of one or more of the provisions of the contract (units bought and sold—a quota—within specific time frames as the criteria for maintaining a franchise or dealer exclusivity in a market-place area or region and parameters of aging within which the customer's account balance must be maintained). If the customer is in violation of at least one of the sections or subsections of the agreement, you might want to proceed to terminate the agreement under provisions for such action which should be a part of any such agreement. The customer is in violation of two or more areas of the agreement? Now is the time to use them to leverage your position.

Zampher: If you're going to try to squeeze us for money, there isn't any to be squeezed.

Campbell: No, no. All I'm going to do is cite our agreement and what you are obligated to do for us if your company wants to continue to handle our line of products.

Zampher: Oh, come on now! Your company's products are an important part of the diverse selection we offer to our customers!

Campbell: It won't be yours to offer much longer, Mr. Zampher, unless account aging is reduced to parameters set in the agreement that was signed when we gave you an exclusive in your marketplace area.

Zampher: I don't remember the contract figures. How much money are we talking about, and how far beyond the allowable time frame are we?

Campbell: (Compares photocopy of applicable page of the agreement with the aged trial balance report of the account) My company needs a check for $_____ to bring past-due aging within parameters set in the agreement.

Zampher: Good Lord! That much?

Campbell: That's the figure. Now—I can work with you up to a point. Give me a check today for $_____ (half the above total) and send a second check for $ _____ so it arrives within two weeks from today. But let me be sure that there is no misunderstanding. After those two checks, your account will either remain within the parameters for receivables aging set in our agreement or the first time a past-due balance goes more than seven days past those parameters, I'll send you a letter which will terminate your authorization to distribute (or retail) our products.

Zampher: Do you mind if we take a breath? I've just told you about the shortfall in our cashflow and you're telling me we have to come up with this kind of money over a period of the next two weeks!

Campbell: It's taken between three and four months for your company to get itself into this position. I could pull the plug today on our agreement and we would have exceeded by a comfortable margin anything that we are required to do. No, Mr. Zampher, the problem was not created by my company and it isn't one that is going to continue to survive outside the parameters of our agreement.

Zampher: So you're saying that we come up with a check today for the first half of the money or ...

Campbell: The first half today or we pull the line. There are others in the area who would like to have the line, and would do a good job of representing us. The call is yours.

Zampher: Can you give me until the day after tomorrow for the first $_____? If I have today and tomorrow, I can get the money together—then I can send you a check by overnight UPS (Federal Express, etc.).

Campbell: The day after tomorrow for sure?

Zampher: Yes.

Campbell: Alright. The check arrives at my company the day after tomorrow. No games and no delays.

Zampher: Agreed.

Collection Visit 6

Remember what was said regarding this customer at the start of Collection Visit 5? Hammersley-Fields owes your (Francis Campbell's) company *a significant sum of money*, of which 80 percent is past due 10 to 45 days. Orders are being held, promises of payment have been broken consistently, and there is no resistance at your company to any action you feel is appropriate.

We give the basic premise a different slant. This time there isn't the leverage of an agreement between your company and the customer. Although the customer is a frequent buyer of your company's products, your line is not unique in the industry or indispensable to the customer. You (Francis Campbell) must persuade Larry Zampher to pay his company's past-due obligation or you will have to use other methods to force payment. When this major change is applied to the supplier-customer relationship, the thrust of your collection effort is somewhat different.

Campbell: If we can't resolve something today that reduces your past-due receivables balance and puts cash in my company's till, nothing is going to move until we collect *all* of the past-due balance—and then all sales will be on COD terms.

Zampher: You seem to be forgetting one thing.

Campbell: What's that?

Zampher: We don't have to carry your products.

Campbell: True, but you also don't need a collection agency hammering you for money while the credit reporting agencies (Dun & Bradstreet, National Association of Credit Management, etc.) are picking up on your problems and spreading the word to suppliers with a volley of special reports.

Zampher: We don't need that! What would it take to satisfy your company?

Campbell: A check for $_____ (one-third of the past-due balance by [date], a second check for $_____ (one third of the total) by [date], and a third check for $_____ by [date].

Zampher: That's a lot of money in a short period of time! I think you're going to have to give us something with more flexibility than that.

Campbell: We aren't talking about flexibility. Any chance for that was squandered with promises that were not kept. No—I want firm payment dates and firm amounts of money.

Zampher: Why don't I send you $_____ (20 percent of the total) by the end of next week and follow with four more checks of the same size at intervals of, oh, say every two weeks?

Campbell: Past-due balances wouldn't be cleared fast enough to make a real impact on the total balance. I like more money over a shorter period of time. The best I can do is $_____ (40 percent of the total) by the end of this week and three payments of $_____ at ten-day intervals.

Zampher: Forty percent by [date]?

Campbell: Yes, but once you get past the hurdle, you're only looking at three payments that are half the size of the first one.

Zampher: I don't know. The last three payments aren't so bad but that first 40 percent will strip our cashflow to the bone.

Campbell: Alright. You can change the percentages from 40/20/20/20 to 35/25/20/20. That's as much flexibility as I can give you.

Zampher: I can't have every supplier in the industry talking about our cashflow problem. We'll clean up your account balance on the 35/25/20/20 percent schedule—then your products are out of here.

Campbell: The choice is yours. We aren't anxious to have your company continue to handle our products if the past-due problems we've had for the past several months are going to continue into the future.

Wind down and conclude collection visit.

Collection Visit 7

The premise for this collection visit involves the very real potential for a future problem rather than an immediate one. It is collection related in that you—your company's credit and collections manager—are attempting to gather as much information as you can regarding a major change in the ownership of an important customer.

You are visiting the place of business of Peterson, Lackman and Company. This company has been a customer for more than ten years, has always paid within or close to terms, and may continue to do so in the future. There is, however, some question regarding the future direction of this firm because of the death earlier in the preceding week of Morris Lackman, one of the founding and managing partners.

You knew both partners quite well but probably have a closer relationship with the surviving partner, Frank Peterson, than you did with Morris Lackman. Both men had talked in recent years of selling the business and retiring. With the stability of the partnership shattered, there are questions to which your company must have answers if it is to continue the current credit line. The credit line is, for your company, a major one and there must be appropriate assurances (verbal and other) that the financial integrity of the company will not be compromised by the unfortunate death of partner Morris Lackman.

Some of the questions that follow are what you must ask Frank Peterson during your face-to-face meeting.

1. Is there a buy-and-sell agreement funded by life insurance issued on the lives of the two partners? (Your file on the company indicates there is but you must verify it.)

2. Will Frank Peterson continue to operate the business or will he sell it and retire?

3. If Peterson elects to keep the business, will the amount of insurance adequately fund the buy-out or will Peterson have to ask for bank support to complete the buy-out?

4. If Peterson borrows some money from the bank, will this new debt compromise the ability of the business to meet the financial demands placed upon it?

5. Of enormous importance to the continuity of the business under the sole proprietorship of Frank Peterson is the following question: Can the business afford to hire a replacement for Morris Lackman (the financial and business half of the partnership) and avoid seriously impacting a cashflow that could become considerably less dependable without Lackman's steadying hand?

6. Does Frank Peterson think he will consider the possibility of taking a younger partner (younger in age) or a junior partner (in terms of investment); a partner who would come into the business with good experience in the areas that were Morris Lackman's strengths and who would come into the business with an agreement that would give him a specific number of years in which to exercise an option to buy the business.

7. Morris Lackman was more involved with the customers on a day-to-day basis than was Frank Peterson (product design, testing, and manufacturing). Is there potential for a significant loss of customer support because Lackman will not be there to ensure that customers get what they need when they need it—and at a fair price?

Your meeting with Frank Peterson will address all of the problem areas, real and potential, that have arisen automatically with the death of partner Morris Lackman. It is your responsibility to collect receivables dollars for your company. It does not follow automatically that the company founded and operated successfully by Peterson and Lackman will have the same level of success without the services of Morris Lackman. You will use your friendship with Frank Peterson to ask (with an appropriate level of sensitivity) the necessary questions regarding continuity of the business.

When you have as much information as Peterson is able to give you (he will obviously have decisions to make that must come later than a few days after the death of his partner), you will decide whether your company should continue the current credit line. Unless it is obvious that there may be serious financial problems (no funded buy-out agreement, etc.), you will probably continue the current credit line as you increase dramatically the monitoring of an account that has previously given your company no cause for more than routine monitoring.

Until there is clear-cut evidence of the direction this company will take, you will make a point of visiting this firm on a regular basis (every four to six weeks). It is in the interest of your company to maintain your relationship with Frank Peterson and to develop an early rapport with the person Peterson bring in to take over for Morris Lackman. It doesn't matter whether the person (man or woman) comes into the business as an employee, a potential junior or full partner, or a person who comes into the business with an agreement to buy it all. Your job is to establish with the new person the importance to his (or her) firm, and to yours, a continuation of the within-or-near-terms payment relationship that has been a highlight of the relationship. Position your company to be as helpful to the surviving partner as you possibly can. Be tolerant (but watchful) of a short period following Lackman's death when invoices are not paid as rapidly as they were. This should not be a problem unless it extends beyond the short term (two or three months). Should the problem continue beyond a relatively short time frame—and especially if the aging of the receivables balance begins to break new ground for the account—close monitoring of the account should enable you to take action appropriate to moving the account back into a pattern of aging that is compatible with the requirements of your company's credit plan and the ongoing changes at Petterson, Lackman Company.

Collection Visit 8

New owners take over a company/business that has been successful for 12 years. Your company has sold to the customer for 10 of those years, and the relationship (payment and otherwise) has been excellent.

But now there are questions, some of which can be answered now but many that only time can answer effectively. What will the new owner(s) bring to the business, or take from it? Will they be active in managing it? How many of the current experienced personnel will be retained? Do the new owners have the training and/or the skills necessary to continue this successful business? After committing to buy the business, do the new owners have the financial strength to generate a cashflow adequate to finance acquisition debt and pay suppliers within terms—or within parameters that will be satisfactory to the suppliers?

Whether your first visit to this company is a combination collection call and fact-finding one will depend on how the former owners handled payment for their purchases. If the balance at the time of sale is minuscule, forget *collection visit* and concentrate on getting to know the person (one of the owners, a new financial manager, etc.) with whom you will be communicating if there is a payment or other problem.

If the balance at the time of sale is substantial and much of it is past due, you will want to know how the contract of sale handles the matter of payables balances that were incurred by the seller(s). Does the contract of sale assign responsibility for these balances to the seller or are they a part of what the buyer(s) has agreed to assume? And if the seller is responsible for paying all debts through the date of sale, how does the escrow handle the disbursing of the purchase funds? Is a sum equal to the payables responsibility of the outgoing owners being withheld within the escrow to pay a list of creditors furnished to the title company (or other transfer agency) by the seller?

Do not drop in unannounced unless you are unexpectedly in the area. Get the name of the person who will be handling financial matters for the new owner(s) (if it is an employee, it could be the same person you contacted before), and call to set up an appointment. When new owners come into a business, there can be a certain amount of disfunction that relates to new people becoming comfortable not only with each other but with employees who have been retained. There are multiple meetings designed to integrate what has gone before with ideas and procedures that the new ownership want to install.

Give the new owners and their management staff the courtesy of a visit that has been scheduled for a time that is best for them. Ask questions relevant to the purchase and about the experience and background of people who will be in key management positions. Use the question posed earlier in this section (Additional Benefits), and include any others that seem relevant to your relationship with the customer. The visit should be cordial, should include an offer to help at any time and in any way possible, and should not drag on too long. Leave the office with as much helpful information as you can obtain because, at this point, there is no sure way to predetermine the success new owners will have with the business.

Notifying a Customer in Advance of Your Visit

There are two schools of thought regarding whether you should or should not let a customer know when you will be making a collection visit to his or her place of business. One school says, "No! A thousand times no! Do not give the debtor any advance notice because too many of these people will tell you they'll be there, then find a reason to be away." The other school of thought says, "Sure. Call first. Why should you drive or fly a considerable distance, take time and spend money to get there only to find that the person you wanted to see is away on business, vacation, out sick, etc.?"

It is true that the effectiveness of *call or no call* cannot in all situations be predicted accurately. Experience with past-due accounts will give you some insight into the deviousness of some and the integrity of others.

The Advantages of Calling in Advance

A credit manager who relates well to people can use collection and/or *courtesy and get-acquainted visits* to accrue multiple benefits for his or her company. Sales and marketing people benefit especially from courtesy calls that a credit manager makes on the company's customers. It surprises some people that a credit manager is calling on them just to get acquainted, or to find out if there is anything his or her company can or should be doing to improve its products or service. Many people do not associate a credit manager with anything more than setting credit lines and collecting past-due balances: They are surprised—and pleasantly—to learn that a good credit manager is an extension of the public relations arm of his or her company.

You may think of your company as too small to allow customer visits that are not motivated solely by the need to collect money. That is the primary reason for many visits to customers but it should not be the only one. It can be very worthwhile to put together a half-day or a one-day trip that involves a combination of collection, courtesy, and get-acquainted calls. If you can set up an itinerary that involves six or eight accounts—customers whose paying habits run the gamut from very good to marginal—the long-term advantages can be substantial. You will no longer be talking or writing to faceless names or voices, or wondering about the location and condition of a company's offices, warehouse, or manufacturing area.

The more you know about a company or a business, the better prepared you will be to collect your company's money. By calling on customer companies at times when there is no problem, you will be taking important steps in the building of a rapport between yourself and the person with whom you need to communicate when there is a payment problem. You will have gone beyond the important—but imageless—data from credit reports and the information you get from other suppliers. Data from credit reports and information obtained from other credit managers is enormously important to a proper evaluation of credit accounts but a credit manager's edge in any account relationship is when his or her relationship with a key member of the customer firm is so strong that the person voluntarily gives you information regarding the customer firm that is current, is indicative of their current thinking, and is frequently not a part of any report from a credit reporting agency.

Calling in advance of a collection visit gives you the opportunity to set with your customer contact the parameters of an agenda for what the two of you need to talk about. It gives the customer an opportunity to prepare for the visit by gathering data, forecasts, and other material relative to the customer's near- and long-term prognosis for increasing cashflow and reducing the problem of past-due balances. And if the person who is your contact knows that you will arrive on a specific day and at a specific time, the overwhelming majority of those people will honor their commitment to meet with you.

The Disadvantages of Calling in Advance

It is not to your advantage to call before you make a collection visit to a customer whose business and financial situation is so precarious that the person you would want to see (a partner, financial manager, etc.) does not want to see or talk with you. This person has probably failed to respond to your collection letters and/or has broken payment commitments during your telephone collection calls. The customer is unable to pay any significant part of the past-due balance, or can pay some of it but knows from letters and telephone conversations that the amount will fall far short of what your company says it needs.

If this person is of a mentality that believes it is better to dodge an issue as long as possible before finally being cornered and forced to face up to it, then your best chance to get your message across is to make a collection visit—and do it unannounced! This is the type of individual who would agree reluctantly to meet you at a specific time then leave it to a department underling to explain—after you have arrived for the appointment—why he or she is out of the office for the day.

Remember that a collection visit does not have to be an action of last or near-last resort. It can be the first—or one of the first—collection actions that you take. If the account is located within blocks or miles of your company's offices, or if you have business in the more distant city of another customer, make a collection call on that customer. Early collection visits could lead to avoiding the necessity of writing collection letters and making telephone calls: forms of communication that might be much less productive—in obtaining a check—than your collection visit.

Mix all of the collection tools—letters, phone calls, fax messages, visits to the customer's place of business—and be sure that the mix is appropriate for the account situation. Your collection success rate should increase dramatically.

Follow-Up Collection Letters

The following are examples of letters that can be used as a follow-up to the credit manager's (or the collection manager's) visit to the office of the owner, general manager, treasurer, or controller of a customer/debtor company. These letters are used to confirm what was said during the visit, what the parties agreed to do, and the time frame in which it is to be done. Each of these letters is an attempt by the creditor company to eliminate any chance of a misunderstanding between the two parties.

When your company's collection efforts (letters, telephone calls, fax messages, etc.) have not been productive, legitimate questions might be raised regarding the sincerity of any commitment made by the customer/debtor during a personal visit to the credit and collections manager. If the customer has disregarded your earlier collection efforts and has perhaps defaulted on one or more earlier payment promises, why should you expect a better result now? Unfortunately, you cannot know whether the customer/debtor will take the promised payment action within the agreed time frame until the calendar has brought the customer/debtor face-to-face with his or her commitment. If a check arrives within the specified time frame (or if the first and second of several payments arrives at your office on or about the date specified), then there is reason to rejoice: Unless something unexpectedly negative should occur, you can be increasingly confident that the agreement will hold.

The letters that follow can be adapted easily to the circumstances of your own agreement with a customer/debtor. Should the agreement fail, the customer/debtor should be very aware that a more formal collection effort will follow. Collection agencies, small claims and civil suits, collection attorneys, and the force of judgments and attachments is not a scenario in which most customer/debtors want to become involved.

12.1 [date]

Name of Company
Street Address (or P.O. Box Number)
City, State, Zip Code

Attention: [name and title]

Dear Mr./Ms. _____:

It is my feeling that our meeting in your office on [date] was a significant step toward bringing the relationship between our two companies into a new era of cooperation and understanding.

I appreciate your candor in telling me about the problems that are causing your company to experience more financial difficulty than had been anticipated. Your assessment of the problems, and what is being done to cope with or to avert them, seems to be well thought out. It is planning of a quality that should see your company safely through the current cashflow problem.

As we agreed on [date], payments of $_____ are to reach this office by each of the following three dates: _____, _____, and _____. After the third of these three payments has been received, we shall expect account payments to be made on our regular credit terms of _____.

If there is any negative change in your company's return to a normal level of cashflow, please contact me before the change is reflected in a new problem with payments.

Sincerely,

Credit Manager

12.2   [date]

Name of Company
Street Address (or P.O. Box Number)
City, State, Zip Code

Attention: [name and title]

Dear Mr./Ms. _____:

My thanks for the opportunity to meet and talk with you on [date]. Your candor regarding your company's current financial crunch—which you anticipate will be resolved over the next three or four months—has enabled me to understand more clearly the reason for the past-due status of your company's account.

However, as I stated during our meeting, it is essential that we receive a partial payment of $_____ on the payment due date for each of the next three months. If at the end of that time frame your company is unable to return to a program of payments that is within parameters set in our credit agreement, we shall review the status of the account and decide whether we can continue to accept a payment program that puts our own cashflow at a disadvantage.

Please do everything possible to bring the aging of your account balance within a maximum of 30 days past due. When that parameter has been attained, we can evaluate whether the account is ready to move from a hold order (and/or COD) status to a more conventional account arrangement.

After meeting with you, I feel that your company can move through the problem(s) we discussed and emerge a stronger and a more competitive company.

Sincerely,

Credit Manager

13

Fax Messages as a Collection Tool

The age of electronics has touched or become intimately involved with almost every facet of business life. Computerized data has been with us for several decades but it is no longer necessary to have a giant Univac, IBM, or other room-filling, card-index type of data processing monster to process a large volume of work. Nowadays it is done much more economically and efficiently by much smaller and more powerful computers; computers that long ago outgrew the era of card-index data. Truly, electronic equipment has done wonders for us all, and we are still barely beyond the threshold of its potential.

Among the most recent of the post-threshold electronic wonders to have an impact on business is the fax machine. By giving companies and businesses the capability to transmit letters, documents, and messages from one instrument, to be received in printout form by another instrument at a near or distant point, the fax machine has added a new dimension to business communication. It is now possible for companies to communicate almost instantaneously with one another, or for offices and branches of the same company to send documents, messages, and directives. Sending it by UPS, Federal Express, or Express Mail service? For goods and some types of documents, one of the above is still the service of choice. But when there is an urgent need to get a proposal, a legal document, an agenda for a top-level meeting, and any number of other time-critical situations, fax is becoming an indispensable aid.

Fax has added a 21st-century dimension to the transmission of documents and messages. It is now possible to be in the middle of a collection call to a customer, have the customer attempt to refute the existence or the contents of an earlier collection communication, pull the refuted document from the customer's file folder, and fax it within minutes of the customer's statement.

When the telephone was the one tool for instantaneously exchanging information with a customer, credit management people were grateful for it. With the addition of fax—and the increasing number of businesses of all sizes that have a fax number—credit people are able to integrate notes, memos, invoices, contracts, and documents of all types into their business calls, and specifically into those telephone calls that involve the collection of past-due accounts receivable.

How to Use the Fax

The use of fax can cut hours or days from the transmission of documents (letters, invoices, etc.) via conventional systems of communication (U.S. Mail, UPS, Federal Express, etc.). The customer is unable to refute past statements or deadlines for payment when the document(s) in which that information was included can be transmitted via fax while the conversation between the two of you is still going on.

Example: A customer has failed to pay one or more invoices. The credit person who is charged with the responsibility for that account calls payables, inquires about the invoice, and is told that payables has no record of it.

The credit person inquires if the customer has a fax number. The payables person says that they do and gives the credit person the number. The credit person tells the payables person that a copy of the missing invoice will be faxed to the customer company within the hour.

This customer, whose credit relationship with the supplier has always been excellent, will receive the invoice copy the day the inquiry was made. The invoice can be paid promptly, or entered into the payment cycle, one, two, or three days earlier than would have been the case if the invoice had been sent via the postal service.

The use of fax allows a creditor to expedite a collection letter in which the credit department of the supplier/creditor is requesting payment of a specific dollar amount within a very short time frame. This could be a follow-up to one or two telephone requests for a payment that has not been received. Always note and/or document what was said and/or promised during any telephone conversation with a customer. When the initial collection effort has consisted of one or two telephone calls, and payment promises were made but the date for payment passes and there is none, it is essential that the supplier-creditor escalates the collection effort to the next plateau.

The *next plateau* may, depending upon the customer and the circumstances, be a fax message rather than a conventional letter sent by post. If your next contact with the customer is to be by a fax message, the format for the message can be as flexible as you care to make it. You want to send a collection letter by fax? Do it! Perhaps the preferred communication should be a formal statement of what the account owes, or it could be a photocopy of relevant past-due areas of the customer account. Whichever choice you make, it must be clear to the customer/debtor that time is about to run out. Let the customer know that your company has been patient beyond what should reasonably be expected of it, but that those days are over. The past-due balance is to be paid by the date you set in the fax, and there will be no extension of that deadline.

The Equipment

Fax machines come in assorted sizes, prices, and capabilities. There are the smaller, slower, limited capacity and capability machines that can do an excellent job when they are a fit with the purchaser's needs. (As this manuscript is being written, low-end machines are available in a price range of approximately $249 to $299.) Most of the machines in this price range have a 10-page automatic document feeder, a 50-number speed dial memory, transmit each page in approximately 15 seconds, and may have a page cutter.

Many manufacturers are offering units, but a short list of four units put out by four manufacturers currently have price tags of $399, $595, $1395, and $1595. I would not presume to make any recommendations because (1) I have no knowledge of your specific situation, and (2) technology changes too rapidly for a recommendation today that might not be appropriate eight or nine months from now.

It can be said, however, that for the spread in cost between these four units, there is a comparable spread in capability. The $399 and $595 units differ only slightly in their features (10-page document feeder versus 20-page feeder, 50-number auto dialing memory versus 40-number, etc.) with some of the difference in cost represented by a discount dealers price (low service) versus an older (full service) office equipment dealer. Of the two more expensive units, the $1395 unit uses plain paper, has a 100-number speed dial memory, 20-page document feeder, and fax/telephone switch. The $1595 unit also uses plain paper but has a 118-number speed dial memory, 50-page document feeder, and fax/telephone switch.

Other units are available that offer different groups of features, or as unit prices become more expensive, there is an increase in unit speed, capacity, capability, etc. (Incidentally, for credit managers and credit representatives who are part of a large, multi-branch or multi-division company, it is possible to devise a program that will allow the sender of the message to put one copy of the letter, report, or document into the machine and have copies go to 20 or 25 outlets. This is an enormous benefit when many locations of the same organization need to be contacted quickly with information of importance.)

A fax message can be the first contact in a collection effort that—if the fax is not successful—subsequently might include letters (postal service) and telephone calls. The fax might be used at any one of several points in the collection procedure—but that choice is yours, not mine. What might motivate one debtor to pay almost immediately after he or she receives a telephone call, a collection letter, a fax message, or a collection visit could have no positive effect on another. Collecting money is trial and error, but using the best collection tools available cannot fail to improve your chances for an early settlement of the past-due balance.

Examples of Fax Collection Messages

There is no basic difference between the messages you send as a collection letter and the one(s) you send on your fax machine. They are interchangeable messages but only a fax machine can deliver your message to the customer/debtor hours or days ahead of a posted letter.

13.1   Fax Query of Invoice Missing

[date]

Name of Company
Street Address (or P.O. Box Number)
City, State, Zip Code

Attention: [name and title]

Dear Mr./Ms. _____:

The payment pattern of your company is to pay invoices within our terms which causes us to suspect that one of last month's invoices [invoice number, date, and amount] went astray between our office and yours.

If you find that the invoice copy is missing, please fax us a reply and we shall fax a copy of the invoice back to you within an hour of receiving your message.

Let me take this opportunity to thank you for the record of discount/prompt payments you have established with our company. We greatly appreciate the fact that you adhere to our credit terms. As you probably know, life is much simpler for the supplier/creditor who is fortunate enough to have a high percentage of accounts such as yours.

[signature and title]

13.2   Fax Reply from Customer

[date]

Name of Company
Street Address (or P.O. Box Number)
City, State, Zip Code

Attention: [name and title]

Dear Mr./Ms. _____:

Words of praise or gratitude are always appreciated and we thank you for the ones regarding our payment record with your company. We do our best to give our suppliers the same level of consideration that we would like to receive from our own customers. We don't receive it as often as we would like but—you know that story as well or better than we do.

Please fax a copy of [invoice number, date, and amount]. We do not have the invoice and though we are far from infallible, I suspect that it disappeared somewhere between our two companies.

The invoice will be input with the next batch of payables, which means that your check will be mailed before the end of this week.

[name and title]

13.3   Fax Message to Customer Plus Invoice Copy

[date]

Name of Company
Street Address (or P.O. Box Number)
City, State, Zip Code

Attention: [name and title]

Dear Mr./Ms. _____:

Many thanks for your prompt reply. A copy of [invoice number, date, and amount] will be transmitted at the end of this message.

Please contact me if there is ever a problem with products, paperwork, or anything else.

[signature and title]

Another example of the effectiveness of fax messages between two companies is when there has been a misunderstanding (or a delay) regarding the issuing of a credit memo to correct a pricing error and the customer has attempted to deduct the difference between the correct and the incorrect pricing from a payment(s) to the supplier. In the following example, the credit memo and the customer's payment check (less deductions) have crossed in the mail, creating a difference between the balance shown as still owing on the supplier's accounts receivable aged trial balance report and the customer's payables records. The supplier (your company) initiates this exchange of fax messages.

13.4   Notification That Adjusted Credit Memo to Be Sent

[date]

Name of Company
Street Address (or P.O. Box Number)
City, State, Zip Code

Attention: [name and title]

Dear Mr./Ms. _____:

I apologize for the confusion that has arisen as the result of our pricing error on invoices (several invoice numbers). The credit memo for (amount) that you probably have received by now was intended to correct the errors on those invoices. Understandably, you were not going to pay the incorrect higher price shown on those invoices; but during our respective adjusting of pricing errors, revising sales tax, and arriving at adjusted totals, we arrived at slightly different adjustment totals.

Our adjustment figures are so close, however, that I am going to send you (via fax) a copy of the adjusted credit memo we are using to bring our receivables figure into agreement with yours. The pricing error was ours; the difference between our respective adjustment figures is minimal—but it was ours.

I hope that we do not make this mistake again. If, however, you find that we have made an overcharge error (pricing, arithmetic, etc.) on a future invoice, please notify this office and we will immediately fax a credit memo to your company. This will enable you to pay the invoice as billed but our credit memo for the amount of the overcharge will balance your records with ours.

The adjustment credit memo will follow this letter.

[name and title]

The fax machine is an important tool for communicating between your company and its other branches and divisions. It is ideal for transmitting directives or guideline material to several company locations with the one transmission. The credit manager can send instructions or guideline data to company offices whose credit administrator has limited decision-making authority: relevant data can be transmitted that will enable the credit person in a branch office to explain to the customer why an order or a credit line increase has not been approved—or accept the customer's gratitude if it was. And in a somewhat confrontational collection situation—one in which a customer/debtor attempts to deny the existence of collection letters in which specific deadlines were set, and subsequently acknowledged—a fax machine can put copies of relevant material in the hands of a reluctant debtor within an hour of his or her conversation with the collector.

A creditor company can compress the time frame for responses with a combination of the telephone and the fax machine. The customer claims that an invoice or a collection letter was not received? Within minutes it can be pulled from the file, put in the fax machine, and your customer's real or alleged problem has been eliminated. Your customer gave you a verbal payment promise (telephone conversation) but the date of the payment has come and gone—and no payment? Integrate a fax message into your collection program.

13.5   Request for Customer Reply with Specific Payment Data

[date]

Name of Company
Street Address (or P.O. Box Number)
City, State, Zip Code

Attention: [name and title]

Dear Mr./Ms. _____:

I don't want to embarrass your company or mine by forwarding your account for collection if the payment promised for [date] was mailed but has been delayed in the mails.

Fax the number, date, and amount of the check and the date it was released. Our auditors are pressuring us to follow up more closely on payment commitments that fall through the cracks for several days past the date payment should have arrived.

Your fax reply today—including specific data regarding the payment—will allow us to continue to work with your company. We hate to lose a customer, and the loss of one because of a payment problem is especially unfortunate.

[signature and title]

13.6   **Reply from Customer Regarding Requested Information**

[date]

Name of Company
Street Address (or P.O. Box Number)
City, State, Zip Code

Attention: [name and title]

Dear Mr./Ms. _____:

I have bad news and good news.

The bad news is that the check for $_____ to cover past-due balances—and promised for [date]—has not been mailed. The good news, however, is that the check is being processed today and will be mailed tomorrow afternoon.

        Check Number _____

        Date of Check _____

        Amount of Check _____

        Release Date _____

We are hopeful that the coming month will see an increase in the amount of cashflow generated from accounts receivable. One of our major accounts—an account that has had a financially difficult three or four months—seems to be gaining control of its financial problems.

Improvement in the payment pattern of the one account will not increase our own cashflow to the point where we will have no shortfall, but it will improve significantly our bill-paying capability.

[signature and title]

[date]

Name of Company
Street Address (or P.O. Box Number)
City, State, Zip Code

Attention: [name and title]

Dear Mr./Ms. _____:

I am happy to hear that your cashflow is about to improve. It would of course be a very gratifying turn for your company if the payment pattern of more than the one major account were to improve, but take your gains as they come and be hopeful that it is the beginning of a trend.

My thanks for the data pertaining to the check for $_____ which is to be mailed on [date]. It is appreciated and will improve greatly the aging of receivables balances on your account.

[signature and title]

The preceding exchanges of fax messages is indicative of the speed with which information can be exchanged, problems can be identified and addressed, and how relationship-threatening situations can be handled much faster and less abrasively than may be true when telephone calls and posted letters are the conduits for solving problems and settling differences. The fax machine offers an immediacy and a scope that goes beyond the telephone. A creditor and a debtor can, within minutes, be looking at the same several documents that 10 or 15 minutes before were only in the creditor's files.

Within minutes of transmitting the documents, creditor and debtor (though 1000 miles apart) can have the same relevant documents in front of them; documents that immediately offer the difference between an easy understanding of the problem and the potential for a somewhat contentious discussion. The magic ingredient? A fax machine. When both parties have access to one, it effectively ends an imbalance of important information and allows both parties to bridge the gap not just with words but with words *plus* relevant documents.

Using a fax machine within your own company is a major assist. Assume that your company has a sales office in a distant city. Orders are filled from the plant and warehouse where you are located and routinely cross your desk for approval. A notice arrives from your credit reporting service noting a change in the management of this company, a change that might involve an individual who has been involved in three or four bankruptcy filings in your industry over the preceding 10 or 12 years. His name does not appear as one of the new owners or as the manager but he has allegedly been seen going in and out the warehouse door.

You ask the manager of your sales office to find out what he can and to send any pictures he may be able to take that might help to indicate what is going on (such as too much stock from getting everything it can from the suppliers before selling it, pocketing the money, and filing under Chapter 11 of the Bankruptcy Act). In short, is the scam operator back in town and operating behind the cover of this company?

13.8   Fact-Finding Request

[date]

To: [name of your sales office manager]

From: [your name]

Re: [name of company applying for credit]

I have some serious problems with [name of company], and with the people who allegedly own and manage this company versus the rumors that [name of individual who has master-minded three or four previous bankruptcies] has been seen going in and out of the warehouse door.

We don't want any part of this account if [name of individual] is involved in any way with the management or the ownership of this company or if your visual check of the warehouse indicates an excessive build-up of inventory with the possibility that large quantities of product will be moved at prices that will destroy prices in the area. As you know, we would expect [name of company] to let past-due balances build up as merchandise is bought, sold, and suppliers are paid a small percentage of invoice totals.

Nothing will be released on open-account terms until we have some more answers. The company's net worth is inadequate for the size of orders and the scope of their ambition. It is also not comforting to see that their bank is offering nothing better than a token line of credit.

Whatever you can find out will be helpful.

A day or two later the following fax message arrives in your office from the manager in the distant sales office to whom you addressed the preceding memorandum.

13.9   Memo from Sales Office Manager

[date]

To: [your name]

From: [sales office manager]

Re: [company discussed in preceding memorandum]

It was a shocker to hear that [name of individual] might be involved in the ownership and/or management of [name of company].

I made some inquiries among the sales reps for three of our competitor suppliers. At first there was some reluctance to say much about [name of company] but when I mentioned [name of individual] and the rumors that you have heard, I had trouble turning them off!

Fortunately or unfortunately, none of the three has any information regarding [name of sleazy individual] or whether he is involved with this company. They have not seen him or heard any mention of his name—and that mirrors my own experience. As you point out, however, there is also a problem of credibility with the owners/managers who have been identified. The president, [name], was an employee of [name of sleazy individual] when two companies run by [sleazy individual] went down the road to bankruptcy, so it can be assumed he knows how to run a scam operation.

I'd like to have the sales volume but I understand what you're saying. If you think this company's receivables dollars would be at too much risk, I'm not going to make an issue of it.

13.10   Memo: Customer and Credit Line to Be Terminated

[date]

To: [manager of sales office]

From: [your name]

Re: [name of company applying for credit]

Many thanks for the prompt reply.

I have been trying to get some new information that might add stability to what appears to be a high roller's scenario of what new ownership and management wants to do. My problem, and that of other suppliers, is how they REALLY intend to go about it. Unfortunately, the deeper I try to dig for encouraging facts the more shallow the net worth and the bank's support appear to be. Some of the big boys may feel they can afford to take the risk but our credit policy and our cashflow requirements do not give us the same level of latitude.

Sorry to do this to you but at this point there is no way we can offer them a credit line.

[date]

To: [your name]

From: [sales office manager]

Re: [company discussed in preceding memorandum]

Give yourself a gold star for having your ear to the ground at the right time!

I just got a call from a very agitated sales rep for one of our competitors. He was at [company name] less than an hour ago and as he was about to pull out of the parking lot, [sleazy individual] pulled into a parking space on the opposite side of the lot. This is a sales rep who knows [sleazy] so what we have here is a positive I.D.—and verification of the rumor(s) you heard.

It's anybody's guess where this guy fits into the picture, but it should be obvious to everybody that his presence is bad news for the suppliers and for the area in which his company is operating.

Do you use the fax machine frequently as the conduit of information to-and-from your company's one or several branch offices? It is a natural fit. If you are the credit and collections manager for your company, the responsibility for approving credit lines, releasing orders, and collecting receivables generated within the respective areas of the branch offices is yours. There may be one person in the larger branch office who has been given limited credit authority but your office—the headquarters credit and collections office—conducts the credit investigations, assigns credit lines, approves all orders (or orders above a specific amount), collects accounts receivable (or directs the process of collecting receivables), and is responsible for operating the credit and collections department within parameters set in the company's credit policy. Your office—the headquarters credit and collections office—sets policy for the branches, oversees how that policy is handled, and initiates any changes in that policy.

Simple enough? Only when all the tools are utilized that are available to you—and because communication between offices that are often scattered over considerable distances must be expedited—is fax one of your best and most faithful friends. What other tool offers the capability for combining conversation with the ability to almost instantaneously transmit or receive documents about which you are currently talking? The fax machine gives you that capability and it gives it to you in a simple, easy-to-operate machine. Of the various office aids currently available to the business community, the fax is the *dream machine*. It makes your job much easier because it enables you to act (or to react) much more rapidly; and with a better exchange of information, misunderstandings and hesitation can be minimized to the point where they do not interfere with the decision-making process.

The following is an example of how fax messages from the office of the company's credit manager to the branch offices can expedite the exchange of topical information.

13.12   Memo to Branch Offices

[date]

To: [All branch offices]

From: [your name]

Re: Credit sales that exceed credit limits

The current copy of our accounts receivable aging report contains some surprises that I want to share with you. Understand that this is not *show and tell* in its finest hour. This is, quite candidly, an example of accounts receivable *show and tell* that I do not want to have to repeat.

Some of the branch offices are obviously clearing orders that are well within the limit authorized for branch offices *but* the open-balance totals of some accounts—which are in excess of their respective credit limits—tells me that the open-balance total of these accounts is not being checked before an order is O.K.'d for release. As a consequence of the failure to first check the balance, the new order either pushes the customer's open total over the credit line or adds more dollars to a total that already exceeds the credit line.

Our credit guideline for the branch offices is simple. It allows a level of autonomy appropriate for the credit management experience of people at the branch offices. Please review your credit procedure/guideline to ensure that account balances are not inadvertently pushed beyond credit limits. If there is a situation that should be reviewed—a large order that would exceed an existing credit line or a strong growth company whose performance warrants a higher credit line—fax your information and request to this office. We'll get on it immediately and get back to you promptly.

I know how busy the branches can get. The job of credit control that is being done in the branch offices is generally very good—and who says we can be 100 percent perfect 100 percent of the time? You won't hear it here, but we can do our best to minimize mistakes in the areas of greatest dollar danger.

It would be unusual if your fax message to the branch offices did not generate some questions, including perhaps at least one regarding the past due balance of an account whose appetite for product(s) has in recent months begun to exceed its ability to pay close to terms.

Your credit representative (who also does other work at the branch) has very little credit experience but has always been careful to stay within your guidelines. She (or he) is also not reluctant to contact your office for advice and direction.

13.13   Memo from Branch Office

[date]

To: [your name]

From: [branch office credit person]

Re: [name of problem account]

I have reread your guideline for the branch offices and I think this office is doing what is necessary to keep our accounts within their credit limits.

My problem is [account name], its past-due balances, and the constant badgering for a higher line of credit. When they contact me, I tell them the best thing they can do to get you to increase their credit line is to bring their account balance back to "within terms" or "near terms." I know they understand what I'm saying but the accounts receivable aging report doesn't look like they are doing anything to help their cause.

I know you contacted them about 10 days ago and they did send a check for about half of the past-due balance but where do they—and we—go from here? An order is due to come in any day now for approximately $_____ worth of product(s). Is there anything I can or should be doing to help convince them that you won't ship the order unless they bring the account balance within terms?

Another problem: It's my understanding that the order I've just mentioned will exceed their credit line (with current open balance) by a substantial amount—and that would happen if they pay the rest of the past-due balance and a big part of the current invoicing. How do we handle an account that is trying to get us to do all of these things for them when they don't seem able (or willing) to do much to help themselves?

[date]

To: [branch office credit person]

From: [your name]

Re: [problem account]

The closing line in your memo to me gives a perfect recap of our problem. The account is trying to get us to do many things for them—especially the amount of our inventory dollars they want us to invest with them—but they are not able (or willing) to do much of anything to help themselves look more attractive to us.

It does not seem that we will be able to meet the product requirements of this customer—unless among other things there is a dramatic turnaround in the pattern of payments. From a review of the information available to me, that can only come about if there is an infusion of new money—perhaps a "Daddy Warbucks" type of entrepreneur-partner who would have enough confidence in the business to open his purse strings and give the company the level of cashflow that is needed to sustain their pattern of growth.

Because I do not see that happening, we can save some wear and tear on your ear drums if the next time someone takes a run at you regarding the credit line, refer them to me. Tell the caller that all decisions pertaining to the account are made at this office so there is no point in anyone contacting you.

The Psychology of Closely Monitoring Customer Accounts

Fax messages can be an integral part of your campaign of awareness: a campaign designed to raise the conscience level of your customers to the point where they *know* that you monitor accounts very closely. It should be your intention to make some customers so conscious of account monitoring that, without comment, your company is moved ahead of some others when the customer's payables person (or department) writes checks. Your company should not be reluctant to send a clear and an honest message to its accounts: We supply your company with quality (or good) products or services at a fair price and provide service that is second to none; payment for those products and/or services is expected within terms or near terms.

It is important psychologically to let certain of your customers (new ones, chronic past due, etc.) know that you monitor accounts receivable closely. You might send this message by responding promptly (fax, telephone call, etc.) when a customer who has been contacted regarding a past-due balance sends a check. Thank the customer via a fax message or a telephone call, set or confirm the date when a second payment is due, and put a tight time frame on follow-up fax messages or telephone calls. The speed and the consistency of your responses will impress upon the customer the fact that your company does not accept procrastination, poor management of cashflow, or a failure to communicate properly as an acceptable way of business life.

There are customers who will do nothing to protect their own reputation and credit rating unless they are badgered constantly. Some companies and businesses are so bad—slow to respond and unconcerned regarding the size and age of their account balance—that what you might normally view as unacceptably frequent contact to collect a past-due balance is, for the customer, a way of life. You might get a clue about an account if the company has an eye-opening amount of cash but has far too many accounts who report past-due balances of 30 and 40 days. Why will a company sit on a mound of cash while its credit rating is plunging as the result of consistent and unacceptable aging of payables for services and supplies? There are a variety of reasons but none of them is acceptable to suppliers of products and services who have their own obligations to pay.

Suppose you have just received payment from a new customer for the first month's purchases. The check has arrived eight days past the due date. You know from credit report data and the responses of other suppliers that this customer will pay within terms only if (1) your company establishes that requirement immediately, and (2) only if frequent monitoring of the account—fortified by fax reminder messages and telephone calls—establishes in the mind of this customer that your company does not allow its customers to play games with its sales terms.

Net 30 days? Make it clear to this and other customers that you expect payment within terms or near terms. It is in the best interest of your relationship with new customers—with all customers—to affirm what you expect from the customer at the outset of the relationship. If it becomes necessary later to reaffirm those expectations, you should do it without hesitation or rancor. When unacceptable payment patterns are allowed to develop unchallenged, the customer has some basis for claiming tacit approval on the grounds that weeks and/or months went by before the pattern was challenged.

[date]

To: [name of payables supervisor, controller, VP-finance]

From: [your name and title]

Re: Payment within terms

We received your check today for purchases made during the month of _____ and in the amount of $_____.

I thank you for the check but in the same breath I must point out that our sales terms of Net 30 Days called for the check to arrive by the [date] of [month]. Some companies do not monitor their receivables and receivables payments on an ongoing basis; we do, and we prefer to eliminate future misunderstandings by explaining at the first incident what we expect from our customers.

Cashflow is, for both of us, a critical ingredient in the growth and well-being of our companies, and a tandem goal of my company is to provide products that contribute substantially to the acceptance and growth of our customer companies. When a relationship fails to deliver the quality of results we had anticipated—unacceptable payment pattern, etc.—we are not the only loser. The customer loses also.

It is our hope that the relationship we are entering into is destined to be a long and a mutually successful one. Your "within terms" payment of invoices will indicate to us that your company's dedication to responsible business habits and behavior elevates it to the highest plateau of ethical business enterprises.

We appreciate the opportunity to participate in the growth of your company.

Not every one of your business partners (and the people who owe you money are definitely your partners) has a fax machine but the number who do have one is increasing rapidly. The cost of a unit that can adequately serve the needs of most smaller businesses has become very affordable. And with *affordable* as the key word, many more companies and businesses will inadvertently make collecting their past-due balance a less difficult task.

14

Final Demand Letters

The collection letters that follow are examples of what might be used when telephone calls, fax messages, earlier letters, and a personal visit (or two) have been ineffective. These letters—final demands made to the customer/debtor by your company in a last attempt to get the past-due balance before you take more formal collection action—are not written with the intention of preserving a supplier-customer relationship. Your company's money is at much greater risk than you had anticipated so your only interest at this late stage in the relationship is to get the company's money and move on to other accounts.

A final demand letter should be sent by certified or registered mail; or if the urgency is extreme, it can be sent by overnight service such as UPS, the postal service special handling, etc. The goal is to be sure that the debtor receives the final demand with enough lead time to know exactly what you intend to do, and the date on which you intend to do it, if the specified payment is not received by the deadline date. It is a straightforward, no-nonsense communication that tells the customer the time for a payment plan has passed. There is no time or inclination for your company to buy into something that will probably lead to new broken promises to go with the several it has had already from past experiences with this customer.

When most relationships reach this point—and the collections person has done a thorough job of communicating the creditor company's needs in the letters, telephone calls, fax messages, and visits to the customer's place of business that will have preceded the final demand—there is no relationship to be salvaged. You have already given the account a disproportionate amount of your time. If there is no payment response to this *last call*, then you do exactly what you have told the customer you will do. You will assign the account to a collection agency, file suit in Small Claims Court (if applicable), assign the account to an attorney who is a collection specialist, or move on to whatever action is specified in your final demand letter.

So you have spent more time and effort trying to salvage the account than the customer's attitude deserved, but you didn't know it would lead to that when you began the collection effort. Now you know. Unless the customer has the equivalent of a death-bed revelation and miraculously turns into a bill-paying pussycat (and you wouldn't want more than half a buck riding on that one), give it to the people who spend their workdays trying to collect money from these types. You have many other accounts whose problems have been getting less than a fair share of your time. Get back to doing a total credit and collections job with all of your company's accounts.

Examples of Final Demand Letters

The circumstances of how customers arrive at a point where they are sent a final demand letter varies from one to another, but there is no difference in the urgency and the finality of a final demand. It is the last step before a curtain comes down on a relationship that may have been short or long, could have been contentious or promising from the start, and may even have been mutually rewarding for several months or years. But now it is real trouble—trouble that has escalated from receivables aging that was bothersome and occasionally unacceptable, to an account whose receivables balances have slid into an aging pattern that the customer is either unwilling or unable to change.

At this point, or sooner if the circumstances tell you the timing is right to do it, you will send the customer a final demand from the following selection of letters.

14.1   [date]

Name of Company
Street Address (or P.O. Box Number)
City, State, Zip Code

Attention: [name and title]

Dear Mr./Ms. _____:

There has been no response to our telephone and letter requests for payment of your account balance, which is currently _____ days past due.

We are unwilling to devote anymore in-house time to the collection effort. The account will be referred to our collection agency on [date] if payment in the amount of $_____ has not been received.

It is unfortunate that the relationship has reached this point. The next move is yours.

Sincerely,

Credit Manager

14.2   [date]

Name of Company
Street Address (or P.O. Box Number)
City, State, Zip Code

Attention: [name and title]

Dear Mr./Ms._____:

You have convinced us not to devote any more in-house time to this collection effort.

Receivables aging to _____ days past due is as far as we go. Unless your check for $_____ arrives by the _____ of [month], the account will be assigned immediately to our collection service.

Sincerely,

Credit Manager

14.3   [date]

Name of Company
Street Address (or P.O. Box Number)
City, State, Zip Code

Attention: [name and title]

Dear Mr./Ms. _____:

Approximately five months ago this department assigned a $10,000 credit line to your company; at that time I called to tell you the amount of the credit line and to convey our hope that the relationship would prove to be a mutually beneficial one. You assured me that your company would have no trouble staying within the credit limit and within the parameters of our credit terms.

Unfortunately, I am looking now at account aging that is seriously at odds with that pledge: $3100 between 1 and 30 days past due, $4700 30 to 60 days past due, and $2600 60 to 70 days past due. $10,400 is past due and sliding deeper into the past-due categories.

Three telephone calls resulted in payment promises that have not been honored. Orders are being held and will continue to be held until a check for $_____ is received—and that check must be in this office by [date]. Beyond that date, the account will be assigned to third-party collection.

I hope your company will make the appropriate effort to reduce the receivables balance and work to salvage the relationship.

Sincerely,

Credit Manager

14.4   [date]

Name of Company
Street Address (or P.O. Box Number)
City, State, Zip Code

Attention: [name and title]

Dear Mr./Ms._____:

The relationship between our two companies has (certainly for us) become a major dilemma.

The payment schedule that was discussed and accepted on [date] was designed to enable your company to continue to receive product(s) while past-due balances were being returned to acceptable areas of aging.

The first payment was due by [date], but that date passed without payment or an explanation. The due date for the second payment is [date] and our concern is that it too will not be honored. This is an unanticipated and an unwelcome turn in the relationship between our companies.

I urge you to forward one of the scheduled payments so that it arrives at this office by [date]; and forward a second payment to reach this office by [date]. If this happens, I will reactivate the payment schedule and work through it with you.

Both checks must arrive by the dates listed above to avoid having the account assigned to a collection agency, and assigned with appropriate instructions for protecting our receivables interest.

There is still time to salvage the relationship, but the positive move must come from your company and within the stated time frame.

Sincerely,

Credit Manager

14.5   [date]

Name of Company
Street Address (or P.O. Box Number)
City, State, Zip Code

Attention: [name and title]

Dear Mr./Ms. _____:

We have certainly done our part. The record of telephone calls, fax messages, collection letters, and personal visits says that we gave your company every opportunity to pay what it owes us.

This is not another in the long line of reminders and requests for payment. This is what is known as a *final demand*; the last correspondence before we assign the account to a collection service. The point that is to be remembered is that if your company's check for $_____ has not reached our company by [date], the account will be assigned the following day. No further delays and no last-minute reprieves.

Our policy has always been to treat our customers with courtesy, consideration, and respect; to treat them the way we would like to be treated. We prefer to handle collection matters ourselves, on an amicable basis rather than as a formal, third-party collection effort. But when *amicable* fails, there is no hesitation, because we do expect to collect our money.

Sincerely,

Credit Manager

14.6   [date]

Name of Company
Street Address (or P.O. Box Number)
City, State, Zip Code

Attention: [name and title]

Dear Mr./Ms. _____:

Nothing that we have done to this point—letters, telephone calls, fax messages, and a personal visit—has motivated your company to pay the listed invoices:

Invoice No.	Invoice Date	Invoice Amt.

These invoices range from ____ to ____ days past due, and there is no latitude for further delay. Payment in full (a check for $____) must be in this office by [date] or the account will be assigned immediately to our collection service.

This is not just another reminder or request for payment. It is what is known as a *final demand*: the last correspondence before we assign the account for collection.

Sincerely,

Credit Manager

14.7   [date]

Name of Company
Street Address (or P.O. Box Number)
City, State, Zip Code

Attention: [name and title]

Dear Mr./Ms. _____:

There has been no response to our numerous telephone, fax messages, and letter requests for payment of your account balance, currently ___ to ___ days past due.

We are unable to devote any more in-house time to the collection effort. The account will be assigned to our collection agency on [date] if we have not received payment in the amount of $_____.

Sincerely,

Credit Manager

14.8   [date]

Name of Company
Street Address (or P.O. Box Number)
City, State, Zip Code

Attention: [name and title]

Dear Mr./Ms. _____:

This is a final demand for payment of the $_____ account balance by [date].

If payment has not arrived by the date stated above, the account will be assigned immediately to our collection service. My instructions in situations of this kind are always the same: to proceed on any basis that the collection service feels is appropriate to collect our money.

Sincerely,

Credit Manager

14.9   [date]

Name of Company
Street Address (or P.O. Box Number)
City, State, Zip Code

Attention: [name and title]

Dear Mr./Ms. _____:

Our relationship has not been one that I would categorize as a voyage through untroubled waters. I must tell you, however, that I did not expect the relationship to deteriorate this rapidly or this completely.

We are now at the point where this *final demand* letter is the inevitable culmination of a string of unproductive telephone calls, fax messages, collection letters, and office visits. The message is clear and simple: Your check for $_____ must arrive at this company's offices by [date], or the account will be assigned immediately to our collection service. This means no further delays, no discussions, and no further communication from this office.

The choice is yours. Paying us by [date] will spare your company the experience of dealing with our collection service.

Sincerely,

Credit Manager

14.10   [date]

Name of Company
Street Address (or P.O. Box Number)
City, State, Zip Code

Attention: [name and title]

Dear Mr./Ms. _____:

We have not been successful in our effort to collect past-due balances owed to this company by your firm. Because telephone and letter requests for payment have not been successful, we are unwilling to devote any more in-house time to the collection effort.

I must now tell you that the account will be forwarded to our collection service on [date] if payment in the amount of $_____ has not been received.

Sincerely,

Credit Manager

14.11   [date]

Name of Company
Street Address (or P.O. Box Number)
City, State, Zip Code

Attention: [name and title]

Dear Mr./Ms. _____:

There has been no response to our telephone and letter requests for payment of your account balance, currently ____ days past due.

We can devote no more in-house time to the collection effort. I must now tell you that the account will be referred to our collection agency on [date] if we have not received payment in the amount of $_____.

Sincerely,

Credit Manager

14.12   [date]

Name of Company
Street Address (or P.O. Box Number)
City, State, Zip Code

Attention: [name and title]

Dear Mr./Ms. _____:

It is no major news item to state that supplier-customer relationships frequently start with high hopes but end on a note of frustration and disappointment. So it is with our relationship—or that is the way we see it.

After an assortment of unproductive communications, we have arrived at the *final demand* letter. It brings a clear and simple message to your company: Your company's check for $_____ is to arrive in this company's offices by [date] or the account will be assigned to our collection service. There must be no further delays, no discussion regarding a possible payment program; only the focus on collecting our money as fast as possible.

Would we be interested in selling to your company at some time in the future? If the umbilical cord between our two companies is severed as the result of payment problems, we would not be interested in selling to your company again.

Sincerely,

Credit Manager

Now that you have seen some examples of *final demand*, let us backtrack for a few moments. Remember that a *final demand* is the letter of last resort: something that we do not write until every other tool has been used. When there has been a collection effort consisting of telephone calls, collection letters, fax messages, and a visit(s) to the office of the customer—and no combination has motivated the customer/debtor to pay—then the *final demand* letter is your last motivator.

But before you write that *final demand,* ask yourself the following questions:

1. Did I send the customer/debtor a mix of payment requests suitable for the company and the situation?

2. Was I open and receptive to the legitimate problems and requests of the customer/debtor?

3. Have I contributed in any way to the customer's cashflow problem (holding orders, demanding large lump-sum payments, etc.)?

4. Has the customer/debtor been straightforward in his or her responses to payment requests?

5. Have I given the customer/debtor every reasonable opportunity to arrange a payment plan that will reduce past-due balances and allow limited purchases?

6. If the customer/debtor has been making an honest effort to distribute cashflow as fairly as possible, am I jeopardizing the customer's relationship with other suppliers if I ask for a bigger payment than the others?

If the majority of your answers to these questions substantiates your feeling that the customer has had more than a reasonable number of opportunities to do the right thing by your company—to pay past-due balances that have slipped to unacceptable aging—then it is time to take the next step. The *next step* is, of course, the one in which you assign the customer/debtor account to a collection service and limit your company's future involvement in the collection process to monitoring progress reports forwarded by the collection service.

Letters Notifying Customer of Collection Assignment

When the customer fails to pay the required number of dollars by the date specified in your final demand letter, it is time to assign the account to a commercial collection service or agency. When the responsibility for collecting the account balance has been assigned to others, you are free to devote a higher percentage of your attention to the problems and needs of other customers, and that cannot fail to benefit your company.

Does your company's collection service offer a "ten-day free demand" on all accounts assigned to it? This means that if within 10 days from the assignment date the customer sends a check in full payment of the collection assignment to your office or to the office of the collection service, no collection fee will be charged! There are accounts that will pay during the first ten days of the assignment: Be sure your company receives every dollar of that payment.

14.13   **Collection Assignments**

Account Number	Account Name	Date Assigned	Amount Assigned	Collection Agency	Status of Collection

The letters that follow are examples of what you might send to a customer/debtor whose account has been assigned to a collection service or agency. There is no attempt in these letters to be conciliatory or to hold out any hope that a future supplier-customer relationship might rise from the ashes of this unsatisfactory experience. These are letters that tell the customer what has been done, may occasionally review the reasons why it has been done, and leave no doubt in the mind of the customer that your company's determination to collect the account balance remains strong.

14.14   [date]

Name of Company
Street Address (or P.O. Box Number)
City, State, Zip Code

Attention: [name and title]

Dear Mr./Ms. _____:

Several telephone calls, fax messages, collection letters, a personal visit, and a consistent pattern of broken payment promises add up to an account experience that over the past ___ months has continuously brutalized our credit terms. It is an experience that has brought us to the point where we can no longer afford to devote in-house time to the collection effort.

I have this date assigned your company's account to a third party collection service. The collection service has been instructed to proceed on whatever basis may be necessary to collect our money.

I should add also that from this date forward, our products will not be available to your company.

Sincerely,

Credit Manager

14.15   [date]

Name of Company
Street Address (or P.O. Box Number)
City, State, Zip Code

Attention: [name and title]

Dear Mr./Ms. _____:

Our in-house efforts to get your company to pay its past-due account balance has not been successful; in fact, a review of the telephone calls, fax messages, collection letters, and visits to your office indicates that almost nothing has happened during the course of this collection effort to clear any charges from the account. Open items are listed below:

Invoice No.	Invoice Date	Invoice Amt.

Our records and discussions with your office have confirmed that these are legitimate charges and that there is no credit due or pending against any of them. This information has had no effect on the collection process, so we are taking it to the next—and formal—collection level.

The account has this date been assigned to our collection service for appropriate action. Any further communication regarding these past-due balances will come from the collection service. Questions and/or responses should be addressed to the collection service and not to this company.

It should be understood that from today forward, this company's products will not be available to your company. We do not anticipate that this policy toward your company—and toward others whose account has been assigned for collection—will undergo any future change.

Sincerely,

Credit Manager

14.16 [date]

Name of Company
Street Address (or P.O. Box Number)
City, State, Zip Code

Attention: [name and title]

Dear Mr./Ms. _____:

We are not willing to continue what has for too many months been a one-sided relationship. Numerous payment promises have been made and broken, or a token payment has been forwarded in lieu of the promised larger payment. These are not the tactics of a customer whose business we can afford to retain.

We have this date assigned your company's past-due balance to our collection service. You will be hearing from the collection service within the week, but I would not wait that long to pay the account balance. A collection procedure by a collection service does not enhance the image of the debtor with his or her other suppliers.

Our policy is not to sell to accounts whose payment record has been so poor that we have been forced to assign the account for collection.

Sincerely,

Credit Manager

14.17 [date]

Name of Company
Street Address (or P.O. Box Number)
City, State, Zip Code

Attention: [name and title]

Dear Mr./Ms. _____:

It is obvious that at this late date in our relationship there is very little going on that is acceptable to us. Promises have been made and continue to be made regarding payment for past-due balances but, unfortunately, promises are broken as rapidly as they are made. We can no longer have any confidence in the strength of your company's resolve to do what it promises it will do.

The account has this date been assigned to our collection service with instructions to proceed on any basis they feel is appropriate. I must add, however, that although our collection service conducts its business in an ethical manner, you may want to pay the balance that we have assigned to them before they begin the collection procedure. Why would you do that if nothing we have said previously motivated you to pay? It could be that you prefer to avoid an experience that might be compared to the feeling that your company has a pit bull hanging from the seat of its corporate trousers.

It is probably not a good feeling—and certainly not a good corporate image.

Sincerely,

Credit Manager

Bankruptcy and the Collection Process

This is not a book for a detailed analysis of what occurs when a debtor (or the debtor's creditors) files for relief under Chapter 11 of The Bankruptcy Act (see *Credit Management Handbook* by Cecil J. Bond [McGraw-Hill]). It is relevant, however, for the person who has the responsibility for collecting receivables balances to have more than a minimal awareness of the filing process, how a filing impacts the rights of creditors, and what can or should be done to ensure that the rights of your company are not compromised to the point where the chances for a meaningful recovery are slim-to-none.

The following includes many of the major points in the Chapter 11 process: from the voluntary or involuntary filing, to acceptance or rejection of the plan of arrangement:

1. *Voluntary filing:* The debtor files for relief from creditors under Chapter 11.

2. *Involuntary filing:* Filed by three creditors who have undisputed claims that total $500 more than the value of any lien on the property securing the claim (or if less than 12 creditors, any one creditor can file).

3. *Forms for filing:* Obtained at the U.S. District Court for the district in which the filing is to be made.

4. *Debtor files a petition:* Automatically activates a stay of any legal proceedings that might be working against the debtor, including collection effort of creditors, third-party collection agencies, and attorneys.

5. *Debtor's obligations:* The debtor must furnish a list of creditors (and account balances) to the bankruptcy court.

6. *Schedule of assets:* Debtor furnishes a list to the bankruptcy court, including location and description of the assets, their age, condition, and life expectancy.

7. *Additional reports (two):* One statement details the condition of the company's financial affairs, and the second is a schedule or projection of the company's income and expenses for the next week and month.

8. *Cooperating with trustee:* Debtor's cooperation with the trustee must include surrendering any records or property, etc., which are important to the trustee's work.

9. *Notification to creditors:* Notice of filing is sent to creditors by the bankruptcy court (from list of creditors supplied by the debtor).

10. *Notice for a first meeting of creditors:* Follows shortly after creditors have been notified of the filing. Refer to the Order for Meetings of Creditors, Combined with Notice of Automatic Stay. (If available, a copy of the debtor's proposed *arrangement*—how the debtor proposes to handle creditor balances and how the business would be restructured for continuation—is included with the Notice.)

11. *Court appoints receiver or a trustee in bankruptcy continues:* In possession of the debtor's property.

12. *First meeting of creditors:* Creditor is examined (asked questions) by creditors and attorneys for creditors, hears witnesses, and appoints a creditor's committee.

13. *Mandatory filing of plan of arrangement:* The judge sets the time frame within which the debtor must file the plan of arrangement. First meeting is then adjourned for a minimum of 15 days after date set for the debtor to deliver a *plan of arrangement* to the court.

14. *Time lag:* A minimum of 15 days between delivery of *the plan* and the first meeting of creditors provides for the judge and the creditor's committee to examine the proposed arrangement, to have copies made, to include the

recommendations of the creditor's committee (acceptance or rejection of the proposal), and to mail it with a copy of the notice for the next meeting of creditors.

15. *Jurisdiction of the bankruptcy court:* Has jurisdiction in all areas of the bankruptcy process in the specific district of its authority. Refer to Stipulation Pertaining to Use of Collateral Providing for ...

16. *Appointing a trustee (or conservator):* Interim trustee is appointed immediately after the judge issues his or her order for the petitioner's relief.

17. *Electing a trustee:* Trustee may be elected if creditors who have 20 percent of the allowed, unsecured, liquidated claims request it (to be eligible, none of the claims may be entitled to priority, has no interests materially adverse to the interest of the generally unsecured creditors, and is not an insider).

18. *Types of claims:* Secured (UCC Filings, etc.), unsecured, priority.

19. *The plan of arrangement/continuation plan:* Must deal fairly with all claimants within a framework that offers a reasonable chance for success. (Secured claimants are above *the plan*, already on a plateau above that occupied by the priority, and unsecured claimants.)

20. *Acceptance or rejection of The Plan:* The creditor's committee forwards to those claimants who are eligible to vote its recommendation for acceptance or rejection. If a majority of the creditors eligible to vote request a change(s) in The Plan, the creditor's committee will make the change(s) and return the modified version to creditors for acceptance or rejection. Refer to the following cover letter/ballot from the creditor's committee requesting creditors to accept or reject *the plan* and the second letter/ballot (Modifications to Plan of Arrangement) requesting creditors to accept or reject it.

Author's note: The reverse side of the form on the facing page (Order and Notice) is the Claim Form. Complete it in duplicate, make a copy for your file, and forward the original and a duplicate as instructed.

14.18

CHAPTER 11
IN RE: [CASE NUMBER]

95103   8723987
U.S. BANKRUPTCY COURT
ROOM 906, U.S. COURTHOUSE
312 NO. SPRING ST.
LOS ANGELES, CA 90012-4701

CHAPTER 11
ORDER FOR MEETING OF CREDITORS, COMBINED WITH NOTICE OF AUTOMATIC STAY

To the debtor, his creditors and other parties interest:
An order for relief under 11 U.S.C. Chapter 11, having been entered on a petition filed by (or against) the above named debtor on December 27, 19XX

IT IS ORDERED, AND NOTICE IS HEREBY GIVEN THAT:

1. A meeting of creditors is pursuant to 11 U.S.C., 31(a) shall be held at:

U.S. TRUST HEARING ROOM	DATE
U.S. FEDERAL BUILDING	JANUARY 6, 19XX
300 N. LOS ANGELES ST., RM. 3114	HOUR
LOS ANGELES, CA	3:15 PM

2. The debtor shall appear in person (or, if the debtor is a partnership, by a general partner, or, if the debtor is a corporation, by its president or other executive officer) at that time and place for the purpose of being examined.

YOU ARE FURTHER NOTIFIED THAT:

The meeting may be continued or adjourned from time to time by notice at the meeting without further written notice to creditors.
At the meeting the creditors may file their claims, examine the debtor, and transact such other business as may properly come before the meeting.

As a result of filing of the petition, certain acts and proceedings against the debotr and his property are stayed as provided in 11 U.S.C. 362(a).

The debtor (or trustee) has filed or will file a list of creditors and equity security holders pursuant to Rule 1007. Any creditor holding a listed claim which is not listed as disputed, contingent, or unliquidated as to amount, may, but need not file a proof of claim in this case. Creditors whose claims are not listed or whose claims are listed as disputed, contingent, or unliquidated as to amount and who desire to participate in the case or share in any distribution must file their proofs of claim on or before the last day fixed for filing a proof of claim. Any creditor who desires to rely on the list has the responsibility for determining that his is accurately listed.

LOCAL RULE 3001 (B) PROVIDES THAT A PROOF OF CLAIM, INCLUDING AMENDMENTS THEREOF, MAY BE FILED AT ANY TIME PRIOR TO CONFIRMATION OF THE PLAN UNLESS A DIFFERENT TIME IS FIXED BY THE COURT ON NOTICE AS PROVIDED BY BANKRUPTCY RULE 3003 (C) (3).

FILE CLAIM FORM ON THE REVERSE SIDE IN DUPLICATE WITH
    U.S. BANKRUPTCY COURT
    ROOM 906, U.S. COURTHOUSE
    312 NO. SPRING ST.
    LOS ANGELES, CA 90012-4701

Dated: DECEMBER 2, 19XX   [By the Court]
    AT LOS ANGELES, CA
CHARLES A. MILLER, CLERK OF COURT

14.19 FRAZER, CARTER, WALSH, BENSON & HARRIS

A Professional Corporation
   Franklin Carter
529 California Street, Suite 1350
San Francisco, CA 94111-5879
Telephone (415) 555-9998

Attorneys for North Bay National Bank

UNITED STATES BANKRUPTCY COURT
FOR THE NORTHERN DISTRICT OF CALIFORNIA

In Re:	)	Bankruptcy No. 5-89-16524-M
	)	
XYZ CORPORATION, INC.,	)	Chapter 11
A California Corporation	)	
	)	
Debtor	)	
	)	

STIPULATION PERTAINING TO USE OF COLLATERAL PROVIDING FOR ADE-
QUATE PROTECTION SECURED BY LIEN ON PROPERTY OF THE ESTATE
UNDER S364(c), MODIFICATION OF STAY AND ORDER THEREON

TO: THE HONORABLE WILBUR A. HANSEN, BANKRUPTCY JUDGE:

XYZ Corporation, Inc., the Debtor and Debtor-in-Possession herein, and North Bay
National Bank, the Secured Party, apply to this Court for an Order authorizing use of
collateral, providing for adequate protection and the pledging of collateral in
connection therewith, and to borrow funds pursuant to 11 U.S.C. s364(c) and
pledge collateral in connection therewith.

1. On September 14, 19XX, the Debtor filed its Petition under Chapter 11 herein,
and is Debtor-in-Possession.

2. The Debtor's business consists of a health spa and athletic club. Debtor is the
owner of certain real property, as more particularly described on the deed of trust
attached as part of Exhibit "A" hereto ("Real Property"), rents, issues and profits,
equipment, and proceeds thereof as set forth in Exhibit "A," (collectively the
"Collateral") used in the operation of the business.

3. The Debtor requires funds to operate said business and to preserve the Collateral.

4. The Debtor is presently without funds necessary to operate, other than funds
generated from the operation of the club, restaurant, other facilities, and member
fees.

5. Other than certain ongoing services and supplies provided by trade vendors, the
Debtor is unable to obtain credit on a basis other than under s364(c) of the
Bankruptcy Code.

6. The Secured Party and Debtor acknowledges that the unpaid balance of the loan
by Secured Party to Debtor (the "Loan") as of August 7, 19XX, including principal
and interest only, is $6,945,286. The Secured Party has agreed to consent to use of

its Collateral as provided for hereinafter, on a basis that will provide adequate protection and security. In that connection, Debtor and Secured Party have agreed that adequate protection and the necessary security can be provided through use of Collateral secured pursuant to the Loan and the loan documents ("Loan Documents") previously entered into between the Secured Party and the Debtor (copies of which are attached hereto and incorporated by reference herein and are attached as Exhibit "A"), as modified pursuant to the terms of paragraph 7 hereof and this paragraph. Except as expressly modified herein, the Loan Documents shall remain in full force and effect.

7. The Secured Party and the Debtor hereby agree as follows:

> (a) Secured Party consents to the continued use of Collateral by the Debtor, for use by the Debtor as hereinafter set forth, provided that the Court has approved this Stipulation and the . . .

20. Nothing herein is intended to create any right on the part of any third party to assume the terms and conditions of this Stipulation and agreement, and Secured Party retains its right to declare all principal, accrued interest, associated fees and charges, immediately due and payable upon the sale or transfer by the Debtor of the Real Property, or any interest therein, or upon any change in the ownership of the shares of stock of Debtor in excess of 25% of the outstanding shares, or effective change in control of the Debtor.

WHEREFORE, the parties hereto pray that this Court enter its Order authorizing the Debtor to use cash collateral, to borrow funds under s364(c) of the Code from the Secured Party pursuant to the terms of this Stipulation, and each of the terms of this Stipulation be authorized, and declaring that the notice and opportunity for hearing which has been given in respect to this Stipulation are appropriate in the particular circumstances.

DATE: November 22, 19XX.

NORTH BAY NATIONAL BANK
(Secured Party)

By: _____

Its: _____

DATED: November 22, 19XX.

XYZ CORPORATION, INC.
(Debtor)

By: _____

Its: _____

14.20

IN RE:	)	BANKRUPTCY NO. 8-42-16341-Z
XYZ CORPORATION, INC.,	)	CHAPTER 11
A CALIFORNIA CORPORATION	)	
	)	
	)	
DEBTOR.	)	
_____	)	

NOTICE OF HEARING ON APPLICATION OF DEBTOR-IN-POSSESSION
REQUESTING APPROVAL OF STIPULATION PERTAINING TO USE OF COLLATERAL
PROVIDING FOR ADEQUATE PROTECTION SECURED BY LIEN ON PROPERTY OF THE
ESTATE UNDER SECTION 364c, MODIFICATION OF STAY

TO: THE CREDITORS OF THE ABOVE-NAMED DEBTOR AND OTHER PARTIES IN INTEREST:

NOTICE IS HEREBY GIVEN THAT XYZ CORPORATION, INC., Debtor-In-Possession
herein, has filed an Application with the Court seeking approval of a Stipulation and
Agreement between the Debtor and Urban Bank, and that said Application will be
heard, considered, and passed upon at the courtroom of the HONORABLE CHARLES
C. MONROEL, UNITED STATES BANKRUPTCY JUDGE, ROOM 396, U.S. POST OFFICE
BUILDING, NORTH FIRST & ST. JOHN STREETS, SAN JOSE, CALIFORNIA, on:
WEDNESDAY, OCTOBER 23 , 19XX, AT 2:00 PM.

The Stipulation and Agreement negotiated between the Debtor and Urban Bank
contains a number of provisions, terms, and conditions, under which the Debtor will
continue to operate its business known as the Centurian Club. Because of the
complexity and comprehensive nature of the Stipulation and Agreement between
the parties, a copy of the complete Stipulation and Agreement is attached to this
notice to provide creditors and parties-in-interest with complete information and
details regarding the transaction. Exhibits to the Stipulation are on file with the Court.

Reference is hereby made to all pleadings and documentation on file with the Court with
respect to this Chapter 11 case, which information is available for inspection. Creditors or
other parties-in-interest having any questions, or wishing additional information regarding
the matter, may contact the Debtor's Counsel, CARL M. GREEN, GREEN & GREEN, 19
NORTH MARKET STREET, SUITE 168, SAN JOSE, CALIFORNIA 95113, 408 555-9999.

Dated: September 16, 19XX

GREEN & GREEN
Attorneys for Debtor and
Debtor-in-Possession

(ANY CORRESPONDENCE REQUIRING AN ANSWER FROM THE COURT SHOULD BE
ACCOMPANIED BY A STAMPED, SELF-ADDRESSED ENVELOPE.)

14.21 [date]

To: Unsecured Claimants
From: Creditor's Committee
Re: Plan of Arrangement/Continuation (Dated _____)
Case #14969-XX—Bertran Manufacturing Company

Attention: [name and title]

Dear Mr./Ms. _____:

It is the judgment of your creditor's committee that the attached Plan of Arrangement/Continuation represents the best and most equitable arrangement that the debtor company's position will allow.

Please read it carefully. If you agree that the provisions of the plan are acceptable as presented, indicate your acceptance by marking the space that precedes YES. If you do not agree that the plan is acceptable in its present form, indicate that decision by marking the space that precedes NO. Add your reason(s) for rejecting the plan and what changes would, for your company, make it acceptable.

The creditor's committee urges claimants to approve the plan by the percentages necessary for the court to certify the plan (two-thirds of the total claims dollars of claimants who vote and over 50 percent of the number of claimants who vote).

____ YES, we accept the plan as presented.

____ NO, we do not accept the plan in its present form.

It is our feeling that the following change(s) should be made: _____

_____

_____

_____

For the Committee

_____   _____

Chairman   Date

14.22   [date]

To: Unsecured Claimants
From: Creditor's Committee
Re: Modification(s) to Plan of Arrangement/Continuation (Dated _____)
Case #14969-XX—Bertran Manufacturing Company

Attention: [name and title]

Dear Mr./Ms. _____:

The attached modification of the Plan of Arrangement/Continuation incorporates changes requested by a majority of creditors who responded to the Committee's cover letter and original version of the Plan of Arrangement/Continuation which was dated _____. It includes the two major changes that were requested by the creditors and brings the plan within parameters defined by a majority of the respondents.

The Creditor's Committee requests that claimants approve the modified plan and return the ballot portion of this cover letter by [date].

Your cooperation is appreciated.

_____
Chairman

_____

To: Creditor's Committee
From: [Name of creditor company]

___ YES, we accept the plan as modified on [date].

___ NO, we cannot accept the plan as modified [date].

Signed

_____
Title

Questions and Answers

A voluntary reorganization of a company or business may be changed by a debtor in possession to a liquidation case. If it is requested by a person who has an interest in the case, and if it is in the best interest of the creditors and the estate, the court may grant permission for the change.

Question: How can a voluntary reorganization be dismissed?

Answer: The court may dismiss it or convert it to a liquidation case.

Question: What reasons would justify a conversion or dismissal?

Answer: If the business or estate continues to lose money with no likelihood of a turnaround; the debtor is unable or unwilling to deliver a reorganization plan within the time frame set by the court; the debtor's plan is not confirmed by the creditors; the confirmed plan is not put in place by the debtor; major failure of the debtor in one or more areas of the confirmed plan.

Question: When is a first hearing held?

Answer: Notices are sent to interested parties 10 days before a hearing date, which is set not less than 20 or more than 40 days after the filing date of the petition.

Question: How are creditors notified about *the plan*?

Answer: Creditors and other interested parties are given information adequate for them to make a decision. The court will decide what constitutes a *reasonable disclosure time frame in which creditors may make their decision.*

Question: What is the criteria for acceptance of the Plan of Reorganization?

Answer: A class of creditors accepts the plan by at least two-thirds in amount and more than one-half in number if the allowed claims of the class have voted for the plan.

Question: How is a plan modified?

Answer: The debtor or other proponents of the plan may modify it before the creditors confirm it or after it has been confirmed but before it has been put in place. The bankruptcy court will confirm the modified plan after notice and a hearing, if circumstances warrant it.

Question: Who may object to confirmation of a plan?

Answer: Any creditor or other party in interest.

Question: What is the effect of confirmation?

Answer: It is binding on the debtor, all creditors, equity security holders, or a general partner of the debtor. The debtor is discharged from all debts from the date of the confirmation unless the plan states otherwise.

There is a strong belief among those who extend commercial and consumer credit that the bankruptcy process is too easy. The opinion is held widely that the process of filing for bankruptcy, that is,

1. being examined by creditors and the court,
2. filing a continuation plan or restructuring debt in a format that offers no reasonable expectation for acceptance or success,
3. then ultimately being declared bankrupt and receiving a discharge from debts,

is done too quickly, too frequently, and too frivolously by individuals and businesses who find it a convenient way to escape their legitimate obligations and responsibilities.

Collecting past-due balances is never easy, even when the customer/debtor is conscientiously attempting to do the right thing by the company's suppliers. But when the collection process goes up against an account whose escape hatch—a filing under Chapter 11—is opened quietly and carefully by a management whose personal and business integrity vanishes at the first sign of a crisis, supplier dollars are in very serious jeopardy.

15

Other Collection Devices and Procedures

The basic thrust of most collection efforts consists of a mix of what has been detailed to this point: collection letters, telephone calls, fax (letters, messages, and memos), and personal visits to the customer-debtor's office or place of business. In a great majority of collections situations, one or a combination of these approaches is successful. Past-due balances are collected, the supplier and the customer are able to establish (or reestablish) mutually acceptable ground rules and the relationship can become the good one that it once was—or the good one it had been expected to become.

Beyond the variety of collection techniques and procedures that has been presented and dissected in preceding pages of this book is what we refer to as the *formal collection procedures*. These are the procedures that may not initially involve some form of court action but could escalate rapidly to that level: Account assigned to a collection service; creditor seeks a judgment in Small Claims Court; assignment to a collection attorney, suit if it becomes necessary, or a Chapter 11 petition filed by the customer-debtor. Credit grantors must also consider (before the credit account becomes a problem) the protection offered by the Uniform Commercial Code and Mechanic's Lien Laws. And when a customer evacuates a business and disappears into the night, there is always *skip tracing* (which is described later in this chapter).

Every grantor of credit hopes to resolve problems of past-due balances before they become a matter for the courts. But when all other attempts to collect from the customer have failed, the supplier must use the legal system to recover the money for product(s) that was sold to the customer in good faith. When in-house collection procedures have had no success—have met with a level of success that for the magnitude of the problem is less than appropriate—it is time to move on to a formal collection procedure.

Suing in Small Claims Court

Small Claims Court is *do it yourself* law, the place where a business person handles the suit cycle from forms to filing and on through the court's decision. The forms used to illustrate this section are from the Municipal Court of California, Santa Clara County Judicial District, Small Claims Division, and plaintiffs filing in that judicial jurisdiction should be the only people to use them or to be guided by them. You must sue in the right court and in the right judicial district: a rule called venue. Contact the Small Claims Division (or Court) of the judicial district in which you will file your claim. You will be told where to obtain the necessary forms and instructions.

You might encounter few, or many, variations in the filing procedure from one major jurisdiction to another, but what is included here should be typical of the basic process of filing through judgment (and through appeal, if that option is exercised by the defendant). In the subject jurisdiction (Santa Clara County Judicial District), the number of forms is seven. If the defendant appeals to the Superior Court from a Small Claims Court ruling in favor of the plaintiff, the defendant would activate the eighth form: Notice of Filing Notice of Appeal.

Copies in sequential order follow a brief description of each form. Also included are a copy of the Fictitious Business Name Declaration and an explanation of its importance and relevance in California, and also in many other states.

- *Suit form:* Plaintiff's name, defendant's name, nature of the claim, etc.
- *Proof of service:* States how, where, and by whom relevant papers were served on the defendant.
- *Plaintiff's claim:* Describes the amount of the debt, effort to collect, and rules of the court.
- *Defendant's claim:* Countersuit stating amount owed defendant, effort to collect, etc.
- *Order to appear for examination:* Issued against Judgment Debtor and/or Third Person because the Judgment Debtor claims the Third Person has possession or control of property which belongs to the Judgment Debtor, or concerning a debt owed the Judgment Debtor by a Third Person.
- *Abstract of judgment:* Judgment Creditor or Assignee of Record applies to the court clerk for a certified copy of the Small Claims Court judgment.
- *Memorandum of credits, accrued interest, and costs after judgment:* Self-explanatory. All payments and charges pertaining to the case through the date executed.
- *Notice of filing notice of appeal:* Judgment Debtor appeals to the Superior Court from the Small Claims Court judgment or denial of motion to vacate the judgment.

You will use an additional form, Fictitious Name Declaration, in conjunction with a filing in Small Claims Court in California and many other states. Failure to comply with California Law (and the law in other states) could cause the court to dismiss your claim. To use the example of California, you file the Fictitious Name Declarations with the clerk of the county in which the principal place of business is located or in Sacramento County if the filing firm has no place of business within the state. Whether your state does or does not require the filing of a *fictitious name* or *DBA* statement is information you will want to obtain when you inquire regarding the *how and where* of filing your claim in Small Claims Court.

The thought that you will be acting as your own attorney should not be inhibiting. This court is not a court where silver-tongued oratory is a requisite. Presenting your case does not demand the skills of a Clarence Darrow. The trial itself is informal and the rules simple:

- Be in court on time.
- Bring with you all witnesses, books, receipts, and other papers or things to prove your case.
- Ask the clerk of the court to issue a subpoena if a witness is reluctant or unwilling to come to court. A subpoena requires the witness to appear.
- Be prepared to pay a fee to the witness for his or her court appearance.
- Get a court order requiring that the necessary records or papers be brought to the trial to prove your case (if you do not have them but know where they are).
- File a dismissal form with the court clerk if the case is settled before the trial date or time.
- You might receive the court's decision in the mail or someone might hand-deliver it to you in court when the trial is over. The form used for the decision is called The Notice of Entry of Judgment.
- The person who wins the case is called the judgment creditor; the loser, and the one who owes the money, is called the judgment debtor.
- You cannot enforce judgment until after the period for filing an appeal has ended. After judgment has been rendered, and if the judgment is appealed in Superior Court by the judgment debtor, both parties may be represented by attorneys.

Other requirements are necessary before the Clerk of the Small Claims Court can accept a filing (making a final demand on the debtor, etc.). Every jurisdiction should offer some advice and assistance in the preparation of claims cases. In California, it is the Department of Consumer Affairs, Small Claims Advisor, Sacramento. In your city or state there is probably a similar source for information and assistance. If the court in which you would file a claim does not provide such assistance or advice—and I question whether any court that does not permit attorneys to appear would be so insensitive to the needs of litigants—then you should be directed to the appropriate source for such information.

INFORMATION FOR THE SMALL CLAIMS PLAINTIFF

This information sheet is written for the person who sues in the small claims court. It explains some of the rules and some general information about the small claims court. It may also be helpful for the person who is sued.

WHAT IS SMALL CLAIMS COURT?

Small claims court is a special court where disputes are resolved quickly and inexpensively. The rules are simple and informal. The person who sues is the **plaintiff**. The person who is sued is the **defendant**. In small claims court, you may ask a lawyer for advice before you go to court, but you cannot have a lawyer in court. Your claim cannot be for more than $5,000 *(*see below)*. If you have a claim for more than this amount, you may sue in the civil division of the municipal court or you may sue in the small claims court and give up your right to the amount over $5,000. You cannot, however, file more than two cases in small claims court for more than $2,500 each during a calendar year.

WHO CAN FILE A CLAIM?

1. You must be at least *18 years old* to file a claim. If you are not yet 18, you may ask the court to appoint a **guardian ad litem**. This is a person who will act for you in the case. The guardian ad litem is usually a parent, relative, or adult friend.
2. A person who sues in small claims court must first make a **demand** where possible. This means that you have asked the defendant to pay, and the defendant has refused. If your claim is for possession of property, you must ask the defendant to give you the property.
3. Unless you fall within two technical exceptions, you must be the **original owner** of the claim. This means that if the claim is assigned, the buyer cannot sue in

the small claims court. You must also appear at the small claims hearing yourself unless you filed the claim for a corporation or other entity that is not a natural person.

4. If a corporation files a claim, an employee, officer, or director must act on its behalf. If the claim is filed on behalf of an association or other entity that is not a natural person, a regularly employed person of the entity must act on its behalf. A person who appears on behalf of a corporation or other entity must not be employed or associated solely for the purpose of representing the corporation or other entity in the small claims court.

WHERE CAN YOU FILE YOUR CLAIM?

You must sue in the right court and **judicial district**. This rule is called **venue**.

If you file your claim in the wrong court, the court will dismiss the claim unless all defendants personally appear at the hearing and agree that the claim may be heard.

The right district may be any of these:

1. Where the defendant lives or where the business involved is located;
2. Where the damage or accident happened;
3. Where the contract was signed or carried out;

4. If the defendant is a corporation, where the contract was broken;
5. For a retail installment account or sales contract or a motor vehicle finance sale:
   a. Where the buyer (defendant) lives;
   b. Where the buyer (defendant) lived when the contract was entered into;
   c. Where the buyer (defendant) signed the contract;
   d. Where the goods or vehicle are permanently kept.

SOME RULES ABOUT THE DEFENDANT

1. You must sue using the defendant's *exact legal name*. If the defendant is a business or a corporation and you do not know the exact legal name, check with: the state or local licensing agency; the county clerk's office; or the Office of the Secretary of State, corporate status unit. Ask the clerk for help if you do not know how to find this information. If you do not use the defendant's exact legal name,

the court may be able to correct the name on your claim at the hearing or after the judgment.

2. If you want to sue a government agency, you must first file a claim with the agency before you can file a lawsuit in court. Generally, you must do this no later than *six months* after the act or event you are suing about.

HOW DOES THE DEFENDANT FIND OUT ABOUT THE CLAIM?

You must make sure the defendant finds out about your lawsuit. This has to be done according to the rules or your case may be dismissed or delayed. The correct way of telling the defendant about the lawsuit is called *service of process*. This means giving the defendant a copy of the claim. **YOU CANNOT DO THIS YOURSELF.** Here are four ways to serve the defendant:

1. **Service by a law officer**
   You may ask the marshal or sheriff to serve the defendant. A fee will be charged.
2. **Process server**
   You may ask anyone who is *not a party* in your case and who is at least *18 years old* to serve the defendant. The person is called a *process server* and must personally give a copy of your claim to the defendant. The person must

also sign a proof of service form showing when the defendant was served. Registered process servers will do this for you for a fee. You may also ask a friend or relative to do it.

3. **Certified mail**
   You may ask the clerk of the court to serve the defendant by certified mail. The clerk will charge a fee. You should check back with the court prior to the hearing to see if the receipt for certified mail was returned to the court. **Service by certified mail must be done by the clerk's office. You cannot serve the defendant this way yourself.**
4. **Substituted service**
   This method lets you serve another person instead of the defendant. You must follow the procedures carefully. You may also wish to use the marshal or sheriff or a registered process server.

---

* The $5,000 limit does not apply, and a $1,500 limit applies, if a "defendant guarantor . . . is required to respond based upon the default, actions, or omissions of another."

(Continued on reverse)

Form Adopted by the
Judicial Council of California
SC-150 (Rev. January 1, 1993)

INFORMATION FOR THE PLAINTIFF
(Small Claims)

Rule 982.7

4. Substituted service *(continued)*

A copy of your claim must be left
— at the defendant's business with the person in charge;
— or, at the defendant's home with a competent person who is at least 18 years old. The person who receives the claim must be told about its contents. Another copy must be mailed, first class, postage prepaid, to the defendant at the address where the paper was left. The service is not complete until *10 days* after the copy is mailed.

No matter which method of service you choose, the defendant must be served by a certain date or the trial will be postponed. If the defendant lives in the county, service must be completed at least *10 days* before the trial date. This period is *15 days* if defendant lives outside the county.

The person who serves the defendant must sign a court paper showing when the defendant was served. This paper is called a **Proof of Service**. It must be signed and returned to the court clerk as soon as the defendant has been served.

WHAT IF THE DEFENDANT ALSO HAS A CLAIM?

Sometimes the person who was sued (the **defendant**) will also have a claim against the person who filed the lawsuit (the **plaintiff**). This claim is called the **Defendant's Claim**. The defendant may file this claim in the same lawsuit. This helps to resolve all of the disagreements between the parties at the same time.

If the defendant decides to file the claim in the small claims court, the claim may not be for more than \$5,000 (***see reverse**). If the value of the claim is more than this amount,

the defendant may either give up the amount over \$5,000 and sue in the small claims court or file a motion to transfer the case to the appropriate court for the full value of the claim.

The defendant's claim must be served on the plaintiff at least *5 days* before the trial. If the defendant received the plaintiff's claim *10 days* or less before the trial, then the claim must be served at least *1 day* before the trial.

Both claims will be heard by the court at the same time.

WHAT HAPPENS AT THE TRIAL?

Be sure you are on time for the trial. The small claims trial is informal. You must bring with you all witnesses, books, receipts, and other papers or things to prove your case. You may ask the witnesses to come to court voluntarily. You may also ask the clerk of the court to issue a **subpena**. A subpena is a court order that *requires* the witness to go to trial. The witness has a right to charge a fee for going to the trial. If you do not have the records or papers to prove your case, you may also get a court order prior to the trial date requiring the papers

to be brought to the trial. This order is called a **Subpena Duces Tecum**.

If you settle the case before the trial, you must file a **dismissal** form with the clerk.

The court's decision is usually mailed to you after the trial. It may also be hand delivered to you in court when the trial is over and after the judge has made a decision. The decision appears on a form called the **Notice of Entry of Judgment**.

WHAT HAPPENS AFTER JUDGMENT?

The court may have ordered one party to pay money to the other party. The party who wins the case and collects the money is called the **judgment creditor**. The party who loses the case and owes the money is called the **judgment debtor**.

Enforcement of the judgment is **postponed** until after the time for appeal ends or until after the appeal is decided. This

means that the judgment creditor cannot collect any money or take any action until after this period is over. Generally, both parties may be represented by lawyers after judgment.

More information about your rights after judgment is available on the back of the **Notice of Entry of Judgment** form. The clerk may also have this information on a separate sheet.

HOW TO GET HELP WITH YOUR CASE

1. Lawyers

Both parties may ask a lawyer about the case, but a lawyer may not represent either party in court at the small claims trial. Generally, after judgment and on appeal, both parties may be represented by a lawyer.

2. Interpreters

If you do not speak English, you may take a family member or friend to court with you. The court should also keep a list of interpreters who will interpret for you. You may choose an interpreter from the court's list. Some interpreters may be free, and some may charge a fee.

3. Waiver of Fees

The court charges fees for some of its procedures. Fees are also charged for serving the defendant with the claim. The court may excuse you from paying these fees if you cannot afford them. Ask the clerk for the **Information Sheet on Waiver of Court Fees and Costs** to find out if you meet the requirements so that you do not have to pay the fees.

4. Night and Saturday Court

If you cannot go to court during working hours, ask the clerk if the court has trials at night or on Saturdays.

5. Parties Who Are in Jail

If you are in jail, the court may excuse you from going to the trial. Instead, you may ask another person who is not an attorney to go to the trial for you. You may mail written declarations to the court to support your case.

6. Advisors

The law requires each county to provide assistance in small claims cases free of charge. Here is some important information about the small claims advisor program in this county:

MUNICIPAL COURT OF CALIFORNIA
SANTA CLARA COUNTY JUDICIAL DISTRICT
SMALL CLAIMS DIVISION

☐ Santa Clara Annex
  1675 Lincoln St., SC 95050
  (408) 246-0510

☐ Palo Alto Facility
  270 Grant Ave., PA 94306
  (415) 324-0391

☐ Los Gatos Facility
  14205 Capri Dr., LG 95030
  (408) 866-8331

☐ Gilroy Facility
  7350 Rosanna St., GI 95020
  (408) 842-6299

☐ Sunnyvale Facility
  605 W. El Camino, SV 94087
  (408) 739-1502

CASE NO. S. C. _____

PLAINTIFF HAS DEMANDED THAT DEFENDANT PAY THE SUM AND IT HAS NOT BEEN PAID.

1. My Name (plaintiff) _____

2. My Address _____ ZIP _____

3. My Telephone Number _____ 4. Amount of Claim _____

5. Nature of Claim _____

_____

6. Date and place where damages or injury occured, or where obligation was to be performed _____

_____

   Claim for Automobile Damages: I am _____ the registered owner of the vehicle.

7. THIS COURT IS THE PROPER COURT FOR HEARING YOUR CLAIM. SEE INFORMATION FOR PLANTIFF FORM FOR ASSISTANCE AND INDICATE PROPER LETTER IN BOX ☐.
   FOR F OR G ENTER PROPER NUMBER IN BOX ☐.

8. (a) If you are suing individual, give his full name. (b) If you are suing a business firm, give the firm name and the name of the owner. (c) If you are suing a partnership, you must name the partners. (d) If you are suing a corporation, give its full name, and the name of a director of said corporation. (e) If your suit arises out of an automobile accident, you must name the driver and registered owner.

9. I UNDERSTAND I HAVE NO RIGHT OF APPEAL FROM A JUDGMENT ON MY CLAIM.

10. I have not filed more than one other Small Claims action in California during this calendar year in which the amount demanded is more than $2,500.

11. My claim is against (defendant)

NAME	ADDRESS	CITY	ZIP

DECLARATION OF NON-MILITARY STATUS

The declarant is the Plaintiff in the annexed and foregoing action, and/or he takes this declaration for said Plaintiff and declares the Defendant, and each of them, of more than one, is not now a person in the Military Service of the United States as defined in Sec. 101 of the Soldiers' and Sailors' Relief Act of 1940, and amendments thereto.
I declare under penalty of perjury that the foregoing is true and correct.

Executed on _____   Signature _____

The declaration under penalty of perjury must be signed in California, or in a state that authorizes use of a declaration in place of an affidavit, otherwise an affidavit is required.

ORDER TO PLAINTIFF TO APPEAR

Your case will be tried on _____ at _____ M., in Dept. _____ of said court.

YOU ARE HEREBY DIRECTED TO APPEAR on said date and to bring with you all books, papers and witnesses needed to prove your claim.

> **IMPORTANT:** Please check the Court Calendar in the lobby of the building
> for the Department of this Court that will hear this matter.

REQUEST FOR DISMISSAL

If case is paid or settled before trial, sign below and mail this form to the above entitled court. THIS CASE MAY BE DISMISSED.

Signature _____

Ⓢ 381 REV 2/91

PARTY ☐ PLAINTIFF ☐ DEFENDANT *(Name and Address)*:

TELEPHONE NO.:

FOR COURT USE ONLY

NAME AND ADDRESS OF COURT:

PLAINTIFF(S):

DEFENDANT(S):

PROOF OF SERVICE (Small Claims)	HEARING DATE:	DAY:	TIME:	DEPT./DIVISION:	CASE NUMBER:

1. At the time of service I was at least 18 years of age and not a party to this action, and I served copies of the following:

   ☐ Plaintiff's Claim   ☐ Order of Examination   ☐ Other *(specify)*:
   ☐ Defendant's Claim   ☐ Subpena Duces Tecum

2. a. Party served *(specify name of party as shown on the documents served)*:

   b. Person served: ☐ party in item 2.a.   ☐ other *(specify name and title or relationship to the party named in item 2.a.)*:

3. By delivery   ☐ at home   ☐ at business
   a. date:
   b. time:
   c. address:

4. Manner of service *(check proper box)*:
   a. ☐ Personal service. I personally delivered to and left copies with the party served. (C.C.P. 415.10)
   b. ☐ Substituted service on corporation, unincorporated association (including partnership), or public entity. By leaving, during usual office hours, copies in the office of the person served with the person who apparently was in charge and thereafter mailing (by first-class mail, postage prepaid) copies to the person to be served at the place where the copies were left. (C.C.P. 415.20(a))
   c. ☐ Substituted service on natural person, minor, incompetent, or candidate. By leaving copies at the dwelling house, usual place of abode, usual place of business, or usual mailing address other than a U. S. Postal Service post office box of the person served in the presence of a competent member of the household or a person apparently in charge of the office or place of business, at least 18 years of age, who was informed of the general nature of the papers, and thereafter mailing (by first-class mail, postage prepaid) copies to the person to be served at the place where the copies were left. (C.C.P. 415.20(b))
   d. ☐ Date of mailing: From *(city)*:

   Information regarding date and place of mailing is required for services effected in manner 4.b. and 4.c. above.
   Certified mail service may be performed only by the Clerk of the Court in small claims matters.

5. Person serving *(name, address, and telephone number)*:
   a. Fee for service: $
   b. ☐ Not a registered California process server
   c. ☐ Exempt from registration under B&P Section 22350(b)
   d. ☐ Registered California process server
        1. ☐ Employee or independent contractor
        2. Registration Number:
        3. County:

6. ☐ I declare under penalty of perjury under the laws of the State of California that the foregoing is true and correct.
7. ☐ I am a California sheriff, marshal, or constable and I certify that the foregoing is true and correct.

Date: ▶

(SIGNATURE OF SERVER)

Form Approved by the
Judicial Council of California
SC-104 [New January 1, 1992]
Ⓢ 4304 REV 12/91

PROOF OF SERVICE
(Small Claims)

Code of Civil Procedure
§§ 415.10, 415.20

15.4

MUNICIPAL COURT OF CALIFORNIA, SANTA CLARA COUNTY JUDICIAL DISTRICT, SMALL CLAIMS DIVISION

SMALL CLAIMS CASE NO.

— NOTICE TO DEFENDANT — YOU ARE BEING SUED BY PLAINTIFF	— AVISO AL DEMANDADO — A USTED LO ESTAN DEMANDANDO
To protect your rights, you must appear in this court on the trial date shown in the table below. You may lose the case if you do not appear. The court may award the plaintiff the amount of the claim and the costs. Your wages, money, and property may be taken without further warning from the court.	Para proteger sus derechos, usted debe presentarse ante esta corte en la fecha del juicio indicada en el cuadro que aparece a continuación. Si no se presenta, puede perder el caso. La corte puede decidir en favor del demandante por la cantidad del reclamo y los costos. A usted le pueden quitar su salario, su dinero, y otras cosas de su propiedad, sin aviso adicional por parte de esta corte.

PLAINTIFF/DEMANDANTE (Name, address, and telephone number of each):

DEFENDANT/DEMANDADO (Name, address, and telephone number of each):

Telephone No.:

Telephone No.:

Telephone No.:

Telephone No.:

Fict. Bus. Name Stmt. No.   Expires:

☐ See attached sheet for additional plaintiffs and defendants.

PLAINTIFF'S CLAIM

1. Defendant owes me the sum of $_____, not including court costs, because (describe claim and date):

2. a. ☐ I have asked defendant to pay this money, but it has not been paid.
   b. ☐ I have NOT asked defendant to pay this money because (explain):
3. This court is the proper court for the trial because ☐ (In the box at the left, insert one of the letters from the list marked "Venue Table" on the back of this sheet. If you select D, E, or F, specify additional facts in this space.)

4. I ☐ have ☐ have not filed more than one other small claims action anywhere in California during this calendar year in which the amount demanded is more than $2,500.
5. I ☐ have ☐ have not filed more than 12 claims in California, including this claim, during this calendar year.
6. I understand that
   a. I may talk to an attorney about this claim, but I cannot be represented by an attorney at the trial in the small claims court.
   b. I must appear at the time and place of trial and bring all witnesses, books, receipts, and other papers or things to prove my case.
   c. I have no right of appeal on my claim, but I may appeal a claim filed by the defendant in this case.
   d. If I cannot afford to pay the fees for filing or service by a sheriff, marshal, or constable, I may ask that the fees be waived.
7. I have received and read the information sheet explaining some important rights of plaintiffs in the small claims court.

I declare under penalty of perjury under the laws of the State of California that the foregoing is true and correct.

Date:

▶

....
(TYPE OR PRINT NAME)

(SIGNATURE OF PLAINTIFF)

ORDER TO DEFENDANT

You must appear in this court on the trial date and at the time LAST SHOWN IN THE BOX BELOW if you do not agree with the plaintiff's claim. Bring all witnesses, books, receipts, and other papers or things with you to support your case.

		DATE	DAY	TIME	PLACE	COURT USE
TRIAL DATE	1.					
FECHA DEL JUICIO	2.					
	3.					
	4.					

Filed on (date):   Clerk, by_____, Deputy

— The county provides small claims advisor services free of charge. Read the information on the reverse. —

Form Adopted by the
Judicial Council of California
SC-100 (Rev. January 1, 1992)

PLAINTIFF'S CLAIM AND ORDER TO DEFENDANT
(Small Claims)

Rule 982.7

15.5

MUNICIPAL COURT OF CALIFORNIA, SANTA CLARA COUNTY JUDICIAL DISTRICT, SMALL CLAIMS DIVISION

☐ Palo Alto Facility   ☐ Los Gatos Facility   ☐ Gilroy Facility   ☐ Santa Clara Annex   ☐ Sunnyvale Facility
270 Grant Ave., PA 94306   14205 Capri Dr., LG 95030   7350 Rosanna St., GI 95020   1675 Lincoln St., SC 95050   605 W. El Camino, SV 94087
(415) 324-0391   (408) 866-8331   (408) 842-3111   (408) 246-0510   (408) 739-1502

SMALL CLAIMS CASE NO.

— NOTICE TO PLAINTIFF — YOU ARE BEING SUED BY DEFENDANT	— AVISO AL DEMANDANTE — A USTED LO ESTA DEMANDANDO EL DEMANDADO
To protect your rights, you must appear in this court on the trial date shown in the table below. You may lose the case if you do not appear. The court may award the defendant the amount of the claim and the costs. Your wages, money, and property may be taken without further warning from the court.	Para proteger sus derechos, usted debe presentarse ante esta corte en la fecha del juicio indicada en el cuadro que aparece a continuación. Si no se presenta, puede perder el caso. La corte puede decidir en favor del demandado por la cantidad del reclamo y los costos. A usted le pueden quitar su salario, su dinero, y otras cosas de su propiedad, sin aviso adicional por parte de esta corte.

PLAINTIFF/DEMANDANTE (Name, address, and telephone number of each):

Telephone No.:

Telephone No.:

DEFENDANT/DEMANDADO (Name, address, and telephone number of each):

Telephone No.:

Telephone No.:

☐ See attached sheet for additional plaintiffs and defendants.   Fict. Bus. Name Stmt. No.   Expires:

DEFENDANT'S CLAIM

1. Plaintiff owes me the sum of $ not including court costs, because *(describe claim and date)*:

2. a. ☐ I have asked plaintiff to pay this money, but it has not been paid.
   b. ☐ I have NOT asked plaintiff to pay this money because *(explain)*:

3. I ☐ have ☐ have not   filed more than one other small claims action anywhere in California during this calendar year in which the amount demanded is more than $2,500.

4. I understand that
   a. I may talk to an attorney about this claim, but I cannot be represented by an attorney at the trial in the small claims court.
   b. I must appear at the time and place of trial and bring all witnesses, books, receipts, and other papers or things to prove my case.
   c. I have no right of appeal on my claim, but I may appeal a claim filed by the plaintiff in this case.
   d. If I cannot afford to pay the fees for filing or service by a sheriff, marshal, or constable, I may ask that the fees be waived.

5. I have received and read the information sheet explaining some important rights of defendants in the small claims court.

I declare under penalty of perjury under the laws of the State of California that the foregoing is true and correct.
Date:

▶

.... (TYPE OR PRINT NAME)   (SIGNATURE OF DEFENDANT)

ORDER TO PLAINTIFF

You must appear in this court on the trial date and at the time LAST SHOWN IN THE BOX BELOW if you do not agree with the plaintiff's claim. Bring all witnesses, books, receipts, and other papers or things with you to support your case.

		DATE	DAY	TIME	PLACE	COURT USE
TRIAL DATE FECHA DEL JUICIO	1.					
	2.					
	3.					
	4.					

Filed on *(date)*:   Clerk, by _____, Deputy

5171 REV 1/92

— The county provides small claims advisor services free of charge. (Advisor phone no: 299-4216)—

Form Approved by the
Judicial Council of California
SC-120 [Rev. January 1, 1992]

DEFENDANT'S CLAIM AND ORDER TO PLAINTIFF
(Small Claims)

Rule 982.7

ATTORNEY OR PARTY WITHOUT ATTORNEY *(Name and Address)*:	TELEPHONE NO.:	FOR COURT USE ONLY

ATTORNEY FOR *(Name)*:

NAME OF COURT:

STREET ADDRESS:

MAILING ADDRESS:

CITY AND ZIP CODE:

BRANCH NAME:

PLAINTIFF:

DEFENDANT:

APPLICATION AND ORDER FOR APPEARANCE AND EXAMINATION	CASE NUMBER:

☐ ENFORCEMENT OF JUDGMENT   ☐ ATTACHMENT (Third Person)

☐ Judgment Debtor   ☐ Third Person

ORDER TO APPEAR FOR EXAMINATION

1. TO *(name)*:
2. YOU ARE ORDERED TO APPEAR personally before this court, or before a referee appointed by the court, to

    a. ☐ furnish information to aid in enforcement of a money judgment against you.

    b. ☐ answer concerning property of the judgment debtor in your possession or control or concerning a debt you owe the judgment debtor.

    c. ☐ answer concerning property of the defendant in your possession or control or concerning a debt you owe the defendant that is subject to attachment.

Date: Time: Dept. or Div.:   Rm.:

Address of court ☐ shown above ☐ is:

3. This order may be served by a sheriff, marshal, constable, registered process server, or the following specially appointed person *(name)*:

Date: ▶ _____

                                     (SIGNATURE OF JUDGE OR REFEREE)

This order must be served not less than 10 days before the date set for the examination.

IMPORTANT NOTICES ON REVERSE

APPLICATION FOR ORDER TO APPEAR FOR EXAMINATION

1. ☐ Judgment creditor   ☐ Assignee of record   ☐ Plaintiff who has a right to attach order applies for an order requiring *(name)*:   to appear and furnish information to aid in enforcement of the money judgment or to answer concerning property or debt.

2. The person to be examined is

    ☐ the judgment debtor

    ☐ a third person (1) who has possession or control of property belonging to the judgment debtor or the defendant or (2) who owes the judgment debtor or the defendant more than $250. An affidavit supporting this application under CCP §491.110 or §708.120 is attached.

3. The person to be examined resides or has a place of business in this county or within 150 miles of the place of examination.

4. ☐ This court is not the court in which the money judgment is entered or *(attachment only)* the court that issued the writ of attachment. An affidavit supporting an application under CCP §491.150 or §708.160 is attached.

5. ☐ The judgment debtor has been examined within the past 120 days. An affidavit showing good cause for another examination is attached.

I declare under penalty of perjury under the laws of the State of California that the foregoing is true and correct.

Date:

            ▶

....   _____

             (TYPE OR PRINT NAME)   (SIGNATURE OF DECLARANT)

Form Approved by the
Judicial Council of California
AT-138, EJ-125 (New July 1, 1984

**APPLICATION AND ORDER
FOR APPEARANCE AND EXAMINATION
(Attachment—Enforcement of Judgment)**

CCP 491.110, 708.110, 708.120

APPEARANCE OF JUDGMENT DEBTOR (ENFORCEMENT OF JUDGMENT)

NOTICE TO JUDGMENT DEBTOR If you fail to appear at the time and place specified in this order, you may be subject to arrest and punishment for contempt of court, and the court may make an order requiring you to pay the reasonable attorney fees incurred by the judgment creditor in this proceeding.

APPEARANCE OF A THIRD PERSON
(ENFORCEMENT OF JUDGMENT)

(1) NOTICE TO PERSON SERVED If you fail to appear at the time and place specified in this order, you may be subject to arrest and punishment for contempt of court, and the court may make an order requiring you to pay the reasonable attorney fees incurred by the judgment creditor in this proceeding.

(2) NOTICE TO JUDGMENT DEBTOR The person in whose favor the judgment was entered in this action claims that the person to be examined pursuant to this order has possession or control of property which is yours or owes you a debt. This property or debt is as follows *(Describe the property or debt using typewritten capital letters)*:

If you claim that all or any portion of this property or debt is exempt from enforcement of the money judgment, you must file your exemption claim in writing with the court and have a copy personally served on the judgment creditor not later than three days before the date set for the examination. You must appear at the time and place set for the examination to establish your claim of exemption or your exemption may be waived.

APPEARANCE OF A THIRD PERSON (ATTACHMENT)

NOTICE TO PERSON SERVED If you fail to appear at the time and place specified in this order, you may be subject to arrest and punishment for contempt of court, and the court may make an order requiring you to pay the reasonable attorney fees incurred by the plaintiff in this proceeding.

APPEARANCE OF A CORPORATION, PARTNERSHIP, ASSOCIATION, TRUST, OR OTHER ORGANIZATION

It is your duty to designate one or more of the following to appear and be examined: officers, directors, managing agents, or other persons who are familiar with your property and debts.

AT-138, EJ 125
(New July 1, 1984)

APPLICATION AND ORDER FOR APPEARANCE AND EXAMINATION
(Attachment—Enforcement of Judgment)

Page two

15.7

Information regarding additional judgment debtors:

10.   Name and last known address

Driver's license no. & state: ☐ unknown.
Social Security no.:   ☐ unknown.
Summons was personally served at or mailed to *(address)*:

14.   Name and last known address

Driver's license no. & state: ☐ unknown.
Social Security no.:   ☐ unknown.
Summons was personally served at or mailed to *(address)*:

11.   Name and last known address

Driver's license no. & state: ☐ unknown.
Social Security no.:   ☐ unknown.
Summons was personally served at or mailed to *(address)*:

15.   Name and last known address

Driver's license no. & state: ☐ unknown.
Social Security no.:   ☐ unknown.
Summons was personally served at or mailed to *(address)*:

12.   Name and last known address

Driver's license no. & state: ☐ unknown.
Social Security no.:   ☐ unknown.
Summons was personally served at or mailed to *(address)*:

16.   Name and last known address

Driver's license no. & state: ☐ unknown.
Social Security no.:   ☐ unknown.
Summons was personally served at or mailed to *(address)*:

13.   Name and last known address

Driver's license no. & state: ☐ unknown.
Social Security no.:   ☐ unknown.
Summons was personally served at or mailed to *(address)*:

17.   Name and last known address

Driver's license no. & state: ☐ unknown.
Social Security no.:   ☐ unknown.
Summons was personally served at or mailed to *(address)*:

18. ☐ Continued on attachment 18.

982(a)(1) [Rev. July 1, 1983]   **ABSTRACT OF JUDGMENT (CIVIL)**   Page two

MUNICIPAL COURT OF CALIFORNIA
SANTA CLARA COUNTY JUDICIAL DISTRICT
SMALL CLAIMS DIVISION

☐ **Santa Clara Annex**
1675 Lincoln St., SC 95050
(408) 246-0510

☐ **Palo Alto Facility**
270 Grant Ave., PA 94305
(415) 324-0391

☐ **Los Gatos Facility**
14205 Capri Dr., LG 95030
(408) 866-8331

☐ **-Gilroy Facility**
7350 Rosanna St., GI 96020
(408) 842-6299

☐ **Sunnyvale Facility**
605 W. El Camino, SV 94067
(408) 739-1602

TITLE OF CASE (ABBREVIATED):	FOR COURT USE ONLY
ATTORNEY(S) NAME AND ADDRESS	

ATTORNEY(S) FOR:	TELEPHONE:	CASE NUMBER:

MEMORANDUM OF CREDITS

CREDIT for payments and partial satisfaction of judgment, including direct payments and executions partially satisfied: $ _____
(IF NONE, STATE NONE)

INTEREST ACCRUING AFTER JUDGMENT

INTEREST ACCRUING AFTER JUDGMENT at 10% from date of judgment on balances due after dates of payments or credits acknowledged above: $ _____ .

MEMORANDUM OF COSTS AFTER JUDGMENT

1. COSTS AFTER JUDGMENT CLAIMED ON MEMORANDUM FILED HERETOFORE: .... $ _____
2. CLERK'S FEES: .... $ _____
3. .... $ _____
4. SHERIFF OR MARSHAL'S FEES: .... $ _____
5. .... $ _____
6. SERVING SUPPLEMENTARY PROCEEDING'S: .... $ _____
7. .... $ _____
8. NOTARY FEES: .... $ _____
9. .... $ _____
10. OTHER ALLOWABLE COSTS: (PLEASE SPECIFY) .... $ _____
11. .... $ _____
12. .... $ _____
13. .... $ _____
14. .... $ _____
15. .... $ _____

***COSTS MAY BE CLAIMED NO LATER THAN 2 YEARS AFTER THE COSTS HAVE BEEN INCURRED   **TOTAL $** _____

I, the undersigned, say: I am the Judgment Creditor/Attorney for Judgment Creditor (CIRCLE ONE) in the above entitled action and to the best of my knowledge and belief, the items in the within memorandum are correct and the said disbursements have necessarily incurred in said action.
I declare under penalty of perjury that the foregoing is true and correct.

Executed on _____ at _____ , California

(Signature)

NOTE: A notice of motion to tax costs shall specify the items of the cost bill to which objection is made:

MEMORANDUM OF CREDITS, ACCRUED INTEREST
AND COSTS AFTER JUDGMENT

***C.C.P. 685.070 (a)
***C.C.P. 685.070, 1033

15.9

DECLARATION OR CERTIFICATE OF SERVICE BY MAIL
C.C.P. Sec. 1010. et seq. 2015.5

DECLARATION OF SERVICE BY MAIL

My _____ address is _____
    (BUSINESS/RESIDENCE)

I am, and was at the time herein mentioned mailing took place, a citizen of the United States, _____
    (EMPLOYED/RESIDENT)

in the County where said mailing occurred, over the age of eighteen years and not a party to the above-entitled cause.

On _____, I served the foregoing Memorandum of Costs by depositing a copy thereof, enclosed in

separate, sealed envelope, with the postage thereon fully prepaid, in the United States mail at _____
    (CITY OR POSTAL AREA)

County of _____, California, each of which envelopes was addressed respectively as follows:

Executed on _____, at _____, California.
    (DATE)   (PLACE)

I declare under penalty of perjury that the foregoing is true and correct.

_____
    (SIGNATURE OF DECLARANT)

ATTORNEY'S CERTIFICATE OF SERVICE

I, the undersigned, certify: that I am an active member of the State Bar of California and not a party to the above-entitled cause,

and my business address as _____

_____, California:

that on _____ I served the foregoing Memorandum of Costs by depositing a copy

thereof, enclosed in separate, sealed envelope, with the postage thereon fully prepaid, in the United States California, each of

which envelopes was addressed respectively as follows:

Name: Address:

_____
    (SIGNATURE OF ATTORNEY)

ACKNOWLEDGMENT OF SERVICE

Received copy of the foregoing Memorandum of Costs

on _____, _____, Attorney for _____

on _____, _____, Attorney for _____

MUNICIPAL COURT OF CALIFORNIA, SANTA CLARA COUNTY JUDICIAL DISTRICT, SMALL CLAIMS DIVISION

☐Palo Alto Facility   ☐Los Gatos Facility   ☐Gilroy Facility   ☐Santa Clara Annex   ☐Sunnyvale Facility
270 Grant Ave., PA 94306   14205 Capri Dr., LG 95030   7350 Rosanna St., Gl 95020   1675 Lincoln St., SC 95050   605 W. El Camino, SV 94087
(415) 324-0391   (408) 866-8331   (408) 842-3111   (408) 246-0510   (408) 739-1502

SMALL CLAIMS CASE NO.

PLAINTIFF/DEMANDANTE *(Name, address, and telephone number of each)*:

DEFENDANT/DEMANDADO *(Name, address, and telephone number of each)*:

Telephone No.:

Telephone No.:

Telephone No.:

Telephone No.:

☐ See attached sheet for additional plaintiffs and defendants.

NOTICE OF FILING NOTICE OF APPEAL

TO: ☐ Plaintiff *(name)*:
     ☐ Defendant *(name)*:

Your small claims case has been APPEALED to the superior court. Do not contact the small claims court about this appeal. The superior court will notify you of the date you should appear in court. The notice of appeal is set forth below.	*La decisión hecha por la corte para reclamos menores en su caso ha sido APELADA ante la corte superior. No se ponga en contacto con la corte para reclamos judiciales menores acerca de esta apelación. La corte superior le notificará la fecha en que usted debe presentarse ante ella. El aviso de la apelación aparece a continuación.*

Date: _____

Clerk, by _____, Deputy

NOTICE OF APPEAL

I appeal to the superior court, as provided by law, from
☐ the small claims judgment   or   ☐ the denial of the motion to vacate the small claims judgment.

DATE APPEAL FILED *(clerk to insert date)*:

▶

. . . .
            (TYPE OR PRINT NAME)

(SIGNATURE OF APPELLANT OR APPELLANT'S ATTORNEY)

☐ I am an insurer of defendant *(name)* _____ in this case. The judgment against defendant exceeds $2,500, and the policy of insurance with the defendant covers the matter to which the judgment applies.

. . . .
            (NAME OF INSURER)

▶

(SIGNATURE OF DECLARANT)

CLERK'S CERTIFICATE OF MAILING

I certify that
1. I am not a party to this action.
2. This Notice of Filing Notice of Appeal and Notice of Appeal were mailed first class, postage prepaid, in a sealed envelope to
    ☐ plaintiff
    ☐ defendant
    at the address shown above.
3. The mailing and this certification occurred
    at *(place)*: _____ California,
    on *(date)*: _____

Clerk, by _____, Deputy

Form Adopted by the
Judicial Council of California
SC-140 (Rev. January 1, 1992)

NOTICE OF APPEAL
(Small Claims)

Rule 982.7
Code of Civil Procedure, § 116.710

MUNICIPAL COURT OF CALIFORNIA, SANTA CLARA COUNTY JUDICIAL DISTRICT, SMALL CLAIMS DIVISION

☐ Palo Alto Facility
270 Grant Ave.,PA 94306
(415) 324-0391

☐ Los Gatos Facility
14205 Capri Dr., LG 95030
(408) 866-8331

☐ Gilroy Facility
7350 Rosanna St., GI 95020
(408) 842-3111

☐ Santa Clara Annex
1675 Lincoln St., SC 95050
(408) 246-0510

☐ Sunnyvale Facility
605 W. El Camino, SV 94087
(408) 739-1502

SMALL CLAIMS CASE NO.:

— INSTRUCTIONS —

A. If you regularly do business in California for profit under a fictitious business name, you must execute, file, and publish a fictitious business name statement. This is sometimes called a "dba" which stands for "doing business as." This requirement applies if you are doing business as an individual, a partnership, a corporation, or an association. The requirement does not apply to nonprofit corporations and associations or certain real estate investment trusts. You must file the fictitious business name statement with the clerk of the county where you have your principal place of business, or in Sacramento County if you have no place of business within the state.

B. If you do business under a fictitious business name and you also wish to file an action in the small claims court, you must declare under penalty of perjury that you have complied with the fictitious business name laws by filling out the form below.

C. If you have not complied with the fictitious business name laws, the court may dismiss your claim. You may be able to refile your claim when you have fulfilled these requirements.

FICTITIOUS BUSINESS NAME DECLARATION

1. I wish to file a claim in the small claims court for a business doing business under the fictitious name of *(specify name and address of business)*:

2. The business is doing business as
   ☐ an individual
   ☐ a partnership
   ☐ a corporation
   ☐ an association
   ☐ other *(specify)*:

3. The business has complied with the fictitious business name laws by executing, filing, and publishing a fictitious business name statement in the county of *(specify)*:

4. The number of the statement is *(specify)*:   and the statement expires on *(date)*:

I declare under penalty of perjury under the laws of the State of California that the foregoing is true and correct.

Date:

▶

....
(TYPE OR PRINT NAME)

(SIGNATURE OF DECLARANT)

Form Approved by the
Judicial Council of California
SC-103 (Rev. January 1, 1992)
Ⓢ 9022 REV 2/92

FICTITIOUS BUSINESS NAME DECLARATION
(Small Claims)

Rule 982.7(b)
Code of Civil Procedure, § 116.430

15.12

MAIL TO THE JUDGMENT CREDITOR
DO NOT FILE WITH THE COURT

TO JUDGMENT CREDITOR *(fill in name of judgment creditor)*:

FROM JUDGMENT DEBTOR *(fill in your name)*:

SMALL CLAIMS CASE NO.

JUDGMENT DEBTOR'S STATEMENT OF ASSETS

The judgment debtor in this small claims case is the person (or business) who lost the case and owes the money. The person who won the case is the judgment creditor.

TO THE JUDGMENT DEBTOR:

The small claims court has ruled that you owe money to the judgment creditor.

  1. You may appeal a judgment against you only on the other party's claim. You may not appeal a judgment against you on your claim.

     a. If you appeared at the trial and you want to appeal, you must file a Notice of Appeal within 30 days after the date of mailing on the Notice of Entry of Judgment or the date you received it in court.

     b. If you did not appear at the trial, before you can appeal, you must first file a **Motion to Vacate the Judgment** within 30 days from the date the Notice of Entry of Judgment was mailed or delivered to you, and the judgment cannot be collected until the motion is decided. If your motion is denied, you then have 10 days from the date the notice of denial was mailed to file your appeal.

  2. Unless you pay, appeal, or move to vacate, you must fill out this form and send it to the person who won the case within 30 days after the Notice of Entry of Judgment is mailed to you by the clerk.

  3. If you file an appeal or a Motion to Vacate, you do not need to fill out this form unless you lose your appeal or motion to vacate. Then you will have 30 days to pay or complete this form and deliver it to the judgment creditor.

If you fail to follow these instructions you may have to go to court to answer questions or the court can impose penalties on you.	Si usted no sigue estas instrucciones es posible que tenga que presentarse ante la corte para contestar preguntas, o la corte puede imponerle multas.

If you were sued as an individual skip this box and begin with no. 1 below. Otherwise, check the applicable box, attach the documents indicated, and complete no. 12 on the reverse.

  a. ☐ (Corporation or partnership) Attached to this form is a statement describing the nature, value and exact location of all assets of the corporation or the partners, and a statement showing that the person signing this form is authorized to submit this form on behalf of the corporation or partnership.

  b. ☐ (Governmental agency) Attached to this form is the statement of an authorized representative of the agency as to when the agency will pay the judgment and any reasons for its failure to do so.

EMPLOYMENT

  1. What is your occupation? *(Please provide job title and name of division or office in which you work.)*

  2. Name and address of your business or employer *(include address of your payroll or human resources department, if different)*:

  3. How often are you paid?

     a. ☐ daily ☐ every two weeks ☐ monthly
        ☐ weekly ☐ twice a month ☐ other *(explain)*:

  4. What is your gross pay each pay period?
     $

  5. What is your take home pay each pay period?
     $

  6. If your wife or husband earns any income give the name and address of the business or employer, job title, and division or office:

(Continued on reverse)

Form Approved by the
Judicial Council of California
SC-133 (Rev. January 1, 1992)

Ⓢ 2782 REV 12/91

JUDGMENT DEBTOR'S STATEMENT OF ASSETS
(Small Claims)

Rule 982.7

CASH, BANK DEPOSITS

7. How much money do you have in cash? .... $

8. How much other money do you have in banks, savings and loans, credit unions, and other financial institutions either in your own name or jointly *(list)*:

Name and address of financial institution	Account number	Individual or joint?	Balance
a.			$
b.			$
c.			$

PROPERTY

9. List all automobiles, other vehicles, and boats owned in your name or jointly:

Make and year	Value	Legal owner if different from registered owner	Amount owed
a.	$		$
b.	$		$
c.	$		$
d.	$		$

10. List all real estate owned in your name or jointly:

Address of real estate	Fair market value		Amount owed
a.	$		$
b.	$		$

OTHER PERSONAL PROPERTY *[Do not list household furniture and furnishings, appliances, or clothing.]*

11. List anything of value not listed above owned in your name or jointly:

Description	Value	Address where property is located
a.	$	
b.	$	
c.	$	
d.	$	
e.	$	
f.	$	
g.	$	
h.	$	
i.	$	
j.	$	

12. I declare under penalty of perjury under the laws of the State of California that the foregoing is true and correct.

Date:

▶

....
(TYPE OR PRINT NAME)   (SIGNATURE)

Mail or deliver this completed form to the judgment creditor at the address shown on the Notice of Entry of Judgment form,

SC 133 [Rev. January 1, 1992]   **JUDGMENT DEBTOR'S STATEMENT OF ASSETS**   Page two
                                                        (Small Claims)

INFORMATION AFTER JUDGMENT

HOW DO YOU FIND OUT ABOUT THE COURT'S DECISION?

When your small claims case has been decided, the court clerk will mail or deliver to you a form called the **Notice of Entry of Judgment**. The **judgment** or decision of the court appears on the front of the form. The court may have ordered one party to pay money to the other party. The winner of the case and the person who can collect the money is called the **judgment creditor**. The loser of the case and the person who owes the money is called the **judgment debtor**.

Enforcement of the judgment is postponed until after the time for appeal ends or until after the appeal is decided. This means that the judgment creditor cannot collect any money or take any action until after this period is over. Generally, both sides may be represented by lawyers after judgment.

WHAT HAPPENS IF YOU LOSE THE CASE?

1. If you lose the case on your own claim and the court does not award you any money, the court's decision on your claim is **FINAL.** You may not appeal your own claim.

2. If you lose the case and the court orders you to pay money, your money and property may be taken to pay the claim unless you do one of the following things:

   a. **PAY THE JUDGMENT**
   The law requires you to pay the amount of the judgment. You may pay the judgment creditor directly, or pay the judgment to the court for an additional fee. You may also ask the court to order monthly payments you can afford. Ask the clerk for information about these procedures.

   b. **APPEAL**
   If you disagree with the court's decision, you may appeal the decison *on the other party's claim*. You may not appeal the decision on your own claim. However, if any party appeals, there will be a new trial on **all** the claims. If you appeared at the trial, you *must* begin your appeal by filing a form called a **Notice of Appeal** within *20 days* after the date this Notice of Entry of Judgment was mailed or handed to you at the time of the small claims hearing. Your appeal will be in the superior court. You will have a **new trial.** You may be represented by a lawyer.

   c. **VACATE (OR CANCEL) THE JUDGMENT**
   If you did not go to the trial, you may ask the court to vacate (or cancel) the judgment. To make this request, you must file a **Motion to Vacate the Judgment** *within 30 days* after the date this Notice of Entry of Judgment was mailed to you. If your request is denied, you then have *10 days* from the date the motion was denied to appeal the denial.

   The period to file the **Motion to Vacate the Judgment** is *180 days* if you were *not properly served* with the claim. The 180-day period begins on the date you found out or should have found out about the judgment against you.

WHAT HAPPENS IF YOU WIN THE CASE?

1. If you were sued by the other party and you win the case, then the other party may not appeal the court's decision.

2. If you win the case and the court awards you money, here are some steps you may take to collect your money or get possession of your property:

   a. **COLLECTING FEES**
   Sometimes fees are charged for filing court papers or for serving the judgment debtor. These extra costs can become part of your original judgment. To claim these fees, ask the clerk for a **Memorandum of Costs.**

   b. **VOLUNTARY PAYMENT**
   Ask the judgment debtor to pay the money. If your claim was for possession of rental property, ask the judgment debtor to move out. **THE COURT WILL NOT COLLECT THE MONEY OR ENFORCE THE JUDGMENT FOR YOU.**

   c. **STATEMENT OF ASSETS**
   If the judgment debtor does not pay the money, the law requires the debtor to fill out a form called the **Judgment Debtor's Statement of Assets.** This form will tell you what property the judgment debtor has that may be available to pay your claim. If the judgment debtor willfully fails to send you the completed form, you may ask the court to impose penalties.

   d. **ORDER OF EXAMINATION**
   You may also make the debtor come to court to answer questions about income and property. To do this, ask the clerk for an **Order of Examination.** There is no fee for this order, but there is a fee if a law officer serves the order on the judgment debtor.

   e. **WRIT OF EXECUTION**
   After you find out about the judgment debtor's property, you may ask the court for a **Writ of Execution.** A writ of execution is a court paper which tells a law officer to take property of the judgment debtor to pay your claim. Here are some examples of the kinds of property the officer may be able to take: **wages, bank account, automobile, business property, or rented property.** For some kinds of property, you may need to file other forms. See the law officer for information.

   f. **ABSTRACT OF JUDGMENT**
   The judgment debtor may own land or a house or other buildings. You may want to put a lien on the property so that you will be paid if the property is sold. You can get a lien by filing an **Abstract of Judgment** with the County Recorder in the county where the property is located. The recorder will charge a fee for the Abstract of Judgment.

   g. **AFTER PAYMENT**
   If you are paid in full, you must fill out a form called an **Acknowledgment of Satisfaction of Judgment.** The form is located on the back of the Notice of Entry of Judgment. When you have filled out the form, you must mail it to the court *immediately* or you may be fined. If an Abstract of Judgment has been recorded, you must use another form. See the clerk for the proper form.

Form Adopted by the
Judicial Council of California
SC-131 (Rev. January 1, 1990)
5364 REV 1-90

INFORMATION AFTER JUDGMENT
Small Claims)

Rule 982.7

Statute of Limitations

Collection procedures should never be so poorly organized that an account which you carry as active—a receivables balance on your aged trial balance report—is lost because the statute of limitations has run out. You must be aware of the statute in any state or jurisdiction in which you might want to use Small Claims Court or a conventional civil suit to press for a judgment against the customer-debtor. Take appropriate collection action, but initiate it within the period of years prescribed by the appropriate jurisdiction. Virtually no set of circumstances could provide justification for such a level of inattention to the aging of a receivables balance.

If your best in-house collection efforts have not been effective—telephone calls, collection letters, fax memos and letters, personal visits, and a *final demand* letter—then assign the account to your collection service. If the collection service is unable to locate the debtor or determines that there are no assets against which you could hope to levy a judgment, charge the account balance against your company's bad-debt reserve. At that point you will have made every reasonable effort to collect your company's money.

Under certain circumstances, a debtor might surface after the statute of limitations has seemingly pushed your old account balance—now a bad-debt item—beyond your reach. Unless you are notified that the individual, partnership, or company filed for bankruptcy, and your debt was among those listed and discharged by the bankruptcy court, there is the possibility of life after the statute of limitations. Other pieces also must fit the criteria for reviving the account balance, and it is imperative that you have your company's attorney make that decision. Let him or her tell you whether there is hope, what must be done to make reviving the account a possibility and if there is a possibility that you can return the debt to the category of a legally collectible item. Find out if now there are assets against which you could obtain a judgment and collect.

Your time is split in too many directions to waste it attempting to revive accounts that are as dead as your bad-debt assignment indicates, or as dead as a judgment, with no assets against which to levy it. If there is a sudden and an unexpected window of opportunity, seize it; if, however, it is not a rare situation—one in which there is evidence of attachable assets—you are well advised to move on past accounts such as the above and focus your time and attention on your active accounts.

The Remedy of Replevin

Replevin is much too broad a subject to discuss in any detail in these pages. It is important to mention it, however, because it is the remedy used to recover a chattel by one who has a general or a special property in what has been taken or detained. The rules regarding replevin vary from one state to another, so it is not possible to do a neat *one statement covers all* package on the subject. However, to recover in replevin is not that much different from certain types of litigation where recovery of a chattel is the goal. To recover in replevin, a plaintiff is required to show a possessory right or a title superior to that of the defendant.

The problem of replevin occurs most commonly in conditional sales and chattel mortgage contracts. Credit people have a real problem when both title and possession of a chattel have passed to the buyer; the seller company is suddenly faced with the fact that it has no right to maintain a replevin action. It is, in that circumstance, a done deal. When does the seller maintain the right of a replevin action? Only when the sale is made on conditions which are performed by the buyer (the buyer's failure to perform prevents a title from passing to it) does replevin remain an option.

If your company encounters a situation where it seems possible that the *remedy of replevin* might be used, or if you have any questions regarding the rules governing replevin in your state or the states in which you do business, let me urge you to consult your company's attorney. Any attempt to apply generalities to a specific situation could have the effect of damaging or diminishing your company's options to the point where it must deal from weakness rather than strength.

Skip Tracing

This is the name attached to a procedure that is used to locate a debtor who closes his or her business between dusk and dawn, cleans out the place, leaves no forwarding address, and is obviously interested only in disappearing from the sight and jurisdiction of the creditors.

Skip tracing is a standard part of the work done by commercial and consumer collection agencies, and also by some independent specialists who work for more than one agency, when the creditor assigns an account but has no current address for the proprietor, partners, or principals in a company or corporation. Some of the tools used to trace include social security records; motor vehicle registration records; bank records; personal, payroll and property tax records; friends and relatives of the debtor; and other sources of information.

It is not a procedure that most credit grantors are set up to handle in-house; most in-house skip tracing is done by retail merchants (single store or multi-store chains) who have a charge account system of their own in addition to VISA, MasterCard, American Express, or another. Grantors of commercial credit carry their own accounts (unless there is a factoring agreement which means that funds are advanced by a factor on a *recourse* or a *non-recourse* basis). If the account agreement is set up so the factor has recourse against the manufacturer/distributor if the account does not pay within terms, there is additional pressure on the factor's client (the creditor) to see that the accounts make on-time payments to the factor.

Mechanic's Lien Laws

This is a very complex area of the law. Just as the Uniform Commercial Code is not uniform in what the 50 states, the District of Columbia, and the Virgin Islands require to have a perfected filing, so Mechanic's and Materialmen's Lien Laws vary from one state to another.

The majority of states accept the premise that any person who furnishes material or does work on a property can file a lien. An individual, a partnership, or a corporation can file a lien, and no regulation states that a person or an entity must be a resident of the state in which they wish to file the lien. Labor or material is the basis for a Mechanic's or Materialmen's Lien. To qualify, both must have become part of the property or added value to it.

The filing of liens by subcontractors and materialmen is governed by two different concepts. A filing is made not because one concept or the other is the choice of the person or company filing, but because it is based on whether the state in which you are filing the lien follows the New York or Pennsylvania requirements to qualify a given situation as eligible for exercising lien rights. The New York concept sets the allowable lien limit to the amount owed by the owner to the general contractor. If the amount owed to the general contractor doesn't cover the subcontractor's claim, the burden of proving that the owner owes the greater amount rests with the subcontractor. Pennsylvania and the states that follow its concept do not limit the amount of the subcontractor's allowable lien to the amount owed by the owner to the general contractor. Pennsylvania and its followers give the subcontractor a direct lien regardless of whether there is proof that the owner has made payments to the general contractor.

The same warning applies here as with a UCC filing. Do not try to file a Mechanic's or Materialmen's Lien unless you are familiar with the procedural requirements in the jurisdiction where you are filing. Filing requirements do differ from state to state; the schedules of filing fees are not consistent; the duration of liens may vary; the requirements for what must be included in the lien notice itself are often complex. Until you have gone through the filing process enough times and in enough jurisdictions to know how and where to look for the guidelines, let your company's attorney guide you through the process. And as you listen to him or her, also become familiar with NACM's Credit Manual of Commercial Laws.

Uniform Commercial Code Filings

A person whose job it is to manage credit accounts must have a working understanding of the *when and how* of UCC filings, and to do that requires some recognition of the Code's component parts. The credit manager, administrator, and/or collector should be able to identify and locate which of the Divisions (or Articles) is applicable to a specific problem or need. It is not necessary for a credit manager to be able to recite Sections and subsections of a Division of the UCC, but it is appropriate for a credit manager to know where to look to locate the applicable part of the Code.

A *perfected filing* under the Uniform Commercial Code means that the secured position of the creditor adds a safety net to transactions protected by the filing, and makes it much easier for the supplier-creditor to collect if the customer's financial position worsens to the point where there is a filing under Chapter 11 of the Bankruptcy Act. Whenever an account balance becomes so large that the loss of it would result in a major financial problem for the supplier-creditor, it is mandatory that the supplier company protects its security rights with appropriate filings under the provisions of the Uniform Commercial Code.

The Uniform Commercial Code

The purpose of this book is to assist creditors to collect accounts receivable balances, and one of the key ways for a creditor to collect those balances is to make enlightened credit decisions, avail himself or herself of every protective device appropriate to the size and type of the risk, and to have some familiarity with the options for protecting receivables balances in advance of any type of collection problem. What follows is a list of the provisions of the section of the Code used most frequently by grantors of commercial credit. Other sections cannot be disregarded, but Division 9 is the area of major interest.

Division 9: Secured Transactions; Sales of Accounts, Contract Rights, and Chattel Paper
    Chapter 1: Short Title, Applicability, and Definitions
        9101. Short Title
        9102. Policy and Scope of Division
        9103. Accounts, Contract Rights, General Intangibles, and Equipment Relating to Another Jurisdiction; and Incoming Goods Already Subject to a Security Interest
        9104. Transactions Excluded from Division
        9105. Definitions and Index of Definitions
        9106. Definitions: "Account"; "Contract Right"; "General Intangibles"
        9107. Definitions: "Purchase Money Security Interest"
        9108. When After-Acquired Collateral Not Security for Antecedent Debt
        9109. Classification of Goods: Consumer Goods; Equipment; Farm Products; Inventory
        9110. Sufficiency of Description
        9111. Applicability of Bulk Transfer Laws
        9112. Where Collateral Is Not Owned by Debtor
        9113. Security Interests Arising under Article on Sales
            Chapter 2 :Validity of Security Agreement and Rights of parties Thereto
        9201. General Validity of Security Agreement

The preceding list presents a comprehensive look at the Divisions and major sections of the Uniform Commercial Code. I did mention, however, that the Code is loaded with sections and subsections which break each of the Divisions and major sections into categories that define the statute. The reader who has an interest in a specific section or subsection should refer to the Uniform Commercial Code for his or her state. If you have any problem understanding the legal language or interpreting the meaning of certain phrases, subsections, or sections, contact your attorney for whatever assistance or clarification seems appropriate. Do not assume that you understand areas of the Code if they are not crystal clear. The consequences of an erroneous interpretation can be too costly to proceed on the basis of assumptions or guesswork.

UCC Filings and Your Company

The UCC has been in effect for a varying number of years in each of the 50 states, the District of Columbia, and the Virgin Islands. State legislatures have put a personal imprint on the resulting legislation, diluting to some degree the original concept of a *uniform code*, but what has been passed by the various state legislative bodies is still much more effective than were prior controls. Suppliers are now able to protect their intrastate and interstate interests in goods via a Purchase Money Security Agreement with a subsequent UCC filing. This procedure not only gives companies or individuals a security interest in their goods until payment has been received and the filing cancelled, but also gives protection for an appropriate dollar interest in proceeds from the sale of those goods.

If your company sells to a variety of customers and those customers are located in your immediate service area or scattered throughout one or more states, it is probably wise to avail yourself of the protection of the UCC. It can provide some of the protection you need to sell to businesses and companies that have potential, but are not fully established; it can enable your company to stock new distributors or dealers at levels you could not consider were it not for the UCC; it can protect the interests of your company with appropriate filings to cover consumer goods, crops, business equipment, etc.

UCC filings enable companies to sell goods or services to customers whose credit records (payments to suppliers, etc.) might, under conditions of an unsecured sale, be too uncertain for the supplier(s) to take the risk. Not that a UCC filing automatically ensures payment or payment in full—not so. There are elements of risk that can be minimized, but not totally eliminated, and there is credit management work that must be ongoing after a perfected filing has been made. A credit manager should ask questions such as the following:

1. Are there UCC filings on record ahead of the one I would file to protect my company? Contact the appropriate authority to obtain a list of the prior filings. You may also want to obtain copies of individual filings to determine whether they have been prepared and filed properly.

2. If the bank was the first to file, what was included in that filing?

3. Have other suppliers established a priority with their filing? And again, what exactly do these filings cover?

4. If there are prior filings, have the companies that filed established a valid priority claim? You might want to order copies of these filings to be sure that they are proper (or perfected) filings.

5. In the event of a Chapter 11 filing by the customer, would your company's UCC filing put it in a priority position in the line-up of secured customers?

There are other questions that should be asked, but the above are typical of what a credit manager must look at before he or she makes a protective filing under UCC, ships any product, or performs any service that should be covered by a filing. If your company is not making the first filing, you must know who stands ahead of your company and what asset or assets is covered by the one or more filings that are ahead of yours. Do not file just for the sake of filing. If a filing is not going to give your company the protection it needs, then the priority position of other suppliers and creditors could put your company too far down the line. If that is the situation, you should reevaluate the account (or the order for goods and services) before deciding whether it is an acceptable risk.

15.14

Uniform Commercial Code Filings–Current/Closed

Name and Location	Filing Date	City, State Where Filed	Acknowledgment Copy in File	Renewal Date	Date Financing Statement Terminated

16

*What to Do When
the In-House Collection
Effort Is Not Successful*

There are times when your best in-house efforts to collect an account balance will be unsuccessful. You will have exhausted your in-house collection tools (letters, telephone calls, fax messages, visit(s) to the customer's place of business, a final demand) and must reluctantly assign the account to a commercial collection agency. Most companies will have one or two whose work over the years has been satisfactory. But if your company or business is fairly new, or the collection service(s) you have been using is not doing as well for you as you think it should, how do you decide which of the many to try?

One of the better ways to determine which agencies are doing a good job for suppliers and service companies in your industry is to make inquiries of fellow credit managers. You may get a broad variety of opinions about a number of collection services, but you may also get good reports about certain ones which will help you to narrow the field from which you will select one to represent your company or business. The responsibility for sorting information and arriving at a decision is your responsibility but when the information is based upon the experiences of suppliers in your own industry, the probability that you will make a satisfactory choice is enhanced greatly.

There are agencies who specialize in collecting commercial accounts; other agencies specialize in collecting consumer accounts. Most commercial credit reporting services and industry credit associations offer a collection service to their subscribers and/or members. Two such commercial credit organizations that come immediately to mind are Dun and Bradstreet and the National Association of Credit Management. They offer members a collection service that covers national and international accounts, although the leverage for collecting international accounts that have been sold on an *open account basis* (no confirmed letter of credit or other secured arrangement) does not offer a strong chance for success.

Other collection agencies may offer personal collection service in only one city, or perhaps in an area such as the Rocky Mountain States or the Pacific Western States. When a client of one of the local or regional collection services assigns an account that is located beyond the agency's normal geographic boundaries, it (the original assignee) will assign the account to a collection service with which it has a working agreement in the home area of the client's customer-debtor.

Every full-service collection agency must have the capability to service the needs of its clients. To do that effectively means that the smaller agencies must network with others scattered across the country. Whether this is an especially good or effective way for collections to be handled, with one agency or service enlisting the services of another, depends primarily upon the collection service to which the customer assigned the account. If the collection agency has a good record of success, is aggressive in its pursuit of creditor dollars, and is careful to operate with integrity, there is every reason to assume that the primary agency only associates itself with agencies whose professionalism and performance are comparable to the standards it sets for itself.

If an assignment to one collection service evolves into an effort that brings a second service into it, the combined efforts may or may not result in your company's money being collected but there is little question that it greatly improves the chances for success. And if the collection effort is successful, does the presence of a second collection agency increase the amount of the collection fee? It does not. The fee for a successful collection should be based upon a printed schedule of fees (which translates into a percentage of the amount collected). The primary agency deducts the fee from funds received from the debtor, remits the balance to the client, and shares the fee with the secondary agency on the basis of their agreement.

When to Use a Commercial Collection Agency

It is the function of a credit department to see that merchandise is sold (or services provided) to companies and businesses that have been evaluated and accepted as *creditworthy* within parameters set for the specific account (a credit line, etc.). A commercial collection agency should not be brought into the picture until every in-house effort has been made to collect the creditor-supplier's money. Does this mean that a collection service does not earn its fee if it collects the balance(s) your in-house effort failed to collect? Not at all. It means that the expense of a collection fee increases the loss (in-house expense of trying to collect, etc.) your company must absorb as it attempts to get out of the unsatisfactory relationship with the highest percentage of its receivables dollars intact.

Having made the pitch for a total in-house collection effort, I must now temper that thought with one that is equally relevant: Do not continue an in-house collection effort beyond the point where it becomes obvious that nothing your company can say or do will motivate the customer-debtor to send a check for the past-due (or account) balance. It is easy to waste additional time and effort in a collection situation that has gone beyond the point where any further in-house effort might have a chance to succeed. At some point in the chain of in-house collection procedures, the obvious will become evident to even the most tenacious (or stubborn) collection person. Assign the account to a commercial collection agency and turn your time and energies toward other accounts and other problems; and unless you are an amazingly perceptive credit person, there will be accounts whose balance(s) could become a problem unless you make it a point to work with them.

The in-house collection procedure should be effective in all but a very few of your collection situations. If your company has several hundred or several thousand credit accounts and you are assigning more than a few per year to your commercial collection service, one or more of the following is out of synch with a good credit and collections program:

1. Accounts are not being screened properly. Accounts are being accepted that are not *creditworthy on the background, bank, and supplier data.*

2. The credit line is too high for the quality of the account. Account should be reviewed periodically and the credit line should be adjusted (up or down) when the facts indicate it is appropriate to do so.

3. Accounts are not monitored frequently enough, or they are being monitored frequently but the person doing the monitoring is failing to pick up early signs of an account that is beginning to slip, or an account has problems of a temporary nature but problems that your company should know about and include in the evaluation.

4. The credit report data from reporting agencies and from other suppliers, banks, and service companies is not being updated. (Unless data is updated, changes in the business and financial condition of a customer could go unnoticed until a major problem has surfaced.)

5. Credit lines are not being reduced (or reduced rapidly enough) when all the signs point to a serious business and/or cashflow problem. Decreasing sales will certainly impact cashflow but the customer's slow-paying receivables will also seriously impact cashflow.

6. The sequence of in-house collection tools selected are not appropriate for (a) the situation or (b) the company. (Your experience with the account will be your biggest asset when a collection problem surfaces. How well you know a key person (a partner, the financial officer, etc.) will influence the sequence and the variety of the in-house collection tools that you use.)

7. When one tool (telephone calls, letters, etc.) is not generating a payment commitment, try a fax message or a personal visit. Most companies are receptive to the same basic collection techniques; others require a much more innovative approach.

8. When nothing you have done has motivated the customer-debtor to give any indication of a serious desire to fulfill that company's payment obligation to your company, it is time to assign the account to a commercial collection agency.

   Example: You have an account whose five-figure past-due balance has been adding aging as you progressed through the collection procedure. There have been several promises of payment but only two of those commitments resulted in a check, and both checks were for considerably less than the amount promised. You have done everything possible to avoid assigning the account to an outside collection service but it has become obvious that the in-house collection effort is not going to succeed.

   If there has been no payment response within ten days after the date the final demand letter was mailed, or no payment for the amount specified in the final demand, it is time to assign the account to your collection service. You might get lucky. Sometimes the surprise of having the account assigned to a third party collection service is enough to get the customer-debtor to send a check for the amount assigned. At other times the standard "10 days free demand" (the period immediately after the date the account is assigned and during which no fee is paid to the collection service if the debtor pays the assigned balance) will pass with no indication from the debtor that notice of the collection assignment has been received.

   Before an in-house collection effort fails, and to avoid a repetition of a situation that might have been avoided, you will want to determine what went wrong with the account, with your company's relationship with the account, and what the credit department might have done to avoid putting a five-figure receivables balance in the kind of jeopardy that leads to a third-party collection assignment. Were there early signs that cash flow was becoming more restricted, and were those signs visible some time before it became a critical problem? You will want to know how you could have seen it, why you did not see it, and how you can avoid a future repetition by applying the lesson to your company's other receivables accounts.

   Credit managers are not infallible. There are valid reasons why a credit manager could be in a situation where the potential for a receivables loss becomes lost in the cumulative pressures of spiraling growth: an inadequate and inexperienced staff, pressure from executive management to release orders to high volume/high risk customers, too little time to properly evaluate applicants for a credit line, and various other reasons.

How to Select a Collection Agency

   The criteria for selecting a collection agency should be based upon the requirements and standards of the company that is about to select an agency. Not all collection agencies work to the same high standard of ethics, but some agencies that flirt with questionable collection practices have a high rate of collection success. If your company practices a consistently ethical approach to business, then it is obvious that a collection service whose approach to collecting debts is scrupulously ethical would be a fit. But is your company high on the ethical approach in its own business but less demanding when it comes to the tactics used by an agency to collect money owing to your company? If a double standard is applicable, the criteria is suddenly much wider.

Example: Your company is a one-location manufacturer of metal pipe for stoves, furnaces, water flumes, etc. The dealer base is in the Rocky Mountain states with a few customers in states adjoining the Rocky Mountain area. Nobody has ever raised a question regarding the business ethics of your company, but it should be noted that your company does know how to brawl in a back alley when a business situation calls for that type of behavior. So what type of collection might your company select?

Because the customer base is regional, it is not essential that the collection service have offices in key areas of the country (You may still opt for one of the national agencies because there is the perception that it does the job faster and more effectively than the competition, but the geographic requirement does not mandate it.) Inquire of other credit managers regarding regional agencies whose area of activity may be in the Rocky Mountain states. Ask if their regional agency is doing an effective job of collecting accounts, and if it is doing the job on the same percentage scale (based upon the amount of the collection assignment) as the national agencies or perhaps for less?

If the agency's credentials (ask for references) seem to be a fit for the requirements of your company, assign one or two accounts to it. If your evaluation of agencies indicates that two or three offer approximately the same level of service and client satisfaction, and if you have more than one account to assign, give one account to each of two or three of the collection agencies. Then step back and see which one does the best job of skip tracing (if necessary), keeping you informed of progress, and collecting your money. An example of an assignment agreement appears in Letter 16.1.

Remember also that it isn't possible usually to give three facsimile accounts to three different agencies and assume that all three are operating on the same level playing field. Problems in one of the accounts may not be present in the other two; or may not be factors to the same degree as in the others. But what you will be looking for is the overall balance of the collection effort: Is it being handled in a professional manner? Is the agency moving steadily forward with the collection procedure, increasing the amount of pressure on the debtor as the collection effort moves closer to a settlement? And give an agency high marks if it picks up something that your in-house procedure did not, something that enhances the possibility for an early settlement of the problem. When a collection agency certifies its high level of professionalism with a thorough evaluation of the case before it begins the collection process, the chances for success increase significantly.

Compare the fee structures of collection agencies you consider to be candidates for your company's referrals but do not be unduly influenced by minor variations in the percentages of assigned balances that would be withheld from monies collected by the agency. The fee structure is important because you would not assign accounts to an agency whose fees for collecting accounts is out of line with others who perform the same service. You should not, however, judge the quality or the effectiveness of the service by the collection fee that would be charged.

The first priority is to select the collection agency that seems to be the best for your company: the agency whose methods, track record, personnel, and area of operation should be the most effective for what your company will expect of it. It is wise to stay away from an agency whose image is of a "hired gun"; choose one whose standards and methods are comfortably within the statutes that define and govern fair collection practices. Remember that the agency of choice is your representative and as such it can involve your company in the most embarrassing and costly litigation resulting from unfair and illegal collection practices. The goal of your company is to have a collection assignment resolved in a professional manner; being named by a debtor in a suit for damages is not an appropriate result.

16.1   Assignment

FOR VALUE RECEIVED (I/We) hereby sell, assign and transfer unto _____
all (my/our) right, title and interest in and to (my/our) claim and demand against
_____ standing in the amount of $_____,
with full power to sue and collect the same. We hereby certify that this is a valid and subsisting claim and no defenses, counterclaims, cross-complaints or offsets exist as of this date on this account. Assignee shall not be liable for any claim so made. Assignor shall furnish such witnesses and such testimony of such of its officers, employees or agents as may be reasonably required.

(SEAL)   _____

Dated: _____   _____

When returning this assignment, it is essential that we are advised on the following:

1) Are you a corporation?   ( ) Yes   ( ) No

If a corporation, advise State in which incorporated:

2) Are you a copartnership?   ( ) Yes   ( ) No

If a copartnership, give names of partners:

_____

_____

3) A you an individual transacting business under a fictitious name? ( ) Yes ( ) No

4) Has trade style been filed?   ( ) Yes   ( ) No

If yes, under what name:_____

Retain Overview Control of the Agency's Collection Effort

When your company assigns an account to a collection agency, it takes itself out of the day-to-day collection effort but not out of the collection loop. You should know in advance of assigning the first account (a) how frequently the agency forwards a progress report, (b) how much you are to be told regarding the nuts and bolts of the collection procedure, (c) at what point in the agency's effort is it appropriate for the account to be assigned to an attorney for suit, (d) and if you do not want the collection agency's attorney to file suit, the form used to assign the account to the agency should include a line (or an area for special instructions) for you to include that instruction. If your company does not state in full the limitations of the assignment, the collection agency is justified in forwarding the case to an attorney of its choice.

The objective of any assignment is to free your company credit department from the day-to-day responsibility of the collection effort. It is not, however, a farewell to responsibility. Any account that is still judged to be collectible—one that has not gone down the long, sad road and into the category of bad debt items—is never totally out of mind. Meaningful reports from the collection agency are essential not only for the possibility that money will be collected which will then be added to cashflow, but also as the company's fiscal year-end approaches and decisions must be made as to which customer accounts are potential bad debt items (essential when projecting a bad debt total for the next fiscal year and to minimize bad debt losses for the purpose of having the year-end financial statement reflect the best and biggest bottom line figure). If a credible determination is not made in advance of the preparations for budgeting and year-end financial statements, the charges made to the bad debt account, and the projections made for the following year, may be out of phase with what should be appropriate charges and projections.

Accounts Assigned to an Attorney

Whether the attorney who handles the collection suit is one chosen by the plaintiff (creditor) company or by the collection agency is irrelevant to the costs involved in the filing of a suit. There are up-front costs which require an advancement of funds for future disbursement which must be paid to the attorney prior to filing suit to obtain a judgment against the defendant (debtor). In fact, it is illegal in many jurisdictions for an attorney to advance fees or expenses of litigation on behalf of a client. It should also be remembered that any delay in furnishing the attorney with funds for costs or disbursements could delay proceedings against the debtor.

1. Services of a process server (serving notice of filing on the defendant, serving subpoenas, etc.)

2. Filing fees (suit fees, etc.)

3. Posting security for costs (generally mandated by law if the plaintiff is not a resident of the jurisdiction) (Refer to Memo 16.2 for a sample memo regarding this type of situation.)

4. Trial fees (court costs, etc.)

5. Jury fees

6. Cost of entering judgment (when a verdict has been rendered)

The attorney cannot be expected to go forward with a filing if he or she has not been provided with documentary evidence basic to proving the plaintiff's case. Some of the key documents are listed below:

1. Copies of the defendant's original purchase order.

2. Three copies of the original invoices (invoice copies should show the date of delivery, signature of the person who received the merchandise, terms of sale, a description of each separate item or category of merchandise, quantities of the various items, and a total of the dollars to be collected).

When the plaintiff's attorney has the debtor served with a summons to appear in court on a specific date and at a specific time, it can be the first in a series of actions by both plaintiff and the defendant.

1. Plaintiff's attorney serves the debtor with a summons and a statement of the claim in the form of a complaint (another procedure may be prescribed by the law of the jurisdiction in which the suit is to be filed).

2. After being served, the debtor has a time frame in which to respond to the allegations as set forth by the plaintiff-creditor.

3. Debtor may offer defenses to the plaintiff's claim, or may deny the allegations.

4. Debtor may claim an offset or make a counter claim.

5. If the defendant introduces new material, the plaintiff may be required to file a reply.

The trial will be held before a judge or a jury. Judgment is then entered in accordance with the decision or verdict, and either for or against the plaintiff or defendant. The judgment becomes a part of the permanent records of the court and, when entered, it becomes (in most states) a lien against any real estate owned by the debtor. In some jurisdictions, the lien may become effective against the personal property of the debtor.

The statutes are not uniform among the jurisdictions as to what constitutes an effective lien again real and personal property. In all instances, what determines when and how the judgment will be executed are the laws of the jurisdiction in which the judgment is entered.

16.2　　　　　　　　　　**Memorandum**

To: Branch Offices

From: Corporate Credit Manager

Re: Suits Filed Against Nonpaying Out-of-State Customers

In any account situation where this company is doing business in a state other than one in which it is qualified (or licensed) to do business and we have a collection problem with an account that ultimately requires the services of a local or an area attorney, corporate legal counsel has advised that we proceed in the following manner:

We do not initiate a suit as The _____ Corporation representing itself in the matter. Prior to the filing of suit against the customer, the account will have been assigned to any one of several collection agencies for a conventional run at collecting the company's money. If that approach fails, the collection agency will then refer the account to an area attorney. The attorney will notify our company via the collection agency of his or her requirements: suit fee (refundable court costs) and contingency fee. The licensed and bonded collection agency with whom we do business in California will send an assignment form (similar to the attached) which transfers ownership of the account to the collection agency. The form empowers the collection agency to assign the account to the licensed in-state agency (customer's state) for whom the attorney works. He or she will then proceed to file the suit.

The attorney will deal directly with the collection service. In the event a settlement offer evolves from pretrial or trial, that offer will be transmitted to this company via the non-California agency to the California agency with whom we have direct contact. The California agency will then contact this company with the settlement offer, this company will respond favorably or with a counteroffer, and the information will be sent back through the chain to the attorney.

Whether this company's status in the customer's state is classified as qualified or nonqualified, this company's position in these matters, when handled as outlined, is alleged to give us maximum protection under procedural law.

Corporate Credit Manager

Attachment–and Attachable Assets

Attachment of an asset that if liquidated would generate enough cash to pay the plaintiff's judgment against the debtor, is the goal of every plaintiff. A *writ of attachment* is the legal instrument that places real or personal property in the custody of the law to secure the creditor's interests. It is the step that occurs when an asset has been located and against which an attachment may be levied. The attaching party is generally not required to obtain a bond because the attachment is issued as a right acquired when a decision or a judgment is rendered in favor of the plaintiff. There are, however, jurisdictions that do require the attaching party to obtain a bond so, once again, nothing can be done on the assumption that because it is done in some jurisdictions, it must be right in all of them. It should be mentioned that many states do not allow a writ of attachment to be issued as a matter of right. In these states, statutes specify the classes of action in which a writ of attachment may be issued and the circumstances and relationships that must exist before the writ is issued.

A debtor does not have the same level of flexibility as that enjoyed by most plaintiffs. When a debtor company wants to get an attachment released, it must file a bond. The bond takes the place of an attachment on the property and provides the plaintiff with security against which a recovery of the judgment amount may be made.

Suffice to say that although there is some uniformity among the states, there are enough differences, of sufficient importance, to require the services of an attorney. This is not an area for "do it yourself" law, and no one should yield to the temptation to try. The law in every state is explicit as to its requirements; any deviation from those requirements could result in a hard-won attachment being terminated at the defendant's request.

When a Judgment Has Been Satisfied

The statutes of almost every state mandate that a *satisfaction* (an acknowledgment that the judgment has been paid) must be filed by the creditor within a specific period of time after the debtor satisfies the judgment (pays the account balance plus court costs, etc.). This mandate applies to payment(s) received as the result of judgment enforcement proceedings as well as voluntary payment(s).

Though the requirement is virtually universal among the states, the time frame in which the filing of satisfaction must be accomplished varies from a few days in some states to as long as 30 and 60 days in others. California is among the states that requires a notice of satisfaction to be filed within a specified number of days after payment in full and upon written demand of the debtor. Guidelines for how satisfaction is to be recorded range from the specific statutory requirements, to the more informal entry of a creditor's satisfaction upon the judgment record.

It is imperative that creditors, or the attorneys who represent them, know the law in the state where the original judgment was entered and the law in each of the states where a certified copy of the judgment was or is to be filed. If there is a breakdown in this process, there is the potential for a creditor to get the court to set aside the judgment.

Liquidating an Asset

Locating one or more attachable assets of a debtor can be a difficult task. Some debtors are cooperative; others will swear that they have no assets other than the none, one or few that are known or have been declared. But when an asset has been located and a writ of attachment (or applicable procedure) has allowed the creditor to seize legally or to take possession of the asset, the creditor is not without his or her own considerable responsibility. While functioning as the caretaker of an asset that has been seized, or one that has been frozen at its location, the creditor must ensure that it does not deteriorate in appearance, utility, or value as the result of inadequate or inappropriate care or handling. If the asset has been seized with the objective of liquidating it, then there are other cautions that must be addressed.

If the fair market value of a seized asset is alleged to be $30,000 and the creditor's judgment against the debtor is for $21,000, the creditor will not sell the seized item for less than the appraised or fair market value. If the item has been carried on the debtor's records at a book value of $30,000, and if it is sold for a price at or only slightly above the judgment figure of $21,000, which is alleged by the creditor to be the fair market value, a qualified appraiser or appraisers should have been brought in to set the fair market value. Creditors who do not document the value of property (land, buildings, equipment, vehicles, jewelry, etc.) may find themselves being sued, by the debtor for the difference between $21,000 (or the sale figure) and the alleged true and/or fair market value of $30,000.

A judgment is not a license that gives a creditor the right to abuse a debtor. Debtors often have a higher level of interest in an asset(s) than the amount of a creditor's judgment and although a creditor's primary interest in an asset is to convert it to cash as quickly as possible, it is never permissible for the self-interest of the creditor to damage the interest of the debtor. The hasty sale of an asset often brings a lower price than would be true if the creditor examined the options and scheduled the sale for a more favorable time and place.

When an in-house collection effort is unsuccessful, it generally hardens the attitude of the creditor toward the debtor. By the time the in-house effort has been recognized as a failure, the creditor's credit manager will have spent hours attempting to get the debtor to pay—hours that in retrospect might have been spent more productively with other accounts and other problems. But the creditor company's frustration with the debtor cannot be allowed to color the relationship to the point where a vengeful creditor disregards the rights of the debtor. The court system does not turn its back on the debtor's rights because a judgment has been granted to the creditor.

Although the debtor company's owners or management may be hip-deep in unethical business practices, it is unlikely that criminal action can or should be brought against the debtor firm unless there is provable evidence of intent to defraud the creditors. If the asset(s) that has been located is not valuable enough to cover, when liquidated, the amount of the judgment, the case will remain open until another asset (or assets) can be located and converted into enough cash to clear the balance on the judgment.

The goal of the creditor is to recover all or most of the judgment figure, thereby eliminating or minimizing the uncollectible balance that must ultimately be charged to the bad debt account. No creditor is happy when an account balance must be charged to the bad debt account but if a creditor is not being excessively restrictive in the granting of credit, a small amount of unhappiness goes with the territory.

Part 3

Bad-Debt Write-Offs

The subheading for Part 3 implies a straightforward question: "Is it possible for a bad debt to have life after a write-off?" Although the answer is "Yes," the subject is much more complex and requires an answer in more detail than just the one word.

Let us set the parameters for life after a write-off by stating that it is unwise for a credit department to invest time trying to revive any small balance(s) that has been charged to the bad-debt account. If, however, there is at some future point (within the statute of limitations for your state) a sudden possibility that one of your company's largest bad-debt write-offs might be revived, you would have to explore the possibility of a partial or a full recovery.

When a collection effort has run its course (from in-house to-and-through a collection agency or an attorney and judgment), and an account balance has been charged to the bad-debt account, there is a period of years during which the account might be returned to the status of an active collection item. The time limitation for civil actions varies from one state to another and from one type of debt to another (Open Book Accounts, Contracts of Sale, Contracts in General, Bills and Notes, etc.), and the time limitation for these and other categories of debt starts from the date that a cause of action begins. *Example:* If the debt was incurred as an open account or an open book account, the clock begins to tick against the statute of limitations for filing a civil action from the date the last entry was made in the account.

Statutes of the various states prescribe specific periods of time within which a creditor may bring an action to enforce a legal right. This forces litigation to commence within a time frame that takes into consideration (1) allowing too much time to pass, during which important evidence and records are lost, and (2) the possibility that potential witnesses may be removed from the legal process by death or a move from the jurisdiction. Not the least of elements important to any criteria for an effective legal action is the ability of witnesses or key people to recall events clearly, and memory views events with less clarity as time passes.

For an accounts receivable balance to have life after it has been charged to the company's bad-debt account is comparable to any situation in which there is the possibility for success, but the odds are long. But if the dollar total that was charged to the bad debt account is large enough to be meaningful, then the possibility that some or all of the debt might be collected is well worth a long, close look.

17

How to Revive Some Bad-Debt Write-Offs

As I mentioned in the introduction to Part 3, the circumstances under which a bad debt write-off might be revived are quite limited. And because it is an area that has a limited potential for success, it would be unwise to invest additional time in any but the largest of the bad-debt write-offs.

Statute of Limitations

Let me state first that collection procedures should never be so poorly organized that an account which you carry as active—a receivables balance on your aged trial balance report—is lost because the statute of limitations has run out. You must be aware of the statute in any state or jurisdiction in which you might want to use Small Claims Court or a conventional civil suit to press for a judgment against the customer-debtor. Take appropriate collection action but initiate it within the period of years prescribed by the appropriate jurisdiction. Virtually no set of circumstances could provide justification for such a level of inattention to the aging of a receivables balance. If the collection service has been unable to locate the debtor or determines that there are no assets against which you could hope to levy a judgment, charge the account balance against your company's bad-debt reserve. You will at that point have made every reasonable effort to collect your company's money.

There are certain circumstances under which a debtor might surface after the statute of limitations has seemingly pushed your old account balance—now a bad-debt charge—beyond your reach. Unless you are notified that the individual, partnership, or company filed for bankruptcy, and your debt was among those listed and discharged by the bankruptcy court, there is the possibility of life after the statute of limitations. Other pieces must also fit the criteria for reviving the account balance, and it is imperative that you have your company's attorney make that decision. Let your attorney tell you whether there is hope, what must be done to make reviving the account a possibility, and if there is a possibility that the debt can be returned to the category of a legally collectible item. Also find out if there are now any assets against which you could apply your judgment and expect to collect.

The statutes in some states allow for the limitation to be suspended if the defendant is out of the state or a false name or identity is being used. Another reason for extending the period of limitations is when the existence of a cause of action is concealed fraudulently by a party who is liable. The death of a claimant may not terminate the limitation until a specific number of months after his or her death. As it is with so many of the subjects that I have discussed in this and other books, there is seldom uniformity between the statutes of the various states. So I must say again: Consult your attorney before making a decision that might prove costly to your company.

When the Clock Begins to Tick

The statute of limitations (the time limit beyond which your company or its authorized collection representative(s) cannot file a civil suit to obtain a judgment) begins to tick from the last date on which the debtor account had an order shipped (and billed) or the last date on which the creditor received payment against the receivables balance. If an account has a major payment problem, try to set up a payment program that will deliver a small payment every month, or on some schedule. A payment program is the commercial equivalent of a respirator; it keeps the patient's (your customer) account active as it gradually chips away at the account total.

Get as big a payment each month (or every 15, 30, or 45 days) as you can, but if there is no realistic chance that the debtor will be able to pay the account balance in one, two, or three monthly payments, try to get the debtor to commit to small payments at regular intervals over a longer period of time. Such a program will put the statute of limitations on hold, will add some cash to the company's cashflow, and will defer the possibility that some part of the account's past due balance is probably destined to be a bad-debt item.

When a company seems to be slipping toward a Chapter 11 bankruptcy filing, it is usually not possible to work out a payment plan that has a realistic chance to succeed. Faced with that situation, your company should do what it can to maximize the amount of money it collects before the debtor files for the protection of the bankruptcy court. When the filing has been made, your company is either a secured creditor (if its interests have been protected with filings under the appropriate section(s) of the Uniform Commercial Code) or it will be wallowing around at the bottom of the pit with other unsecured creditors.

If the customer does not respond to any collection attempts (in-house, Small Claims Court, collection agency, collection attorney, etc.), protect what chance your company may have of collecting part or all of the receivables account by taking the debtor to court and obtaining a judgment. It is wise also to pursue larger account balances through the judgment process because if there is ultimately some part of the balance that must be charged to the bad-debt account, proof of a vigorous collection effort is essential if the IRS is going to accept the write-off as a valid bad-debt item.

What Statute Governs When the Parties Are in Different States?

How does the law react to the problem of parties who live in different states and sue over a contract or an obligation that was created in a third? The location where the suit is maintained determines whether the claim is timely (within the time frame allowed for such an action) as defined by the laws of that jurisdiction. There are some states, however, that will not allow an action to be brought if the action was not allowed by the statute of the state in which the cause of action arose. Interestingly, the places (states) in which the contract was negotiated and/or signed does not determine where, when and how an action may be maintained.

Length of Judgments

When a judgment is entered against one of the parties to the action, the judgment may be effective, depending upon the statute of the state and the court rendering the decision, for a period of years ranging from two to 20. The period of years during which these judgments are effective varies from state to state and from the types of accounts or contracts that form the basis for the suits (Promissory Notes, Open Accounts, Instruments and Contracts Under Seal, Ordinary Contracts, Domestic Judgments in Courts of Record, Domestic Judgments in Courts Not of Record, Foreign Judgments in Courts of Record, and Foreign Judgments in Courts Not of Record).

The following information is relevant to the types of judgments and the meaning of terminology that might be somewhat misleading or difficult to interpret:

1. A domestic judgment is one secured in the state in which the suit was brought.
2. A foreign judgment is a judgment that was secured in a jurisdiction other than the one in which the suit was brought.
3. Courts of Record are generally courts that keep a permanent record.

4. Courts Not of Record usually include justices of the peace, and in some cases, municipal courts.

5. Statutes of limitations are usually longer for judgments of courts of record than for judgments of courts not of record.

Exemptions from Judgments

Many exemptions still on the statutes of the various states do not offer justice to the rights of creditors. It is a weakness in the law that a debtor who has made every effort to bilk a creditor should be allowed to exempt much or all of his or her personal property from the power of a judgment. Why should that same person or persons be allowed to homestead a piece of property to escape what should be a just liquidation of assets?

Homestead property is limited as to the value that can be exempted but some states require a creditor to fulfill certain statutory requirements before the creditor can proceed to levy against a property with value above the allowable limit. A creditor may have to file an affidavit describing the property, the name of the person who filed the homestead, when any other claim has been filed against the property from the same judgment, and attach the affidavit of an independent professional appraiser to verify the true value of the homestead property.

Documenting Your Collection Efforts

When your company loses a receivables balance to the bad-debt account, the credit department must be able to substantiate its claim that every effort was made to collect the money before it was written off. There must be no question regarding the diligence and the continuity of your company's effort to collect. Your company will use these legitimate write-offs to reduce the annual tax obligation, but the IRS will not accept the validity of these write-offs unless there is indisputable documentation to support the statement that there was a total, aggressive collection effort before the balance or balances were charged to the bad-debt account.

The credit department should have a special section in its file cabinet for accounts that have been written off. In each of these account folders there should be copies of all correspondence pertaining to payment of the obligation that was sent by your company, and any letters or notes that were received from the debtor should also be in this folder. There should be a copy of the form for recording telephone calls that were made to the debtor, a recap of each conversation, and a statement regarding any promises of payment that were made by the debtor to a member of your credit department.

It is imperative that the record of telephone calls and letters should reveal a consistent pattern of increasingly insistent and/or urgent messages and statements from your company to the debtor. There should be clear evidence that your company made every reasonable effort to get the debtor to pay his or her obligation to your company. A copy of the letter or form that was used to refer the account to third-party collection, including your company's instructions to the agency or attorney, plus copies of any notes or memorandums received by your department or initiated by it should also be available. And finally, if the agency or attorney returned the account with an explanation of what it had done to try to collect (or if the business had closed and there had been an unsuccessful attempt to skip trace the owner, owners, or partners), covering that phase of the collection effort should also be a part of the file.

The IRS could challenge one or each of the items that your company claims as a bad-debt loss as the company attempts to reduce its obligation for a specific tax year. If the information received by the IRS is not complete, the IRS might demand more data pertaining to the effort made by your company to collect from the debtor. If the debtor filed a Chapter 11, then failed to produce a plan for continuing the business that was acceptable to the creditors and the court, the subsequent transferring of the Chapter 11 to a straight bankruptcy and subsequent liquidation of assets should provide all of the documentation necessary to verify final disposition of the case.

The situation does not, however, ensure that your company will be allowed to deduct an account balance as a bad-debt loss, unless there is sufficient documentation (letters, records of telephone calls, third-party collection assignment, etc.) to prove that your company's collection effort prior to the filing by the debtor of a Chapter 11 meets the criteria of the IRS for diligent and aggressive collection effort. You must do your job, and be able to provide the back-up data to prove that you did it as effectively as circumstances would permit.

When a list of potential bad-debt customers and balances is prepared from the company's accounts receivable aging report, it is often difficult to project the time frame within which certain of the company's problem customers will complete their demise. It is also difficult to project whether the percentage of loss to your company will be 10 percent, 25 percent, 50 percent, 75 percent, or more of what is owed when the account is declared to be uncollectible, a certified bad-debt balance. The provision for bad-debt items should be as accurate as possible, but to project whether an uncollectible balance will become a bad-debt item this year or the next is, in the instance of some accounts, a very difficult situation.

The following are examples of what should be considered when the credit manager sets out to provide a bad-debt provision against which write-offs can be charged on a quarterly or annual basis. Will your company be able to collect a part of the account balance, or will it be a full or partial write-off?

1. Has the account been in Chapter 11 for several months?

2. Have the company's creditors been unwilling to accept any of the proposed continuation plans?

3. If a continuation plan has been offered and accepted by the creditors, how does the plan deal with prior debts?

4. Have prior debts been deferred for one or two years with payments of 5 percent per year scheduled to be paid from third- and subsequent-year profits, if any?

5. Has there been a change in management personnel or in the business philosophy of the company that would seem to give the continuation plan a reasonable chance to succeed?

6. Will the company be issuing stock for a major part of the debt owed to creditors?

7. If stock is a part of the restructuring of old debt, what is the time frame and the criteria for selling the stock?

8. If a continuation plan has been accepted, has it been accepted because the alternative would be to liquidate the company and pay some of the secured creditors as much as the liquidated assets would cover, with nothing left for some of the allegedly secured creditors and all of the unsecured creditors?

9. If your own evaluation of the debtor's chances for pulling out of the Chapter 11 is not optimistic, review the monthly bad-debt accrual to ensure that funds will be available to accommodate the write-off.

10. Do not be intimidated by the wishes of credit committee members who have their own personal and/or company agenda for wanting creditor companies to accept a specific plan or recommendation. Do remember, however, that what has been worked out by a creditor's committee and approved by the bankruptcy court is probably the best solution for the majority of the creditors and should be viewed from that perspective. Almost no plan that a creditor's committee might devise would please every creditor; so a plan that is acceptable to a majority of the creditors is generally a plan that represents the best interests of creditors. What about your own company? If you are a smaller creditor, you might prefer another plan, something that might be more favorable to the smaller creditors, but the rule of the majority (in number, dollars owed, etc.) is virtually certain to prevail.

When a Bad Debt Cannot Be Revived

Unless a bad-debt item represents an unusually high loss based upon the size and liquidity of a creditor company, it is not generally productive for a credit department to try to breathe life into that account. If the collection effort was a comprehensive one—the full gamut of in-house collection tools and options plus the best efforts of an outside collection service and/or collection lawyer—there is no good reason for a credit department to spend additional time on the account.

But what if you, a member of the your company's sales staff, or a credit manager from another company tells you that one or more of the principals in that earlier, somewhat questionable bankruptcy have surfaced in your company's headquarters city, a nearby city, or a city several hundred miles from your company's headquarters? Do you push the information out of your mind on the grounds that you did everything possible to collect the account; and although you discovered subsequent to the bankrupt being discharged from debts that your company's debt was not on the list, there is no reason to assume that the debtor has new assets against which you can use your judgment (which is still within the statute of limitations).

There is some truth in the rumor, but not what you had hoped. One of the former partners in what became a bad-debt write-off for your company is with another company in a nearby city but after checking the business license to get the names of owners (or after going to the state commission for corporations in the home state of the company being investigated), it may be found that there is nothing to connect your bankrupt debtor with an ownership interest in this business. He (or she) is an employee unless or until there is irrefutable evidence to the contrary, and so you return the account folder to the section reserved for bad-debt accounts.

What Is an Allowable Write-Off of a Bad Debt?

When an account has reached the point where it is no longer considered to be collectible, the major thing to be salvaged is a write-off of the account balance to the bad-debt account, a write-off that must be able to withstand the scrutiny of an IRS audit. Guidance will be provided by your company's accounting firm (the firm that performs an annual audit as a part of the process of preparing certified year-end financial statements), but the behind-the-scenes work and documentation must be done by your company.

This is a book on collections and collection techniques, but how a failed collection effort reaches write-off has relevance to the subject. A collection effort that was less than diligent and forceful will not persuade your own auditors or auditors from the IRS that the charge you have made to the bad-debt account is an allowable one. To be sure that your collection effort is in compliance with the criteria for an allowable bad-debt charge, your company should be able to verify and/or document that most of the following steps were taken as the account moved unsuccessfully through the various stages of the collection process:

1. A record of all collection telephone calls to the debtor (date of the call, a recap of what was said, whether a payment commitment was obtained, and what follow-up was to be made on what date).

2. A record of all collection letters to the debtor (copies of each of the letters should be in the customer file folder). If there was a reply (telephone call, fax, or letter) to any of your company's letters, it should be in the file folder.

3. A copy of all outgoing and incoming fax messages should be in the folder (also any responses that might have been made).

4. A record of any collection visits to the offices of the debtor company (including a recap of conversations or meetings with people who have the authority to authorize payments of the past due balance).

5. Assignment to a collection agency (copies of periodic reports from the agency pertaining to actions being taken by the agency to locate the debtor, to force the debtor to pay, etc.).

6. Assignment by the collection agency to an attorney for the purpose of filing a suit and obtaining a judgment against the debtor (or per instructions given by the creditor when the account was assigned to the collection agency, the collection agency having failed to collect balance, returns the account to the creditor company. The creditor company assigns the account to its own collection attorney.)

7. A judgment is obtained but the creditor is unable to find assets against which to levy an attachment (after searching for a period of several months, the judgment is put in the debtor's file folder and the collection effort is closed).

8. The account balance is charged to the company's bad debt account (and the bad-debt reserve).

It is not possible to know in advance which account balance(s) will be among the very few to be brought out of the bad-debt account. Unforeseen circumstances can intervene and give the creditor a second chance, a chance to use the judgment and levy an attachment against property not known to exist when the judgment was granted.

What are the chances that one of your company's bad-debt accounts will rise from the black hole of bad debt and give you a chance to collect some or all of your company's money? Let me put it another way. In the 30-plus years of my own experience in credit and collections, the number of accounts that I was able to bring back from a bad-debt write-off and collect some or all of the balance was not more than a dozen.

Not a very high percentage of the total number of account balances I wrote off during those 30-plus years? That's true, but when I tell you that assets I was able to find, attach, and sell generated something over $250,000 from accounts that had been buried in the bad-debt account, it becomes obvious that the major bad-debt balances should never be totally out of your mind, not until the statute of limitations has had the last word.

17.1   [date]

To: The Reader

Fr: Cecil Bond

Attached Recap of Bad-Debt Charges—19XX

The letter that follows is a photocopy of the one I prepared for the auditors, state and federal tax reports, and the company's records.

The cover letter total of $48,023.43 was supported by three pages of itemized bad-debt charges, the first page of which I have attached to the cover letter. Pages two and three were a continuation of the same format and involved listing a total of 31 accounts. The total of the three supporting pages—the 31 accounts—equalled the cover letter total of $48,023.43.

Each write-off was supported by the weight of our effort to collect from these 31 accounts: an effort that was documented in the file folders of these accounts with copies of collection letters, a call sheet which detailed all collection calls (date called, person with whom the credit department member talked, the questions asked and the responses and promises given in return), a record of the collection agency's efforts to collect (or copies of Chapter 11 proceedings, a conclusion of bankruptcy, etc.).

By the time the account had reached the point of becoming a bad-debt item, all steps possible had been taken to collect the balance.

17.2   [date]

This recap of bad-debt charges for the year 19XX includes all items that qualify for the category, plus an adjustment for old credit balances.

BAD-DEBT CHARGES	$47,874.39
(Total includes major balances plus various very old, small balances.)	
ADDITIONAL BAD-DEBT CHARGES	516.70
(Numerous small sales tax, freight, and quantity discrepancy charges not documented by customer. Average individual balance is less than $5.00.)	
CREDIT BALANCES	–367.66
(Various small credit balances such as overpayments of invoices, sales tax added to payments, etc.)	
TOTAL	$48,023.43

Bad-Debt Charges–19XX

Account Name & Location	Amount	Remarks
Acctg. Equip., Inc. 1896 Rock County Rd. Casper, Wyoming	$734.97	March & April 19XX invoices. Assigned third-party collection on 10/4/XX. Many broken payment ment promises. Debtor has no money.
Action Planning, Inc. P.O. Box 439 Paoli, California	$212.62	April 19XX invoicing. Collection assignment on 10/14/XX. Paid $350.00 of $562.62. Collection Association is working on the balance. Collection doubtful
American Systems 1314 Piedmont Blvd. Bushnell, Montana	$507.04	Nov. & Dec. invoices. Company reorganized in Jan. 'XX. New problems in late 'XX and early 'X1.
Business Applications 949 Acorn Drive San Francisco, California	$912.53	Oct. & Nov. invoices. Could not locate this business when I was in the San Francisco area in Feb. 'XX. Out of business.
Carmichael Corp. 1791 Carter Way Roanoke, Virginia	$14,953.3	April & June 'XX invoicing. Repeated efforts to get debtor to pay. Balance of $16, 195.28 reduced to current total when $1241.90 received 4/5/XX. Sent another letter 11/2/XX. Payment not expected at this late date.
Computer Research, Inc. Dunham Drive Phoenix, Arizona	$912.53	Oct. 'XX invoice. Out of business via bankruptcy. Nothing left for creditors.
Computer Space 1599 Temple Drive Ogden, Utah	$1515.07	Dec. 'XX & Feb. 'X1 invoices. All assets were assigned as collateral for an SBA loan. The corporation failed in the early part of 19X1 with no assets available for distribution to the unsecured creditors.

Prepared by: _____
              Credit Manager

Approved by: _____

Part 4

Collection Techniques: Consumer Accounts

There are differences and similarities between the techniques used to collect past-due commercial accounts versus past-due consumer accounts. Some of the obvious similarities include a series of reminder letters; telephone calls (generally to the consumer-debtor's home unless the customer has failed to respond to other contact efforts); a suit in Small Claims Court; assigning the account to a collection agency; and initiating a civil suit for the purpose of obtaining a judgment against the assets of the debtor.

Past-due commercial accounts? These pages have taken you through almost all the same tactics and techniques as those that are used to collect past-due consumer accounts. The past-due balance of a commercial account is usually much higher, and the letters, collection calls, and other phases of the collection process can become more intense and accelerate more rapidly to a demand for payment or an assignment to a collection agency. But the granters of commercial credit and consumer credit are interested in the same result, which is the prompt resolution of a past-due payment problem.

18

Before the First Letter Is Mailed

Consumer accounts may range from a balance of less than $100 to a balance of several thousand dollars (for an automobile, household furnishings, and other big ticket items). Although most consumer purchases are paid for in cash or on a major credit card (VISA, MasterCard, American Express, Discover, etc.), other noncash purchases are made on a sales contract (automobiles, major purchases of household furnishings, etc.), or on the in-house charge account offered by an area, regional, or national retailer (Macy's, Sears, The Emporium, Penney's, Mervyn's, etc.).

Collecting for purchases that have been made on one of the major credit cards is not a problem for the retail merchant.

Collecting for purchases that have been made on the retail merchant's in-house credit account can be a problem if accounts have not been screened properly. The average annualized interest or carrying charge of 18 to 22 percent that is assessed to the in-house credit accounts of retail merchants will not offset very many poor credit decisions. But when it is administered properly, an in-house credit system that has a monthly interest or carrying charge of 1.5 to 1.8 percent per month can be an important profit center. The potential for good earnings is especially strong when the cost of money borrowed to finance the program is in the area of 6 to 9 percent.

Consumer Credit Terms–In-House Credit Accounts

The number and variety of imaginative credit terms offered by retail merchants whose company's feature an in-house credit program is virtually endless. Here are a few taken from the daily newspaper:

1. *Six Months Same As Cash!* The fine print tells the consumer that any purchase not paid in full in 180 days will be subject to an APR (annual percentage rate) of 21.6 percent accruing from the date of purchase.

2. *0 percent Financing for 6 More Weeks!*

3. *Six Months—No Payment/No Interest/No Finance!*

4. *Free Carpet For 6 Months! No Interest/No Payments! 90 Days No Interest—3 Payment Plan Without a Finance Charge!*

6. *Take 38 Months to Pay!*

7. *90 Days Same as Cash!—Or Take 22 Months to Pay—Instant Credit to $2000!*

8. *90 Days Same as Cash! No interest for 90 days for qualified buyers.* Purchases not paid in full during the 90-day period are subject to finance charges that will accrue at APR 21.96 percent in California; 21 percent in CO; 20.4 percent in PR; 19.8 percent in IA1 and 18 percent in ME, NC and WI.

9. The J.C. Penney Company issued the following Credit Card Disclosure information on notice dated Rev.(7/92):

> *Annual Percentage Rates (Finance Charge)* — Texas (21%); Alabama (21% $750 or less; 18% over $750); Arkansas (18% $1,000 or less; 7.92% over $1,000); California and Iowa (19.8% the entire balance); Arizona (7.92% the entire balance); FL, MA, ME, MN, PA, WA, WI (18% the entire balance); DC (21% the entire balance); accounts in other states have been assigned APR (finance charge rates) that range from 18% to 21%. In most states there is a late payment fee of 5% of the late payment (excluding any insurance premium, returned check fee and previously assessed late payment fees). There is no annual fee for the credit card and no finance charge if there is no balance from the previous billing period or if the billed balance is paid within 25 days of the billing date.

The credit card operations of department stores or other types of merchants (national tire companies, etc.) are usually centralized in a city in each of the company's sales and service regions. Data pertaining to credit accounts—recording sales to accounts, preparing and mailing statements, processing payments, and collecting past-due account payments—is handled by a staff whose principal ally is an imposing array of high-tech equipment. Although it is costly to set up a processing center for the credit card operation, the long-term return from such an operation has enabled many major retailers to improve the bottom line of their financial statement.

Immediate advantages for a retail merchant of an in-house credit card system over one of the national cards, includes elimination of handling fees, avoidance of processing time, and the elimination of the time delay between forwarding credit card receipts and reimbursement for them. And there is of course the biggest incentive of all, which is that all of the profits from carrying charges belong to the retail merchant. But the national cards are a must because retailers must offer their customers a full choice of merchandise, locations, prices and credit services. No merchant can afford the luxury of losing a sale because the store or business does not accept VISA, MasterCard, American Express, Discover, or some of the other national and internationally recognized credit cards.

The Credit and Collections Philosophy

Credit and collections people who are alleged to have been trained properly are often instilled from day one of their training with the thought and belief that you should always assume that the debtor will pay. It is a statement that if carried to absurd limits, will cause an experienced credit and collections person to wretch and contribute no small number of new entries to the bad-debt account.

There are customers that a perceptive credit and collections person will soon, gradually, or suddenly realize are (a) not going to be able to pay; (b) are not particularly interested in paying; (c) might pay some of the account balance over a long period of time; and (d) are not terribly worried about your collection procedure because the customer is about 48 hours away from taking his belongings and disappearing into the night.

It is true that the initial stages of most collection efforts should appear to convey a confidence on the part of your company that a debtor (individual, business, or company) intends to pay the account balance. It would be less than professional to initially use a less positive or understanding approach, but there is a point at which the weight of evidence begins to indicate clearly that the account is not destined to be one of your company's winners. Your company's experience with the customer plus the experience of others (the bank, other retailers, etc.) will tell you that the collection effort must be intensified or the account balance could become the victim of a personal bankruptcy.

When You Say It, Mean It!

When collection calls and letters reach the point where there is a payment ultimatum, be crystal clear as to your intentions, and how and when you intend to implement them. Never threaten a customer with assignment of the account to a collection agency or a collection attorney unless you intend to do it. And when the date for the threatened (or promised) action arrives, and the customer has not met the conditions that would allow you to avoid the stated action, you must follow through without delay. There is no such thing as a hollow threat; you either do what you say you are going to do when you say you are going to do it or a street-wise customer will have his or her attorney suing for harassment and sundry other charges.

Suing to Obtain a Judgment

When other attempts to collect have failed, a creditor must sue a debtor to obtain a judgment. This does not ensure that the creditor will recover the amount of the debt but if the suit is successful (judgment in the amount of the debt is granted to the creditor), the creditor has a vehicle for moving to collect from the debtor.

1. *Jurisdiction:* A creditor must determine whether he or she can obtain jurisdiction over the debtor. This determines in which jurisdiction a suit can be filed.

2. *Attachment:* Property of a defendant may be impounded by an officer of the court and held pending the outcome of the suit.

3. *Garnishment:* When a third party holds property that belongs to a defendant, or is indebted to the defendant, garnishment can, in some jurisdictions, allow a judgment to be directed against the third person in order to reach property of the defendant.

4. *Wage garnishment:* The employer of a debtor is served with a process (a paper issued by the court) which directs the debtor's employer to deduct a specific sum from the debtor's wages (one time, weekly, monthly, etc.) and remit that money directly to the judgment creditor.

5. *Judgment:* A judgment in favor of a creditor is the result of a civil suit brought by a creditor against a debtor who has refused to pay what the creditor alleges is due and owing. (This does not guarantee that the creditor will recover the money awarded by the judgment but it gives the creditor the tool with which to attempt a legal recovery.)

6. *Execution and levy:* An *execution* is an order of the court which directs the sheriff or other designated law officer to seize the defendant's property to satisfy the judgment. A *levy* is the process by which the sheriff or other law officer takes possession and control over property which is to be used to satisfy the judgment.

7. *Supplementary proceedings:* Initiated by a creditor when the court's officer has been unable to find property upon which to levy, or when an "execution" has been returned as unsatisfied. A creditor may by subpoena or court order, direct the judgment debtor or others who might have knowledge of assets to appear before the court (or a referee) to be examined by the judgment creditor.

8. *Judgment liens:* A judgment lien does, in most states, give to judgments the status of liens, giving judgment creditors who are otherwise unsecured priority over all subsequent judgment lien creditors and over all unsecured creditors. The proceeds from the sale of any property are applied first to the satisfaction of the creditor's claim whose judgment was the first to attain the status of a lien (when lien status occurs, the scope of the lien and the means of enforcing it vary from one state to another).

The Opening Line(s)

No stand-up comedian is under more pressure to deliver than the collection person who—with the opening line of the collection letter—must grab and hold the attention of the customer-debtor. When your company sends collection letters to a customer, there is a strong probability that other creditors are doing the same thing. And because there is undoubtedly a limited number of dollars available to pay creditors, the creditor whose approach is the most innovative and/or attention grabbing has the best chance of getting a good share of the available cash.

What about the collection letters that you have been using? Do you write the kind of collection letters that get the attention of the customer? And if the letter gets the customer's attention, will it also motivate the customer to send your company or business a check for the past-due balance or installment? If your letters can and are doing both, there is a good chance that life for the person(s) collecting your consumer credit accounts is not going to be burdened with too many heavy problems.

Get the customer's attention *immediately*, with the opening line, but do not squander that advantage! Whether the approach uses humor or concern regarding the health or personal welfare of a customer whose account has always been excellent, you must take advantage of a strong opening line and parlay it into a winning, motivational letter.

The Basic Approach

Unlike the collection procedure for commercial accounts where a telephone call is frequently the first contact, the basic format of a consumer collection usually involves a series of collection memos or letters. Some are stock reminders that are mailed routinely when an account is five or ten days past due, with subsequent memos or letters of increasing intensity as the number of past-due days increases.

If these types of letters and memos are not effective, the consumer creditor will use the telephone to contact the customer to determine the reason for the failure to make the account payment. If this is still not effective, a personal letter and/or a collection telephone call (made to the customer's home during the evening hours) should ensure that (1) a representative of the retailer's credit department is able to talk with the customer, and (2) get a payment commitment from the customer.

The Wisdom of Being Innovative and Flexible

As this is being written in mid-1993, there is some evidence to support the thought that the economy is turning upward. However, people who would normally pay their bills on time are in too many instances struggling to put food on the table.

This, then, is the time for credit and collections people, who are the guardians of their company's internally generated cash flow, to use innovative concepts to help good people to maintain their self-respect in the face of crippling personal economic problems.

Example: One of your customers has lost his or her well-paying job in business or industry and is struggling to adjust, and to survive, on a new job that pays 60 percent of what he or she earned previously. The customer owes your company almost $4500 for home furnishings that were purchased when the customer's job seemed secure. Your job is to help the customer and your company to a middle-ground accommodation.

The customer's monthly payment has been $195 a month, but the customer has slipped to 40 days past due with no prospect for improvement. You will do your company and the customer a genuine service if you suggest a reduced payment of $100 a month; or if the customer was unemployed for a period of 3 to 6 months before getting the new but lower paying job (60 percent of the previous salary), suggest a payment of $75 a month for the next two or three months (to give the customer some help in bringing order out of the chaos from the "no income" months into the "low income" ones). Then suggest a payment of $100 a month from the fourth month through the twelfth month.

If by the end of the twelfth month the customer's economic situation has not improved markedly, tell the customer that you will take the account balance and refinance it into a new payment program of 30 or 36 months, a payment program that will continue to reflect the customer's more restricted economic circumstances, and spotlighting the fact that your store, business, or company knows how to lend a helping hand to its customers and to itself. Your company will retain the goodwill of the customer while salvaging an account balance that might eventually have been referred to a collection service or a collection attorney.

Anything positive that your store or business can do for the customer, something that does not add a new and a major element of jeopardy to an existing situation, should be done. You should be willing to do anything that is reasonable to assist customers who, through no fault of theirs, are struggling to survive in an economic climate that may have taken on new and serious personal consequences. Treat the customer right today and the customer will remember you favorably when conditions improve and there is a need for new merchandise or services.

Scripted Telephone Calls—Consumer Credit

The reminder and/or the collection telephone call has its place in consumer credit just as it does in commercial credit. How a collection call is used—at what point in the collection process and the level of urgency and/or insistence that it must convey—is a decision that should be based upon individual credit account circumstances.

An account whose payment performance is spotted with late payments and/or late payment charges (and whose performance is becoming increasingly slow) should not receive the level of consideration that is extended to the account whose payment record shows no more than one or two minor deviations from the payment due date. A chronic slow pay is one problem but a chronic slow pay whose monthly payments begin to arrive at an increasingly slower pace may raise concerns for the safety of the account balance. Suppose the account has no more than one or two minor deviations from the due date. Unless your company has picked up something from the retail credit association, or from another store, merchant, or business, your call should not be heavier than a courteous reminder.

The following five scripted telephone calls should be directed toward customers whose accounts have never been a payment problem: a record of on-time payments with no more than one or two minor past-due payments.

Jack Farben places a call to the home of Ms. Alice Weston.

Weston: Hello?

Farben: Is this Ms. Alice Weston?

Weston: Yes, it is.

Farben: Ms. Weston, this is Jack Farben at The Merchandise Center.

Weston: Yes?

Farben: We haven't received your monthly account payment, Ms. Weston, and I'm calling to ask if you forgot to mail it?

Weston: Oh, my goodness! You know, I don't think I did mail it! Can you hold a minute while I look at my check stubs?

Farben: Certainly. (Silence for a couple of minutes, then ...)

Weston: Mr. Farben?

Farben: Yes, Ms. Weston?

Weston: This is really terribly embarrassing. I did forget to mail the check, but I'll write it now and mail it tomorrow morning on my way to work.

Farben: That will be fine, Ms. Weston. Your account payment is so rarely not on time that we thought it had to be an oversight.

Ms. West: I'm really sorry.

Farben: Please don't worry about it. We appreciate your concern but your credit rating hasn't suffered a bit. Thanks, Ms. Weston.

Weston: Thank you. Goodbye.

Farben: Goodbye, Ms. Weston.

Jack Farben contacts Randy Marshall at his home.

Marshall: This is Randy.

Farben: Randy Marshall?

Marshall: That's me. Is this Masters and Johnson?

Farben: (Gives him benefit of doubt and a quick laugh.) No, this is Jack Farben, Mr. Marshall. I'm with the credit department of The Merchandise Center.

Marshall: What did I do this time?

Farben: I think it's what you've done a couple of times in the past. You seem to have forgotten to send us the monthly payment for your charge account.

Marshall: No! Did I do that?

Farben: (Chuckles.) Come on now, Mr. Marshall. Are you sure you haven't been waiting for this friendly reminder before you put the check in the mail?

Marshall: Well, money has been a little tight these past few months. I string you people out a few days once in a while.

Farben: You aren't always on time but you aren't a problem either. Can you put a check in the mail tomorrow?

Marshall: How about if I put a check in the mail this [day of week]? I get paid that day so I can make out a check the night before and mail it on my way to the bank or after I deposit my pay check?

Farben: That'll work fine for us, Mr. Marshall. Thank you for your cooperation. Goodbye.

Marshall: Sure. Goodbye.

Jack Farben contacts Al Harrington at his home.

Harrington: This is Al Harrington.

Farben: Mr. Harrington, this is Jack Farben at The Merchandise Center.

Harrington: O.K. What have I done?

Farben: It may be what you haven't done, Mr. Harrington.

Harrington: Oh?

Farben: Your monthly credit account payment is five days past due and we're wondering if you forgot to mail the check?

Harrington: Hmmm. You know, I think I did.

Farben: Mailed it or forgot to mail it?

Harrington: No, I forgot to mail it. I was out of town last week and I didn't think about it before I left.

Farben: No problem. Can you mail it to us tomorrow?

Harrington: Sure. I'll write it now and mail it in the morning.

Farben: That's all I need to hear. Thanks very much, Mr. Harrington.

Harrington: You're welcome.

    Farben contacts Will Bryant at his home.

Bryant: Yes?

Farben: Mr. Bryant? Will Bryant?

Bryant: That's me.

Farben: This is Jack Farben at The Merchandise Center, Mr. Bryant.

Bryant: I'm watching a ball game. What is it?

Farben: A quick question. We haven't received your monthly account payment and we're wondering if you forgot to mail it?

Bryant: Damn!

Farben: I beg your pardon?

Bryant: Sorry. Yeah, you're right. I did forget it.

Farben: It's no big problem. Can you put a check in the mail tomorrow?

Bryant: Sure. I'll write it tonight and mail it in the morning.

Farben: Great. Thanks very much, and sorry to disturb you.

Bryant: Ah, it's alright. My team is playing like a bunch of bums tonight anyway.

Farben: Well, better luck next game. Goodbye, Mr. Bryant.

Bryant: Goodbye.

    Jack Farben contacts Ms. Evelyn Hawkins at work.

Hawkins: This is Evelyn Hawkins.

Farben: Ms. Hawkins, this is Jack Farben at The Merchandise Center.

Hawkins: (Lowers her voice.) Why are you contacting me here at work?

Farben: We've been trying to reach you at home, Ms. Hawkins, but we haven't been able to talk with you and our recorded requests that you return our calls have not been answered.

Hawkins: I just couldn't make the payment this month. I've had some problems with my car and I had to use the money for your monthly payment to get my car back on the road.

Farben: I can understand that, and it's no problem.

Hawkins: It isn't?

Farben: (Laughs.) No, Ms. Hawkins, it isn't. If you had told us sooner, we could have saved you the worry that has resulted from your inability to make the payment.

Hawkins: I wanted to call but I was afraid you people would be angry.

Farben: We don't get angry when a customer has an unexpected financial emergency. You do intend to make up the payment, don't you?

Hawkins: Oh, yes. If you agree, I'd like to pay one and one-half payments this months, then do the same next month.

Farben: That's fine. And because this is the first time your payment has been late, we'll waive the late payment charge.

Hawkins: Thank you, Mr. Farben. My next payday is a week from today. If it's alright with you, I'll mail a check for $_____ [one and one-half monthly payments] a week from today, and I'll do the same thing the following

Farben: The second one and one-half monthly payments will be mailed a month from the payday that's a week from today?

Hawkins: That's right.

Farben: I have no problem with that, Ms. Hawkins. Thank you and goodbye.

Hawkins: Goodbye, Mr. Farben.

19

First Collection Letters—Consumer

Major retail merchandisers have traditionally used a program of reminder notes or letters, released at specific intervals to coincide with the aging of a past-due account. Some mail the first gentle reminder within five days of the payment due date; others may wait eight or 10 days before sending the first reminder.

Past-due notices to consumer credit customers are generally mailed within a tighter time frame than the pattern used by grantors of commercial credit. It is of course somewhat easier for a consumer to avoid paying a credit obligation than it is for a company or an established business. Not every consumer is a homeowner so there is always the possibility that a customer whose job has disappeared, and whose financial situation has become desperate, will simply disappear; move to another city, state, or region.

A filing of personal bankruptcy is the avenue of escape taken by too many other consumer debtors. Some consumers use bankruptcy in a way that borders on perpetrating a fraud against merchants and other consumer creditors. There is, unfortunately, far less stigma to a filing of personal bankruptcy than was true some decades ago. It should be added quickly that when a bankruptcy is the result of one or a series of legitimate misfortunes, there should be no stigma. But when it is used by debtors as a convenient ploy to rid themselves of legitimate obligations? It is unconscionable, and every effort should be made to prosecute those who try deliberately to take illegal advantage of the provisions of the Bankruptcy Act.

The Structure of the First Collection Letter

Owing money, or being owed money that is past a payment due date, is not a subject that lends itself to a humor-laced treatment. If you (or your company) are the creditor, the single most important way to put a smile on your face is for the debtor to hand you a check or for one to arrive in the mail. This is a smile of relief, not one to be associated with something bright or amusing. However, a check in your hand or on your desk from a customer whose payment record might be described as "spotty at best"is relief in its purest form.

Whether you do or do not believe that "the customer" (an all-inclusive phrase) will pay eventually, your first collection letters (and there should be several from which to make an appropriate choice) should be very light, very relaxed, and very friendly in their tone. There is in most instances, no justification for any other approach. The overwhelming majority of your customers will pay—and most of them on time—but there are legitimate reasons for a customer to miss a payment due date: out of town for several days and neglected to write a check; illness of the customer or a member of the customer's family; a sudden loss of employment and the customer's unsuccessful effort to make the available money cover all bases. These are just a few of the reasons why first collection letters should do little more than offer a reminder in a format that is steeped in "Oh, by the way—." No push, and definitely no pressure.

Is There a Problem with the Product?

One of the best ways to ease into the matter of a past-due payment is to inquire first whether the product is or is or has been performing in a satisfactory manner, whether it is wearing as well as the customer had reason to expect, and it is giving the appropriate (and expected) level of satisfaction. Many customers will pick up the telephone and register a complaint if what they have purchased is not satisfactory, or if it is not performing as the guarantee indicates it should. Other customers will not say anything to the store or to the manufacturer but will fume silently, and if one of the "silent fumers" is a credit customer whose silent protest manifests itself in the withholding of an account payment(s), the problem can usually be dealt with in a manner that proves eventually to satisfy the customer and does not damage his or her credit rating.

A customer base is at best a very fragile thing so it becomes imperative that retail merchants (goods, services, etc.) make every reasonable effort to placate a customer whose handling of a grievance may not be totally appropriate but whose claim to having a problem with the product(s) is certainly correct. So the customer insists that he or she will not make a payment until the store (or the manufacturer has either corrected the defect or has received a replacement unit. This may or may not be a customer with whom your company or business has a long-standing credit account relationship, but if, from the viewpoint of a customer, the position taken can be justified, the obligation to correct the problem rests with you (your company or business) and not with the customer.

If you correct the problem and the customer still does not pay, then that is another story, one that should receive your company's standard collection treatment.

A Policy of Customer Satisfaction

When a customer has had a long-standing and satisfactory relationship with a store or a business, it is usually much easier for the credit department (or the customer relations department) to remind the customer of the store's well-advertised and well-documented policy of customer satisfaction. Most customers will be less inclined to take a measure as drastic as withholding a payment(s) if:

1. The store's reputation for customer satisfaction is known widely.
2. Corrective steps are initiated immediately upon the store being notified of a problem.
3. The product is fixed to the satisfaction of the customer.
4. If the purchase cannot be made to perform (or wear) as it was represented when the customer bought it, a replacement should be delivered to the customer.

A reputation for giving customer satisfaction is established not over a period of days and months but over a period of years. When the handling of a complaint is botched (whether the complaint is or is not legitimate), it can result in a flurry of word-of-mouth negativism that will take more than a little of the luster off a reputation that has been years in the building. Give every customer complaint the benefit of a judgment of legitimacy. If a review of the problem indicates that it is not legitimate—perhaps a ploy to avoid and/or to delay the payment obligation—the credit and the customer relations departments must work together to let the customer know that the complaint has been thoroughly investigated and for one or more reasons (explained in detail to the customer) there is no basis for an adjustment or a replacement. And second, the customer should be told that the past and the currently due payments are expected by such-and-such a date. Your company's credit department is a vital link in the chain of customer relations activities. Credit departments must be courteous, understanding, flexible (within the parameters of reason), and, when in the final analysis it becomes necessary to do it—be firm.

The following letters are examples of the soft approach to a past-due balance, an approach that is calculated to get the customer's attention but in a context that is friendly and understanding.

19.1 Dear Mr. George:

One of the primary reasons people do not make a payment or pay a bill is because a purchase has not performed as expected or as advertised.

Your recent purchase of a _____ is the latest credit purchase in a long and a satisfactory credit relationship, or perhaps I should say a credit relationship that has been satisfactory to this point.

The account balance is _____ days past due but our service department reports two calls during the past 10 days regarding warranty-related problems. It is now our understanding, however, that the unit is operating properly and you have expressed satisfaction with it.

If there is an ongoing problem with this unit, or any other current or future purchase, contact me if you do not feel that the problem is receiving the appropriate level of attention. If the unit is no longer a problem, your check for the past-due and currently due payments should be in this office by the [date].

We appreciate your business, and we want our products to give you good service.

Sincerely,

19.2 Dear Ms. Carson:

A funny thing happened on the way to the bank. As I left my office, from somewhere within me a sharp, nasal voice rattled my eardrums.

"You don't have her account payment on the deposit slip, do you?"

I found myself answering myself—and doing it aloud.

"I don't have whose account payment?"

The voice was not only sharply nasal but wrapped in a sneering tone.

"Don't play dumb with me! You don't have Ms. Carson's check, do you?"

I hate being defensive with myself.

"It's none of your business but, no, I don't have it!"

"So—when are you going to get it?"

My voice filled the parking lot.

"I'll send her a reminder note when I get back to the office! O.K.?"

That was the end of my run-in with the "inner voice," but I would prefer it didn't happen again. People in the parking lot were looking a bit panicky.

Your check by the [date] will be greatly appreciated and should eliminate any recurrence of my problem.

Sincerely,

19.3   Dear Mr. Baker:

We've been watching the incoming mail but so far we haven't seen your check.

If it is in the mail, please forgive this reminder. If it hasn't been mailed, please forward it promptly.

Sincerely,

19.4   Dear Mr. Wilkins:

Did you forget us?

I know we don't socialize during the month or do any of the other things that help to keep a name or a date in mind, so the failure to remember us on a payment date is no big deal.

If your payment hasn't been mailed, we'll appreciate your prompt attention to it.

Sincerely,

19.5   Dear Mr. Arcel:

Your monthly payment is usually timed so well that we could use it as a substitute for our calendar.

This month is different. It is _____ days past the due date and no payment check, and that causes us some concern; not because we don't have your check but because illness or some other problem is always a possibility.

We hope there is no problem, and please contact us if there is one. If it is just an oversight, please forward the check and accept our thanks for your excellent payment record.

Sincerely,

19.6   Dear Ms. Tennant:

It isn't like you to miss a payment date.

If there is a problem, please give me a call. If not, your check by [date] will be appreciated.

Sincerely,

19.7   Dear Ms. Pemberton:

Let me guess. You have been out of town and forgot to write a check before you left? Perhaps there has been a wedding in the family and you were in charge of all the arrangements? None of the above? Well, it must have been something very unusual to cause you to forget to send your account payment.

If everything is back to normal, please forward your check for the payment. If, however, there is a problem that has not been resolved—one that has made it impossible for you to send the account payment—call me and let's see what we can do to help.

We're sure about one thing. A customer whose payment record is as good as yours does not purposely miss a payment. We want to help you maintain that excellent record.

Sincerely,

Credit Manager

19.8   Dear Ms. Garner:

This is new ground for us. We've never sent you a payment reminder before.

Your account payment has always arrived on or before the due date, so we are both surprised and concerned that the payment for the current month is _____ days past due.

If there is a problem—illness, job, merchandise, etc.—please give me a call. Your credit record with us is excellent and we want to do whatever we can to help you keep it that way.

Sincerely,

Credit Manager

19.9   Dear Ms. Talford:

People who make a conscientious effort to maintain a good credit rating are a throw-back to another era—an era when a man or a woman was judged (among other attributes) by how they handled their personal and financial obligations.

Your good credit record tells us that your sense of ethical behavior is as good as any—and better than most. I don't know how you happened to miss sending your monthly account payment but if you will get it to us by the [date] of this month, it will be posted as an "on-time" payment.

We appreciate your patronage.

Sincerely,

19.10   Dear Mr. Lenhart:

I don't know about your personal finances, but all businesses have this terrible preoccupation with cash. I suppose it stems from the simple fact that if we don't have enough of it, our banker turns testy, our suppliers become surly, and our paychecks might set a new record for "altitude per bounce."

Please understand that all of these traumatic events are not your responsibility—not yet, anyway. You're only a few days late with one payment, but if it escalates—Wow!

So there you have it. Although we're happy to say there is no cash crunch here, we'll appreciate your payment by the [date] of this month.

Sincerely,

19.11   Dear Mr. Canfield:

Good customers such as yourself are never a cause for concern regarding their monthly payment. We also know, however, that each of us can become distracted or sidetracked by new or unusual events in our lives. When that happens, almost anything—including a monthly payment—can be overlooked.

We appreciate your business and the way your monthly charge account is handled. If you will take a few minutes to send the payment for the current month, your credit record will remain unblemished.

Many thanks,

19.12   Dear Mr. Rickard:

Some of our customers have a fairly good credit record, and we certainly don't quarrel with that. A few others, people such as yourself, lead the way in setting the standard for what is an excellent credit account.

Of course, there is no such thing as "Excellent (Minus)" because the question then becomes, "How much less than Excellent are we talking about." A tiny bit? A little bit? Almost too much to still warrant incorporating the word "excellent" into the description? These "minus" designations are hard to sort out.

But you can avoid all of this "minus" talk with your check for the past-due monthly payment. I know there is a good reason for the delay but if you will get the past-due payment to us by the _____ of this month, the payment will be considered as "on time."

Why not! After all these months and years of "on-time" payments, we owe you one!

Sincerely,

Credit Manager

19.13   Dear Ms. Sheffield:

Say it isn't so! Not you, Ms. Sheffield! Not one of our most faithful and dependable credit customers!

Actually, what we have in the above paragraph is a bad case of overreaction to what we're sure is a simple case of a payment that is only a few days past due. And because your account is *never* past due (well, almost never), we thought a little frantic phrasing would help to make your day and ours.

If you will send the payment so we can enter it before the [date] of this month, I'll make a notation on the account that will preserve your "on time" payment record.

Sincerely,

Credit Manager

19.14   Dear Mr. Martin:

Just a note to remind you that your account payment is _____ days past the due date.

Please forward a check so we can apply it to the account before [date].

Sincerely,

Credit Manager

19.15   Dear Mr. Santos:

Your excellent payment record tells us that the past-due payment is an oversight.

If you have not mailed the payment, please do so. If this reminder and your payment cross in the mail, please accept our thanks.

Sincerely,

Credit Manager

19.16   Dear Ms. Abbott:

Checks are sometimes written in plenty of time to meet a payment due date but are inadvertently pushed under some papers and do not get to the post office.

I don't know if this has happened to your payment but we'll appreciate it if you will verify whether a check has or has not been written? If it has not been written, please send it at once and we'll give it a proper greeting.

We appreciate your business.

Sincerely,

Credit Manager

19.17   Dear Ms. Wallace:

I really think we should stop meeting this way, and especially at this time of the month.

Our problem is that this is the _____ time in the last _____ months that your account payment has been _____ days (or more) past due.

If something has happened that makes it difficult for you to make the account payment on the due date, please contact me. I'll be happy to change the payment date to one that is more convenient for you, which should then eliminate the pattern of late payments.

Sincerely,

Credit Manager

19.18   Dear Ms. Bannister:

An occasional past-due of 3, 4, or 5 days from an account whose credit history is excellent? No real problem. But a consistent pattern of a few days past the payment due date? It isn't something we like to see.

Our credit manual tells us to remind our customers that an account balance is overdue when it is _____ days past the due date. This is your reminder, Ms. Bannister, and I know your check for the payment will arrive by [date]

Sincerely,

Credit Manager

19.19   Dear _____:

We've looked and looked, but it hasn't arrived.

Please take a few minutes and mail a check for the past-due monthly account payment.

Sincerely,

Credit Manager

19.20   Dear Mr. Denby:

I don't think there is a person who has not, at some time, forgotten to do something that is usually done routinely.

Your account payment has apparently slipped through the crack of forgetfulness mentioned above. If you will put it in the mail by [date] , it will be posted as an "on-time" payment.

Sincerely,

Credit Manager

19.21   Dear Ms. Gorman:

A reminder notice is something we haven't sent to you before. It is, however, an automatic when an account—even one as good as yours—is _____ days past due.

Please forward your check so I can delete your account from our list of past-due payments.

Sincerely,

Credit Manager

19.22   Dear Mr. Reese:

We know that payments do go astray in the mails. We know also that good, conscientious people such as yourself forget occasionally to mail a check.

If the stubs in your checkbook tell you that one has not been written and mailed, please attend to it when you receive this note. If you did mail one and it has apparently gone astray, a stop payment on the first check and another to replace it will take care of the situation before it can become a problem.

Sincerely,

Credit Manager

19.23   Dear Mr. Yancey:

Reminding a good customer that a monthly payment is _____ days past due isn't all bad.

It gives us an opportunity to thank you for being such a good customer, and for handling your account so well that your name is a stranger to the collections section of this department.

We'll appreciate your check by the [date].

Sincerely,

Credit Manager

19.24   Dear Ms. Emerson:

I have told my staff not to panic, that they must have faith. Any customer, I have told them—even our Ms. Emerson—can be distracted and fail to make an account payment.

They do seem to be bearing up quite well but if you can mail your payment by [date], staff confidence will be restored.

Sincerely,

Credit Manager

19.25   Dear Mr. Rosen:

It is a tribute to your excellent payment record that after _____ months (or years), you are receiving your first payment reminder.

This tiny glitch in an otherwise exemplary payment record is not going to do anything to your credit rating. We are pleased with the relationship and, more important, hope that you are pleased with our merchandise and our service.

If your account payment has not been mailed, please send it along.

Sincerely,

Credit Manager

The preceding group of letters give the customer the benefit of the doubt; there is, in fact, nothing in any of them that suggests that the customer is reluctant to pay. These letters assume that the customer has forgotten to mail the payment, has been ill, has been away, or has for some other nonroutine reason, failed to forward the account payment. There is no pressure on the customer beyond the confidence expressed that the customer will pay immediately when he or she receives the reminder.

As I have mentioned before, it would be foolish to assume that every customer who fails to make a payment is as conscientious as the preceding group of letters seem to indicate. Too many credit customers do not respond until they have received a reminder or two; others need to be jogged with a reminder that presents the past-due problem in language that is much more collection-oriented.

The following examples stress the importance of not allowing the past-due balance to become a problem, and not allowing it to deteriorate into a pattern of monthly confrontations.

19.26   Dear _____:

The account balance is $_____ and was set up to be paid in _____ monthly installments of $_____ each. Unfortunately, the first of these payments is _____ days past due and, if not paid promptly, could jeopardize the integrity of the payment program.

We appreciate your interest in our products but we would be unable to continue to offer credit terms if payments to the account are not made as agreed.

Sincerely,

Credit Manager

19.27   Dear Mr. Penn:

A good credit rating is accepted generally as one of the most reliable indicators of a person's character, and your on-time account payments have put you solidly in that category.

For the first time in _____ months (since the account relationship began) the monthly payment is _____ days past due. It is not a major concern, and we do not want it to become one. So we would be remiss if we didn't send you this reminder.

Please mail the payment in time to reach this office by the _____ of this month.

Sincerely,

Credit Manager

19.28   Dear Ms. Ashford:

I'm afraid we have a problem.

This is the third time in the last four months that your monthly payment has missed the due date by several days, and it appears that the time frame between due date and the arrival of your payment is lengthening.

Please contact the undersigned if there is a financial problem that is not going to resolve itself before the next monthly payment comes due. We want to help to protect your credit rating, but we can't be helpful if we don't know the problem.

Forward the past due payment so it arrives at this office by the [date]. Call me when you release the check so we can discuss the problem and see what can be done to alleviate it.

Sincerely,

Credit Manager

19.29   Dear Ms. Banes:

Have you stopped recently to think about your good credit rating and the effort you've put into establishing and maintaining it?

The unfortunate part of any good credit rating is that it can be destroyed in a much shorter period of time than the time it took to establish it, and if you don't reverse the recent pattern of past-due account payments, all of that hard work will disappear with your good rating.

If the payment problem is going to last longer than the current month, call me when you receive this reminder. If there is no call, your payment is expected in this office by the [date].

Sincerely,

Credit Manager

19.30   Dear Mr. Barrett:

A good credit rating is something that has to be earned. It ranks in importance somewhere behind good health, a job that gives personal satisfaction, and one that pays well enough to meet the obligations of the consumer's lifestyle. Good credit ranks somewhere behind those things, but not far behind them.

The pattern of "on-time" payments that you established over a period of _____ months [_____ years] has in recent months begun to slide into a pattern of increasingly slow payments. This is not good for us, and not good for your credit rating.

Please mail the past-due payment so it arrives at this office by [date]. When the payment arrives, I will call you. We can then discuss the problem and decide what can be done to ease it.

Sincerely,

Credit Manager

19.31   Dear Mr. Orland:

I wonder if you are aware that your account payment has not been on time _____ of the last _____ months? In fact the payment that was due on the _____ of the month is now _____ days past due.

We can usually help a good customer with a temporary or a permanent payment restructure program that will enable you to make a smaller monthly payment to us while freeing some cash to pay other obligations.

We need your payment now. And we need also to talk about your payment problem. Call me when you receive this reminder notice.

Sincerely,

Credit Manager

19.32   Dear Ms. Ellred:

The pattern of "on time" payments that you established over a period of _____ months (_____ years) has in recent months been eroding into a pattern of increasingly slow account payments.

Call me when you receive this notice. It is to our mutual benefit if we can work out something that will protect your credit rating.

Sincerely,

Credit Manager

19.33   Dear Mr. Quigley:

It is always our intention to work with a customer who is experiencing payment problems, but we must know first what is happening to the customer before we can suggest or approve a change.

Payments to your account have become increasingly less prompt and as of this moment, we don't know why it is happening. Let's discuss the problem (call me when you receive this), and we'll try to offer some meaningful help.

Sincerely,

Credit Manager

The short reminder letter is the correspondence of choice for many stores and businesses, especially when it is the first or second. These reminders get the message to the customer in a straightforward, nonconfrontational manner and leave the door open for a dialogue if the customer feels there is a current or a looming problem that can impact the customer's ability to pay.

It is assumed that the customers to whom these payment reminders will be sent are honest people who want to pay what they owe. In most situations where it becomes necessary to contact the customer regarding a past-due payment, you will have had prior contact with the customer (payment on time, occasionally slow, constantly slow, etc.) and should know whether there is a desire to pay. When a customer makes an obvious effort to do the right thing, the credit policy of the.store, business, or company should allow the credit manager an area of latitude broad enough for him or her to work with a conscientious, "cash poor" customer.

Here are some examples of short reminder letters.

19.34   Dear Ms. Cannon:

Just a reminder that your account payment is now _____ days past due.

Please forward your check today.

Sincerely,

Credit Manager

19.35   Dear Mr. Danson:

A friendly reminder that your monthly account payment of $_____ is _____ days past due.

Please accept our apology if your check is already in the mail.

Sincerely,

Credit Manager

19.36   Dear Ms. Kemp:

We don't have your check, which means that your account is days past due, and that is a major deviation from your usual "on-time" payment pattern.

Please verify that you have mailed the check. If you have not, please forward it today.

Sincerely,

Credit Manager

19.37   Dear Mr. Willett:

Did you mail the $_____ payment that was due on [date]? If you did, we'll continue to watch for it; if you have not, please take care of it today.

Sincerely,

Credit Manager

19.38   Dear Ms. Hazeltine:

Know what? You wouldn't be the first person to forget a payment. But if you have, will you send it to us today?

We'll appreciate it.

Sincerely,

Credit Manager

19.39   Dear Ms. Ellison:

I can appreciate the possibility of forgetting something that is normally done routinely (like mailing your check for the [date] account payment?).

That's alright, Ms. Ellison; you're still one of our good customers. Just put the check in the mail and all will be forgiven.

Sincerely,

Credit Manager

19.40   Dear Mr. Isleton:

I have checked your payment record and this [has never happened before / has happened very seldom]. That's right. You forgot to send a check for the [date] account payment.

But something like this doesn't cause us to rave, rant, or put voodoo signs on an account. You mail the check today and we'll go on about our business.

Sincerely,

Credit Manager

19.41 Dear Ms. Farley:

Which lucky merchant got our check? You know, the one you always send to us on the [date].

We aren't hard-nosed, unforgiving types, Ms. Farley. You mail the check today and we'll be sure to be smiling when it arrives.

Sincerely,

Credit Manager

19.42 Dear Ms. Carstairs:

The _____ of the month has come and gone but the department's welcoming committee refuses to disband. They say your check is bound to arrive today, tomorrow for sure.

If you have forgotten to mail the payment, please do so immediately. It will allow some good people to relax their vigil and get on to other work.

Sincerely,

Credit Manager

19.43 Dear Ms. Zinke:

Please excuse the payment reminder but because we haven't received your payment for [date], it is our procedure to send a past-due notice.

This does not mean that you are no longer one of our favorite accounts. The check you are about to mail to us (you are, aren't you?) will protect that status.

Sincerely,

Credit Manager

Some customers become so upset when a purchase fails to meet their expectations (or their interpretation of a limited warranty/guarantee) that they (1) withhold their monthly account payment and (2) fail to notify the creditor why they are not paying. This has the effect of crawling into a cave, setting off a charge of dynamite at the entrance, bringing down a few tons of earth, and sealing yourself in the cave. It is a self-destructive technique that should be dealt with before it can become a problem.

The letters that follow address the fact that an account balance is past due and remind the customer that the store or business wants its customers to be satisfied with their purchases. And if they are not? The merchant (business or service) needs to know so an appropriate adjustment, or a replacement, can be made.

19.44   Dear Mr. Jarvis:

Customers are reluctant sometimes to tell us that a purchase is not performing as well as the customer had expected or had been led by the warranty or guarantee to believe that it would. And customers often withhold both their complaint and their payment, which is not the way to resolve a problem and protect your credit standing.

If one of your current purchases (or a future purchase) is letting you down, let us know so we can do something to eliminate the problem. Meanwhile, whether there is or is not a product problem, please forward the past-due payment when you receive this notice.

Sincerely

Credit Manager

19.45   Dear Ms. Raymond:

Is there a problem with your most recent purchase (one of your most recent purchases)?

The reason I ask is that some customers withhold an account payment when they're dissatisfied with the way a product is performing. But they neglect to tell us about it! If we don't know that the product isn't giving satisfaction, we not only can't do anything about it, but the customer's credit rating may suffer as well.

If there is a product problem, now or in the future, let us know about it. Meanwhile, please send your past-due payment today.

Sincerely,

Credit Manager

19.46   Dear Mr. Jason:

What is a man with a payment record as good as yours doing in a neighborhood populated with past-due accounts?

If there is a problem with a product, make the account payment now but tell us what is happening so we can take whatever steps are necessary to correct it.

"Customer Satisfaction." It isn't just a slogan; it's a key part of our success, and we're proud of our record in that area.

Sincerely,

Credit Manager

19.47   Dear Ms. Gardner:

I get concerned when a good customer fails to make an account payment on time.

Customer satisfaction is the key to our continuing success. If a product or a purchase ever fails to deliver within the parameters of its guarantee—as you or one of our people interpreted the guarantee when you bought the product—do not withhold your monthly account payment. Call us, explain the problem, and we'll see that the wheels are set in motion to do what is necessary to eliminate the problem.

Please forward your payment when you receive this notice.

Sincerely,

Credit Manager

19.48   Dear Ms. Langford:

Some people make the mistake of withholding account payments when a purchase fails to satisfy them. And while they're doing this, they somehow forget to tell *us* that there is a problem!

We like satisfied customers, and we do everything reasonable to keep them satisfied. Please forward your check today, and if there is a problem—any problem—let us know about it.

Sincerely,

Credit Manager

Often, the customer has the ability and the willingness to pay. But one of the strongest of the other requisites for getting a customer to pay on time is the widely publicized strength of the store, business, or service company's policy of customer satisfaction. After competitive prices and good service, nothing bonds a customer more firmly to a business than the knowledge that when a purchase does not perform as it should, there will be a quick, hassle-free adjustment. Knowing how the store handles such matters adds a level of satisfaction and security that is very important to the customer.

In most situations where there is a past-due payment owing to the monthly account, the first reminder-collection letter is all that is needed. The customer will respond immediately to the payment request and letters two, three, and "final demand" are never sent. But when there is no response, the second, third, and "final demand," letters must be sent as a prompt follow-up to the first one.

Chapters 20, 21, and 22 contain many examples of what can be used to prod customers whose dedication to an on-time payment record is less than solid.

20

Second Letters: Reminder and/or Collection

The second letter, usually a reminder or notice of a past due payment or balance, should reflect the difference between the first letter-reminder and a follow-up that has become necessary because there has been no response to the first letter. Unless the customer is on an extended business or vacation trip, the first reminder should be enough to jog the customer to an awareness of his payment responsibility.

Courtesy and consideration for the feelings of the customer, and for your relationship with the customer, is still the primary consideration when forming the content of a second notice or letter. Always remember that a customer with whom your store or business has had a long and a satisfactory relationship could be in the middle of a situation that is personally devastating. When faced with such moments of trauma and crises, the most well-adjusted person can be shaken to their roots by the magnitude of an event(s) over which they have no control. These good people with whom your business has had a good credit relationship do not need the added burden of an insensitive credit person chastising them about something that, for the moment, is of minor importance.

Credit and collections people have two important duties: the first duty is to the employer's business (or, if an entrepreneur who handles credit and collections, to his or her business), and the second duty is to the customers of the employer's (or entrepreneur's) business. People who administer credit and collections have an obligation to ensure that although customers must pay within the time frame set for their account, the effort to accomplish that result must be done in a way that preserves a good creditor-customer relationship.

A tactful approach to collecting past-due balances is the best way to ensure that a customer whose payment or balance is past due does not become offended and slide into the area of former customers. No customer is immune from an event or a happening that might disrupt what has always been a dependable pattern of *on-time* payments. The job of any credit and collections person is to get the

407

customer to tell you (1) the nature of the problem; (2) how long the customer expects the problem to continue; (3) how it will impact the customer's ability to pay, and (4) what you can do to help a good customer (and we'll assume this is one) through what may be a difficult financial and emotional time.

Second notices or letters should be a little stronger than a reminder; you've already done that with the first one. Customers should be reminded of possible charges for late payments; the potential for an account slipping from a credit rating of excellent or good to good or fair; and, if the trend of late payments were to continue, the possibility that the credit privilege could be limited or withheld until the account balance is current or has been paid. Whatever part of the above is incorporated into the second letter should be in the nature of an advisory only, a nonthreatening reminder written in the context of "you've done so well for so long, why allow yourself to take a risk that can only have results that diminish rather than enhance?"

The following are examples of letters that build from the base of the first letter. The second letter is the time to be more specific about what the customer should be doing to keep the relationship running smoothly. You do not want the situation of a past-due balance to escalate into an account problem, and you should convey the assumption that the customer has the same goal. Be sure the customer knows that the dialogue goes both ways and that you want to help.

20.1   Dear Ms. Michael:

Our [date] notice regarding your monthly account payment, which was due on [date], has not generated a check. This is a surprise because your account has always been one that is consistently on-time.

If you have been out of town, please forward the payment as soon as you see the two notices. If there is another reason why we have not received the check, contact this office immediately so we can help to work you through whatever the financial or other problem may be.

Please do not hesitate to call. We are ready to help in whatever way we can.

Sincerely,

Credit Manager

20.2 Dear Mr. Morgan:

Unfortunately, we seem to be breaking new ground. A second notice regarding a past-due balance isn't something we have sent you before.

If there is a problem that will be influencing current and future payments, please contact me and let's talk about it. Your good credit rating is too important for this situation to continue unaddressed.

Sincerely,

Credit Manager

20.3 Dear Ms. Albright:

I was sure that one reminder would be enough to bring your past-due account payment.

If the payment is on its way, please accept my apology. If it has not been mailed, please protect your credit standing and send it today.

Sincerely,

Credit Manager

There are as many ways to motivate people as there are reasons for the appeal. Can a particular customer be reached by appealing to a number of things:

Fairness: The "do unto other" approach.
Self-interest: Unless I pay my account as agreed, I risk losing the credit privilege, etc.
Honor: Doing what I agreed to do when-and-as I agreed to do it.
Reputation: My word is the cornerstone of my reputation.
Duty: I have an obligation to do what I agreed to do.

In addition to the above, creditors can appeal to consumers on the basis of a number of other motivational factors, but the fact is that the majority of past-due customers will pay when they receive the first reminder. And those who receive a second reminder? Most will respond to something from the preceding or following group of examples.

20.4   Dear Ms. Walker:

Department employees have been watching the incoming mail but to date no check has been received. There are a number of reasons why this could occur but because we have not had this experience with your account, I am at a loss to know which reason is applicable.

Please mail your payment when this letter arrives. If there is a problem, call me so we can work out a mutually acceptable solution.

Sincerely,

Credit Manager

20.5   Dear Ms. Willows:

Your account payment is _____ days past due and is rapidly approaching the point where we must add a late charge.

Please protect your good credit standing by forwarding the payment when this reminder arrives.

Sincerely,

Credit Manager

20.6   Dear Mr. Findlay:

This would be a perfect time for you to send a check. The account payment is _____ days past due, we are rapidly approaching a late payment charge, and the increasing number of past-due days is working against what is still a good credit rating.

If you have not mailed the payment by the time this second notice arrives, please do so immediately. If you do, the check should arrive in time to avoid any major blemish on your account.

Sincerely,

Credit Manager

20.7   Dear Ms. Anderson:

A second past-due notice is one more than we thought would be necessary.

Your check for the $_____ payment by [date] will return the account to on-time payment status.

Sincerely,

Credit Manager

20.8   Dear Ms. Warner:

Our records do not indicate that we have ever had to send you a second payment reminder notice, not until this one.

We can live with one such incident but it is to our mutual advantage if you will mail your check today.

Sincerely,

Credit Manager

20.9   Dear Ms. Leeds:

Payment reminders do go astray so we are sending you a second notice.

Your check by the [date] will be appreciated and will take the account off of the list of past-due accounts.

Sincerely,

Credit Manager

20.10   Dear Mr. Marsten:

Your reputation with our store (company, business, etc.) is that you are a man who honors his obligations.

Please keep that record intact by forwarding your check today.

Sincerely,

Credit Manager

20.11   Dear Ms. Nelson:

Fairness is something that your payment record tells us is as important to you as it is to us.

Please forward your check for the past-due payment so we can close this small glitch in an otherwise excellent credit record.

Sincerely,

Credit Manager

20.12   Dear Ms. Olcott:

When we think of cooperation, we are reminded of the long record of on-time payments that has been our experience with your account.

This second reminder of your past-due payment should be all you need to mail the check today.

Sincerely,

20.13   Dear Ms. Barnes:

You have every reason to be proud of the payment record you have established with our store (company, business, etc.). You obviously do not want to do anything that would tarnish or put a blemish on that record.

If there is some reason why the past-due payment cannot be paid immediately, call the undersigned at once. The past-due payment is an oversight? Please forward the check today.

Sincerely,

Credit Manager

20.14   Dear Mr. Milburn:

Most of us are proud of the work and effort that has gone into our good credit rating.

This second notice of a past-due payment does not change the excellent credit rating you have with us. Please send your check for the payment today, and we'll do the rest.

Sincerely,

Credit Manager

20.15   Dear Mr. Jackman:

Every person has their own special set of motivators, words that cause a person to react in a certain way at a certain time.

We are not sure which of these is your magic motivator (honor, duty, fairness, etc.) but this second notice of a past-due account payment should activate the one that does it for you.

Please send a check for the payment today.

Sincerely,

Credit Manager

20.16   Dear Mr. Zachary:

We find ourselves in one of those situations that cannot be allowed to continue. In a nutshell, your account balance is becoming larger because your monthly payments are becoming more irregular.

It has always been the policy of our store (business, etc.) to help our customers in every reasonable way whenever a financial problem makes it difficult for a customer to meet his or her monthly account payment. It's something that we're very happy to do, but the customer must take us into his or her confidence and tell us what is going on so we can make a positive contribution toward alleviating the problem.

The present situation cannot continue. We need a check for the past-due account payment, and we need to talk. Call me when you receive this letter and let's discuss the nature of your financial problem.

Sincerely,

Credit Manager

20.17   Dear Ms. Vincent:

Past due accounts cost us money, which means that we must increase the cost to our customers of goods and services to pick up the loss in revenue.

We don't mean to make it appear that your account is or could be the cause of a future cash flow problem—nothing like that—but your check for the past-due payment will be greatly appreciated.

Sincerely,

Credit Manager

20.18   Dear Ms. Canby:

Your good credit standing is on the line, Ms. Canby.

You have a financial problem? Please call me. There is no financial problem? Let this second payment notice remind you to send a check today.

Sincerely,

Credit Manager

20.19   Dear Mr. Rush:

We grant credit on the basis of an applicant's experience with other merchants and businesses, and on the basis of our own perception of the customer as a person of integrity who other creditors tell us honors his (or her) commitments.

We are not infallible. We make an occasional error in judgment, but I have no doubts regarding you and your account. You are a person who pays his (or her) obligations, but I suspect that at the moment you may be having a cash flow problem.

If when you receive this letter you have not sent a check for the past-due payment, or you are financially unable to do so, call me without further delay. We'll work out some way to keep the account above water until your financial situation improves.

Sincerely,

Credit Manager

20.20   Dear Mr. Belson:

A long-term relationship with customers—one that is mutually satisfactory—is the goal of every merchant (business or service). Satisfied customers are the backbone of any successful business, and our goal is to build an ever-larger base of customers who are satisfied with what we sell and how we sell it.

On-time monthly payments are an important part of the two-way street that links the customer to our store (business or service). When this letter arrives, please take the time to mail a check for the past-due account payment.

Sincerely,

Credit Manager

20.21 Dear Mr. Jansen:

Why should we waltz around the subject? Please send us a check for the past-due account balance.

Sincerely,

Credit Manager

Most credit grantors (merchants, banks, service businesses, etc.) assess a late charge if a payment is received and/or posted more than a specific number of days past the due date (usually 10 or 15 days).

The mention of a late charge in a collection letter can be presented as a positive. When it appears that your primary interest is to alert the customer to the fact that his or her account will be assessed a *late payment charge,* if the past-due balance is not paid within a specific number of days after the payment due date, you can take on the appearance of a white knight. And you do want the customer to pay, although the primary motivation is a realistic desire to collect the past-due payment. The fact that the customer can save himself or herself a late charge by paying within a prescribed number of days is an added benefit.

When a customer does not respond with a payment or a telephone call before a second payment becomes due, it is obvious that the credit person has to take more initiative than has gone into the first two letters. Any customer who does not respond to two collection letters is (1) on an extended vacation; (2) has a serious financial problem and does not know how to deal with it; (3) has been jolted out of a stable job and life scenario due to the sudden loss of employment; or (4) suffers from an illness that has led to one or two episodes of surgery, etc.

Help the customer to deal with an unaccustomed shortage of cash as detailed in some of the letters that follow.

20.22 Dear Mr. Pemberton:

It is unlike you to allow your account to reach the point where a late payment charge is about to be imposed, the payment has still not been paid, and a second payment is almost due.

We have no desire to make things more difficult for you than they must be currently. But we must know what is going on; the nature of the problem, how long you expect it to continue, and what we can do to help you through it.

Please contact the undersigned as soon as you receive this letter.

Sincerely,

Credit Manager

20.23   Dear Ms. Danton:

No business is more customer-oriented or is more appreciative of its customers than we are. There is, however, a feeling of frustration when a good customer misses a payment and does not respond to a subsequent reminder.

Many people experience temporary financial problems. If that is your current dilemma, please do not be embarrassed by it. We can help you through it, and do it so there is no residual damage to your credit rating.

Please contact me when you receive this letter. We do not want to impose a late payment charge if a temporary change in your monthly payment schedule (and/or the amount of the monthly payment) will help to see you through the problem.

Sincerely,

Credit Manager

20.24   Dear Ms. Gaines:

The expression "money talks" is applicable to a variety of situations but it never has a louder, more forceful voice than when it is expected to speak, but it remains silent.

We have not heard the voice of your money and it is now several days past the date when your monthly account payment was due. What is even more puzzling is the fact that there has been no response to our payment reminder, which was mailed on [date].

It is imperative that we hear from you immediately so the current problem—whatever it may be—is not allowed to unfavorably impact your good credit rating. We want to help you but we must know what is going on before we can offer help that is meaningful.

Please call me when you receive this letter.

Sincerely,

Credit Manager

20.25   Dear Mr. Norval:

Money can be a big problem in personal life as it is in business, and there are few people or businesses that are not susceptible to an unexpected financial problem.

Your payment record has been so good that I cannot visualize anything causing you to miss a scheduled payment short of a major financial problem. If you were financially unable to send the payment that was due on [date], you may have felt additional embarrassment when the payment reminder arrived.

Please do not be embarrassed. We are anxious to help but we must know the problem before we can channel our help in a constructive manner. You do not need late payment charges or a damaged credit rating.

Give me a call when you receive this notice.

Sincerely,

Credit Manager

20.26   Dear Ms. Beatty:

For a good account such as yours to suddenly (and inexplicably) nose-dive into a past-due status of _____ days past due, face an imminent late payment charge, and make no response to a payment reminder, indicates to us that something unexpected has occurred in your financial picture.

We are here to sell you good merchandise at fair prices but we are not here to make it hard for you to maintain your good credit rating. You have a financial problem? Tell us about it and we'll do what we can to make it easier for you. But if we don't know what is going on, we can't do anything to help to ease your problem.

If you can send the payment, please do it now. If you can't send it, give me a call when you receive this letter.

Sincerely,

Credit Manager

20.27   Dear Mr. Valley:

Financial problems are not the exclusive burden of one group of people or another. Our experience has shown that there is hardly an individual or a group that is immune from unexpected financial problems.

We know that it is usually something unexpected and serious when an account whose consistent on-time payment record suddenly slides into a past-due of several days, does not respond to a payment reminder, and is in imminent danger of having a late payment charge added to the account balance. In this scenario, there is no question that something has happened that is beyond the immediate control of our customer.

We want to help, Mr. Valley, but we need to know what is going on before we can offer something meaningful. The best first step is to call me as soon as you get this letter, and we'll go from there.

Sincerely,

Credit Manager

20.28   Dear Mr. Ambrose:

Money may be the root of all evil, but we all scrape and struggle to get enough of it to meet our needs. But sometimes something happens and there isn't enough of "the root" to go around, and we're wondering if you are experiencing such a problem.

You have been a valued customer for many months (several years, etc.) and this is the first time you have missed a monthly account payment; there has also been no response to the past-due notice that was mailed on [date].

Please do us both a favor and contact me when you receive this letter. Doing and saying nothing about the past-due payment, or the late charge that has been added to the account balance, is the way good customers lose the credit rating they have worked so hard to earn.

I don't want that to happen to your account.

Sincerely,

Credit Manager

20.29   Dear Ms. Quigley:

What can I say after I've said, "Your account is past due"?

Well, I can urge you to call me when you receive this letter. A customer who has always paid the monthly account payment when it is due does not suddenly miss a payment and disregard a past-due notice unless something very serious has occurred.

We want to help but we can't suggest anything meaningful until we know the nature of the problem. If you'll give me a call, we can do something that will help.

Sincerely,

Credit Manager

20.30   Dear Ms. Eggers:

We find that some of our customers are consistent in their inconsistency; in other words, they consistently fail to make their monthly account payment on time.

Not true with you, Ms. Eggers. You have always been one of the consistent ones—until the last payment due date. The payment is now _____ days past due, there has been no response to the past-due notice, and I have just had to add a late payment charge to the account balance.

It is obvious to us that a serious financial problem has occurred but because we have not heard from you, we do not know how to offer help that will be meaningful.

Please give me a call when you receive this letter. The very worst thing you can do is to ignore the problem of the past-due payment, and the problem of another payment date rapidly approaching, when we are ready and willing to do what we can to help you work through the problem.

And do not be embarrassed. Your excellent credit rating with us, and with others, is the type of character reference that motivates us to want to help.

Sincerely,

Credit Manager

20.31   Dear Ms. Paisley:

If it was our policy to use "canned" correspondence and/or past-due notices, we might now be at the "Good gracious! Did we forget to mail our payment?" stage in this first episode of a past-due payment.

We don't do the above because each of our customers is an individual, and each person is important to us. When you miss a payment and we follow with a payment reminder that doesn't bring a payment or an explanation, we know that you have a financial problem.

Don't be embarrassed. Please contact me when you receive this notice. If we know the problem, we can help to work out a meaningful solution.

Sincerely,

Credit Manager

20.32   Dear Ms. Gilbert:

A review of your file reminds me that your work takes you out of town for days and weeks at a time, so I suppose I am a little surprised that you have not forgotten to send a payment before the one that was due on [date]. You must be a very well organized person (a trait that some of us have in very short supply!).

Please forward the payment when you receive this notice. I am waiving the late charge because it seems obvious that this will not be a recurring problem.

Sincerely,

Credit Manager

20.33   Dear Mr. Horan:

I've said this before, Mr. Horan, but this time I really do mean it: We simply must stop meeting like this!

Your account is at a point where it no longer seems to be a question of whether the monthly payment will be on time but rather how many days or weeks it will be past due.

Credit is never granted with the expectation that a customer is going to consistently fail to pay on time. Late payment charges? We assess them but we do not expect that they will become a way of life for any of our accounts.

Please call me when you receive this notice. We need to talk about your account, any financial problem(s) that may be impacting your ability to pay on time, and work out a more satisfactory approach to the future.

Sincerely,

Credit Manager

20.34   Dear Mr. Chaplin:

It has just been brought to my attention that what we knew was a very unusual situation (your failure to send a check for the payment that was due on [date], had a very unusual, serious, and painful reason for there being no payment.

A member of our staff showed me a newspaper account of the recent (auto, pedestrian, etc.) accident that hospitalized you for several days. I understand that, fortunately, you are now up and recovering quite rapidly. That is good news!

Don't be concerned about the past-due payment. Mail it when you get around to catching up on those items. Incidentally, I am waiving the late payment charge; hopefully there will be no recurrence of this misfortune.

Sincerely,

Credit Manager

20.35   Dear Ms. Lomax:

Roses are red, violets are blue—and green is still the color of money.

Please check your records. If you have not sent a check for the payment that was due on [date], send it today. If we have it before [date], a late payment charge can be avoided.

Sincerely,

Credit Manager

20.36   Dear Ms. Parsons:

Very unusual, the fact that we haven't received your check for the [date] account payment and you haven't responded to the reminder notice that was mailed on [date].

Call me when you receive this notice. If there is a problem (financial or other), we should talk. We are always happy to help a good customer but if we don't know the problem, we can't suggest help that is meaningful.

Sincerely,

Credit Manager

When the first past-due notice has addressed the possibility that a customer is withholding a monthly account payment because there is dissatisfaction with a product (or the alleged failure of a product to perform to the warranty of the manufacturer and/or the expectations of the customer), it should not be necessary to mention that possibility in a second letter/notice—or should there?

A customer who has built a case against a product (and indirectly against the seller, dealer or merchant) is sometimes so angry that he or she is not addressing the problem in a rational manner. Because of this anger, it may become necessary for the store (seller, dealer, etc.) to pursue every possible reason for the customer's abrupt change in the pattern of payments until the reason has been determined and has been addressed successfully.

The following second letter-notices continue to address the possibility of dissatisfaction with a product or purchase as the reason for withholding the monthly account payment—and the many good reasons for continuing to pay on the account while relying upon the excellent reputation of the store (seller, dealer, etc.) to deliver on a long-time pledge of customer satisfaction.

20.37   Dear Mr. Jarvis:

There has been no direct reply to our first payment reminder regarding the past-due monthly payment, but we have heard a rumble or two that seem to confirm that you are dissatisfied with the product.

As I mentioned in the first letter, withholding your payment is not the way to do it. We want you to be satisfied and if the problem is not something that can or should be handled in our own repair department, we are happy to be your advocate with the manufacturer for any warranty-related problem.

Your good payment record is important to you and to us. Please forward the past-due payment now, then give me a call. When we have information from you regarding the problem, we can see that the appropriate steps are taken to correct it.

Sincerely,

Credit Manager

20.38   Dear Ms. Raymond:

I am more convinced than before that a recent major purchase is not performing properly or is not giving you the level of satisfaction that was expected of it.

If that is the reason for failing to forward the [date] account payment, it is the wrong way to do it. Your credit standing suffers, late payment charges could be assessed, and the whole process is a negative for you and for us.

Send the payment now, and call me when you do. Our reputation for customer satisfaction (in addition to any manufacturer's warranty) is your assurance that we are going to be sure that any problem is adjusted fairly, and we won't take forever to do it.

Sincerely,

Credit Manager

20.39   Dear Ms. Gardner:

We have not received the account payment that was due on [date], and there has been no response to the reminder we mailed on [date].

As I said in the reminder letter, we expect our customers to pay when and as agreed and if there is a problem—financial, product, etc.—guarantee of customer satisfaction will take over in the event a product fails to measure up to the warranty.

But before we can help, we must know the nature of the problem, so before your good credit rating goes riding off into the sunset, give me a call. The sooner we talk, the sooner we can return the relationship to its former level of mutual satisfaction.

Sincerely,

Credit Manager

20.40   Dear Ms. Langford:

There has been no response to our payment reminder dated [date].

Please contact me when you receive this second notice. Silence is jeopardizing your good credit rating, and it is also about to cost you a late payment charge.

We need to know whether your problem is financial or product performance. If it is financial, we can do several things to help you through a crunch. If it is product performance, that too is tied directly to our pledge of customer satisfaction.

Sincerely,

Credit Manager

The creditor generally does not know what to expect from the second reminder letter. Will the customer's response be immediate and positive? Will the customer be apologetic, citing an extended business or pleasure trip as the reason for forgetting to send the payment? Or will the second reminder notice be no more successful than the first one?

The second reminder can be the turning point in a creditor-customer relationship. If the customer does not respond to two reminder notices, both of them friendly to the point of expressing a desire to help the customer over a financial (or other) hurdle, then there is good reason to assume that for an unexplained reason, the account has gone from good or satisfactory to a problem account and a rating of unsatisfactory.

Until there is conclusive evidence that the customer is not making a reasonable effort to comply with the credit agreement, the customer should be given the benefit of the doubt, especially if this is a customer whose good relationship with your company goes back many months (or years). Do everything possible to get to the bottom of the customer's problem. When you do, the good customer you have always known may be waiting for your helping hand, too embarrassed to accept your earlier offer of help but now willing to unburden himself or herself of the problem.

Working with good people is always rewarding and if you have screened your customers properly, the overwhelming majority of them should meet the criteria for that category.

21

Third Letters:
Collection, Not Reminder

It should not be necessary to send a customer more than two reminders that he or she has failed to mail a monthly account payment. If it is necessary to send a third letter, the difference between the second and third letters should be obvious.

There can be valid reasons why a customer fails to send a check (business or vacations trip, etc.) but the time frame between first and third letters is generally broad enough to allow for absences from home or office. A third letter should push on past the softer *reminder* technique and confront the problem of a past due payment, a late payment charge, and the approach of the due date of another payment. If this is an account whose record prior to the current problem has always been excellent, it is not an acceptable excuse for the customer failing to respond (check, telephone call, etc.) to either of the friendly payment reminders sent by your store (business, etc.). Use the third letter to increase the pressure for money, for a response to your reminders, or for some contact that will give you a dialogue with the customer.

As a merchant dealing in a product (or a business dealing in a service), your company cannot afford to assume that a customer whose payment record has always been satisfactory is going to momentarily resume that payment pattern. Customers change; their circumstances change. The business or merchant who attempts to walk too fine a line between *soft notices* and firmer collection letters may be dealing with a customer whose job and financial situation has changed, and he or she is too embarrassed to say anything about it.

When first and second reminder letters fail to bring results, the third letter (which is really the first collection letter) must build on the two reminder letters. And when there has been no response from the customer, it is imperative that third letters stress the seriousness of the situation and the necessity for immediate payment and/or communication. The tactful, understanding approach of the first and second notices should not be totally abandoned. It should, however, be overshadowed by a firm statement of the damage that is being done to the credit rating of the customer. Make it known to the customer that this is an unacceptable change by a customer whose payment record with your firm, and with other merchants and businesses, has always been good.

As your company's administrator of credit and collections, it is your responsibility to protect the company's interests. You have, in the first two reminder letters, recognized and acted upon the obligation to give the customer every opportunity to fulfill his or her payment responsibility. Your best efforts have been rebuffed with a curtain of silence, and it is a form of disregard and discourtesy that should not receive indefinitely the "kid gloves" treatment. After two reminder letters the customer still isn't doing the things that a good faith customer should be doing? Forget "nice" as you projected it in the first two reminder letters. The third letter should be a collection letter, and there should be no doubt as to its intent.

The following examples of third letters involve sharpening the focus on collecting the past-due payment rather than the theme in reminder letters one and two of finding or suggesting reasons why the customer has failed to pay. At this point there is much less interest in why the customer has not paid because the customer has made no effort to give the creditor a reason for that failure. It is difficult to generate sympathy or support for a customer whose silence might be construed as indifference to the creditor and to the creditor's best efforts to be helpful.

21.1   Dear Mr. Marsh:

We dislike having to shift from reminder letters to collection letters but because there has been no response to our reminder letters dated _____ and _____, we have no other option.

Your good credit rating is being jeopardized because you have not sent the past-due payment or called to tell us why you have not paid. As I said before, if we do not know why you have not or cannot send the payment, there is nothing we can do to help you to protect your credit rating.

Do not delay another day. If you cannot send a check for the past-due payment today, call me as soon as you receive this letter. One late payment charge has already been added to the account balance; another charge would begin to unravel the fabric of good credit that you have worked hard to establish.

Sincerely,

Credit Manager

21.2 Dear Ms. Canfield:

We can accept the fact that one reminder of a past-due balance fails to trigger a payment or a call. We may even accept the fact that a second reminder fails to trigger a payment or a call, although our acceptance is tempered with several questions and a small amount of skepticism. A third letter (this one a collection letter) that fails to trigger a payment or a call? We do not accept it, and neither does any other company, store, or business.

A customer who does not give us the consideration of a call after two letters from us in which the tone is set with offers of help? This tells us that the customer has problems that we want to hear about—and *now.*

What happened to Mr. Nice Guy, you ask? He began to disappear at some point after reminder letter number two was received and it became obvious that a check had not been put in the mail, and no telephone call had been made. At that point there is a downgrading of the customer's credit rating that only a dramatic change in attitude can reverse.

Contact me at once. It is not too late to salvage your good credit rating.

Sincerely,

Credit Manager

21.3 Dear Ms. Maples:

It isn't often that we send two reminder letters (such as those we sent to you on _____ and _____) and get nothing in return. No payment? An explanation might be an acceptable substitute. No telephone call? It is difficult to come up with an acceptable explanation.

Whatever your reasons for not replying to the two reminder letters, let me strongly urge you to respond to this collection letter. No one likes to be asked for money but when an account begins to put as much distance between itself and the creditor as you are doing, we begin to think more about our investment in you than we do about any problem you may be having, and about which we have been unable to get any information. Yours has always been one of our on-time accounts. Now? No response to the two reminder letters is not good.

This problem of payment(s) and communication has escalated to the point where your good credit rating is at serious risk. I'll say it one more time: if you cannot send the past-due payment, call me as soon as you get this letter!

Sincerely,

Credit Manager

21.4   Dear Mr. Malone:

There are conditions under which silence may be considered golden, but after two reminder letters and a monthly payment that is _____ days past due, there is no more time to waste.

Pick up the phone and call me *now!*

We're still waiting to hear why you are unable to make your payment. Call and tell me about it today. Nothing can be resolved when you disregard reminders or fail to take advantage of the opportunity to call and discuss the problem.

Sincerely,

Credit Manager

21.5   Dear Mr. Winthrop:

Your account may be breaking new ground, Mr. Winthrop, but it is new ground that is no longer acceptable. The account is _____ days past due, a late payment charge has been added to the account balance, and we have not had a reply to either of our two reminder letters.

Another payment will be due in _____ days. If the current past-due payment is not paid before the next payment is due, the account will be shut down until on-time payments have been resumed.

Give me a call now. The account has strayed too far from the terms you agreed were acceptable. It is time the two of us did something positive to resolve this problem.

Sincerely,

Credit Manager

21.6   Dear Ms. Sheffield:

Nothing in the background of your credit relationship with us has prepared us for the following: two unanswered letters reminding you that the account payment is past due; a late payment charge added to the account balance; another payment, due in _____ days, and no telephone call from you to advise us of the reason(s) for this dramatic change in your account.

This is not just another reminder letter, Ms. Sheffield. This is a collection letter and it means that we are very serious about the problem that has developed with your account. We want to be helpful and we want to retain you as a good customer, but everything seems to be working against it.

Call me when you get this letter. The time frame for arriving at an amicable settlement is getting short.

Sincerely,

Credit Manager

21.7   Dear Mr. Pollack:

When a customer does not respond to reminder notices of a past-due balance, we begin to have some concern regarding the possibility that the customer's financial situation may have changed since he or she entered into a contract for the purchase of (furniture, clothing, a vehicle, services, etc.).

The suggestion that there may be a change in your financial status is offered as a possible explanation for the fact that you have not responded to our reminder letters dated _____ and _____.

The decision not to contact us with an explanation for the past-due status of your account is not a good one. It is seriously flawed and should be terminated immediately.

We must have your check for the past-due payment or an explanation for your inability to send it, and this must be done immediately. This is jeopardizing your credit rating and is narrowing the options that we think of as "user-friendly."

Sincerely,

Credit Manager

21.8   Dear Ms. Varney:

A customer begins to jeopardize his or her credit rating when it becomes necessary for us to send a third collection letter.

I have asked you in letters one and two to contact me if there is a problem with any of your purchases; if there is a personal financial problem that is making it impossible for you to send the monthly account payment, or if there is some other reason for the worsening past-due situation. To this date, we have not had the courtesy of a reply.

We have not given up on you or your account but there is no way we can help if you do not call me, tell me what is going on, and give me a chance to help you.

Time is running out, Ms. Varney. A desire to help someone can only be sustained when there is a two-way dialogue, and for the past _____ days, we have been talking to ourselves.

Do both of us a favor. Pick up the telephone and call NOW!

Sincerely,

Credit Manager

21.9   Dear Mr. Lewiston:

We do not enter lightly into a credit relationship with a customer. It is a relationship that we want to see become successful and toward that end we do whatever we think will work to the customer's advantage. We pride ourselves on being a business that doesn't just give lip service about being customer-oriented. This business sees that it is a reality.

All of these good intentions miss the mark, however, when we send two notices reminding a customer of a past-due balance; ask the customer to send a check (or if there is a financial problem, to call us so we can arrange something that will give the customer some payment relief), and do all of this with the expectation of a two-way dialogue with the customer.

It is unfortunate but you have not responded in any of the areas mentioned above: payment, telephone call, explanation of the past-due payment, etc. We have heard nothing from you, Mr. Lewiston, and I must tell you that at this point in our relationship, "nothing" is far short of being good enough to satisfy our need for information.

Before the present situation reaches a point where our options become so narrow that we can offer very little in the form of payment relief, pick up the telephone and give me a call. Do it now, when you receive this letter.

Sincerely,

Credit Manager

21.10   Dear Ms. Volkers:

I am very surprised that you have not responded to our _____ and _____ reminder letters. Silence solves nothing. It only ensures that the past-due period gets longer; the embarrassment over nonpayment increases, and our sincere wish to help you through your problem (whatever it may be) begins to erode.

This is not the way to do it. There is still time, and we still have the desire to help.

Don't delay any longer. Call me when you receive this letter.

Sincerely,

Credit Manager

21.11   Dear Mr. Northrup:

It is always disappointing when reminders of a past-due balance are not answered. This is especially true when the communications gap involves a customer with whom we have had a very good payment relationship.

Problems of this nature usually occur when there is a change in the financial status of a customer that makes it difficult for the customer to meet a payment commitment that had previously presented no problem.

We have made every reasonable effort to get you to tell us the nature of the problem and without that information, there is no way we can help you to overcome it or work through it. Your good credit rating is being jeopardized, and that is something you should not allow to occur.

Time is running out. Call me when you receive this letter so we can discuss the problem and work out something that is mutually helpful.

Sincerely,

Credit Manager

21.12   Dear Ms. Abbott:

We cannot continue to accept your silence as a substitute for the past-due account payment or for an explanation of why you are unable to pay it.

The past-due payment must be in our hands before [date]. After that date, nothing can be added to the credit account until (1) past-due payments have been paid and (2) we have a satisfactory explanation for the payment problem.

It is important that you call me when you receive this letter.

Sincerely,

Credit Manager

21.13   Dear Mr. Rosemont:

Credit is a privilege that we are happy to extend to qualified customers. Unfortunately, the question of whether you are now a qualified customer is giving us more trouble each day.

Your past-due payment is getting older and the date for the next payment is rapidly drawing nearer. We have asked you to contact us with an explanation of the problem so we can arrange to revise your current payment program, but we can't do anything until we hear from you.

The problem has escalated to the point where it is very much in your best interest to call me when you receive this letter. Too much time has been lost already sending past-due notices that have been unproductive.

Sincerely,

Credit Manager

21.14   Dear Mr. Percy:

Your account is _____ days past due, we have sent two reminder-letters, and to date there has been no reply.

It is not unusual for people to have financial problems. What is unusual—and not productive of any positive result—is for a customer to avoid having any contact with the creditor. This tactic only increases the creditor's level of apprehension over the possibility that the account is or has deteriorated to the point where this is a danger of loss.

Don't wait any longer. Call me when you receive this letter. We can try to arrange a program that will ease your problem and move you off our past-due list.

Sincerely,

Credit Manager

21.15   Dear Mr. Darby:

Two things, Mr. Darby. We need your check for the past-due payment by [date] and we need to talk with you regarding the reason(s) for the past-due status of the account.

The purpose of the two past-due notices was to help you to protect your credit rating. It can still be done but I need to hear from you by [date], which is _____ days before the next account payment is due.

Sincerely,

Credit Manager

21.16   Dear Mr. Voltman:

This is very disappointing. It has been my impression that we have a better relationship than events of the past _____ days seem to indicate.

There has been no response to the past-due notices that were mailed on _____ and _____, and that begins to pose a real problem. When we urge you to call, to talk with us, and to let us help you work out a solution to the account problem, and there is no response from you, we are suddenly in the position of being unable to wait longer for answers. We need them now—and that can only happen when you pick up the telephone and call me.

We have done our part. It is now time for you to do yours. It is time for you to reread the two past-due notices that we sent to you on _____ and _____, send a check for the past-due payment, or call me and tell me about your financial problem(s).

We are a customer-friendly company. A telephone call will enable you to experience it yourself.

Sincerely,

Credit Manager

The contents of the preceding collection letters make it quite clear that the customer has not responded, either with a payment or a telephone call, to either of the two reminder letters that preceded the third or collection letter. The best efforts of the creditor's representative to establish a two-way dialogue with the customer has been unsuccessful, and without a two-way dialogue, nothing has come from the letters. Of course a customer may send a payment and elect not to include an explanation with the payment or call to discuss the problem (or reason) with the credit representative. This is not a wise decision because the creditor needs to know why the payment was late. The problem (or reason) could foretell whether one or more future account payments might be caught up in the web of delay.

The customer has a simple choice: either pay or talk, and it is to his or her advantage to do both. A past-due payment that arrives without an attached explanation, or no telephone call, conveys an absence of responsibility that the creditor does not appreciate. It may also be construed as the customer's disinterest in maintaining a good credit rating, and that is not an attitude calculated to ease the concerns of a creditor.

The appeal to fairness or to fair play is not generally a major motivator. It is effective in enough situations, however, to make it a worthwhile addition to any program of collection notices and letters. The following examples of fairness collection letters should be used when there has been no response to a first and a second past-due notice. There is cause for concern when you have sent the customer two friendly reminders of a past-due payment, have offered to help the customer work through his or her financial (or other) problem, and there has been no response. When that is the background, it is time to get serious.

21.17   Dear Ms. Lapham:

I don't like to invoke the Doctrine of Fairness but what can I say that is more pertinent in the light of our two past-due notices (mailed _____ and _____; your failure to respond to either of them; a late payment charge that has been added to the account balance, and another payment due in _____ days.

You are not the first customer who has had to miss a payment because of a financial problem. We understand—or we probably would understand—if you had called as we suggested in the two past-due notices. But until you join us in putting "fairness" into this situation, we do not know what has happened to put you in this bind.

Do the right thing by us and by yourself. Call me as soon as you receive this letter so we can revise the date and amount of the payment until you have worked through your financial problem(s).

Sincerely,

Credit Manager

21.18   Dear Ms. Swift:

One of the cornerstones of our relationship with our customers is the belief that we must be fair to the customer at all times and under all conditions. Our reputation for being a customer-friendly store [business, etc.] attests to the fact that we continue to be successful in that area.

We would like it if our customers were fair with us, both for the sake of their credit standing and for the fact that we can do so much for them if we know the reason(s) for a sudden deviation from on-time payments. But if we are not contacted—or when there is no response to our requests for payment or information—our dilemma becomes one that can assume proportions that are a serious threat to our relationship.

Please call me as soon as you receive this letter. It is time for you to give us the answers we need to help you through what must be a serious and a sudden problem.

Let's activate "fairness" and enjoy the helpful things that can result from it.

Sincerely,

Credit Manager

21.19   Dear Mr. Mahoney:

When a customer who has a good payment record fails to send a payment, does not respond to two past-due notices, and does not call to tell us what is going on, we begin to get concerned.

We cannot help you with your problem if we have no information upon which to formulate some suggestions. The most important element in bringing problems into focus is fairness—a reciprocal type of relationship in which we are notified when or before the customer is about to have a financial problem.

Contact me as soon as you receive this letter. The one payment is now _____ days past due, a late payment charge has been added to the account, and a second payment will be due in days. Our mutual goal should be to protect your credit rating, but that is going to be very difficult unless we have your cooperation.

There is still time to work out a mutually satisfactory solution—but it must be done now.

Sincerely,

Credit Manager

21.20   Dear Ms. Vale:

Most merchants and businesses are anxious to help their customers when a financial crunch makes it difficult—or impossible—for the customer to make his or her monthly payment.

We have a well-deserved reputation for doing everything within reason (and more) to help our customers cope with a financial problem. Good customers are in short supply and we would never do anything to complicate their lives. We are, in fact, a store (business, etc.) whose policy of fairness to our customers is something of an industry standard.

Fairness is something that we value very highly, and we are especially appreciative when our customers extend it to us. At the moment it is missing in our relationship. Two past-due notices, a payment that is _____ days past due, and a second payment due in _____ days, and two requests that you call me with an explanation of the problem falls short of what we need to help you protect your credit rating.

Too much time has gone by during which there has been no communication. Call me when you receive this letter.

Sincerely,

Credit Manager

21.21   Dear Mr. Raven:

Your account payment, which was due on _____, is still unpaid. Even more disturbing is the fact that there has been no response to our two past-due notices, and two requests that you call me and give us an explanation of the problem.

We cannot help you, or help to preserve your credit rating, if we don't have information regarding the problem. Your best interest is not being served when we have no information, one account payment is past due _____ days, and a second payment will be due in _____ days.

We need an explanation now.

Sincerely,

Credit Manager

Series Reminder Collection Letters

Letters for a series can be selected from the examples of first, second, and third reminder-collection letters in Chaps. 19, 20, and 21. They can also be a special series of short reminders (numbers one and two) and, if necessary, a collection letter (number three) tailored to the specific situation.

There are customers who will never get their payment to a creditor on time. It is also true that very few of the customers in this category will default on their obligation. These are usually people who are rather casual about their obligations, are not especially well organized, meant to mail the check last week but it somehow slipped their mind, and frequently attach a one-line message to the check apologizing for not sending it sooner. These people pose no special problems beyond the conventional parameters for a credit risk.

Examples of the series form of past-due notices and collection letters are shown on the following pages.

21.22   **First Past-Due Notice**

Dear Ms. Cramden:

Did you forget to mail a check for the [date] payment?

If you haven't mailed it, please send it when you receive this reminder.

Sincerely,

Credit Manager

21.23   **Second Past-Due Notice**

Dear Ms. Cramden:

We have been watching the incoming mail but your check has not arrived.

A late payment charge will add several dollars to your account balance and put a blemish on your account record. You don't want that to happen.

If there is a financial problem that makes it impossible for you to pay the past-due payment, call me when you receive this letter. We'll help you work through the problem.

Sincerely,

Credit Manager

21.24   **Third Past-Due Collection Letter**

Dear Ms. Cramden:

There hasn't been a reason to send you a collection letter before this one but because there has been no response to past-due payment reminders mailed on _____and _____ we have no choice.

The payment is now _____ days past due, a late charge has been added to the account balance, and another payment will be due on [date]. Another disturbing element is that our request that you call us and give us the details of your financial problem has not been acknowledged, and we cannot help you if we do not know what is going on.

If it were to continue, this is the type of situation that can cause permanent damage to a credit rating. We do not want this to happen, and we assume that you do not either.

Call me when you receive this letter. There is no latitude for delay.

Sincerely,

Credit Manager

Other sets of reminder notices-collection letters might mention the possibility of a problem other than financial (a defective purchase, a purchase that has not performed to the purchaser's expectations, a manufacturer's warranty that has not been honored to the purchaser's satisfaction, etc.).

None of these are valid reasons for withholding a monthly payment but when a customer is upset with a product, the store (merchant, business, services company, etc.) is the most convenient target upon which to vent his or her frustration.

21.25   First Past-Due Notice

Dear Mr. Farnsworth:

We have not received the account payment that was due on [date].

If it has been overlooked because of the many distractions during (the Christmas Season, vacation time, etc.), please mail the check when you receive this reminder.

Sincerely,

Credit Manager

21.26   Second Past-Due Notice

Dear Mr. Farnsworth:

I'm surprised that you have not responded to the reminder of your past-due payment, which was mailed on [date].

If there is a problem with a purchase, or you are unable to make the monthly payment, call me when you receive this notice. An oversight? Your check should be in this office by [date] to avoid a late payment charge.

We are anxious to help but you must tell us what the problem is before we can be helpful.

Sincerely,

Credit Manager

21.27   Third Past-Due Notice

Dear Mr. Farnsworth:

As you begin to read this, you will notice that there has been an escalation from past-due notices _____and _____ to this one, which is a collection letter.

Time is not on our side. You have not responded to either of the past-due notices so we must go to a straightforward request for money. We must have a check for the past-due balance by [date], but if you are unable to pay, I want you to call me as soon as you get this letter. We can't help you, and we certainly can't understand your problem, if we don't know what it is!

Sincerely,

Credit Manager

21.28 **First Past-Due Notice**

Dear Ms. Welch:

An oversight can happen to any customer and if it is corrected promptly, there is no residual effect.

Please forward your check for the payment that was due on [date]. If it arrives by[date], there will be no late payment charge.

If there is a financial problem and you are unable to make the payment, call me when you receive this letter. We are anxious to help you but we must have information upon which to build suggestions and solutions.

Sincerely,

Credit Manager

21.29 **Second Past-Due Notice**

Dear Ms. Welch:

This has been a surprise. You have not replied to our [date] reminder of a past-due payment and there has been no telephone call to tell us what is going on.

We need information from you, and you need it from us. If there is a problem with a product, tell us about it. If there is a financial problem, we are prepared to help you through it, but we must have information before we can offer anything helpful. And if we don't get that information from you? An unsatisfactory situation will get worse rapidly.

Call me when you receive this letter. Valuable time has been lost already so we must move quickly to preserve your good credit rating.

Sincerely,

Credit Manager

21.30   Third Past-Due Notice

Dear Ms. Welch:

This is one of those unpleasant surprises. I would not have put you in the category of a customer who fails to make a monthly payment, disregards two past-due notices, does not call as requested, and succeeds in conveying an impression of disinterest in a situation that is declining rapidly.

One of two things must happen now: send a check for the past-due payment or if your financial problem is such that you are unable to send the payment, call me immediately and tell me what is going on.

If you call now, we'll do our best to help you work your way through the problem.

Sincerely,

Credit Manager

21.31   First Past-Due Notice

Dear Ms. Cleve:

Have you forgotten to mail your check for the [date] payment?

If the check is in the mail, please forgive this reminder. If it has been forgotten, please mail it when you receive this reminder.

Sincerely,

Credit Manager,

21.32   Second Past-Due Notice

Dear Ms. Cleve:

This is a new experience. We have never had to send you a second reminder of a past-due payment so we are wondering what has caused this lapse in your good payment record.

If there is a financial problem and you are unable to send the payment, please call me when you receive this reminder. If the problem is something other than financial (a problem with merchandise, etc.), we need to know about that too.

Sincerely,

Credit Manager

21.33   **Third Past-Due Notice**

Dear Ms. Cleve:

When two reminders of a past-due payment fail to motivate a customer to mail a check, we have to move beyond payment reminders and address the problem with a collection letter.

Your payment is _____ days past due, a late payment charge has been added to the account balance, and another payment will be due in _____ days. I don't know why you have not called, but now is the time to do it.

One of the worst things a customer can do is to ignore a creditor's attempts to give the customer an opportunity to explain the problem and proceed to a mutually acceptable adjustment in the amount and structure of payments. A creditor can do no more and when a customer fails to respond, it damages the customer's credibility and credit rating.

Don't allow your credibility and your credit rating to be diminished. Contact me as soon as you receive this letter.

Sincerely,

Credit Manager

Telephone Calls

Many of the larger retail firms have area collection centers that employ various numbers of people who do nothing other than call past-due customers for their payments. Calls are made generally to the home of the customer, although calls can be made to the customer at his or her place of employment if the customer cannot be reached at any other location. Care must be taken to ensure that collection telephone calls do not fall or ease into the category of harassment. If calls are made to the customer-debtor's home, they must be made during the early evening hours and involve language that is appropriate for a professional (and legal) collection effort (no threats, harassment, etc.).

Telephone calls do not usually enter the consumer collection picture until the customer has failed to respond to payment reminder notices one and two. When the first and second reminder notices are mailed to a customer whose account has not been a serious collection problem, there is the expectation that the customer will pay before the past-due payment becomes a problem. If payment is not mailed as a result of the two reminder letters, a first telephone call to the customer might be made between the second reminder notice and the third written request (the reminder-collection letter), or it could be made between the reminder-collection letter and the final demand.

A final demand can be made during a telephone collection call but it would be wise to follow with a formal written demand. If the demand is in writing and the collection procedure escalates to an outside collection agency (or to a suit in Small Claims or civil court), there is never a question regarding the time frame, the intent, or the content of a final demand for payment.

The creditor's records should be complete as to all collection actions taken, including copies of reminder notices-letters, reminder-collection letters, the content of any telephone conversations with the customer-debtor, and notes pertaining to any conversation in which a verbal final demand for payment was made prior to the mailing of a written demand.

All collection actions taken by a creditor (whether verbal or written) must be a part of the credit history of that customer. It is essential that individual account records include everything relevant to the history and current status of the account. When records are kept in this manner, any member of the credit and collection team can look at the customer file and know almost immediately what is being done, what has been done, and how successful or unsuccessful each step in the collection process has been.

Telephone calls are not usually used routinely in the early phases of a collection effort. The telephone is a collection tool that is used to contact consumer accounts when routine reminder notices and letters have not been successful. At that point in the collection procedure, some one in the creditor's credit and collection department will pick up the telephone and attempt to close what has become a widening gap between the creditor and the customer's payment responsibility to the creditor. With some customers, personal contact such as a telephone call is all that is needed to get them to send a check; with many others, a reminder note or letter is enough to do the job.

Large, multistore retail organizations have a high degree of success with their in-house *collection center* approach. It is a collection effort that has a goal of salvaging the customer-creditor relationship *if* the customer is cooperative and the problem is resolved quickly and satisfactorily. Large individual stores, or chains of two, three, or four stores, will also have the goal of retaining some of the customers who have payment problems. The collection effort for these stores or merchandisers will either be centered in the individual stores or in a centrally located area serviced by the two, three, or four stores.

Whether the credit account is with a large, multistore chain or a one-store company, the goal is to collect the money as quickly as possible while retaining the good will of those customers whose problem was not of their own making or are not likely to occur again.

Mix and Match

Example: A retail customer whose charge account has been a problem from the first purchase on credit terms is not going to receive the same level of consideration when a problem occurs as the customer whose account has seldom (if ever) been past due.

When account payments have been consistently on time over a period of months or years, a creditor will go beyond the usual parameters to accommodate a customer who suddenly has a financial problem because of his or her job, health, or some other problem that impacts the customer's ability to pay. If it is projected to be a problem of relatively short duration (something no longer than one to three or four months), the creditor will rearrange the customer's payment schedule—amount of the payment and date or frequency of the payments—to help the customer through a trying financial time.

The retail customer whose charge account receives a disproportionate amount of collection attention from the credit department's collection person(s), may be a higher risk than most under financial conditions that are normal for the account is not a good candidate for special consideration when new financial problems surface, which may continue to erode the financial strength of the individual if the solution does no work out exactly as it is being projected.

Give the account (person) every reasonable opportunity to address his or her financial problem in a way that you believe can be successful but do not go along with a plan, an idea, or a program in which there is less than a reasonable chance that your company will receive the money owed to it—and receive it within a reasonable period of time.

Following are examples of letters from customers who have a problem (health, job, family, etc.) and the responses from credit and collections managers. These letters are indicative of how the creditor's representative can respond to the quality of the customer and the needs of these customers.

Credit and collections people appreciate candor such as that expressed by Betty Kelton in the following letter.

21.34   **Letter from Someone Whose Job Was Eliminated**

Henry Franklin, Credit Manager
Barkley Department Store
Street Address (or P.O. Box No.)
City, State, Zip Code

Dear Mr. Franklin:

I hardly know where to begin. My finances are in a terrible mess but I want to tell you how they got that way and what I hope to do to get myself out of this situation.

My job was eliminated two weeks ago because of cuts in defense-related spending. I held that job for nine years but, unfortunately, until I am able to locate new employment, my income will be less than 50 percent of what it has been. That is considerably less than what I need to live and to maintain my schedule of monthly payments.

I have no idea what your company's position is in a situation of this type but I will certainly appreciate any consideration you may give me that will help me through this major financial crisis. Paying your company and my other creditors is very important to me but it is not going to be possible for me to make my regularly scheduled payments until I find another job.

I should add that during the past several days I have had two employment interviews for jobs comparable in salary and responsibility to my previous job. Whether either of those interviews will result in a job offer is something that should be resolved during the coming week or ten days.

Please call or write at your earliest convenience.

Sincerely,

Betty Kelton

Henry Franklin, Barkley's credit manager, called Betty Kelton the day her letter arrived.

Kelton: This is Betty Kelton.

Franklin: Ms. Kelton, this is Henry Franklin, credit manager at Barkley's Department Store.

Kelton: Oh, thank you for calling, Mr. Franklin. I've been terribly worried over losing my job and what I'm going to do to satisfy my creditors.

Franklin: I understand your concerns, Ms. Kelton, and we appreciate the fact that you didn't let the problem develop into something more serious than it is already. Too many people don't tell us they have a problem until they miss a payment and we call to find out what is happening. It's only then that we hear about the problem.

Kelton: I don't know how long it's going to take me to find another job. I have excellent references and, as I mentioned earlier, I have had two job interviews that seemed to go very well.

Franklin: You're projecting the need for some payment relief over the next two or three months, or perhaps even longer if it should become necessary?

Kelton: Yes, but I think three months should be enough time, and if I go back to work within the next month or two, I'll resume my regular payment schedule.

Franklin: Do you think you could pay half of your regular monthly payment for the next three months, or for whatever part of that time period you need to get your finances in order?

Kelton: Yes, I think I can manage that.

Franklin: If you find that a 50 percent payment is still a little more than you can manage, send a check for 35 or 40 percent of the amount of the regular payment _____ to my attention. I'll see that the person who would normally contact you regarding a past-due or a partial payment has the guidelines from this conversation.

Kelton: I do appreciate this, Mr. Franklin. I couldn't get through this traumatic period in my life without the kind of help you're giving me.

Franklin: We're glad to be able to help, Ms. Kelton. I hope you get a suitable job offer real soon.

Kelton: Thank you. Goodbye, Mr. Franklin.

Franklin: Goodbye, Ms. Kelton.

The next example involves a person who suddenly finds himself in the position of having been in the hospital for several days, has returned home, but faces the prospect of being unable to go back to work for an indeterminate period of time.

As in the preceding example, this is a person who wants to do the right thing by his creditors and has the good sense to contact them at the earliest opportunity; fortunately, that is before the account has become past due.

Wallace Benson (the customer) makes a telephone call to Larry Clarkson, credit manager of the Schneider-Compton Furniture Company.

Benson: Mr. Clarkson?

Clarkson: This is Larry Clarkson.

Benson: My name is Wallace Benson, Mr. Clarkson. I'm a credit customer of your company's store.

Clarkson: Yes, I know your account. What can I do for you, Mr. Benson?

Benson: Well, I have a health problem and I need to talk to you about getting some payment relief for a few months.

Clarkson: I'm sorry to hear about the health problem, Mr. Clarkson. Can you tell me something about it and what we can do to help you?

Benson: I had triple by-pass surgery 12 days ago and because my job as a marketing manager is so stressful, I've been advised to stay away from it for three months—and possibly as long as six.

Clarkson: And you won't be on salary during the period of time you just mentioned?

Benson: No. The company is fairly small, but I wouldn't expect them to pay my salary even if they could afford to do it. I am going to do some work at home; some market research that we can use when I go back to full-time management again. Meanwhile, I'll be getting 50 percent of my regular salary during the two or three months that I'll be doing the market research. That won't pay all the bills, but it will help.

Clarkson: Your doctors are projecting that you'll be able to return to full time employment at some point three to six months after the by-pass operation?

Benson: That's right. They tell me it went well and I should be able to resume my regular job activities. But what I need during the period of half salary is some payment relief; not a moratorium on payments but a reduction in the amount of the monthly payment.

Clarkson: With your credit record, it will not be a problem. If you're going to be on half salary, it won't be possible to reduce some of your living expenses by 50 percent so you'll need more than 50 percent relief from creditors, such as ourselves. I'm looking at your account record and your current monthly payment is $ _____. If we reduce it to $ _____ (one-third of the regular monthly payment) for the next three months, then review your job and income status at the end of the three months, do you think a payment of $ _____ [see above] is something you can handle?

Benson: Yes. Fifty percent of my regular salary is going to call for some tight money management but I can handle a payment that's one third of what I have been paying.

Clarkson: Good. Then let's consider it an agreement.

Benson: Thank you, Mr. Clarkson. Your cooperation is a big help.

Clarkson: I'm glad to be able to do it. Take care of yourself and have a speedy and a complete recovery.

Benson: Thank you. Goodbye.

Clarkson: Goodbye, Mr. Benson.

Does Larry Clarkson make the appropriate note in the customer's file and go on to other matters? He does make the appropriate note in Mr. Benson's file but before he goes on to other customers and other problems, he takes the time to write a short letter.

21.35   Dear Mr. Benson:

Many thanks for your call today. I'm sorry that our telephone meeting came as the result of your health problem but I cannot let the moment pass without acknowledging formally my appreciation for your call—and for your candor.

Too many customers let their account slip into a past-due situation before they let us know that something negative and unforeseen has happened in their lives. Perhaps the fault is not the customers as much as it is the lingering perception of credit and collections people as unbending and unforgiving. Whatever the reasons, it is unfortunate that more people do not seek a solution to their problem before it casts a shadow over the relationship.

We are pleased to accept a payment of $ _____ for each of the next three months and will review your health and job status with you at the end of the third month.

Best wishes,

Credit Manager

The last example in this series involves two customers—a man and a wife who have filed for a divorce. Their charge account at a large local department store is in both names, but the wife (Carol Jones) contacts the credit manager (Paul Benson) to advise him of the pending divorce and to terminate her responsibility for any new charges to the account that might be made by her soon-to-be exhusband (Tim Jones).

Jones: Is this Mr. Benson?

Benson: Yes it is.

Jones: This is Carol Jones, Mr. Benson. My husband, Tim and I have a joint charge account with your store.

Benson: Yes, Mrs. Jones. What can I do for you?

Jones: I want to notify you that Mr. Jones and I are divorcing. I want to be sure that I have no further responsibility for any charges he might make to the account after this date.

Benson: You want your name removed from the account effective this date?

Jones: Yes. Until we've reached a property settlement, anything I buy will be a cash purchase.

Benson: That's no problem, Mrs. Jones. I hope that after a settlement has been reached you'll open another account with us.

Jones: I probably will. My husband and I have agreed to pay all of our outstanding obligations from stocks and bonds that we've accumulated, so the present account total won't be a problem. I just don't want that miserable—

Benson: I understand, Mrs. Jones. I'll take care of it.

Jones: Thank you, Mr. Benson. Goodbye.

Benson: Your welcome. Goodbye, Mrs. Jones.

Final Demand Collection Calls

Collection telephone calls that can be categorized as *final demand* may be made before a final written demand is sent to the customer. When a collection call of this type is made to a customer, the person making the call should record accurately (1) what he or she said to the customer (payment requirements, deadline(s) for receiving money, etc.) and (2) what the customer said (any payment commitments, dates, etc.). This information or key parts of the conversation should be a part of the final demand letter.

Many creditors do not use this type of collection call. They feel that a telephone demand for payment at this late point in the collection effort is a waste of time and effort. They feel that after two reminder letters, an earlier telephone call, and a collection letter (or some mix of the preceding), a final demand collection call is a very low percentage effort that should be by-passed. Creditors who have no faith (or very limited faith) in the final demand collection call will go from the preceding collection letter to the written final demand.

For those who see an occasional situation where a final demand collection call might be appropriate, a few scripted examples of these calls follow.

Lawrence Kelsey calls Ms. Patricia Caulfield at home.

Caulfield: Hello?

Kelsey: Is this Ms. Patricia Caulfield?

Caulfield: Yes.

Kelsey: Ms. Caulfield, this is Lawrence Kelsey at the Merchandise Warehouse.

Caulfield: Oh. What is it?

Kelsey: We've sent you several reminder letters regarding your past-due account payments—two of them at this date—and we haven't heard from you.

Caulfield: I don't have the money to pay you right now.

Kelsey: You aren't able to pay anything on the account? Not even a percentage of the monthly payment that is in your credit agreement?

Caulfield: No, no. I just have too many other demands on my money to worry about paying your account.

Kelsey: (Pauses for several seconds.) I'm sorry to hear that, Ms. Caulfield, because this is an opportunity for you to make some form of payment commitment before we assign the account (to our central collection bureau, to an outside collection agency, etc.).

Caulfield: Assign the account to a collection bureau? That could ruin my credit! Why would you do that?

Kelsey: We certainly don't want to do it, Ms. Caulfield, but we don't have any alternative. You haven't responded to our requests for payment, and now you tell me that you really can't be bothered to make regular payments to your account with us because of unspecified other -demands on your money.

Caulfield: I don't think that's at all fair!

Kelsey: Ms. Caulfield, we have been fair beyond the necessity for it. If you can't commit today to an acceptable payment arrangement, the account will be assigned (to our collection center, to an outside collection agency, etc.) by [date].

Caulfield: I don't have the money. I have rent, car payments, food, clothing, entertainment, health care—there isn't anything left after I pay those things.

Kelsey: It sounds like a typical lineup of household expenses to me and, frankly, Ms. Caulfield, others manage to take care of their monthly obligation to us. No—that isn't good enough—and it does nothing to solve the problem. I'm going to have to assign the account for collection by [date] if you haven't brought it up to date.

Caulfield: Get lost, Mr. Kelsey!

Kelsey: Goodbye, Ms. Caulfield.

Lawrence Kelsey calls James Wilton at his home.

James Wilton: Wilton here.

Kelsey: Is this James Wilton?

James Wilton: Yes. What is it?

Kelsey: Mr. Wilton, this is Lawrence Kelsey at the Merchandise Warehouse. We have sent several reminder letter about your past-due monthly account payments but we haven't received a reply.

James Wilton: That's because you people aren't near the top of my payment priority list. My wife and I are in the process of getting a divorce; she bought whatever it is that's on your account, and I'm not about to pay any more of her debts.

Kelsey: This isn't just her debt, Mr. Wilton. The purchases on this account were made several months ago so the obligation to pay is a joint one—yours and hers.

James Wilton: Hey—I don't care! By the time the divorce settlement is finalized, I'll be lucky if I have enough left to pay my own monthly expenses!

Kelsey: I have to tell you, Mr. Wilton; if we can't come to some payment agreement, I'll have to send you a written final demand for payment. If payment isn't made by a specified date, the account will be assigned (to our central collection bureau, to an outside collection service, etc.).

James Wilton: Do what you have to do. I'm not paying a dime of what she spent with you people.

Kelsey: I'm sorry to hear that. It's obvious we'll have to assign the account so we won't be talking again.

James Wilton: Fair enough.

Kelsey: Goodbye, Mr. Wilton

James Wilton: Goodbye.

Lawrence Kelsey calls Bonnie Franken at home.

Franken: This is Bonnie Franken.

Kelsey: Ms. Franken, this is Lawrence Kelsey at the Merchandise Warehouse.

Franken: Oh-oh.

Kelsey: Well, it is kind of an "Oh-oh" situation, Ms. Franken. We've sent you several payment reminders but we haven't had any response from you.

Franken: I know. The truth is I've been sick. Some of my monthly obligations have become past due, and I just didn't know what to tell you.

Kelsey: This is a pretty good start, Ms. Franken. We aren't interested in creating more problems for you. Our goal is to work with our customers but if we don't know the kind(s) of problems they're having, we can't be very helpful.

Franken: I'd like to pay—I intend to pay—but I've just gone back to work and money is really tight.

Kelsey: I can appreciate that. Could you make a small payment—say one-third (or one-half) of your scheduled monthly payment—for the next three months? Would that help you to handle your other obligations and continue a good relationship with us?

Franken: Yes. I could pay you one-third of my regular monthly payment for the next three months, then go back to my regular monthly payment schedule.

Kelsey: Great! And we'll add two payments (the unpaid two-thirds of three monthly payments) to the end of your account payment schedule.

Franken: Oh, that's fine! I get paid on [date]. Will it be alright if I mail you the first one-third of my regular payment on that date?

Kelsey: Certainly. Ms. Franken, I'm glad we were able to work it out.

Franken: Me too.

Kelsey: Good health and good luck, Ms. Franken. Goodbye.

Franken: Goodbye, Mr. Kelsey.

Lawrence Kelsey calls Burt Benson at his home.

Burt Benson: Yes?

Kelsey: Is this Burt Benson?

Burt Benson: Right.

Kelsey: Mr. Benson, this is Lawrence Kelsey at the Merchandise Warehouse.

Burt Benson: Look. I told you people I wasn't going to pay another dime on your account until you or the manufacturer fixed the washer!

Kelsey: I know, and our records indicate that our service department fixed the washer on [date]. That was _____weeks ago, and your wife's signature on the serviceman's report indicates it is working just fine.

Benson: You're kidding!

Kelsey: No, I'm not. Your wife hasn't told you that there hasn't been a problem since [date] ?

Benson: If she did, it didn't register with me.

Kelsey: Your account is past due two months, Mr. Benson. If you mail a check for the two payments so we get it by [date], I can keep the account from being assigned (to our central collection bureau, to our outside collection service, etc.).

Benson: If the washer has been fixed, I'll send you the two payments. I don't want my credit rating to be damaged over what has turned out to be nothing.

Kelsey: Get the check for $ _____to us by [date] and there won't be a problem with your credit rating, Mr. Benson. Thanks for your cooperation. Goodbye.

Benson: Thank you.

And Lawrence Kelsey makes the following telephone call to Brad Thaxton after Mr. Thaxton fails to keep the agreement he made in an earlier telephone conversation with Lawrence Kelsey to send a check for two past-due monthly payments by [date].

Thaxton: Brad Thaxton

Kelsey: Mr. Thaxton, this is Lawrence Kelsey at the Merchandise Warehouse.

Thaxton: Oh, yeah.

Kelsey: When we talked on [date], you agreed to send a check for the two past-due payments by the _____ of [month]. It's the _____of [month] and we still haven't received the check.

Thaxton: Yeah. Well, I was just about ready to send it when something came up and I had to use the money for it.

Kelsey: That's too bad. The agreement was for the check to be in our hands by [date] or the account would be assigned (to our central collection division, to an outside collection service).

Thaxton: I can probably get the money for you by this time next month.

Kelsey: That won't do, Mr. Thaxton. It's too long a period of time and too uncertain. At this point our only course of action is to assign the account for collection.

Thaxton: That's going to raise hell with my credit rating!

Kelsey: I'm sorry. We gave you every opportunity to prevent it but you didn't take advantage of it.

Thaxton: That's it?

Kelsey: I'm afraid so. Goodbye, Mr. Thaxton.

Thaxton: Yeah. Have a nice day!

Lawrence Kelsey makes a second call to Barbara Wallace after Wallace sends half the amount (one of two past-due payments) she promised during their first telephone conversation. It is important to note that Ms. Wallace did get the check for the one payment to Lawrence Kelsey by the date promised, and she attached a note of explanation to the check.

Barbara Wallace: Barbara Wallace.

Kelsey: Lawrence Kelsey at the Merchandise Warehouse, Ms. Wallace.

Barbara Wallace: Oh, I'm so glad you called, Mr. Kelsey. Did you get my check and the explanation for why it was for one of the past-due payments instead of two?

Kelsey: I. did, Ms. Wallace. I would have preferred to have you pay both of the past-due payments but I understand why you were able to send just the one.

Barbara Wallace: And it will be alright if I send two payments next month instead of this month?

Kelsey: I don't see any reason why we can't live with that. The fact that you sent a check for one payment by the date you said you would tells us that you are sincere in wanting to maintain a good credit rating.

Barbara Wallace: I won't fail you, Mr. Kelsey.

Kelsey: No, I don't think you will, Ms. Wallace. You're a good customer and we hope your problems disappear soon.

Barbara Wallace: Thank you.

Kelsey: Two payments on the _____of next month then?

Barbara Wallace: Absolutely.

Kelsey: I appreciate it, Ms. Wallace. Goodbye.

Barbara Wallace: Goodbye, Mr. Kelsey.

22

Final Demand Letters

When over a period of several weeks an account has been given an opportunity to pay, and has failed to come to any agreement with the creditor, the creditor will give the customer one final opportunity to pay before the account is referred to a collection service (or to the special collection unit of a large retail store or chain). This is done with what is called a *final demand letter:* a letter in which the customer/debtor is told that a specific payment must be made by a stated date or the creditor's credit department will assign the account to a special internal collection unit or to an outside collection agency.

This is not a move that pleases a creditor nor is it one that delights the customer. Any time a creditor assigns an account to an outside collection service, there is the loss of a percentage of any money that is collected by the agency (or service). An assignment of an account to a collection service is also an admission that the merchant (store, business, service company, etc.) has misjudged the quality or credit worthiness of the customer. And finally, there is the loss of the customer, and that might be the biggest loss.

The customer's responsibility in all of this is to work out a payment arrangement with the creditor that allows him or her to avoid having the creditor assign the account for collection. Retail credit bureaus receive reports of these assignments from members and include this data in reports that are compiled and made available to others who do a consumer credit business. To have the account assigned for collection is a black mark against the credit record of a consumer and it alerts other retailers to the possibility that their credit account might suffer a similar fate.

Final demand letters should state clearly what is going to happen to the account if a specific sum of money is not received by a specified date. It is not a time for ambiguity or for coddling the customer/debtor. If you have followed a procedure of past-due notices-letters and the customer has failed to respond or has not responded in a way that has resolved the situation, then you must do what you feel is necessary to protect the interests of your store or business. The final demand letters that follow cover a variety of past-due situations and the options that are available to the creditor. There are letters that introduce the possibility of:

A suit in Small Claims Court (with the goal of obtaining a judgment).

Assignment of the account to a collection service or transfer of the customer's account from the store's credit department to the chain's area collection center.

A suit in civil court to obtain a judgment in the amount of the unpaid balance (plus costs).

Assignment of the account to an attorney who specializes in collection matters.

A final effort to work out a revised payment schedule with the customer.

These are all options that have significant negatives for the customer. Reason demands that the customer should make every effort to work out an adjusted payment schedule—one that will keep the creditor from escalating the collection process to the point where it unfavorably impacts the customer's credit rating and casts a shadow of doubt on the customer's status as an acceptable credit risk.

One major problem with one creditor is enough to cause other merchants and businesses to back away from granting credit to a known problem account.

Small Claims Court

Dear Ms. Knabe:

Two payment reminders and one collection letter should have been more than enough to awaken you to the negatives that can accrue when your credit rating begins to slide. It is unfortunate, but that has not been the case.

Our series of reminders and letters (phone calls if any were made) stressed the fact that we wanted you to call—to tell us about the problem so we could help you work your way through it. Each letter stressed the necessity for communication, not just us to you but the kind of feedback from you that would make it possible for us to help you preserve your credit rating.

None of what we hoped would happen has happened, so this is our final effort to get you to respond. It is, in fact, what we in the credit profession refer to as a "final demand ": the final effort to get you to recognize that to speak up is in your own best interest.

Two payments are now past due: a total of $_____. A check in the full amount of the two past-due payments must be in this office by [date] or the account will be assigned to (our area collection office, an outside collection service, etc.). When that occurs we are no longer involved in the collection process; your account is, at that point, transferred into the hands of strangers, people who are less concerned with you and your credit rating than they are with the dollars you owe this company.

Do yourself a favor. Send us a check for $_____by the _____ of [month]. If the account is assigned for collection, there can be no resolution of the account problem that will be a positive for you.

Sincerely,

Credit Manager

22.2   Dear Ms. Knabe:

There is only so much we can do to influence a past-due customer to take some positive action.

Our two past-due notices, a telephone call, and a collection letter have been unsuccessful; we have, in fact, not heard a word from you during this period of time. It is disappointing and alarming: disappointing because your account had (prior to this episode) never been a problem; alarming because although we have asked repeatedly for information, we still have no data regarding the magnitude of the problem.

There is always a time frame with problems of this type during which time something positive must happen. It has not happened, and time has run out. This letter, then, is a final demand for the two past-due payments ($_____) before the account is assigned to (our area collection office, an outside collection service, etc.). A check for the $_____ must be in this office by [date] if there is to be any chance of salvaging your relationship with this company.

We still want to help you, but if it becomes necessary to assign the account for collection, the focus will shift to an all-out collection effort. You will suddenly be in the company of strangers, whose only thought will be to collect the money that you owe this company.

Sincerely,

Credit Manager

22.3   Dear Ms. Knabe:

Time has run out, Ms. Knabe. If you do not pay the two past-due account payments ($_____) by the _____ of [month] your account will be assigned to (our area collection office, an outside collection service, etc.).

To have that happen would be an unsatisfactory ending to a customer relationship that, until recently, has never been a problem. I urge you not to let your credit rating be swallowed up in a collection effort that could be easily avoided.

Sincerely,

Credit Manager

22.4   Dear Ms. Knabe:

There are many reasons why a customer might be unable to make one or more monthly account payments. All of the reasons will, however, ultimately have their roots in an ongoing financial problem, so it is imperative that a customer who has a financial problem contact the creditor at the earliest possible moment.

It is obvious that you have a financial problem, Ms. Knabe, but we have been unable to get you to tell us what it is or if it might be of short or long duration. Past-due reminder letters (2), a telephone call, and a collection letter have resulted in a zero response, and we can no longer excuse or accept your silence as an answer.

Your check in the amount of $_____ must be in this office by [date] or the account will be assigned to (our area collection office, an outside collection service, etc.). We have given you several opportunities to call this office and give us an explanation of your financial problem(s), but unless you call me before [same date as above], the account will be assigned for collection. Until the last two months your account has had a good record of on-time payments. It is our thought, therefore, that although the current financial problem may be serious, it is possible that a turnaround can come at some point during the next few months. On that basis, there is every reason to assume that we can work out a payment plan that includes lower monthly account payments until a more normal cash flow has been restored.

I urge you to give me a call when you receive this letter. At this point you have nothing to lose and a great deal to gain.

Sincerely,

Credit Manager

The objective of a final demand letter is to reinforce the seriousness of the situation and to make known the imminent danger of an escalation of the collection procedure. You are making it known that because the customer has not responded with the required payment(s), has not called to explain the reason(s) for not sending a check, or has failed to work out a plan that would allow for temporary payment relief (a program of reduced monthly payments, a restructuring of a contract to extend it over a longer period of time, etc.), your company is on the point of escalating the collection process by assigning the account for collection.

Why a customer should be willing to allow a credit account relationship to erode to the point where it becomes a no-win situation is seldom the same for any two customers. The reasons can range from embarrassment on one end (and the hope that "something will happen" to miraculously turn the situation around), to the opposite end of the spectrum where a customer's personal integrity and desire to do the right thing deteriorates to the point where there is no longer an active sense of responsibility.

Most customers do not consider the ramifications of their failure to try to work out a mutually satisfactory solution with the creditor. If they considered some of the following negatives, there would be a much higher level of cooperation.

Has the customer thought about the potential for imminent and long-term damage to his or her credit rating?

Has the customer considered the short- and long-term impact of a garnishment of wages or salary?

Is the customer prepared to cope with a Small Claims or a civil suit, the granting of a judgment against the customer/debtor, and the levying of that judgment against the customer/debtor's personal property (or assets)?

22.5   Dear Ms. Garner:

Our telephone conversation on [date] regarding the two past-due account payments seemed to be the solution that we had been hoping for: your commitment to send a check for the two past-due payments so it would reach this office by [date] would then enable us to cancel the scheduled assignment of your account (to our collection division, to our collection service, etc.).

Unfortunately, there is many a slip between the promise of a check and its arrival. The _____ of [month] has come and gone and we do not have your check for the two past-due monthly payments. And because the payment agreement on [date] was a final effort to keep your account from becoming a collection assignment, we have now lost the flexibility of that option.

I'm sorry to tell you, Ms. Garner, that the account will be assigned to collection (in-house collection division or a collection service) on [date]. From that date forward, you will have no credit privileges with us and there will be no contact between this office and the people who will be collecting your account balance.

Can you still do something to keep the account out of the hands of the collectors? Only if you get a check for $_____ to us before [date]. If the check arrives after that date, it will be too late to avoid a collection assignment.

Sincerely,

Credit Manager

22.6   Dear Ms. Garner:

Your check for $_____ (one third of the total amount of the two past-due payments) arrived this morning.

The suggestion that you be allowed to pay a second one-third of the total amount of the two past-due payments on [date] the third one-third on [date], and then resume your regularly scheduled payment one month from [the date of the third one-third payment] is acceptable.

Sincerely,

Credit Manager

There are times and situations when it is impossible to reach an amicable resolution of an account problem with a customer. Past-due notices and letters may get no response, and a payment commitment made during a telephone call from the merchant's credit department may ultimately prove to be worthless.

How do you differentiate between accounts that should be assigned for collection (in-house collection center or a collection service) and the very few you may decide should be sued in Small Claims Court? Use Small Claims Court very sparingly, especially if yours is a credit department that has little time (or personnel) for other than the normal flow of departmental activities. It takes some time to gather and prepare the records you will need to present your company's case; to prepare the forms for filing the suit (serving the defendant, etc.); to take them to the clerk of the Small Claims Court jurisdiction in which you will file the suit; and for appearing in court to present your company's case, which may include attempting to refute successfully any conflict or controversy over the amount of the debt and the defendant's efforts to have it decreased or thrown out.

The following letters are examples of what can be used to try to convince a customer/debtor that it makes no sense to allow himself or herself to be put in the position of a defendant in a Small Claims Court consumer credit action. It is time-consuming, embarrassing, and is detrimental to the credit rating of the customer-defendant. Some reasons you may want a Small Claims Court action include:

1. If there is any thought that the customer might be thinking of leaving the area, a Small Claims suit can deliver a judgment (which may then be levied against an asset or assets) while a collection assignment to an in-house collection center or a collection service is just beginning to apply pressure to the customer/debtor.

2. Does the customer/debtor have items of value that are readily accessible and could be attached quickly once a judgment has been obtained? If so, this is an incentive for the creditor to sue in Small Claims Court (and especially if there is any concern regarding the conditions stated in 3.

3. There is the subtle factor of self-imposed intimidation when a customer faces the possibility of appearing in Small Claims Court, a venue wherein the defendant must represent himself or herself. Attorneys are not allowed to participate during in-court proceedings, which can be an unexpectedly strong incentive for a customer-defendant to come to a last-minute, presuit agreement with the creditor.

22.7 Dear Ms. Abbott:

Our effort to collect the unpaid account balance has not been a satisfactory experience. There is a past-due balance of $_____, another payment of $_____will be due on [date], and your failure to respond to past-due notices and collection letters has left us with the feeling that you are not committed to the payment program.

This final demand letter is a courtesy to you and one which I hope will motivate you to pay past-due monthly account payments. If we do not receive your check for $_____by [date] a suit will be filed in Small Claims Court. We will ask the court for a judgment in the full amount of the account balance and will then levy an attachment against whatever asset(s) we can use to offset the debt.

If you are interested in maintaining a good credit rating among the area's consumer stores and businesses, allowing a credit account to deteriorate to the point where the creditor feels compelled to sue for a judgment in Small Claims Court is definitely not the way to do it. There is the feeling among granters of credit, whether the credit is commercial or consumer, that one creditor's problem with an account is indicative of a potential for a similar problem with other creditors. In short, it is not a healthy procedure.

You can avoid being the defendant in a suit in Small Claims Court by forwarding your check for $_____in time for it to arrive in this company's credit office by [date] If the requirement of dollars and arrival date is not met, we will proceed to suit in Small Claims Court.

Sincerely,

Credit Manager

22.8   Dear Mr. Langley:

The primary reason for nonpayment of a scheduled obligation is a financial problem, something brought on by sickness, loss of employment, or one of several other reasons. We don't know your reason(s) because there has been no reply to past-due notices and collection letters, and the telephone commitment that you made on [date] for a payment of $_____ by [date] did not happen.

Because the collection effort has been unsuccessful, our recourse is to file suit in Small Claims Court if we do not have your check for $_____ by the ____ of [month]. We will ask the court for a judgment in the full amount of the account balance and will then levy an attachment against whatever asset(s) we can use to offset the debt.

We do not enjoy having to take this action. It is time-consuming for us and for you, and it ultimately reflects unfavorably on your credit rating. Other stores and businesses may become concerned that our problem with your account is indicative of a potential for a similar problem with them.

A suit in Small Claims Court can be avoided if your check for $_____is in this office by [date]. If we do not receive the check by [date] , we will proceed to sue in Small Claims Court.

Sincerely,

Credit Manager

22.9   Dear Mr. Dempster:

Final demands are not something that we like to make on a customer but when our other collection efforts have failed (past-due notices, collection letters, and collection telephone calls), we are left with a very limited number of options.

Your monthly account is currently two payments past-due. If we do not have your check for $_____ by [date] , we will file suit in Small Claims Court for the total amount of the obligation. The reason for filing suit for the full amount is because the account is in default, which allows us to proceed to ask the court to award us a judgment for that amount.

Small Claims is an effective but a somewhat time consuming procedure for us and for you. It has the added disadvantage (for the defendant) of being an action that has an unfavorable impact upon the credit rating of the person being sued. Most stores and businesses are justifiably concerned when they receive a report from their credit association of this type of action because it raises questions regarding the quality of their own relationship with the person being sued.

Your check for $_____ by [date] will enable us to back away from this type of collection action.

Sincerely,

Credit Manager

22.10   Dear Mr. Simpson:

After our telephone conversation on [date], I thought I should verify in a letter what was said during the several minutes of our conversation.

You have agreed to send a check for $_____(one and one-half of the two past-due monthly payments) by the ____ of [month]. The unpaid one-half of the second past-due payment will be included in your check for the next regularly scheduled account payment, which is to be in this office by [date].

Please do not fail to honor this commitment. If this agreement does not work, our recourse will be to file a suit for the unpaid balance in Small Claims Court. We will ask the court for a judgment in the full amount of the unpaid balance, and then proceed to levy an attachment on whatever assets are available to offset the debt.

Your cooperation is crucial as we work jointly to protect your credit rating.

Sincerely,

Credit Manager

22.11   Dear Mr. Jonas:

Probably the worst thing a credit customer can do is fail to pay one or more monthly account payments, receive several past-due notices and collection letters, and disregard the creditor's request for information pertaining to the problem.

Creditors do not want to assign accounts to an in-house collection bureau or to an outside collection agency. It is a negative for the customer because an account assignment—or a suit in Small Claims Court—is picked up by the area retail credit bureau and made available to other stores and businesses. The impact on the customer is to cause other stores and businesses to question whether their own credit balances are at unusual risk, and to cause merchants and businesses that are not currently granting credit to the account to decline any request for credit.

Our telephone conversation on [date] concluded without your firm commitment to send a check for $_____ by the _____ of [month]. I cannot stress too strongly the importance of this payment as it relates to your credit relationship with us and with many of the other stores and businesses in this area. The damage has, to this point, been manageable; if it escalates into a suit in Small Claims Court (or a collection assignment), the damage to your credit rating will be much more extensive and longer-lasting.

Sincerely,

Credit Manager

22.12   Dear Mr. Jonas:

We did our best to work with you to resolve the problem of past-due account payments, but it takes the cooperation of both parties. Unfortunately, we did not have yours.

A suit will be filed in Small Claims Court within the next seven days. You will be served shortly thereafter with the details of our suit, which will include the court's instructions regarding the defendant's responsibility to the court and to the plaintiff (ourselves).

I regret that you have apparently failed to appreciate the seriousness of your failure to honor your responsibility to this company and to your credit standing.

Sincerely,

Credit Manager

22.13 Dear Mr. Jonas:

What can I say that hasn't been said before? I told you in my letter of [date] that suit would be filed in Small Claims Court within seven days of the date of the letter. You now know that it has been done.

The only circumstance under which the suit can or will be withdrawn is if before the trial date, you hand-deliver to this office a cashier's check in the amount of $_____ That amount covers the unpaid account balance; expenses we incurred during the process of filing suit papers, and other suit-related costs.

I am sure you understand that we did not file this suit as a frivolous action. It follows, therefore, that the only way we will abort it before trial is if the payment and manner of payment are as stated in the preceding paragraph.

Sincerely,

Credit Manager

Whether a credit customer is a questionable credit risk probably has nothing to do with the collection procedure once the debtor has allowed his or her account to face the creditor's final demand. The question of credit risk is probably equally relevant whether the creditor's collection procedure involves a collection effort by the credit and collection team of one store (or business); a centralized area collection section to which all delinquent accounts are sent; assignment of the account to an outside collection service; a suit for judgment against the customer/debtor filed in Small Claims Court; an assignment to an attorney whose specialty is collections, or a suit filed in civil court for balances in excess of those eligible for Small Claims Court. The inevitable result of any one of these collection procedures is to put the customer/debtor in the position of being at best a questionable risk for credit.

When a customer's creditworthiness is being evaluated by a store, a service, or a business other than general merchandising, the creditor must satisfy himself or herself that the person who is asking for credit does not represent an unusual and/or an unacceptable level of risk. The nature of credit involves the taking of risks by the credit grantor but the objective is to establish a level of risk appropriate for each account and manage it so well that it does not slip out of parameters that meet the criteria for the credit grantor's store or business.

The final demand is a critical point in the relationship between creditor and credit customer. If at this point the customer fails to respond to the finality of the credit grantor's appeal, the credibility of the customer is not only irrevocably diminished in the eyes of the creditor but must ultimately experience varying levels of the same diminution in the eyes of other creditors. The exact moment when a creditor loses faith in one of his or her accounts may not be identifiable but it can be narrowed to a set of specifics that should guarantee no repetition of the circumstances that led to the credit problem.

Give the customer/debtor every reasonable opportunity to respond to your requests for payment or for information regarding a problem that is not expected to correct itself for a period ranging from two or three months to several months. When the customer responds immediately to your past-due notice and is forthright in offering information pertaining to a temporary problem (one that you feel confident the customer can handle successfully), you can monitor the customer's account and also be grateful that the customer's sense of responsibility toward his or her credit obligations is such that you have no less than a reasonable chance of seeing the account return to on-time payment status.

Is there another positive to this happy ending? There certainly is. Your store or business has every opportunity to retain the good will of a customer who is indeed a creditworthy person.

23

Other Collection Devices and Procedures

A cardinal rule for any credit professional is to never assign an account to an outside collection service until your own credit and collections department has exhausted every in-house possibility. You do not want to give away a percentage of the account balance if your own collection effort, or that of a credit and collections department, can get the job done.

There is, however, a point beyond which an in-house collection effort can begin to become too time consuming, too costly, and too nonproductive. If the time and energies of a department member (or members) is being diverted to a collection effort that is dragging on and on, and there is no indication that a resolution of the problem is near, then you are well-advised to assign the account to an outside collection service and invest the time and energy of department members in other credit and collection duties.

The following list of options is available to credit departments whose in-house attempt to collect a past due balance has not been successful. Some of these options stand alone, others are intertwined, and not every option is applicable in every collection situation. But there is in this selection an assignment procedure that is appropriate for almost any of your collection problems that have not responded to the in-house collection effort.

1. Assign the account to a collection agency (and how to select one).
2. Skip tracing.
3. Cosignatory.
4. Small claims court (suit fees, court costs, etc.).
5. Civil court (suit fees, court costs, attorney's fees).
6. The customer files personal bankruptcy.

7. Assigning an account to an attorney who is a collection specialist.

8. Securing a judgment (small claims or civil court).

9. Attaching an asset.

10. Individual repayment plans (Bankruptcy Act).

The credit manager (or the collections manager) should use his or her best judgment to match the account with the assignment that seems to offer the best chance for a full recovery of the account balance. Remember, too, that when an account is assigned for collection, or a suit is filed in small claims or civil court, the amount of the assignment or suit should be the full amount of the account balance and not just the sum of past due monthly payments.

An account should not be assigned to a third party for collection (or a suit filed during the in-house phase of collection) unless there is no longer any realistic expectation that the in-house collection effort will be effective. But suppose the customer has told you why he or she is unable to make the monthly account payment, has given you a verifiable reason(s) why it may be two, three or four months before payments can be resumed, and suppose the customer's story has the ring of truth and your prior experience with the customer has not been unsatisfactory. The customer should not be thrown to a collection agency. It would be foolish to give a collection agency-service 25 or 35 percent to collect an assigned balance when, with some patience and perhaps an innovative approach to the payments problem, your store or business should eventually receive 100 cents on the dollar, plus has a financially healthy customer who loves you for staying with him or her during a period of financial trauma.

The timing of a suit, a collection assignment, or any action that is taken to collect an account balance must coincide with the customer's financial condition. If the customer has been candid with the details of his or her problem, there is no incentive to assign the account or to take any other formal collection action. Retain the account and work with the customer to get small monthly payments (some small percentage of the regularly scheduled payment). If even that small payment is not possible, do nothing to put more pressure on a customer who is trying to cooperate with you. A candid customer and constant monitoring of the account should enable you to know when there are signs of financial improvement. At that point you may call on the customer to begin to make good on his or her promise to resume the original payment schedule, and to begin to pick up some of the past due dollars that accumulated during the several months when no significant payment was being made.

A generation only slightly older than mine would, at such a moment, invoke the phrase "You can't get blood out of a turnip." It should not take a rocket scientist to realize that both the "turnip" phrase and the act of trying to force payment from someone who wants to pay but temporarily cannot are obvious impossibilities.

Having made a case for the selective use of patience and restraint, I must hasten to add that the majority of customer accounts whose payment performance gets slower as the past-due balance gets older are legitimate candidates for any of the remedies outlined earlier in this chapter. This is especially true of customers with whom you have had no contact, no satisfactory contact, or no indication that the customer has an appropriate sense of responsibility toward the account balance.

Assigning an Account to a Collection Agency

A collection agency is an extension of your own store, business or company. When you assign an account to a collection agency, the assignment form that you complete, sign, and forward to the agency authorizes them to take certain actions and certain levels of action in the name of your store, business, or company. The agency is your authorized representative in specified (in the assignment form) phases of the effort to collect from the customer.

Would you threaten a customer? Would you make defamatory statements or slanderous remarks about a customer? If you would not (and you should not) then you do not want to be aligned with a collection agency whose operating procedure does not exclude them. These are all illegal actions for which the customer has the right to sue your company and the collection service for damages.

As the designated agent for your business, the collection agency-service incurs liability for itself and for your business when it makes false and defamatory statements or ventures into areas that are not legally, morally, or ethically acceptable. Federal and state statutes define what is legally acceptable: there is no provision in any statute for assigning to an individual, a store or a business the right to do or say whatever he or she pleases about another party.

Select an agency about whom you have heard good things (from other merchants, businesses, etc.), and whose philosophy for doing business is compatible with yours. Are the personnel those with whom you could work comfortably? Do they go about their job with an appropriate level of professionalism? If the agency seems to be a fit, try one or two accounts, preferably accounts whose backgrounds and reasons for nonpayment (if any have been given) are dissimilar. These are test assignments and you want to see whether the collection agency can handle successfully a variety of challenges.

Collection agencies usually furnish their clients with assignment forms and other relevant data. Letters 23.1 and 23.2 are examples of assignment letters written by the creditor which is also serving as a cover letter for the assignment form furnished by the collection agency.

23.1   [date]

Collection Agency Company Name
Street Address (or P.O. Box No.)
City, State, Zip Code

Gentlemen:

We are assigning the listed account to you effective this date.

Ms. Agnes Beresford
3333 Northridge Lane
San Francisco, CA

Amt. of Assignment—$2378.59.

Proceed with collection calls and letters. If your efforts in these two areas are not successful, the account is to be returned to this office. We shall use our own attorney to pursue the collection process in civil court.

I have signed and attached your company's assignment form to this letter. The form reflects the instructions given to you in paragraph two of this letter.

Sincerely,

Credit Manager

You may want to limit further the parameters within which the collection agency is to work. Write your own letter of assignment and if the collection agency does not want to accept the parameters (or restrictions) imposed by your company, contact another collection agency.

23.2   [date]

Collection Agency Company Name
Street Address (or P.O. Box No.)
City, State, Zip Code

Gentlemen:

Subject to your acceptance of the guideline conditions set forth in this letter, we are assigning the following account to your agency effective this date.

Ms. Agnes Beresford
3333 Northridge Lane
San Francisco, CA

Amt. of Assignment—$3278.59

You may proceed with the collection process through telephone calls and letters. The account is not to be assigned to an attorney (collection specialist) until this office has received, reviewed, and approved progress reports forwarded by your office. The collection attorney must be one who is acceptable to us; and if we do not think the customer has enough assets to warrant the time and trouble that is involved in obtaining a judgment, we will instruct you to terminate the collection effort.

Unless I hear from you within 10 days from the date of this letter, we understand mutually that your agency accepts the instructions, and the limitations, imposed upon it in paragraph two of this letter and as that paragraph is applicable to the conduct of your agency in this matter.

Sincerely,

Credit Manager

A good collection agency is worth the fee (a percentage based upon the dollar amount of the assignment) that the creditor company obligates itself to pay if the agency is successful in collecting the assigned balance. But what if the customer pays part of the assigned balance immediately after the creditor assigns the full amount of the account balance, and before the collection agency has had an opportunity to make the first telephone call to the debtor? The creditor is still obligated to pay a collection fee on that part of the assignment. An assignment to a collection agency becomes effective (binding) on the date stated in the assignment letter or on the assignment form, and for the full amount of the assigned balance.

If you have worked with the agency for a period of time and have given the agency some profitable business, you should not be reluctant to ask for a waiver of their claim to a payment for which they did no work. This is considered leverage which is not entirely unfair. The agency made no contribution to the amount that was collected, and if they fail to accede to your request, there is the back-of-the-mind thought that this is a collection firm whose lust for a fee has caused it to lose its good judgment and its sense of fair play. The thought might establish itself in your mind that this is the type of greed that you don't appreciate from a firm that is working for you. You know what? The collection agency may decide that earning their money, and keeping a good customer, is much healthier for their bottom line!

Skip Tracing

This is a function of the collection procedure that is done only occasionally by a small credit and collections department. If the store, business or company is large and it does a high volume credit account business on the company's own credit card (or conventional charge account), the collection section may employ people whose sole responsibility is to skip trace assigned customers.

Skip tracing is the process followed by a creditor (or the creditor's representative) when a customer leaves the only address the creditor has for the customer; he or she fails to make a regularly scheduled payment or fails to pay a bill by the due date; there is no response or contact as the result of reminder notices and telephone calls; mail is or may be returned stamped "return to sender—no forwarding address"; or the telephone has been disconnected. A creditor who is faced with this abundance of bad news knows that he or she is looking at a "skip."

If the creditor has personnel who have been trained in skip tracing procedure, an in-house effort will be made to locate the customer. But whether the creditor does or does not have a specialist in skip tracing, one of the basic actions that any store or business can take is to refer to the customer's credit application for the names of (1) close relatives or friends, and (2) other stores or businesses that were given as references. These contacts offer the most efficient base from which to try to locate the customer.

You do not have to be a long-time credit professional to understand that any customer who moves from the only address known to your store or business (and does not advise you of the address change) is not going to do anything to help you locate him or her. The objective of the skip is to lose himself or herself so that any creditors—and there are usually several—will have a very difficult time trying to locate him or her. Your skip is no different than the others. He or she hopes generally to melt into the background of a city or a state several hundred miles away, and locating such an individual can prove to be a time-consuming process.

Is it possible that the skip forgot to notify one or more creditors? Anything is possible but if your store or business is dealing with an honest customer who recognizes the obligation to your store or business and expects to pay what is owing, that honest customer will remember within a few days or two or three weeks at the maximum. The honest individual who forgot to notify you of the move will send you the new address before enough time has elapsed for you to send up a red alert.

The number of skips who genuinely forget to notify their creditors of their move is a very tiny percentage of the whole. When you discover that an account is a skip, and unless your office has the time and the experience to try to locate the customer, assign the account to an agency whose specialty is skip tracing, or a collection agency whose staff is experienced in skip tracing.

The following are some examples of letters a creditor might send to relatives, friends, and other merchants whose names were given as references on the skip's new account information sheet. With these letters, you can try some of this work within your own department.

23.3   Letter to a Brother

Dear Mr. Collins:

Our current attempts to contact your sister, Emily Collins, at her 1694 Margot Place address have not been successful.

We will greatly appreciate any information you may be able to provide to us regarding her current residence or business address. If you do not have that information, perhaps you know the name of a friend or an acquaintance who might be able to help us?

Your reply will be appreciated.

Sincerely,

Credit Manager

23.4   Letter to Another Store or Business

Attention of Mr. Clint Martin, Credit Manager

Dear Clint:

We are currently running into a blank wall with the account of Margaret Dunne (formerly residing at 15986 Wisteria Drive, San Jose, CA 95123), I am wondering if you have a more current address, and if you do not have one, I am afraid we are looking at a lady who within the past 30 or 40 days has become a skip.

If you have a current address and will be good enough to share it with me, I will greatly appreciate it.

Sincerely,

Credit Manager

Letter to a Friend or an Acquaintance

Dear Ms. Wilson:

Your name appears on the new account application form of Mary Warner (15792 Milton Place, Los Angeles), as a friend for more than 10 years.

Our problem is that we are unable to locate Ms. Warner at the Milton Way address. We are wondering if you might know what has happened to her or what her current address may be.

Ms. Warner has always been a good customer. We are concerned that something may have happened to her, or that she has an experienced an unexpected financial problem.

Your reply will be greatly appreciated.

Sincerely,

Credit Manager

23.6 **Alternate Letter to a Friend or an Acquaintance**

Dear Ms. Wilson:

We are unable to locate Mary Warner at the 15792 Milton Way address and are wondering if you know what has happened to her, and where she can be reached.

It is important to her and to us that we locate her. Any information that you may care to share with us will be greatly appreciated.

Sincerely,

Credit Manager

Cosignatory

This is a form of protection that is popular with banks, automobile dealers, borrowers who use land or other chattels as security, and certain other major purchases or loans that offer a potential for major risk to the credit grantor. It is a procedure that can be used when (1) the purchaser's equity in an automobile or a property is less than the percentage or dollar amount required by the seller or the financing institution, or (2) a credit check raises doubts regarding the purchaser's ability to sustain the required monthly payments when aligned against income, living expenses, other obligations, and the length of time the purchaser (or borrower) has been employed. The stability of the employer and of the industry also has bearing on the decision.

When the layer of buyer equity (the percentage of equity versus the value of the object or property) in a home purchase loan, an automobile, an expensive piece of jewelry, or some other type of major purchase does not allow the buyer or borrower to qualify on the strength of his or her own credit standing, the seller or the person or institution financing the purchase may require an acceptable cosignatory (a cosigner). The person who needs a cosigner usually turns to a close relative who is willing to accept the factors of risk that are a part of such an obligation.

A *cosigner* is a guarantor who, by his or her signature on a financing agreement, contract, etc., agrees to accept payment responsibility for any delinquency (or deficiency) that might occur during the span of the contract or payment program; this could occur as the result of the purchaser's failure to make monthly or other payments as required by terms of the purchase or financing agreement. The cosigner, by affixing his or her signature to the purchase or financing agreement, accepts payment responsibility for the full amount of the contract and/or responsibility for the unpaid portion of the contract or agreement at the time there is default (under terms of the agreement) by the signatory.

A person who accept a cosigner's signature does not have an obligation to discuss the cosignatory's obligations under the terms of the contract or agreement beyond what is spelled out in the contract or agreement itself. It is well to remember, however, that family members (grandparents, parents, siblings, close friends, etc.) are susceptible to the perils of a cosignatory's position. Many do not realize that their own assets and credit standing can change almost overnight if what was considered to be merely a helpful gesture to a relative or close friend turns suddenly into what could become the nightmare of full responsibility for an obligation in the thousands (or tens of thousands) of dollars.

The terms of the agreement will specify what constitutes *default* by the primary signatory to the agreement or contract. It will state clearly when and how responsibility for the unpaid obligation shall become the responsibility of the cosigner, and it will detail the procedure that may be invoked by the lender, seller, etc., to collect from the cosignatory.

It is understandable that a cosigner's (cosignatory's) financial status may be given the same level of scrutiny as that of the primary signatory. There is no point in accepting a cosigner whose financial condition would not be adequate for the financial requirement that would be his or hers in the event of a default or of a deficiency.

The person, business or institution that is the beneficiary of a cosigner's agreement should move aggressively to protect that interest, and without regard for the position of the cosigner. Collecting an obligation by whatever legal means is available is the responsibility of every good credit and collections person. Collecting from a cosigner who is a wide-eyed parent or grandparent may not give you any personal comfort but you have a job to do.

If the primary signatory defaults on the obligation, you must take the steps prescribed in the agreement or contract (notification of default, etc.) to transfer payment responsibility to the person whose signature as cosigner made it possible for you to accept the credit risk. Remember that you would not have entered into an agreement with the primary signatory if there had been no financially acceptable cosignatory. However, there was one so it becomes your obligation to see that the interest of your store, company, business, bank, etc. is protected as prescribed under the terms of the contract or agreement.

Credit Cards and Charge Accounts

The competition is intense among the various chain stores to get customers to keep VISA, MasterCard, American Express, and other nonproprietary cards in their pockets and reach instead for the card issued by the department store or the chain store. A first thought is that this is a strange program for a store to be pushing because the funding of a proprietary credit card (or charge accounts) could tie up millions of dollars of the company's cash flow in credit card accounts or conventional charge accounts. But when one gets down to the question of what is in it for the store or the chain, the answer is strong. There is plenty!

During the period when I was focusing mind and effort on the consumer credit section of this book, an interesting piece of information arrived in my mail. It was a kit from one of the nation's oldest and biggest department store chains advising me that a preapproved credit card could be mine in exchange for my signature on an acceptance form. The kit included the company's Credit Card Disclosure Table, which listed the APR (Annual Percentage Rate) paid by this company's customers for the privilege of charging purchases. If I had not known before receiving this material why department stores and store chains push their own credit cards, the Credit Card Disclosure Table would have supplied the answers to my questions.

Residence	APR	Range of Balance	Minimum Finance Charge
AL	21%	$750 or less	50¢
	18%	Over $750	
AK	18%	$1000 or less	50¢
	7.92%	over $1000	
AR	7.92%	Entire	None
CA, IA	19.8%	Entire	50¢
DC	21%	Entire	None
FL, MA, ME, MN, PA, WA, WI	18%	Entire	50¢
CT, HI, NC, ND, RI	18%	Entire	None
KS	21%	$1000 or less	50¢

Residence	APR	Range of Balance	Minimum Finance Charge
	14.4%	Over $1000	
MI	20.4%	Entire	50¢
MO	20.04%	Entire	50¢
NE	21%	$500 or less	None
	18%	Over $500	
WV	18%	$750 or less	50¢
	12%	Over $750	50¢
All other states	21%	Entire	50¢
Outside U.S. 50 states	21%	Entire	50¢

The credit card disclosure rate for this chain in the state of Texas is 21 percent with a 50¢ finance charge. The rate is, however, a variable rate and is the market competitive rate ceiling as determined by the Texas Consumer Credit Commission and published in the Texas Register in September of each year. Any published change becomes effective October 1 of the same year.

As this book is being written, bank money to support an in-house credit card or charge account system is available at nominal single-digit interest rates. If consumer credit grantors such as the one cited in the preceding paragraphs do a reasonably good job of screening account applicants, the difference between the cost of bank money and the APR charged by the store(s) for financing customer purchases should add up to a substantial annual addition to the bottom line.

Another example is a California chain of retail stores whose product emphasis is on the spectrum of consumer electronics products (television sets, CD players, word processors, etc.). This chain has its own charge account system and markets it aggressively. An advertisement in May of this year offered "0 percent financing for two more weeks" and "6 months the same as cash." This financing was offered on purchases of $250 or more on the firm's Revolving Charge Account. No finance charge is payable if the charge is paid in full within 180 days: purchases not paid within 180 days are subject to an APR of 21.6 percent accruing from the date of purchase.

The above paragraph says at least two things about this California retailer of electronics products, and about all of the other stores (large individual stores or chains) and businesses who have their own charge card or charge account program. Volume sales is the life blood of their operation, but there must be enough profit built into the price via sharp buying practices (manufacturer rebates, volume discounts, etc.), to finance the store's credit card or charge account program versus the interest rate (APR) charged to customers.

It is true that an in-house credit card and/or charge account program involves considerable additional expense. An in-house program requires more credit department personnel to screen applicants and to process and collect credit card and charge account payments. Additional office space and equipment (furniture of all types, electronic office equipment, etc.) is essential to prepare charges for input into data processing and posting to individual customer accounts. There are end-of-the-month statements which must be prepared and mailed, plus the cost of envelopes and postage.

These are not items that, as a combined total, are of small financial consequence. When taken as a whole, the number of dollars is substantial and can be expected to diminish the warm glow that occurs when the potential for a profitable credit card and/or charge account operation is being considered. When limited to the simplistic formula of money borrowed at a low rate versus a much higher financing charge (APR) to the customer, it equals a substantial profit from the in-house credit operation. The net profit from this type of operation is diminished substantially when all of the various new internal costs are subtracted from the gross revenue generated from the in-house program.

There is no question that, when all facets of an in-house credit program are in synch, it can make money for the store, chain, or business. It can, however, have a very different result if management of the in-house operation does not involve an appropriate level of experience. Controls must be in place to monitor and adjust all phases of the operation. The quality of the basic ingredient, the credit card customer, must be consistent with what is necessary to have a profitable credit card-credit account operation.

The Customer Files Personal Bankruptcy

Chapter 13 of the Bankruptcy Code provides for the adjustment of debts of an individual with regular income. It allows for the development of individual repayment plans to satisfy the claims of creditors and provides some small businessmen with Chapter 13 relief; the criteria being a specific dollar limit on secured and unsecured debts.

A filing under Chapter 13 is voluntary. A debtor cannot be forced into a repayment plan by his or her creditors. It is the debtor's exclusive right to propose a plan, which may take a conventional three years of payments or it may be extended by the court to a maximum of five years. A debtor who files for protection under Chapter 13 has the advantage of retaining his or her property while enjoying the protection of assets while paying creditors over a period of time. It is not necessary for the debtor to surrender nonexempt property as is required in a liquidation case.

Cosigned Consumer Debt Claims

A Chapter 13 repayment plan may treat cosigned consumer debt claims differently than other unsecured claims. This is because cosigners are usually relatives or close friends, and debts of this type (debts with a guarantor) would be collected by the creditors. This category of debts may have a separate payment schedule because the presence of a solvent cosigner-guarantor virtually ensures that these balances will be liquidated.

Six Separate Requirements For Plan Confirmation

Compliance with the listed requirements ensures that the plan meets the criteria for arrangements of this type.

1. To meet the requirements for confirmation, the plan must meet the requirements of Chapter 13 and any other applicable provisions of the Bankruptcy Code.

2. All fees relating to the filing and subsequent procedures must be paid.

3. If the trustee or the holder of an unsecured claim objects to the plan, the value of the property to be distributed under the plan must be equal to and/or exceed (a) the amount of the claim or (b) all of the debtor's projected disposable income to be received in the three years beginning when the first payment is due.

4. The value of property distributed under the plan for allowed unsecured claims must not be less than the amount that would have been paid under a liquidation plan.

5. With respect to each allowed unsecured claim, the holder of the claim must accept the plan, or the holder of the claim must retain his or her lien or recover the value of the claim, or the debtor must surrender the property securing such claim to the claim holder.

6. The debtor must be able to comply with the plan. Payment under the plan must begin within 30 days after filing the petition.

The court must grant the debtor a discharge as soon as practicable after completion of payments under the payment plan. Waiver of the discharge, with court approval, is permitted. The court may also grant a *hardship discharge* when the debtor has not completed payment if:

1. The debtor could not be held accountable for the circumstances precluding his or her payment.

2. The debtor has paid at least liquidation value.

3. Modification of the plan is not practicable.

Modification of a Chapter 13 plan may be made only if the request is made by the debtor, the trustee, or the holder of an allowed unsecured claim.

Unlike Chapter 7, the Chapter 13 debtor is not prevented from seeking another discharge at any point during the six years after a discharge under a prior liquidation or repayment plan.

The Consumer Credit Bureau

There are local and regional member-supported credit bureaus whose function it is to gather and maintain credit files (and ratings) on the consumers in their respective service areas. Credit, work, and financial information on consumers is gathered on a relatively constant basis from input provided to the bureau from employers, other merchants, businesses, and financial institutions. This input is then used to establish or to update the credit ratings of individual consumers, which then serves to inform credit grantors of (1) an excellent credit risk, or (2) an account whose risk factors may be changing as evidenced by nonconforming payment patterns experienced by retailers and businesses who have an ongoing credit relationship with the customer.

The merchant and business-supported credit bureau is not as universal an organization as it was before the proliferation of VISA, American Express, Master-Card, and other national charge card accounts. Stores and businesses who do not offer their own credit card or charge card service have no need for a consumer credit bureau. A telephone call to the service or verification center for the credit card being presented will provide the merchant with the information regarding creditworthiness that is necessary to complete the sale. In many communities or service areas, there is no longer enough demand to support a consumer credit bureau.

In areas where there is no consumer credit bureau, a store or a business that has its own credit card or charge account program must do a thorough job of gathering credit information, contacting personal and business references, and evaluating information gathered from these sources. It puts responsibility for good credit decisions squarely on the shoulders of the store's own credit department.

24

Lessons of the Unsuccessful Collection Attempt

It is the hope of credit and collections professionals that every in-house collection effort can be resolved successfully before time and the absence of in-house success make it necessary to assign the account to an outside collection service. A collection assignment is never a moment for joy because it represent a failure of the in-house system to do the job for which it was created. It represents also the loss, in the form of a collection fee, of a percentage of the assigned receivables balance (usually 25 to 40 percent). That is in itself enough to cause a conscientious credit manager to review the data that went into the original credit decision and the subsequent monitoring of the account. Perhaps it was unavoidable; a case of something unforeseen occurring weeks or months after the credit line had been approved. Whatever the reason for the in-house failure, the credit and collections department will learn from the problem and phase the probability of such a future occurrence into evaluations of new accounts and the monitoring of existing ones.

The Hazards of a Restricted Cashflow

When a business (either consumer or commercial) drifts into increasingly more difficult financial problems, the variety of goods and services available from its suppliers may become increasingly less attractive to the customer base. Key suppliers will not maintain the integrity of the selection of merchandise or services if they are not being paid within parameters that are acceptable. And if the cashflow deteriorates to the point where some suppliers are selling only on COD terms, or are holding orders until specific past due balances have been paid, the warehouse and the shelves will begin to take on the look of a "going out of business" sale. It will, in fact, be a true reflection of what is an involuntary situation.

So what does a company or a business do to maximize the flow of cash from its accounts receivable? The process starts with the first credit customer and builds on that customer by adhering to the principles of account strength and the guidelines for determining whether an applicant meets that criteria. The requirements and the goals of your company, and the credit policy that was formulated to help it to achieve those goals, must be implemented to ensure that the business benefits from a strong flow of cash. Nothing less than the fulfillment of that goal is acceptable if the vision of a successful venture is to become, and remain, a reality.

In-House Credit Cards and Credit Accounts

Any individual store, business, or chain of stores whose goal it is to get customers to open a charge account opens the window on a different area of consumer credit. When stores and businesses set up their own credit account systems, they face the sometimes daunting task of trying to collect an overdue account balance from a customer who cannot be persuaded to pay.

When the chain of stores or businesses is large, there is usually an area or a regional collection division to which past due accounts are forwarded by stores located within the geographic boundaries of the collection office's service area. Large independent stores will have their own credit and collections department, and when the collections department has been unable to collect a customer's past due balance, the account will be assigned to a consumer collection service. The in-house credit departments of independent stores and businesses generally do not have the personnel to pursue every in-house collection problem to a conclusion. It is important, therefore, for businesses to choose their collection agencies on the basis of a reputation for success in the industry or business area of interest; a reputation for staying within the legal parameters for collecting accounts, and for the ability to cut through a customer's list of reasons why paying the account balance is a financial impossibility. There are collection agencies whose success ratio is phenomenal, and that speaks well for the expertise of the staff and those who direct it. Other agencies may seem to have a good record of success until an analysis of their performance reveals a failure to collect from too many debtors whose situation (poor cashflow, decreasing volume of business, etc.) is deteriorating and who require an innovative and/or a hard-nosed collection effort. The collection agency of choice must be a fit with the philosophy of your business, store, or company; and it should be versatile, innovative, inspired, tenacious, persuasive—and successful!

Is It the Chicken or the Egg?

Although every credit professional will concede that there can be no payment unless there has been a sale, the importance of collecting for the sale (merchandise, services, etc.) is indisputable. The sale of products or services during a specific period of time (a month, a quarter, etc.) might generate some impressive figures but if credit customers do not pay, or do not pay rapidly enough to make a timely contribution to the cashflow needs of the creditor company or business, that company or business is not going to generate internally the percentage of monthly cashflow necessary for it to minimize reliance on borrowed money.

When this situation occurs (a constant need for borrowed money to supplement cashflow generated in-house), the victim is the creditor company's bottom line. The cost of borrowed money can be devastating to a company that operates in an industry or an area of business where profit margins are thin. Good management in all areas of every business is a primary requisite if the enterprise is to enjoy long-term success: Good management of accounts receivable is one of the most important keys to successful management of the cashflow of a company or a business.

Small Claims Court

The procedure for obtaining a judgment against a consumer creditor (and the forms used in that process) is the same as the procedure used to obtain a judgment against a commercial debtor. The plaintiff must prepare and file his or her own forms (see Chap. 15); appear in court to present the case (no attorney is allowed to appear with a plaintiff or to speak for him or her); and, if a judgment is rendered in favor of the plaintiff(s), it is the responsibility of the plaintiff to locate any assets of the debtor and levy an attachment against them.

Obtaining a judgment does not ensure a successful end to the collection effort. If assets cannot be located when the judgment is granted, the plaintiff (creditor) may wait months or years for something to surface, only to have the debtor file a petition in bankruptcy court. But if the creditor is able to locate an asset and levy an attachment against it (take possession of the asset), the creditor may either sell the asset and retain the amount of the judgment or force the debtor to pay the judgment from other (hidden) sources to preserve the integrity of the targeted asset. If the debtor is able to satisfy the judgment before the creditor can liquidate the asset, the creditor is obligated to promptly release the attachment and notify the court that the judgment has been satisfied.

Rather than repeat the sequence of the procedure for obtaining a judgment and levying an attachment on property (an asset) of the debtor, refer to Chap. 15. This chapter outlines the procedure, which is the same for commercial and consumer accounts, and includes the forms used by the plaintiff (creditor, the court, and the debtor (defendant). A suit in civil court, however, normally involves attorneys (yours and the defendant's); a case that is argued before a judge (who may also render a verdict), and a decision that either grants or denies judgment for a specified number of dollars to the creditor-plaintiff.

Small Claims Court is one of the few areas in the credit and collection process where commercial credit grantors and grantors of consumer credit follow the same guideline criteria. Consumer credit balances do not generally involve as many dollars as do commercial credit accounts, resulting in more Small Claims Court activity in the consumer credit area.

An example of the pressure on the court systems in many states is what has occurred in California. The Small Claims Court statute for California was changed effective January 1991 to reflect higher levels of credit activity and to remove hundreds of cases from increasingly cluttered civil court calendars. The California legislature raised the limit for small claims actions to $2500 and revised the statute to place a limit on suits filed by individuals to two per year for amounts that do not total more than $5000; no limit was placed on the number of suits that can be filed when the amount is less than $2500. (Consult the statute of your own state or jurisdiction for applicable limits and guidelines for filing.)

Correspondence Relating to Collection Assignments

When the relationship between a store or business and the consumer account has reached the point where it has become obvious there is no point in continuing the in-house collection effort, the creditor (if a store or business that does not have its own area or regional collection center) must assign the account to a collection service, or to an attorney whose specialty is collections. If the choice is a collection agency whose specialty is consumer accounts, Letter 24.1 at the top of page 485 is an example of an assignment letter and the special instructions that might be included.

If your business is notified by the collection service that the customer has failed to make the second $2000 payment, Letter 24.2 at the bottom of page 485 might be your instructions to the agency.

What Can You Learn from a Failed Collection Effort?

It is not possible to collect every account balance, but any person who is charged with the collection responsibility should go into a collection effort expecting to get the money. Anything less than that attitude is unacceptable. If you do not move confidently and aggressively, advantages or opportunities that might have been yours could be lost.

Do not fault yourself or other members of the company's credit and collections staff if the in-house collection effort was handled in a professional and an efficient manner. So it was not an effective effort. Of course, there is no reason to be satisfied, but thinking about "the one that got away" is productive only to the point where something has been learned from the experience.

24.1   Consolidated Collection Service
Street Address (or P.O. Box No.)
City, State, Zip Code
Attention of Mr. [or Ms.] _____:

Dear Mr./Ms. _____:

The following account was assigned to your company on the [day] of [month], with instructions that you were to begin collection action promptly.

Account: Harry and Mabel Klutz
Address: 1326 Universal Lane
City/State: Any City, Any State
Account Balance: $4874.16
Aging of Account Balance: 40 to 95 days past due

It is not surprising that the customer did not follow your or our instructions to send payment(s) to your office. We have this date received a cashier's check in the amount of $2000; an attached note promises a second $2000 next month (on the same date as this payment) and a payment of $874.16 one month after the second one.

The arrangement is acceptable. Please monitor the account to see that the customer keeps his (or her) promise of two more payments ($2000 and $874.16) on the dates specified.

Sincerely,

Credit Manager

24.2   Consolidated Collection Service
Street Address (or P.O. Box No.)
City, State, Zip Code
Attention of [name of manager]:

Dear Mr./Ms. _____:

We have your letter of [date] in which you state that Henry and Mabel Klutz (our account number _____) did not make the promised payment of $2000 by [date].

If the overdue payment of $2000 does not arrive within 10 days from the date of this letter, escalate the collection effort to include your attorney and a civil suit to obtain a judgment.

Sincerely,

Credit Manager

When the hired gun (the collection agency to whom you assigned the account) proves to be no more effective than your department's in-house collection effort, there is some small satisfaction in the knowledge that the customer was every bit as uncompromising as your in-house collection effort indicated.

Before you turn away from the experience, take a few minutes to review the customer's credit file.

1. Was there anything in the applicant's personal, employment, or credit history that should have been a warning?

2. Had the applicant's employment been with the same employer, and continuous for a reasonable period of time?

3. What did the applicant's credit references have to say about their experience with the account?

4. Did the bank reference indicate that the applicant handled his or her obligations in a satisfactory manner, while maintaining adequate to good account balances?

Were there any indicators from your own experience with the account that might have been indicative of trouble ahead?

1. Was your company's early experience with the customer very good, good, or satisfactory?

2. In retrospect, were there indications that it would be downhill from the start?

3. Did the customer's payment pattern begin to deteriorate at any one specific point? (If it did, should somebody have noticed the change and began to monitor the account on a more frequent basis?)

4. A satisfactory account will occasionally change very suddenly and dramatically. If this was your company's experience, what do you now know about the change in this account that might have been a clear warning if it had been known *before* the sudden change?

Index

DISK WARRANTY

This software is protected by both United States copyright law and international copyright treaty provision. You must treat this software just like a book, except that you may copy it into a computer to be used and you may make archival copies of the software for the sole purpose of backing up our software and protecting your investment from loss.

By saying, "just like a book," McGraw-Hill means, for example, that this software may be used by any number of people and may be freely moved from one computer location to another, so long as there is no possibility of its being used at one location or on one computer while it is being used at another. Just as a book cannot be read by two different people in two different places at the same time, neither can the software be used by two different people in two different places at the same time (unless, of course, McGraw-Hill's copyright is being violated).

LIMITED WARRANTY

McGraw-Hill warrants the physical diskette(s) enclosed herein to be free of defects in materials and workmanship for a period of sixty days from the purchase date. If McGraw-Hill receives written notification within the warranty period of defects in materials or workmanship, and such notification is determined by McGraw-Hill to be correct, McGraw-Hill will replace the defective diskette(s). Send request to:

Customer Service
TAB/McGraw-Hill
13311 Monterey Avenue
Blue Ridge Summit, PA 17294-0850

The entire and exclusive liability and remedy for breach of this Limited Warranty shall be limited to replacement of defective diskette(s) and shall not include or extend to any claim for or right to cover any other damages, including but not limited to, loss of profit, data, or use of the software, or special, incidental, or consequential damages or other similar claims, even if McGraw-Hill has been specifically advised to the possibility of such damages. In no event will McGraw-Hill's liability for any damages to you or any other person ever exceed the lower of suggested list price or actual price paid for the license to use the software, regardless of any form of the claim.

McGRAW-HILL, INC. SPECIFICALLY DISCLAIMS ALL OTHER WARRANTY, EXPRESS OR IMPLIED, INCLUDING BUT NOT LIMITED TO, ANY IMPLIED WARRANTY OF MERCHANTABILITY OR FITNESS FOR A PARTICULAR PURPOSE. Specifically, McGraw-Hill makes no representation or warranty that the software is fit for any particular purpose and any implied warranty of merchantability is limited to the sixty-day duration of the Limited Warranty covering the physical diskette(s) only (and not the software) and is otherwise expressly and specifically disclaimed.

This Limited Warranty gives you specific legal rights; you may have others which may vary from state to state. Some states do not allow the exclusion of incidental or consequential damages, or the limitation on how long an implied warranty lasts, so some of the above may not apply to you.